The 'Empty' Church Revisited

ROBIN GILL
University of Kent, UK

ASHGATE

Published by
Ashgate Publishing Limited
Gower House
Croft Road
Aldershot
Hants GU11 3HR
England

Ashgate Publishing Company
Suite 420
101 Cherry Street
Burlington, VT 05401-4405 USA

Ashgate website: http://www.ashgate.com

British Library Cataloguing in Publication Data
Gill, Robin
  The 'empty' church revisited. – (Explorations in practical, pastoral and empirical theology)
  1. Church attendance – Great Britain – History – 19th century 2. Church attendance – Great Britain – History – 20th century I. Title
  274.1'0908

Library of Congress Cataloging-in-Publication Data
Gill, Robin
  The 'empty' church revisited / Robin Gill.–2nd ed.
    p. cm. – (Explorations in practical, pastoral and empirical theology)
  Rev. ed. of: The myth of the empty church. 1993.
  Includes bibliographical references and index.
  ISBN 0–7546–3462–0 (alk. paper) – ISBN 0–7546–3463–9 (pbk. : alk. paper)
  1. Church attendance–Great Britain–History–19th century. 2. Great Britain–Church history–19th century. 3. Church attendance–Great Britain–History–20th century.
  4. Great Britain–Church history–20th century. I. Gill, Robin. II. Title. III. Series.

BR759 .G535 2003
274.1'08–dc21
                                                                            2002034529

ISBN 0 7546 3463 9 (Pbk)
ISBN 0 7546 3462 0 (Hbk)

Explorations in Practical, Pastoral and Empirical Theology

Typeset in Times by LaserScript Ltd, Mitcham, Surrey
Printed and bound in Great Britain by MPG Books Ltd, Bodmin, Cornwall

Contents

Preface

In the original Preface to *The Myth of the Empty Church* I wrote:

> For more than three years this book has been a grand obsession. I have broken journeys, made vast detours, and searched through numerous archives, record offices and, occasionally, bishops' studies. I have pestered librarians and taxed the patience of those dealing with interlibrary loans. I have bored numerous colleagues and vigorously hunted down other specialists in this area. It has all been wonderful!

However, the truth was that the book was not just an obsession but also a liberation. After sixteen enjoyable years as lecturer at Edinburgh University I was ambitious for a chair of theology. But chairs were not plentiful in the late 1980s and anyway Scotland was not the obvious hunting ground for an Englishman. So when the unique opportunity of the William Leech Professorial Fellowship at Newcastle University emerged, I leapt at it. Not only could I now be called 'professor' (such vanity) but I could also concentrate for five years wholeheartedly upon research. In the event I held the fellowship for four years before moving to Canterbury. Yet one of the greatest privileges about my time in Newcastle was getting to know and respect the late William Leech himself. He was a self-made millionaire builder who read the Bible every day and was determined to give away most of his wealth to charities, especially those connected with hospitals or churches. I shall always remain grateful to him.

The Myth of the Empty Church was published in 1993, but by the time anyone had noticed it, it had sold out. So it has been out of print now for almost a decade. I am most grateful to Ashgate for encouraging me to produce a new edition. I have incorporated many changes in it. Scholarship has moved on since 1993 at both the theoretical and empirical levels, so it was obviously important that I addressed this properly. I have also revisited all of my original case studies (North Northumberland in Chapter 1, Glan-llyn in Chapter 2, and York in Chapter 9), made radical changes to Chapters 8 and 10 (incorporating in the latter material first published in a briefer form in Richard K. Fenn (ed.), *The Blackwell Companion to Sociology of Religion*, Blackwell, Oxford, 2000), updated Tables 18 and 19, and added Table 20 (itself updated from that first published in Robin Gill, C. Kirk Hadaway and Penny Long Marler, 'Is Religious Belief Declining in Britain?', *Journal for the Scientific Study of Religion*, 37:3, 1998).

In the original book I thanked a number of scholars for their enormous help, particularly the social historians Callum Brown, Hugh McLeod, Edward Royle, and Peter Catterall, the sociologist Jon Davies and the statistician Chris Stephens. Most amazing of all was Clive Field with his huge knowledge of bibliographical and census sources. Now with the new edition I would particularly like to thank the series editors Leslie Francis and Jeff Astley, both valued friends and colleagues.

Finally, as I wrote in the original Preface:

> One of the main problems about grand obsessions is the effect they have on families. My own family have been more than supportive, and only sometimes have they rolled their eyes heavenward. Frequently they have teased me: obsessives need to be teased. Occasionally they have looked mildly convinced, but that is much more dangerous for obsessives. So finally my love to Jenny, Martin and Judy. I will have more time for them now ... that is, until the next obsession.

Adding that I now have a grandson, William ... and even he is beginning to roll his eyes.

Introduction

Where do empty churches come from? Or, perhaps more accurately, when did British churches and chapels start to appear more empty than full, and why did this happen?

I am going to struggle with these seemingly naïve questions throughout this book. I have deliberately chosen the empty church as a focus, rather than some broad concept of church decline or (worse still) religious decline. There is an obvious physicality about the empty church that avoids the usual wrangles about what does or does not constitute 'religion' and whether largely invisible features of Christianity still permeate British society. I do not intend to decry the latter. Rather, I believe that too little scholarly attention has been paid to churches in all their religious physicality. In contrast to an immense literature on the architecture of churches, and a growing literature on church furnishings, it is a rare book that sets out to study the social history of church buildings as places of worship.

And it is surely the very physicality of largely empty churches and chapels in Britain that plays such a powerful role in popular perceptions of 'religion'. Regular churchgoers and the clergy themselves may become partially blind to this. Time and again I have been assured by clergy in particular that, from a theological perspective, churchgoing and the provision of church buildings are relatively unimportant activities.

Viewed from the planet Uranus this assurance would, I suspect, appear strange to its inhabitants. Surely what they must notice is that especially Anglicans and Methodists spend a large proportion of their time maintaining church buildings and go to great lengths to provide accommodation and, with decreasing success, a stipendiary minister for even the smallest populations to go to church. In many towns and cities they might even notice whole rows of churches and chapels built side by side. But being inhabitants of Uranus, they might mistakenly conclude from this that such proximity derived from deep bonds of mutual love between these churches and chapels.

When journalists write about religious decline, they characteristically cite the empty church as the primary evidence of this decline. They might or might not discover longitudinal membership statistics, or single-point measurements of belief or of churchgoing, but, without fail, they draw attention to the empty church. Thus they argue, as religion is churches, and churches are empty, so *ipso facto* religion is no more. Such an implicit syllogism may then inspire clergy to fresh denials of the religious significance of churches and churchgoers.

It is obvious to most people that a majority of churches and chapels in Britain today are more empty than full. Of course there are some striking exceptions – in particular Catholic churches and some charismatic evangelical churches. These apart, Sunday congregations are seen as characteristically sparse. Furthermore, the elderly often remember their churches being much fuller in the past.

1

If there is widespread agreement about all of this, there is little consensus about the factors that have led to these sparse congregations. In the extensive interviews I have conducted, many people attribute the empty church to a single cause and often do this with considerable vehemence. However, the causal factors (predominantly cultural) offered differ very widely from person to person. Many people seem to *know* why churches are empty, even though they cannot agree among themselves why this is so. Thus a questionnaire-survey of current opinions on this would be a very unreliable method for discovering the origins of empty churches.

Much more reliable might be to start from a consensus that has developed among many sociologists of religion and social historians. Here, at least, is a group of scholars who have taken a long-term view of empty churches and have frequently set them in a context of an overall process of secularization. To understand the origins of empty churches, and perhaps of church decline generally, it would seem necessary first to understand the complex ways that secularization has transformed British culture.

This consensus might be expressed schematically in terms of ten propositions:

1   Before the First World War a majority of churches in Britain were full.
2   The Victorians built extra churches because they needed them to meet the demands of rapidly expanding urban and rural populations.
3   Competitive church building between denominations raised the general level of churchgoing throughout the nineteenth century.
4   Urban church building never quite kept pace with late nineteenth-century urban population growth and thus excluded significant sections of the urban working classes.
5   Churchgoing started to decline generally in proportion to the population only after the First World War.
6   Disillusionment resulting from the war was a significant factor in causing this decline, especially among urban working-class men.
7   Secularization – the product of nineteenth-century developments in science and rational thought and spread in the twentieth century through better education – has proved to be the most abiding factor in church decline.
8   Urbanization – involving the breakdown of rural communities upon which churches thrive – has also contributed significantly to church decline.
9   Twentieth-century leisure activities – cars, radios, televisions, etc. – have also contributed to church decline.
10 An accumulative result of these various external factors is that British churches (with the significant exception of competitive evangelical churches) have recently become secularized and increasingly empty.

Taken together, these ten propositions offer a very full account of why churchgoing in Britain has declined and why most churches and chapels are now predominantly empty. They also offer an indication of how, and in what form, religious organizations might survive in the future.

At the heart of this understanding is the notion of secularization. This is seemingly a process that started to affect British society in the nineteenth century and then to affect the institutional churches themselves in the twentieth century. In short, church decline started with a crisis in religious belief. The gradual effect of some of the leading intellectuals of the nineteenth and early twentieth century – notably Darwin, Marx and Freud – has been that religious belief has become increasingly implausible to ever larger sections of the population and that churchgoing has, as a result, slowly atrophied and been replaced by other leisure activities. Empty churches are but the latest visible evidence of this long process of secularization.

Owen Chadwick has characterized this process in cultural terms as 'the secularization of the European mind'.[1] Peter Berger, in his earlier writings at least, viewed it in more structural terms as the process by which religious institutions in an increasingly secular world assume the status of 'deviant cognitive minorities'.[2] For both scholars, although remaining religious believers themselves, secularization started as a crisis of religious belief that gradually eroded religious institutions.

Other explanations of the origins of empty churches are secondary to this process. Once religious beliefs became tenuous, it is hardly surprising that the widespread disillusionment caused by the First World War or the allures of late twentieth-century technology have also had their effect on churchgoing. Without a supporting consensus of belief, churchgoing has naturally become increasingly fragile – so much so that almost any radical social change is now likely to result in further empty churches.

Evidently urbanization has made profound changes. Even fragile religious beliefs might still be supported by face-to-face rural communities. However, once set in the anonymity of urban environments, it is again not surprising to find that they atrophy. This is especially likely when it is also discovered that churches themselves failed to respond fast enough to the rapid urban growth of the late nineteenth and early twentieth centuries. Churches simply failed to provide the sort of supporting network (especially for the new industrial working classes) that might have preserved religious communities in urban areas.[3] In any case, urban areas themselves were probably unsuitable venues for predominantly rural churches. Neither the structures nor the ethos of churches were appropriate for urban areas. Fragile beliefs depend for their survival upon small-scale communities. In the absence of such communities, religious beliefs soon withered in cities and a gradual demise of churchgoing inevitably followed.

This overall process has been plotted in statistical terms by Robert Currie, Alan Gilbert and Lee Horsley in their highly influential *Churches and Churchgoers*.[4] For a number of years it provided an authoritative source for most of the ten propositions just outlined. The authors were well aware of a cluster of factors

---

[1] Owen Chadwick, *The Secularization of the European Mind in the Nineteenth Century*, Cambridge University Press, Cambridge, 1975.

[2] See Peter L. Berger, *The Sacred Canopy*, Doubleday, New York, 1967; published in Britain as *The Social Reality of Religion*, Faber and Faber, London, 1969, and *A Rumour of Angels*, Doubleday, New York, 1967 and Penguin, Hamondsworth, 1969.

[3] See E.R. Wickham, *Church and People in an Industrial City*, Lutterworth, London, 1957.

[4] Robert Currie, Alan Gilbert and Lee Horsley, *Churches and Churchgoers: Patterns of Church Growth in the British Isles Since 1700*, Cambridge University Press, Cambridge, 1977.

affecting churchgoing – economic, political, technological, and those to do with two world wars – yet they maintained that it was secularization that was the primary factor: 'Secularization affects all other exogenous determinants of church growth because the long-term result of cultural changes tending to reduce the appeal of church membership is to minimize the effect of all factors promoting growth and to maximize the effect of all factors inhibiting growth.'[5] By 1977 Currie, Gilbert and Horsley were aware that there were already some powerful sociological critics of the notion of secularization,[6] but they were convinced that their carefully gathered statistical evidence demonstrated the process quite clearly:

> But secularization, in the sense of a diminished resort to supernatural means, can be seen in the British Isles; and this process is manifested in a diminution of both the quantity, and what Wilson calls the 'social significance', of 'religious thinking, practice and institutions'. That very many opinion-poll respondents claim to 'believe in God' is scarcely evidence to the contrary since the very concept of God has undergone, even in the thought of church leaders and theologians, certain well-attested changes which hardly contribute to the perception of God as a concrete, effective supernatural entity ...
>
> Moreover, the widespread claim, again among opinion-poll respondents, to engage in private prayer or other secret devotions is not strong evidence against secularization, both because the claim not to do so is now more widespread, and because over time the incidence of these devotions, as recorded by such data, is decreasing. And of course other forms of religious activity are decreasing also ... the membership of the major British Protestant churches fell from 5 to 4.5 million between 1900 and 1970, while the total British population rose from 37 to 53 million; and though the Catholic population rose through immigration, the number of British recruits to Catholicism also fell. The audiences for religious broadcasts too, have declined ... especially in the case of those broadcasts whose religious content is most overt. Given such evidence, it would seem difficult to argue that 'secularization' is not at work in Britain.[7]

On the basis of a mass of statistical evidence, they argued that the relationship between secularization and church growth/decline could be measured in three distinct periods. In the first of these periods – that up to 1914 – they showed that, although civil marriages increased from 2.6 per cent of all marriages in 1838 to 24.1 per cent in 1914, Protestant church membership increased from 18.4 per cent to 19.6 per cent of the adult population. Thus 'secularization may have delimited the number of church members and potential members ... but it did not greatly affect membership retention'.[8]

In the second period of time – 1914–1939 – civil marriages again increased, from 24.1 per cent to 29 per cent, but Protestant church membership fell from 19.6 per cent to 15.4 per cent. 'In other words, a rise in about a fifth in the civil-marriage rate accompanied a fall of about a fifth in Protestant density; and it seems probable that during this period, secularization, as measured by the civil

[5] Currie, Gilbert and Horsley, *Churches and Churchgoers*, p. 101.

[6] They refer to David A. Martin's classic article 'Towards Eliminating the Concept of Secularisation', reprinted in his *The Religious and the Secular*, Routledge & Kegan Paul, London, 1969.

[7] Currie, Gilbert and Horsley, *Churches and Churchgoers*, pp. 99–100.

[8] Currie, Gilbert and Horsley, *Churches and Churchgoers*, p. 100.

marriage-rate, had begun to affect the behaviour of both church members and potential church members.'[9]

It was in the third period that secularization became most evident:

> After 1940, the loyalty of church members' children began to fall significantly and this development can perhaps be associated with a more rapid secularization of British culture. Furthermore, from 1940 onwards fluctuations in church membership seem to become quite closely connected with fluctuations in support for explicitly secularist organizations ... during this period the short-term increase of rationalists, and the short-term decrease of church members, do for the first time seem to arise from the operation of the same, or very closely connected, causes; and those causes would appear to consist, above all, in short-term changes in the level of secularization.[10]

The strength of the Currie, Gilbert and Horsley analysis is that it was based upon a wealth of statistical data. *Churches and Churchgoers* acted as a pioneer work in attempting to come to an objective understanding of church decline and is now widely used by social historians and sociologists alike. Indeed, it has inspired a new generation of scholars to examine thoroughly statistical data related to churches.[11] Furthermore, from the analysis offered in the book, it should be possible to construct a fairly full account of the origins of the empty church.

This analysis also makes possible predictions about the future of religious organizations. The authors were strictly concerned with analysis, not with prescription. In this respect their aims are different from my own. However, they did offer some hints about the future, on the basis of which churches themselves might form policies:

> The continued secularization of British culture has restricted the churches' opportunities to profit from political crises. For the churches' fundamental problem during recent generations has been to demonstrate the utility of church membership; and the spread of secular attitudes and assumptions has made this problem ever less soluble ... The most striking effect of secularization, so far as the churches are concerned, is simple disbelief in the supernatural. Plainly once such belief becomes widespread, individuals need unusual qualities to be sure of the utility of churches' religious functions ... In recent years many Sunday schools have virtually collapsed, and there is no evidence that the churches have found a satisfactory means of reorganizing their methods of indirect recruitment. The churches' recent difficulties arise not merely from the problems of recruiting members but also from the problems of retaining members once made. Membership termination may be said to arise from two sources. On the one hand, a church member is likely to surrender his membership if he ceases to believe in its utility, or if he regards the costs of membership as greater than the benefits. On the other hand, he is also likely to relinquish membership if he ceases to belong to the church-centred community in which membership was regarded as normal and acceptable.[12]

---

[9] Currie, Gilbert and Horsley, *Churches and Churchgoers*, p. 101.

[10] Currie, Gilbert and Horsley, *Churches and Churchgoers*, p. 101.

[11] e.g. Jeffrey Cox, *The English Churches in a Secular Society: Lambeth, 1870–1930*, Oxford University Press, Oxford, 1982, and Callum Brown, *The Social History of Religion in Scotland since 1730*, Methuen, London, 1987.

[12] Currie, Gilbert and Horsley, *Churches and Churchgoers*, pp. 121–3.

From this it can be seen that the prognosis of *Churches and Churchgoers* for mainstream denominations was bleak. I doubt if the authors would have dissented from Bryan Wilson's judgement that the future of religious organizations lies with sects rather than with churches or denominations.[13] Exclusive forms of sects alone have the powerful control mechanisms needed to reduce the effects of a hostile surrounding culture. It is such sects that characteristically build protective barriers against the secular world. Their exclusive terms of membership, high self-esteem, rigorous organizational structures and exclusive doctrinal positions are all important means to achieve this.[14] In contrast and in an increasingly secular environment, mainstream denominations – with their inclusive forms of membership, lack of particularism, diffuse organizational structures and pluralist doctrinal positions – are destined for virtual, if not actual, extinction.

But since *Churches and Churchgoers* was published, there has been a very considerable change of opinion about secularization among both sociologists of religion and social historians studying religion. Currie, Gilbert and Horsley were clearly aware of some of the early criticisms of the notion of secularization. Yet, like Wilson, they maintained that it was still the main explanatory factor involved in church decline. A quarter of a century later it is difficult to find more than a handful of specialists who still see secularization as an ineluctable process sweeping all things religious before it. In this respect Wilson has become surprisingly isolated.

It is now frequently claimed that secularization is too Euro-centric a notion. Three types of evidence are usually cited in support of this claim.[15] First, there is the evidence of recent fundamentalist resurgences within Christianity, Islam and other religious systems, that have taken place elsewhere in the world. Secondly, there is the evidence about the continuing role of religion as a power within national conflicts – in the Middle East, Northern Ireland and especially in the events following September 11. And thirdly, there is the evidence about the persistence of 'unofficial' or 'implicit' forms of religion within supposedly 'secular' Britain as elsewhere. As a result of these three types of evidence, scholars more usually talk today about Britain as being 'religiously pluralist' not secularized. Some even see secularization as a feature of an outmoded 'modernism': for them we now live in a post-modern or post-industrial society. It is possible that 'dechristianization' rather than secularization may more accurately depict religious changes that are currently taking place in British society.

Furthermore, as I shall point out in several places in the pages that follow, secularization never was a very useful explanation of declines in churchgoing. Not the least of the reasons for this is that it makes little sense of the wholly different

---

[13] See Bryan Wilson, *Religion in Secular Society*, Watts, London, 1966, and *Religion in Sociological Perspective*, Oxford University Press, Oxford, 1982.

[14] See Bryan Wilson, *The Social Dimensions of Sectarianism: Sects and New Religious Movements in Contemporary Society*, Oxford University Press, Oxford, 1990.

[15] See the following collections: Philip E. Hammond (ed.), *The Sacred in a Secular Age*, University of California Press, Berkeley, 1984; J. Obelkevich, L. Roper and R. Samuel (eds), *Disciplines of Faith: Studies in Religion, Politics and Patriarchy*, Routledge, London, 1987; James A. Beckford and Thomas Luckmann (eds), *The Changing Face of Religion*, Sage, London, 1989; and Steve Bruce (ed.), *Religion and Modernization*, Oxford University Press, Oxford, 1992.

American evidence. There, churchgoing increased at just the same time that British churchgoing was declining most rapidly. Yet in both contexts higher education should have ensured the spread of a secular intellectual culture and, supposedly following upon it, the gradual demise of churchgoing.

In the course of this book I will be questioning each of the ten propositions outlined earlier. I will argue that each is vulnerable to surprisingly complete census data on churchgoing. Despite its title, *Churches and Churchgoers* presents very little data on churchgoing as such. For the most part it presents data on church membership and (even worse) affiliation and, as a result, I will argue that it seriously misled a generation of scholars. Specifically, its detailed claims about secularization cannot be sustained in the light of longitudinal census data on churchgoing.

Precisely because these ten propositions have had such a powerful control over academics and others, it is, I believe, appropriate to regard them as 'myths'. In a popular sense myths are purely fictional stories. Even in an academic context 'myths' retain a suggestion of fictionality. However, there is more to myths than that. They are powerful representations in story or epigrammatic form which mould perceptions and understandings. And the process of 'demythologizing' is a process of contesting these representations and replacing them with others that more accurately reflect the evidence of experience and/or data. This is exactly my task.

To give but a small indication of what is to follow, it is worth briefly recasting the ten propositions. In itself, this task will not furnish a full set of alternative explanations of the origins of empty churches. Explanations must emerge slowly from the new data that I will present. But for the moment the counter-propositions are as follows:

1   Before the First World War a majority of churches in Britain were more empty than full. By 1901 in rural areas, despite some very high churchgoing rates, there was a considerable excess of church seating over population. Occasionally this also happened in urban areas. More typically, by the turn of the century urban churches and chapels, with seats sufficient for at least two-fifths of urban populations, were on average only a third full at Sunday services.

2   The Victorians built extra churches and chapels for a variety of reasons, only some of which had to do with expanding populations or expanding congregations. In rural areas in the second half of the nineteenth century they built and restored churches vigorously against rapidly declining populations. And frequently they built mission chapels to counter churchgoing decline, rather than because existing churches were full. The Free Churches in all major urban areas built so vigorously that their chapels were always physically emptier by the 1880s than they had been in 1851, even when their churchgoing rates were still rising. Paradoxically, empty chapels in the Free Churches *preceded* a decline in their churchgoing rate.

3   Competitive church building between denominations may well have raised the general level of churchgoing in the first half of the nineteenth century. However, in the second half it was already proving to be counter-productive, in terms of an increase in empty churches and chapels, in both rural and urban areas.

4   Chapel building by the Free Churches exceeded population growth between 1851 and the 1880s in every major urban area studied. There was always more than adequate provision, across denominations, for the urban working classes. Wickham's pioneer work on Sheffield[16] was, in this crucial respect, misleading. Until the middle of the twentieth century, children used this provision extensively, but adults, even when benefiting from church philanthropy, did not.

5   In most urban areas, the year 1851 represents the highest point of Church of England attendances at services: since then there has been an almost continuous process of churchgoing decline. In the Free Churches the 1880s represent the highest point of attendances; for most of them, also, decline has been virtually uninterrupted since then.

6   There is considerable evidence of disillusionment with the churches long before the First World War. Furthermore, it is difficult to show that this war had any appreciable effect on churchgoing rates. Indeed, the decade immediately following the Second World War appears to have been a period of slight increase in suburban churchgoing.

7   Cultural secularization is a most unlikely cause of churchgoing decline. Suburban middle-class areas have been among the most recent areas to decline in terms of churchgoing, yet their residents should in theory have been among the earliest to have been affected by developments in science and rational thought. The collapse of chapel-going among the adult urban working classes (a group surely least affected by early developments in science and philosophical thought) happened decades earlier. Despite the claims of *Churches and Churchgoers*, evidence from social attitude questionnaires suggests that the decline in conventional Christian belief is far more recent than that in churchgoing.

8   Some urban areas in the nineteenth century recorded significantly higher churchgoing rates than those in the surrounding countryside. Ironically, it was the highly rural district of Haltwhistle in Northumberland that recorded the lowest churchgoing rate in 1851 for any district in England or Wales. Furthermore, areas of middle-class urban churchgoing persisted with very high levels well into the twentieth century. Conversely, churchgoing rates today seem to be declining faster in rural than in suburban areas. Outside Europe, low churchgoing rates have frequently been a feature of rural not urban areas.

9   Twentieth-century leisure activities, although frequently held responsible for empty churches by churchgoers themselves, have not been associated with churchgoing decline in the United States. Urban churchgoing decline in Britain both in the Church of England and in the Free Churches, predates the technological developments of the twentieth century.

10 Over the full period of 150 years for which extensive churchgoing statistics are available, it is British Catholics and not evangelicals who until recently have most consistently maintained full churches. Their pattern of church building is

---

[16] See Wickham, *Church and People in an Industrial City*.

wholly different from that of any other denomination: alone they have never provided sufficient church seating for more than half of their average attendances. Today Anglicans have less attendances nationally than Catholics, but more than five times the number of church buildings. Methodists have only a third of Catholic attendances, but more than twice as many buildings. Not surprisingly, perhaps, both Anglican and Methodist churches today are characteristically empty. Only a very few Anglican evangelical congregations (and even fewer non-Anglican congregations) can match current (albeit declining) attendances at most urban Catholic churches.

These counter-propositions obviously hint at arguments to be elaborated later in the book. I will maintain that inattention to some of the physical factors underlying churches has distorted perceptions and perpetuated misleading myths. Of course I am fully aware of more cultural explanations of churchgoing decline. Furthermore, by focusing upon physical explanations instead, I have no intention of offering a monocausal explanation of this decline. It will become clear that this is not simply an argument about buildings, but also about economics and social space.

In the process a variety of unfamiliar disciplines must be explored. For example, the economics of religion is as yet a remarkably undeveloped field of study, yet it has profound implications for the churches and, as I shall argue, for understanding differing levels of churchgoing. The social geography of religion is slightly more developed as an academic discipline,[17] but not in the area of long-term patterns of churchgoing and church building. The relationship of buildings and church furnishings to the changing needs of worship has also received sustained scholarship.[18] Although even here the dominant interest has been in liturgical change rather than secularization. In short, religious physicality is an area ripe for inspection.

However, the point of this inspection only becomes clear when explanations based upon a notion of an ineluctable process of secularization are seen to be strongly contested. If there is a single key myth that must first be questioned if further analysis is to proceed, it is the following:

Churchgoing decline results primarily from a gradual loss of religious belief, itself resulting from the development of scientific and rational thought in the nineteenth century, and enhanced by war and technology in the twentieth century.

So long as this key myth remains unchallenged, the empty church is not intellectually problematic. Occasional resurgences of churchgoing might still be expected among the gullible and superstitious, but amongst an increasingly educated population churchgoing would inevitably become a declining and socially insignificant form of activity.

---

[17] e.g. *Geographia Religionum: Interdisziplinäre Schriftenreihe zur Religions-geographie*, Dietrich Reimer Verlag.

[18] e.g. Nigel Yates, *Buildings, Faith and Worship: The Liturgical Arrangements of Anglican Churches 1600–1900*, Oxford University Press, Oxford, 1991.

However, once this key myth is contested, empty churches do become intellectually problematic. This is especially the case when they can be seen to be a feature of only some parts, and only some denominations, of the Western world. Once it is no longer acceptable to resort uncritically to a notion of secularization, churches take on a new complexity. The serious scholar is forced to go back to the data and to ask new and unfamiliar questions. Perhaps even a naïve question: Where do empty churches come from?

1

The Data

Until about ten years ago sociologists of religion tended to pay more attention to sects and to new religious movements than to long-established denominations or churches. With a few important exceptions at the time,[1] mainstream churches seldom received the sort of detailed attention that one might expect given their prevalence and greater size. In part this may have resulted from lingering suspicions of 'Religious Sociology' and to the ecclesiastical control often thought to lurk behind it in France. It may also have been a consequence of the sheer difficulty of analysing amorphous religious institutions. Small scale religious bodies, in addition to being frequently more exotic and deviant, are also perhaps more sociologically controllable. Whatever the reason, long-established denominations until recently remained surprisingly unresearched.

Even when sociologists did show an interest in long-established denominations they typically relied upon generalized data. As has been noted already, *Churches and Churchgoers*[2] invaluable as it may be as a source of historical information about national church membership, is notoriously lacking in information about Sunday-by-Sunday churchgoing and tends to put forward factors deemed responsible for church decline in a highly impressionistic manner. And the vast literature on secularization tended to avoid statistical data altogether; or else it used *both* statistics indicating church decline in Europe and statistics showing persisting (but supposedly epiphenomenal) churchgoing in the United States as indications of secularization.[3]

In contrast, it was initially a number of younger social historians who showed an interest in churches as social phenomena. Stephen Yeo's detailed study of Reading in the nineteenth and early twentieth centuries, *Religion and Voluntary Organisations in Crisis,*[4] proved to be a pioneer work and is well known to sociologists of religion. So did Hugh McLeod's *Class and Religion in the Late Victorian City.*[5] Rather less well known is Jeffrey Cox's *The English Churches in a Secular Society: Lambeth, 1870–1930,*[6] James Obelkevich's *Religion and Rural*

---

[1] The most striking exception is Michael P. Hornsby-Smith in his three important books: *Roman Catholics in England*, Cambridge University Press, Cambridge, 1987; *The Changing Parish*, Routledge, London, 1989; and *Roman Catholic Beliefs in England*, Cambridge University Press, Cambridge, 1991.

[2] Robert Currie, Alan Gilbert and Lee Horsley, *Churches and Churchgoers: Patterns of Church Growth in the British Isles Since 1700*, Cambridge University Press, Cambridge, 1977.

[3] e.g. Bryan Wilson in *Religion in Secular Society*, Watts, London, 1966 and *Contemporary Transformations of Religion*, Oxford University Press, Oxford, 1976. I reviewed some of the recent literature on secularization at the time in my *Competing Convictions*, SCM Press, London, 1989.

[4] Croom Helm, London, 1976.

[5] Croom Helm, London, 1974.

[6] Oxford University Press, Oxford, 1982.

Society: South Lindsey 1825–1875,[7] and Callum Brown's *The Social History of Religion in Scotland Since 1730*.[8] Together with a number of research dissertations and doctorate theses that they have often served to inspire,[9] they suggested that there is considerably more statistical evidence available on churches as social phenomena than is often imagined, and that it is directly relevant to understanding the decline of most British churches throughout the twentieth century. Far from being generalized studies, they each show that an intense analysis of churches in specific areas yields insights that cannot be deduced from national church membership statistics.

This use of church statistics has dramatically changed among sociologists of religion in the last few years. I will not dwell on this since I have analysed it elsewhere,[10] but it is worth noting the impact of recent works using a wide range of statistics such as Grace Davie's *Religion in Modern Europe: A Memory Mutates*,[11] Steve Bruce's *God is Dead: Secularization in the West*,[12] and again Callum Brown in his *The Death of Christian Britain*.[13]

1

The accumulative effect of these studies has been to undermine the approach championed by Currie, Gilbert and Horsley's *Churches and Churchgoers*. The latter argued that churchgoing statistics collected through various local censuses 'have contributed little to the formation of time series'.[14] Instead, they insisted that national church membership statistics are the most valuable resource:

> But religious statistics [of local attendance] are, however useful, of secondary importance compared with those collected by the churches themselves. Just as, for example, it would be impossible to study the growth of trade unions or political parties without reference to their own membership series, it is impossible to study church growth unless the churches' own membership returns are used; and these returns are probably unique among those available for organizations in Britain, both in quantity and in variety.[15]

Although this claim might at first seem plausible, on closer inspection it faces a number of formidable difficulties. Not the least of these is that the very concept of 'church membership' is a Free Church concept. Comparison of, say, varieties of

---

[7] Oxford University Press, Oxford, 1976.

[8] Methuen, London, 1987.

[9] For dissertations and theses until 1987, see Clive D. Field, 'Non-Recurrent Christian Data', *Reviews of United Kingdom Statistical Sources*, vol. XX, *Religion*, Royal Statistical Society and Economic and Social Research Council, Pergamon Press, Oxford, 1987, pp. 189–504.

[10] See my *Churchgoing and Christian Ethics*, Cambridge University Press, Cambridge, 1999 and *Changing Worlds*, Continuum, London, 2002.

[11] Oxford University Press, Oxford, 2000.

[12] Blackwell, Oxford, 2002.

[13] Routledge, London, 2001.

[14] Currie, Gilbert and Horsley, *Churches and Churchgoers*, p. 11.

[15] Currie, Gilbert and Horsley, *Churches and Churchgoers*, p. 12.

Methodist membership at a single point of time might have real value. In all probability they shared an understanding of 'church membership' and even had similar procedures for measuring this membership. But the Church of England has never had a comparable concept of 'church membership', nor has the Catholic Church.

This is an obvious, but very long-standing, deficiency. Those attempting to compare the relative strengths of British denominations have been struggling with it for more than 150 years. In what has been termed the first specifically English survey of the relative strength of denominations, the Congregational Union survey of 1834 distinguished between 'hearers' and 'communicants'.[16] However, in the process the survey clearly imposed Free Church concepts on other denominations. Although, as is seen in Chapter 5, the evidence produced in the Congregational Union survey is not worthless, it does have to be approached with considerable caution.[17]

To remedy this deficiency, *Churches and Churchgoers* treated Easter Communions as indicators of Church of England 'membership' – on the basis, presumably, that Easter Communion is supposed to be a requirement of belonging. In reality, despite many attempts by bishops and clergy to make it a requirement (questions about communicants have continuously featured in bishops' questions to their clergy since the eighteenth century), Easter Communion has not been a serious indicator of Anglican belonging, or more accurately 'conformity', since the seventeenth century. Even then, seasonal 'conformity' was compatible with regular attendance at 'dissenting' chapels.

In the pages that follow abundant evidence is provided to show that Easter communicants in the Church of England represented a very small proportion of regular attendances in both rural and urban areas in the mid-nineteenth century. Furthermore, the ratio between regular attendances and Easter communicants show considerable local variations today. In rural areas of England, Easter communicants represent as much as three times the average Sunday congregation; in urban areas they are seldom more than half as much again. Thus, Easter communicants vary as an indicator of Anglican belonging both over time and within time – or, to express this more technically, variations are diachronic as well as synchronic.

Confusion about how the notion of 'membership' applies to Catholics is even more obvious. *Churches and Churchgoers* relies primarily upon 'estimated Catholic populations'. These are based on estimations by local Catholic priests of the number of Catholics living in their parishes, regardless of whether or not they are practising Catholics. Often estimated from baptisms, they are, in most Free Church understandings, affiliation rather than membership statistics. Aware of this difficulty, early versions of MARC Europe's *UK Christian Handbook*[18] relied instead upon regular Mass attendances (measured on the last Sunday every October) to produce statistics that can be compared with 'membership' in other

---

[16] 'A Comparative View of the Hearers, Communicants, and Scholars Belonging to Churchmen, Dissenters, and Wesleyan Methodists in Two Hundred and Three Towns and Villages', *The Supplement to the Congregational Magazine*, 1834.

[17] cf. Field, 'Non-Recurrent Christian Data', p. 236.

[18] Peter Brierley (ed.), *UK Christian Handbook*, MARC Europe, 1989/1990 edition. Christian Research, London.

denominations. Unfortunately this approach confuses membership and churchgoing statistics.

It is evident from this that 'church membership' is a very odd concept for the two largest denominations in England and Wales. Because a number of Free Churches (especially Methodists) have kept national 'membership' figures for such a long period of time, it is understandably tempting to try to squeeze Anglicans and Catholics into the same mould. However, in so doing a minority criterion is transformed into a yardstick for measuring all. As a result, some very curious statistics emerge. Sadly, it cannot be considered to be a serious means of assessing relative interdenominational strengths and weaknesses.

Membership may not even be a very consistent measure of Free Church belonging. Later I show that the ratio of members to quarterly Communion attenders in a number of Free Churches changed significantly over time. The twentieth century has seen a widening gap between official communicant membership rolls and numbers of people actually attending seasonal communion services. Furthermore, the urban churchgoing statistics reviewed later suggest that national Methodist membership statistics at the Union of 1932 considerably exaggerated the strength of Methodism at the time. Many chapels already had a higher proportion of largely dormant 'members' than they would have had in the mid-nineteenth century.

What emerges from this, I believe, is the realization that an intense study of churches at a local level and over a sufficient period of time (using records of local attendances rather than national membership figures) is a prerequisite for investigating the social factors underlying church decline.

This would be a standard premise in the sociological study of sects or new religious movements. Ever since the 1950s, and in particular Bryan Wilson's pioneering *Sects and Society*,[19] the detailed local study of small-scale religious bodies has been preferred to generalized discussions of them as national, or international, institutions. Presumably this is based upon the realization that national information is often partisan and may not accurately represent the way a religious body functions in practice.

But this applies *a fortiori* to churches. The claims that a church makes at a national level may or may not be based upon the way it functions in practice at the local level. Indeed, part of the skill of the social scientist involves comparing claims with actual behaviour. To make such comparisons there is no substitute for detailed empirical research; and it has, perhaps, been the most obvious failing of the literature on secularization that it has seldom been based upon such research.

2

In this book I examine a great deal of data, much from local censuses and most previously uncollated. It is astonishing that so many generalizations about church

---

[19] Bryan Wilson, *Sects and Society*, Heinemann, London, 1955; see also his *The Social Dimensions of Sectarianism: Sects and New Religious Movements in Contemporary Society*, Oxford University Press, Oxford, 1990.

decline and secularization were made without anyone surveying this evidence before. To be honest, I had little concept myself of its extent until I started this research in the late 1980s. I had assumed for years that longitudinal statistics about regular churchgoing patterns were largely unattainable. Certainly I had assumed that little was available outside the three nationwide censuses of church attendances: namely, the 1851 Religious Census,[20] and the 1979 and 1989 (and now the 1998) MARC Europe/Christian Research censuses.[21]

In fact, there is a wealth of data from at least six major sources, as well as an invaluable source guide to most of the data produced by Clive Field.[22] There is the 1851 Religious Census which covered the whole of England and Wales and (with more gaps and no surviving original returns) Scotland. There are independent newspaper censuses for the 1880s, and occasionally for the 1890s and 1900s. There are occasional censuses conducted by statistical societies and individuals for the 1830s and for several points in the twentieth century. There are numerous local clergy returns to bishops, Catholic records and sometimes Free Church records, with information about average Sunday attendances. These often start in the 1850s or the 1860s: in Lancashire they start in the 1820s, in Oxford in the 1830s, and in North Yorkshire they continue without substantial breaks right up to the present day.

Furthermore, several denominations today go to considerable lengths to collect average Sunday attendances on a systematic basis. Ironically, they seldom make much use of this information and recently the Church of England has become distinctly more wary about even collecting the data.[23] Perhaps they too feel that the general decline it illustrates is simply an indication of a broader process of secularization that they are powerless to combat. Finally, there are the churchgoing statistics for the whole of Britain compiled from clergy returns to the censuses directed by Peter Brierley of MARC Europe/Christian Research. There are crucial gaps in the information supplied from local churches to MARC Europe: Independent Churches, perhaps not surprisingly, have proved to be somewhat elusive. For example, some of the 1979 figures were considerably adjusted both at the time and when reported a decade later alongside 1989 figures. Nevertheless, Peter Brierley's work has become an immensely valuable resource – gathering original data, collating research done by others and responding sensitively to changing research methods over a quarter of a century.

Altogether there is a great deal of long-term data on churchgoing in England and Wales going back some 170 years. Up to now, this evidence has never been properly collated.

---

[20] Horace Mann, *1851 Census Great Britain: Report and Tables on Religious Worship England and Wales*, British Parliamentary Papers, Population 10, 1852–3 (reprinted by Irish University Press, Shannon, 1970).

[21] Peter Brierley (ed.), *Prospects for the Eighties*, MARC Europe, 1980, *Prospects for the Nineties: Trends and Tables from the English Church Census*, MARC Europe, 1991, and *UK Christian Handbook: Religious Trends*, No. 2 (1999) and No. 3 (2001), Christian Research, Vision Building, 4 Footscray Road, London SE9 2TZ.

[22] Field, 'Non-Recurrent Christian Data', pp. 189–504.

[23] See further Chapter 6 of my *Changing Worlds*.

In so far as those discussing secularization in Britain referred, until recently, to statistical data at all, they characteristically used the weakest forms of data. Baptism, membership and (worst of all) affiliation statistics of religious institutions tend to be cited. Few made serious use of this much more obvious and, so I argue, more reliable indicator: namely, diachronic regular church or chapel attendance (although in the decade since *The Myth of the Empty Church* was first published, this situation has slowly begun to change).

There are several possible reasons for this extraordinary situation. The first may simply be that sociologists, and to a lesser extent social historians, have often been unaware of the extensive urban census statistics that exist – sometimes well hidden in ecclesiastical archives or in local newspaper reports.[24] The second may be a result of unease about how attendance data (rather than data about separate attenders), collected at different points in the day, can satisfactorily be compared. The third may result from the variability of external factors such as weather, time of year, and methods of collecting the data. For example, can clergy returns (as in the 1851 Religious Census and numerous nineteenth-century and early twentieth-century clergy returns to bishops) be reliably compared with independent enumerations of church attendances (as in the London 1887 and 1903 censuses, many of the 1881 large town censuses, the two Birmingham censuses of 1887 and 1892, and the four Liverpool censuses of 1881–1912)? Can data collected on a fine day in the summer be satisfactorily compared with data collected on a wet day in January?

The second and third of these reasons require a response. However, before giving this it is important to be clear about the sort of evidence that could or could not be gleaned from such data in relation to the secularization debate. Statistics about church or chapel attendances will never provide evidence about non-institutional forms of religiosity. Invisible, implicit, folk or unofficial religion (however characterized)[25] by most definitions is usually contrasted with regular church/chapel attendance. Equally, such statistics tell the researcher nothing about the cognitive world of those attending. Who knows, or will ever know, what was in the minds of all those Victorians who regularly attended churches and chapels? Before the advent of questionnaire surveys, our knowledge of the cognitive worlds of ordinary churchgoers is dependent largely upon the surviving written comments of clerical elites or, frequently partisan, local newspapers.

Churchgoing statistics are valuable rather because they provide evidence about one of the most socially visible aspects of institutional religion (others being church buildings and the presence or absence of clergy). Membership or affiliation statistics would perhaps be known to office bearers in churches and might occasionally (very occasionally in my experience of reading nineteenth-century newspapers) be reported more widely, but they would hardly impinge on the

---

[24] See Nigel Yates, 'Urban Church Attendance and the Use of Statistical Evidence, 1850–1900', in Derek Baker (ed.), *The Church in Town and Countryside*, vol. 16, Blackwell, Oxford, 1979.

[25] See P.H. Vrijhof and J. Waardenburg, *Official and Popular Religion: Analysis of a Theme for Religious Studies*, Mouton, Amsterdam, 1979; Edward Bailey (ed.), *A Workshop in Popular Religion*, Partners Publication, London, 1996 and 'Implicit Religion: A Bibliographical Introduction', *Social Compass*, vol. 37, 1990, pp. 499–509.

consciousness of most people. In addition they varied considerably in their social significance from one denomination to another – some, for example, making a distinction between members and adherents and others not. Within a single denomination, disciplines of membership also could vary over a period of time – becoming less, or occasionally more, strict. Even within those denominations in which the notion of 'church membership' can be used safely, there are still variations. In some cases membership indicates regular participation and /or giving and in other cases it does not.

On the other hand, seasonal conformity would clearly be more socially visible, at least at Christmas and Easter. Again, its nuance has changed considerably over time. Christmas, in popular perception, has today become overwhelmingly more important than Easter. Indeed, even official church statistics for Christmas scarcely give a reliable guide to the proportion of the population involved in carol services – in schools, on streets and even in supermarkets – over the Christmas season. Furthermore, even if it were possible accurately to measure the full extent of present-day seasonal conformity (itself an ambiguous term), by definition it remains an occasional phenomenon. Once a year the British celebrate Christmas in a confusion of sacred and profane activities. This is socially visible, but it comes but once a year.

Crucially, regular churchgoing statistics offer an important means of controlling variables. In addition, they offer the most consistent social manifestation of churches and chapels. Doubtless, individuals attend churches and chapels Sunday by Sunday for a variety of reasons. These reasons may vary over time, between denominations, within denominations, and even within the life-cycle, or just the changing moods, of individuals themselves. Of course very little of this is now accessible for the past. Even in the present it would take a remarkably subtle questionnaire or, better still, qualitative interviews to fathom all the different layers of motivation that encourage individuals to sustain regular churchgoing. However, there is also an obvious physicality about churchgoing and it is this that can be measured over time and across denominations.

What is more, unlike the notion of church membership, churchgoing as a social phenomenon is not primarily a Free Church, an Anglican, or a Catholic construct. Regular churchgoing is encouraged (even if not practised) by all denominations. In addition, all denominations provide buildings and functionaries at considerable expense to maintain regular churchgoing. Finally, it is possible to establish long-term patterns in churchgoing, regardless of the motives of the individuals involved, as a specifically social phenomenon.

In everything that follows it is vital to insist that other non-measurable variables may have been instrumental in general church decline. It would indeed be surprising if such a diffuse subject as church decline, or (broader still) secularization, could be easily resolved by statistical arguments. Yet, having conceded that, it is clearly a prerequisite of a debate in an area such as this, that that which is measurable is indeed measured before the non-measurable (and statistically uncontrollable) is used in any form of explanation. Precisely because so many and varied explanations have been offered in this area already – both by scholars and by the general public – it is imperative that churchgoing statistics are examined carefully.

3

But how can census data on church/chapel attendances be satisfactorily compared? There are several crucial problems that serious researchers soon encounter. Horace Mann's Report on the 1851 Religious Census[26] amalgamated churchgoing and Sunday school statistics, whereas subsequent censuses seldom (Bath is an exception)[27] included, or even gave separately, Sunday school statistics. It is, however, a comparatively simple, although arduous, task to go back to the original 1851 returns (only those for a very few places, notably Bristol and Halifax, are wholly missing) and count the Sunday school statistics separately, removing them from the published results or computing them afresh. For English statistics this entails regular visits to the Public Records Office at Kew, where the original 1851 returns are kept (local returns are sometimes also held on microfilm in County Record Offices or, more occasionally, are published by local history societies[28]). Welsh 1851 statistics, thankfully, have been published in full for every church and chapel.[29]

In all of the 1851 statistics given later, unless stated otherwise, I have already removed the Sunday school statistics. It is important to do this, since it will be seen that urban churchgoing started to decline while Sunday schools were still growing. As can be seen in *Table 6*, Sunday school enrolments in England and Wales (between two-thirds and three-quarters of whom generally attended on a typical Sunday) grew from some 11.5 per cent of the population under age fifteen in 1818, to 38.0 per cent in 1851, to 51.4 per cent in 1891 and to 52.6 per cent in 1901; they then declined to 51.4 per cent in 1911, to 45.8 per cent in 1931, and to 20.4 per cent in 1961.[30] Urban churchgoing, in England at least, started to decline much earlier.

Much more problematic is the long-standing issue of how to relate attendances to attenders. The 1851 Religious Census gave attendances for morning, afternoon and evening, while most subsequent censuses gave those only for morning and evening, despite the fact that in a few areas (e.g. Suffolk) churchgoing was strongest in 1851 in the afternoon. Only the occasional census attempted to estimate the proportion of attenders who were present at two or even three services. Furthermore, there are many indications that the practice of double or treble churchgoing (itself a nineteenth-century innovation compared to the dominant practice of the eighteenth century) faded significantly as the twentieth century developed. Thus total attendances in 1851 might not have represented the same number of attenders as the same amount of attendances in 1881, and they would certainly have been different from those in 2001.

---

[26] See Horace Mann, above.

[27] See *Keene's Bath Journal*, 12 November 1881.

[28] e.g. for Kent see Margaret Roake (ed.), *Religious Worship in Kent: The Census of 1851*, vol. XXVI, Kent Archaeological Society, The Museum, St Faith's Street, Maidstone, Kent, 1999, p. 39.

[29] I.G. Jones (ed.), *The Religious Census of 1851: A Calendar of the Returns Relating to Wales*, 2 vols, University of Wales Press, Cardiff, 1976 and 1981.

[30] The 1818 and 1851 figures have been calculated from *Education (1851) Census* and the 1891–1961 ones from Currie, Gilbert and Horsley, *Churches and Churchgoers*. The latter do not include Catholics or sects.

While recognizing these difficulties, this may not be quite so serious a problem in the context of the secularization debate. If regular churchgoing is regarded rather as an important, comparative indicator of the social visibility of religious institutions, then the amount of attenders as distinct from attendances is not so crucial. Whether and which churches and chapels were seen to be predominantly full or empty on a Sunday is far more apposite. Viewed from the perspective of the consumer, most people would surely have had little or no idea about what proportion of a given congregation attended more than once, or about how great the churchgoing rate was in relation to the total population of the area. Rather, what they would have observed were numerous churches and chapels, staffed by a variety of clergy and ministers, which were predominantly empty or full or something in between. Manifestly most churches and chapels in Britain today, with the exception of Catholic churches and a few evangelical churches, are more empty than full. It is popularly supposed that, at least until the First World War, most were more full than empty. I show presently that this supposition is not confirmed by census data on churchgoing.

Even if the focus, in the context of the secularization debate, is upon the social visibility of religious institutions, problems remain. The absence of Sunday afternoon attendances from most censuses after 1851 is certainly less than desirable. Yet there are several reports that suggest that by 1881 it was no longer so significant a churchgoing time of day,[31] although it remained an important time for Sunday schools. Instead, throughout urban England and Wales, the evening seems to have generally overtaken the morning (and evening overtaken the afternoon in Ipswich)[32] as the time of highest churchgoing. Doubtless this change – which was bemoaned by some commentators at the time – had something to do with the development of urban street lighting. Today this pattern has been fully reversed in most congregations, except in urban Catholic churches that have introduced Saturday evening Mass.

In the context of the secularization debate, the emphasis should be upon diachronic or longitudinal data. Census statistics only become interesting in this context if they can be measured in the same geographical area over at least two points of time. The 'Index', invented by ecclesiastical historians[33] to compare synchronic data in the 1851 Religious Census, is less appropriate for most diachronic comparisons. The Index amalgamates all attendances – churchgoing and Sunday school, morning, afternoon and evening – and expresses them as

---

[31] e.g. *Hampshire Telegraph and Sussex Chronicle*, 24 December 1881, reporting on Portsmouth and Gosport; see also the mission hall returns for London in *The British Weekly*'s *The Religious Census of London*, Hodder, London, 1888, and the afternoon attendances for Chelsea in Richard Mudie-Smith (ed.), *The Religious Life of London*, Hodder, London, 1904.

[32] See *Ipswich Free Press*, 19 November 1881.

[33] See K.S. Inglis, 'Patterns of Religious Worship in 1851', *Journal of Ecclesiastical History*, vol. 11, no. 1, 1960, pp. 74–86; R.B. Walker, 'Religious Changes in Cheshire, 1750–1850, *Journal of Ecclesiastical History*, vol. 17, no. 1, 1966, pp. 77–93; R.B. Walker, 'Religious Changes in Liverpool in the Nineteenth Century', *Journal of Ecclesiastical History*, vol. 19, no. 2, 1968, pp. 195–211; David M. Thompson, 'The 1851 Religious Census: Problems and Possibilities', *Victorian Studies*, vol. 11, 1967, pp. 87–97.

percentages of local populations in order to provide comparators from one area to another. In Chapter 5 it is seen that this can occasionally be useful to compare undifferentiated data from the 1820s and 1830s with the 1851 Religious Census. However, comparisons between, say, 1851 and 1881 more accurately amalgamate only morning and evening attendances, without Sunday school attendances (since the latter seem to have increased faster during this period than general churchgoing).

Alternatively, it is possible to compare the busiest time of day for churchgoing in one census with the busiest time of day for churchgoing in a later census of the same area. Of course, this is likely to be morning in the first census and evening in the second. Yet in both censuses attendances should represent separate attenders. Whichever system is used (the last is useful in Wales where evening attendances in 1881 were often the only ones given),[34] particular attention will be paid in such diachronic studies to changes in average levels of attendance per congregation in relation to seating available.

4

Then, of course, there is the problem of the comparability of censuses themselves. The state of the weather on census days, the time of year, and the method of collecting data all varied. Can data from such varied censuses really be compared satisfactorily? It is often assumed that censuses based upon clergy returns will be considerably exaggerated compared with those based upon independent enumerations (usually in the form of newspaper 'tellers' standing outside churches and chapels). Indeed, clergy reports of parish populations in the twentieth century are notoriously exaggerated.[35] For this reason it is sometimes argued that the 1851 Religious Census can be compared reliably with few subsequent censuses. Some social historians have even written disparagingly about the 'round numbers' that are characteristic of clergy estimations of attendances.[36] Some have also pointed out that bad weather might seriously affect attendances: total attendances on an exceedingly wet day in Cheltenham, 29 January 1882, amounted to 47.7 per cent of the population, whereas those just a week later, but on a fine day, amounted to 61.4 per cent.[37]

Of course such *ad hominem* arguments are seldom conclusive. Numbers can be rounded down as well as up and the sheer difficulty of estimating large congregations may account for the prevalence of such numbers. Furthermore, there are other instances of censuses in bad weather being repeated on more favourable days, but without the dramatic contrast provided by Cheltenham. In

---

[34] e.g. for Llanelly, see *Western Mail*, 25 November 1881, and for Corwen, see *Wrexham Advertiser*, 19 November 1881.

[35] e.g. see the Appendix to Leslie Paul, *The Deployment and Payment of the Clergy*, Church Information Office, London, 1964.

[36] e.g. Hugh McLeod, 'Class, Community and Religion: The Religious Geography of Nineteenth-Century England', in Michael Hill (ed.) *A Sociological Yearbook of Religion in Britain*, no. 6, SCM Press, London, 1973.

[37] Field, 'Non-Recurrent Christian Data', p. 293.

Bradford a census was taken on 11 December 1881. Unfortunately, 'early on Sunday morning there was a heavy fall of snow, which lay on the ground all day in a gradually thawing condition, and rendered the streets and roads most uncomfortable for church and chapel goers'.[38] Consequently the census was repeated on the following Sunday. Despite somewhat better weather, especially in the morning, the newspaper found that the difference in attendances 'was not great': morning and evening attendances combined increased only from 33.8 per cent to 34.4 per cent.

In Chapter 4 it is seen that attendances in 1908 on a wet January Sunday in Caernarfon differed surprisingly little from those on a fine Sunday in July (51 per cent in contrast to 55 per cent). After the first census the local newspaper was apparently much criticized by the local churches for holding it then. The editorial in July stressed that:

> everybody – incredible as it may appear – blamed the weather. The Free Church Council took the matter up, and having closed the doors to the press – presumably for daring to show them that there was work to be done – they went on talking … Refuge was taken in the excuse that the weather was stormy.

'But', the newspaper now triumphantly pointed out, 'as to last Sunday, one feels profoundly thankful for the absence of "weather" as the term is popularly understood, because we can now see how many people attend service when the climatic and other conditions are most favourable'.[39] The results, they claimed, were not impressive.

Fortunately the effects of these external factors on churchgoing rates can be tested more rigorously than this. *Table 8* isolates the effects of weather and census method on a large body of data measured in 1851 and 1881. The censuses for the twenty-eight large towns involved were all conducted on Mothering Sunday in 1851 and in the late autumn of 1881.[40] However, weather and census methods in 1881 varied considerably. *Table 8* suggests that both of these factors did have an effect upon the reported churchgoing rates, but perhaps less than some might expect. The state of the weather apparently had a greater effect upon Free Church attendances than it did upon Church of England attendances, whereas differing census methods seemed to have had a greater effect upon Church of England attendances than they did upon Free Church attendances.

In the six towns[41] that specifically reported fine weather on the day of the 1881 census, Free Church attendances rose to 21.6 per cent of the population compared to 19.4 per cent in 1851. In contrast, Free Church attendances in the nine towns[42] that specifically reported bad weather in 1881 declined from 22.3 per cent to

---

[38] *The Bradford Observer*, 22 December 1881, p. 6.

[39] *The Carnarvon and Denbigh Herald*, 10 July 1908, p. 4.

[40] See Chapter 6, note 7, for a full list and newspaper sources for the twenty-eight large towns in 1881: the earliest of these was held on 6 November 1881 and the latest on 18 December 1881. The 1902/3 London Survey (see Mudie-Smith, *The Religious Life of London*) also reported weather conditions on the census days, but unfortunately the latter were spread over seven months, making control considerably more difficult.

[41] Gloucester, Leicester, Peterborough, Rotherham, Scarborough and Sheffield.

[42] Bolton, Bradford, Burnley, Darlington, Gosport, Hull, Nottingham, Portsmouth and Southampton.

21.0 per cent. On the other hand, Church of England attendances in the eight towns[43] that relied solely upon clergy returns in 1881 increased to 12.6 per cent compared to 11.0 per cent in 1851. However, Church of England attendances in the fourteen towns[44] that had independent enumerations in 1881 declined from 13.0 per cent to 10.9 per cent.

Nevertheless, the overall difference between worst-case and best-case scenarios was not large. In the three towns[45] that reported fine weather and also relied solely upon clergy returns in 1881, both Church of England and Free Church attendances increased. But in those four towns[46] with exactly the opposite conditions, it was only Church of England attendances that decreased. Furthermore, the overall level of Church of England and Free Church attendances in both groups (31.5 per cent in the first and 34.1 per cent in the second) were fairly evenly divided either side of the mean for all twenty-eight towns of 33.1 per cent. Yet unlike the situation in all these towns, attendances in both groups actually increased between 1851 and 1881. The main difference was that they increased faster in those towns that had fine weather and clergy-return censuses (26.1 per cent to 31.5 per cent) than in those that did not (33.0 per cent to 34.1 per cent).

Even at the time the reliability of the 1851 Religious Census was questioned. There were considerable debates about the typicality of Mothering Sunday, about the state of the weather, and about the allegation that some Free Churches deliberately boosted their attendances on the census day. After reviewing these various factors, Clive Field has pointed out that generally there are not huge discrepancies between the actual attendances in the census returns and the average attendances also given in many of these returns. Nor does a comparison of 1848 independent censuses for Canterbury, Carlisle and Lincoln with the data for them in the 1851 Religious Census reveal huge discrepancies: 'morning congregations actually encompassed some four per cent more of the population in 1851 than they did three years earlier'.[47]

Since Church of England clergy returns to bishops frequently contained statistical information about 'average attendances' in the nineteenth century, these can also be compared directly with returns from the 1851 Religious Census, congregation by congregation, and with independent enumerations carried out by local newspapers. Hitherto, scholars have made very little use of this first form of abundant data. There are some gaps and statistical ambiguities in these returns, which must be remedied as objectively as possible. Yet, as will become evident, the same is true of independent enumerations.

Later chapters suggest that, in the urban context, clergy returns do supply additional corroboration of successive decline, as well as synchronic comparisons of these two forms of census data collection. For example, it can been seen in *Table 14* that Church of England morning/evening attendances in Chelsea measured

---

[43] Bradford, Derby, Gosport, Nottingham, Portsmouth, Rotherham, Scarborough and Sheffield.

[44] Barrow, Bolton, Burnley, Burslem, Coventry, Darlington, Hanley, Hull, Leicester, Longton, Newcastle-under-Lyme, Peterborough, Stoke and Warrington.

[45] Rotherham, Scarborough and Sheffield.

[46] Bolton, Burnley, Darlington and Hull.

[47] Field, 'Non-Recurrent Christian Data', p. 289.

19.0 per cent of the total population in the clergy-returned 1851 Religious Census, and in the subsequent clergy returns to the Bishop of London,[48] 14.6 per cent in 1858, 12.9 per cent in 1862, 9.1 per cent in 1883, and 11.1 per cent in 1900. The independent enumerations (which can be charted congregation by congregation) held in 1887 and on a wet day in May 1903 measured 13.9 per cent and 11.7 per cent respectively.[49] In York, too, it can been in *Table 19* that independent enumerations, although not as specific as those for Chelsea, do broadly match the patterns established by long-term clergy enumerations.

Rather surprisingly, then, independent enumerations can sometimes be higher than the nearest clergy returns. While *Table 8* does suggest that clergy returns do somewhat enhance Church of England numbers, nevertheless the overall pattern that they provide appears broadly consonant over time with data from independent enumerations. Scholars may have been rather too quick to assume that clergy would tend grossly to exaggerate their attendances and have thus ignored the independent synchronic and diachronic verification these statistics seem to provide.

Of course the evidence that weather and census method apparently did have some effect upon churchgoing rates must not simply be ignored. It will be necessary at various points in this book to draw attention to these external factors. Yet they need not paralyse all attempts to compare data. This much at least is demonstrated admirably by the four Liverpool censuses of 1881–1912.[50] The evidence from these censuses was controlled internally in four different ways: it was for the same large conurbation; it was all gathered by independent enumerators organized by *The Liverpool Daily Post*; all four censuses were undertaken in the late autumn; and the local weather conditions were reported to have been comparable. These Liverpool censuses thus offer highly controlled, sequential data. Most convincing of all, the diachronic and synchronic patterns of churchgoing and church-building emerging from these four censuses correspond closely to the patterns evident from other major sources. All of this should become clearer in the chapters that follow on urban churchgoing.

5

Churchgoing statistics are clearly more relevant to a study of the origins of empty churches than membership or affiliation statistics, but on their own they give an incomplete picture. Empty churches consist of physical space as well as a lack of attenders. Since it is my aim in this book to take religious physicality seriously, information about the seating capacity of church buildings relative to attendances is obviously crucial.

Fortunately the Victorians were obsessed with the size of their churches and chapels and left behind them a wealth of detail about their various seating

---

[48] Kept in the Library at Lambeth Palace.

[49] Calculated from *The British Weekly*'s *The Religious Census of London*, Hodder, London, 1888, and Richard Mudie-Smith (ed.), *The Religious Life of London*, Hodder, London, 1904.

[50] *The Liverpool Daily Post*, 15 November 1881, 24 November 1891, 11 November 1902, and 13 December 1912.

capacities. Few scholars have given this type of data much attention. E.R. Wickham was an important exception,[51] yet he was often regarded as somewhat quaint for doing so. It has perhaps been generally assumed that all those statistics that Victorians recorded about seating capacities were basically a product of their failing church policies and have very little relevance today.

In complete contrast, I shall argue that these seating statistics provide a vital clue about church decline. Once set alongside churchgoing statistics, they provide crucial, and curiously counter-intuitive, information about the origins of empty churches. Perhaps most critically of all, they show that in some instances *empty churches preceded churchgoing decline*. That, however, is for later.

By comparing church seating, church attendances and population statistics in Sheffield, Wickham argued that an important initial reason for urban church decline was that churches failed to keep pace with the rapid growth of the late nineteenth-century urban population. Church failure was thus a physical one: denominations failed to accommodate the burgeoning industrial working classes. Then, of course, secularization took over. Working classes in Sheffield, who had never been accommodated by churches in the nineteenth century, became largely secularized in the twentieth century. Eventually the urban middle classes followed them in abandoning the churches.

Again, I am going to claim that Wickham's thesis was mistaken at every point. Free Churches actually over-provided in nineteenth-century urban (as well as rural) Britain. Unfortunately, Wickham relied for his thesis on a comparison of the censuses for Sheffield for 1851 and 1881. Had he examined a wealth of data for similar comparisons in other urban areas, he would have realized that that for Sheffield was thoroughly atypical. Indeed, this is very clearly shown in *Table 8*. The smallest group of towns, which had both a fine day for the census and which relied wholly upon clergy returns, was dominated by Sheffield (Rotherham and Scarborough were the other two towns in this group). Thus both the weather and the method of collection for the Sheffield 1881 census[52] were as favourable as possible. Wickham might perhaps have heeded some of the contemporary warnings[53] about this census; strong local rivalries between churches in 1881 and pre-publicity for the census apparently ensured that it represented a high, rather than a typical, point of Sheffield churchgoing. On the Anglican side, *Table 9* seems to confirm this judgement. I analyse statistics here in greater detail in Chapter 6.

While the secularization model was largely unchallenged, Wickham's analysis of Sheffield could be regarded as an interesting, but essentially marginal, contribution to understanding church decline. By adopting the language of secularization himself, he may even have contributed unwittingly to this assessment. The working classes were physically excluded from the urban churches in the nineteenth century, but it was secularization that was the main cause of church decline in the twentieth century. So Wickham's task of relating attendances and seating to local populations was not widely seen as a priority for understanding church decline.

---

[51] E.R. Wickham, *Church and People in an Industrial Society*, Lutterworth, London, 1957.
[52] *Sheffield Telegraph*, 24 November 1881.
[53] See *The Nonconformist and Independent*, 2 February 1882.

Once the secularization model is itself regarded as problematic, the extensive body of data that Wickham touched upon becomes distinctly more interesting. Perhaps it offers some clues to understanding the origin of empty churches that were largely unsuspected at the time. To set this claim into context Chapter 2 reviews and updates the Northumberland case study first presented in 1989 in *Competing Convictions* and Chapter 3 reviews and updates a case study from rural Wales first presented in 1993 in *The Myth of the Empty Church*. However, the main task of the book begins in Chapter 4. Here I present in outline the central evidence on urban churchgoing decline, which is then examined in detail in the subsequent chapters. This statistical evidence is so extensive that it represents about a half of the urban population of England in the second half of the nineteenth century.

2

Rural Churchgoing Decline

The pilot study for my research involved an extended analysis of fourteen adjacent parishes in north Northumberland. Together they represent one of the most deeply rural parts of England, with the Scottish border to their north and west and containing no town much larger than 2000 people at any point since 1801. They stop well short of Alnwick to the south and Berwick-upon-Tweed and the coast to the east. In 1801 the total population of this area was 13 971, at its height in 1851 it was 17 557, and by 1981, after a continuous process of depopulation, it was 7070.

This was an area that experienced considerable Border warfare up to the seventeenth century (most notably Flodden Field in 1513), but that has subsequently been rich, Grade 2, farming land. To study the physical presence of churches in it I divided history since the restoration of the monarchy (when church records first become widely available) into four equal periods of time (1661–1740; 1741–1820; 1821–1900; 1901–1980), simultaneously measuring all changes in graph form as well to avoid the arbitrariness of these divisions. The full data was reported in *Competing Convictions*,[1] but in summary form they were as follows.

1

In the first period it was found that the Church of England was particularly active. In nine of the fourteen parishes an incumbent became resident and a new vicarage was built for him. One church was enlarged and nine others were renovated. In addition, seven Free Church chapels/churches were built, one was enlarged, and four manses were built.

In the second period nine Church of England churches were renovated, five enlarged, and one further parish received a resident incumbent and had a vicarage built for him. In addition, four Free Church chapels were built, four were enlarged, and six new manses were built.

The third period was the busiest of all. In it all but one of the fourteen Church of England parishes renovated their parish church, all but two built new vicarages, seven additional chapels or mission halls were built, and all the parishes now had their own resident incumbent (three of which had total populations of less than 300). Furthermore, twelve new Free Church chapels and three Catholic churches were built, three were enlarged, six were renovated, and seven new manses were built. Ironically, this period also experienced continuous depopulation from 1851.

---

[1] SCM Press, London, 1989.

This depopulation characterized the whole of the fourth period. No new churches were built or enlarged, although seven Church of England churches were renovated, three vicarages were built, and three Free Church chapels were renovated. However, uniquely in this period, in eight Church of England parishes the incumbents ceased to be resident and their vicarages were sold, four mission halls were sold, and thirteen Free Church chapels and eleven manses were sold.

Using the returns from the 1851 Religious Census,[2] it would appear that altogether at that time the churches and chapels in the area had 11 034 seats, sufficient for 63 per cent of the total population (and, in reality far more, since some of the parishioners would have been quite small!). Yet, despite continuous depopulation, denominations continued to build right up to the end of the nineteenth century. By 1901 there would (on the basis of the 1851 Religious Census and subsequent local estimates for additional or enlarged church buildings) have been 13 049 seats for a total population of only 10 970. Of these seats, non-Anglicans had 8704 and the Church of England 4345. Further, an excess of church seating capacity over total population characterized this area from the 1890s until the 1970s.

Unless there was a dramatic rise in churchgoing between 1851 and 1901, churches and chapels, which were on average only 49.3 per cent occupied at their main services on Mothering Sunday in 1851, must have been considerably emptier (despite folk memories) by 1901. If the churchgoing rate had stayed steady, the dual effects of depopulation and increased church seating would have resulted in only 22.1 per cent of these seats being occupied on average at the main services on a comparable Sunday in 1901. If the churchgoing rate had declined, the situation would clearly have been considerably worse. Even if there had been a dramatic increase, the churchgoing rate would need to have reached 58 per cent of the total population for churches and chapels to have appeared as full (but no more) as they were in 1851.

A detailed study of clergy returns to the Bishop of Durham in 1866, 1874 and 1878, and to the Bishop of Newcastle in 1887,[3] suggests that average attendances in the Church of England reached their peak in 1866 and declined thereafter. The 1851 Religious Census asked incumbents to count actual attendances on Mothering Sunday as well as average church attendances over a period of some months. If figures where given for the latter are used, aggregated average attendances in the Church of England for the area (excluding Sunday schools) were 2342 in 1851 (13.3 per cent total pop.), 2884 in 1866 (17.6 per cent total pop.), 2237 in 1874 (15.0 per cent total pop.), 2437 in 1878 (16.3 per cent total pop.) and 2039 in 1887 (15.0 per cent total pop.). Furthermore, attendances at the main service at the three largest churches in the area were in 1887 estimated to be only half those of 1851. In other words, less actual attendances were spread over more church buildings.

---

[2] The original returns are held at the Public Records Office at Kew, but are also available on microfilm at the Northumberland County Records Office, Gosforth.

[3] *Clergy Visitation Returns*, 1866–1878, Auckland Castle Episcopal Records, held in the Department of Palaeography and Diplomatic, University of Durham. Records after the formation of the Diocese of Newcastle in 1882 are held in the Northumberland County Record Office, Gosforth, as are most of those for Free Churches and the Catholic Church in Northumberland.

A very similar pattern emerged from the detailed study of non-Anglican local church/chapel records in the area – albeit with at least one crucial difference. Presbyterian Communion Rolls and attendances (where available), average attendances at Mass at the three Catholic churches in the area, and membership records of the five small Primitive Methodist chapels, each showed a pattern of expansion, followed by a slow reduction of attendance/membership. In each case there was a gradual reduction in the number of ordained ministers serving them. However, there was one key difference from Anglicans. All other denominations closed substantial church buildings. Anglicans closed only their prefabricated mission halls and removed a number of galleries from their parish churches. Only one parish church has as yet been declared redundant in north Northumberland, and it lies just outside the area studied.

Perhaps surprisingly, Catholic attendances declined first. Their combined Easter Mass attendances were 234 in 1849, 480 in 1855, but had declined to 297 in 1861, to 187 in 1892, and to just 109 in 1899. Presbyterian churches characteristically reached a peak of Communion Roll membership in the 1860s or 1870s, and then declined rapidly, closing their first major church (seating over 1000) in 1903. Methodists had a much smaller membership; this expanded later, reaching a high point of 260 in 1888. This figure had reduced to 160 by 1908 and all but two chapels had closed by the 1980s.

When the record of chapel buildings in the area is examined, a remarkable watershed can be observed. The Primitive Methodists were the last denomination to build, opening their final chapel in the little village of Branxton (with a population in 1901 of just 165) in 1898. Built of corrugated iron, it initially had a membership of only fifteen. By the following year this membership had declined to ten, and by the First World War to three. Since the construction of this chapel, no entirely new chapel of any denomination was built in the area until very recently and over half have been closed. At the most, three Free Church chapels were extensively restored; and in every case their seating capacity was at the same time considerably reduced. The large Presbyterian church at Wooler, completely rebuilt in 1878, was the first and most dramatic closure in 1903. Soon afterwards it was turned into a public hall and then finally demolished in 1991. For much of the nineteenth century it was one of three Presbyterian churches serving this small town, with a combined seating capacity almost twice that of its 1901 population of 1336.

Real, and not just perceived, overall decline in attendances has now characterized churches and chapels in the area. A census that I conducted of the remaining twenty-nine buildings in active use (out of a total of forty-five in 1901) at Pentecost 1988 found that there were 676 attendances of all ages (9.6 per cent total pop.) across denominations. On Mothering Sunday in 1851 there were 5436 attendances recorded across denominations at morning services (31.0 per cent total pop.).[4] I repeated this census at Pentecost 2002. In the intervening fourteen years four more churches have been closed. The Catholics have closed their church in Lowick (and now hold services there in the Anglican church), the Brethren have closed two of their three chapels and the Methodists have closed

---

[4] Afternoon/evening services represented 7.9 per cent total population in 1851 but have largely disappeared today.

one of their two chapels. Interestingly, a new evangelical congregation of some fifty people was formed in Wooler in the mid-1990s after breaking away from the United Reformed Church there. Altogether there were now 589 attendances of all ages (8.4 per cent total pop.), with Free Churches showing a decline of 17 per cent, Anglicans a decline of 15 per cent and the smaller group of Catholics holding steady.

It is clear from all of this that there has been a considerable decline in churchgoing in this highly rural area of 13 per cent between Pentecost 1988 and Pentecost 2002. However, it is a rate of decline considerably less than that for usual Sunday attendance. Using that criterion Peter Brierley detects an overall decline of 22 per cent between 1989 and 1998 (and 24 per cent for remote rural areas),[5] and *Table 18* suggests a similar overall decline for Anglicans between 1989 and 1999.

2

When I started this analysis I had no idea that the seating capacity of churches and chapels in north Northumberland had exceeded the surrounding population for most of the twentieth century. Despite living in the area for twenty years and being deeply involved in the churches there, I had never heard anyone mention this fact. If anything, compared with parts of the rural south of England or even rural Lincolnshire, churches and chapels appeared to be few and far between.

Once this surprising discovery was made, several propositions soon emerged. An over-abundance of churches and chapels seemed to be correlated with a number of other factors. Indeed, from this detailed analysis of declining rural churches and chapels, it seemed possible to isolate several factors that directly relate to the phenomenon of over-capacity in the context of ongoing depopulation and that might even be identified as causal factors in church decline.

The first of these factors is the actual closing of churches. Each of the four denominations has closed churches. The Presbyterians (now mostly United Reformed Church), constituting three-quarters of churchgoers in the area in 1851 but now barely a fifth, have closed the most. By examining those Communion rolls that also record individual attendances, it is possible to map out the way individuals respond to a church closing. Characteristically, membership and attendance diminish rapidly as closure nears; only half of the remaining members actually transfer to a neighbouring church after closure; and these transferred members are significantly less regular in their attendance at the new church than they were at their old one.

A second factor, which is particularly evident in some of the local Presbyterian records, is the early presence of debt. Long before they started to close churches, there is evidence that Presbyterians were starting to encounter considerable financial difficulties. Being so close to the Scottish border, this was a highly Presbyterian area.

---

[5] Peter Brierley (ed.), *UK Christian Handbook: Religious Trends*, No. 3 (2001), Christian Research, Vision Building, 4 Footscray Road, London SE9 2TZ, p. 12.42.

Other scholars have also found considerable debt problems emerging in rival Methodist chapels in the 1880s in other parts of Britain.[6]

The village and parish of Lowick well illustrates this problem of debt between rival Presbyterian churches in the 1880s. Lowick had a population of 1941 in 1851, but by 1901 it had reduced to 1138. However, its Free Church chapels expanded very considerably during the same period of time. The Presbyterians, following the Disruption, started a rival congregation in the late 1840s, followed by the Primitive Methodists and finally by the Brethren. In this situation, the two rival Presbyterian churches, not surprisingly, found both membership and economic viability a very considerable problem. Thus, the Lowick Scotch Church declined in communicant membership from 591 in 1858 to 434 in 1878. In its annual report at the later date it announced:

> Throughout the past year the general attendance on the Sabbath at the regular service of the sanctuary has been unsatisfactory. From the complaints heard from other congregations, the careless and sinful habit of neglecting public ordinances appears general throughout the district. Observation within our own communion too easily notes that many are very irregular and infrequent in their waiting upon the ordinances of God's House ... The financial statement at the close of the report shews that the sum of money at the disposal of the Trustees is greatly insufficient to enable them to maintain ordinances as they have hitherto been done.[7]

By 1883 the communicant roll of this church had declined to 255, while at the same time the English Presbyterian church in Lowick had a membership of only 180 and an annual income for all purposes of just £120. Increasing, chapel debt towards the end of the nineteenth century characterized a number of the Free Church congregations in the area. It is seen later that a similar problem can be uncovered in quite a number of other rural and urban areas.

After the initial stages of this research I concluded that, in these circumstances, twentieth-century chapel closures were perhaps inevitable. Now from the vantage point of 2002 it is possible to see just how accurate this initial conclusion was. In 1988 there were still five churches and chapels in the little village of Lowick (with a total population then of 499), whereas today there are just two. It is not difficult to predict that soon there will be just one (the Church of Scotland's church there is clearly struggling to survive with an elderly congregation usually in single figures). If that happens, Lowick will return after some three centuries of religious rivalry to being a village served by a single church, albeit with just a minority of the population now involved actively in the life of that church. One of the products of that past rivalry was that individuals who may well have been debt-free in their private lives were caught up in the growing debts of their own chapels. It is not difficult to understand from this their reluctance to join a neighbouring chapel or church once their own had closed.

---

[6] See Robert Currie, *Methodism Divided*, Faber & Faber, London, 1968; and David M. Thompson, 'Church Extension in Town and Countryside in Later Nineteenth-Century Leicestershire', in Derek Baker, (ed.), *The Church in Town and Countryside*, Studies in Church History, vol. 16, Blackwell, Oxford, 1979.

[7] Report held in the Northumberland County Records Office, Gosforth.

The third factor involves a change in relationship between ministers and congregations. If in 1851 there was one church per minister, today there are three churches per minister (across denominations). The overall ratio of population to minister has changed rather less: in the 1850s there were 605 people per minister, by the 1990s there were 707 per minister. However, multiple charges now characterize all denominations. Leslie Francis's empirical research shows that ministers with three or more churches become significantly less effective and their congregations reduce accordingly.[8]

The fourth factor is small, and increasingly elderly, congregations in large, empty church buildings. At Penetecost in both 1988 and 2002 only five churches recorded congregations of more than 40 and the largest congregation was 75 in 1988 but only 60 in 2002. It is again not difficult to see that it is today more difficult for marginal churchgoers to attend church (without feeling too conspicuous) than it was in 1851.

A measure of this change is the altered ratio between Easter Communions and average attendances on other Sundays in the area. In the Church of England, quarterly Communions represented just 2.1 per cent of the total population in 1810–14, 2.2 per cent in 1857, and 1.8 per cent in 1887. However, in 1986 Easter Communions represented 9.4 per cent of the population. In 1986, though, this was over twice the estimated average attendances (3.6 per cent total pop.), whereas in the 1850s it represented just 17 per cent of aggregated average attendances. Similarly, among Presbyterians today, quarterly Communions represent at least double the average congregations, whereas in the 1850s they were slightly less than aggregated average attendances. In both instances it may be the less committed church members (i.e. the non-communicants) who are now largely absent from regular public worship.

And the final factor that emerged from this study is simple disillusionment. At the end of his important study of the churches in Lambeth, Jeffrey Cox observed:

> In England it was the actual collapse of the churches which allowed the complete triumph of the argument that religion is something which belongs to another age. The empty church is the single most important piece of evidence brought forth by people who argue that religion has become unimportant. They are right, but not for the reasons they think.[9]

This perceptive comment applies equally to my highly rural sample. By analysing vigorous church building and relative seating capacities against continuous depopulation, it is possible to see that empty churches and chapels characterized this area throughout the twentieth century. And soon one notices that the clergy themselves were starting to become demoralized as the twentieth century approached. By 1899 most of the Anglican clergy reported a 'falling off markedly' of congregations; few of them, though, identified depopulation as a factor and not one of them noticed local over-building. The retiring minister of the first

---

[8] Leslie J. Francis, *Rural Anglicanism*, Collins, London, 1985.
[9] Jeffrey Cox, *The English Churches in a Secular Society: Lambeth, 1870–1930*, Oxford University Press, Oxford, 1982, p. 276.

Presbyterian church in Wooler to close was the only ordained minister I have discovered who correctly identified both factors. In his remarkable final sermon (a copy of which I discovered in a loose file only at the end of this case study) in 1903 he said:

> The church at Chatton was built in 1850, and drew away many members from the congregations in Wooler, and in the following year the church at Beaumont Union was built, and drew away members on the West side. During the last 50 or 40 years the rural population has greatly decreased in proportion. At one time, one of the congregations had more members than all the present three put together: Tower Hill, being the smallest of the three Presbyterian Churches, has been the least able to afford a diminution of its numbers, and the time has come when it was considered undesirable that it should continue a burden upon the funds of the Synod, as there was no probability that it would ever again reach a high degree of prosperity.[10]

In extended interviews, few respondents today were able to diagnose the situation as impartially as this. Most bemoaned the present age, looked back to better times in the churches and chapels, and believed that a mixture of clerical failure and general secularism had 'caused' the current demise of churchgoing. Disillusionment is rife.

3

The next stage of my research involved asking two questions. First, why did churches continue to build in the face of depopulation and their own evident decline? Secondly, did this phenomenon of over-capacity, itself apparently leading to factors contributing to the decline in churchgoing (namely, church debts and closures, shared ministers, and sparse, elderly congregations) happen elsewhere in rural Britain? If it did, then perhaps a major piece in the puzzle may have been missed by other scholars. Of course more cultural factors may also have been involved in churchgoing decline, but this factor is at least observable and indeed measurable. Ironically, it has seldom been measured.

To answer the first question I examined in detail the written records left by the four denominations. What emerged is a very considerable degree of inter-church rivalry. Again, this can be reported here only in very summary form.

The Bishop of Durham's questions[11] in 1810 and 1814 to his clergy show that he was as concerned about the presence of 'Papists' as of 'Dissenters': 'Are there any reputed Papists in your Parish or Chapelry? How many, and of what Rank? Have any persons been lately perverted to Popery?' The clergy responses from north Northumberland show instead that they were predominantly concerned about the Presbyterians. By 1861 the Bishop of Durham dropped all reference to 'Papists', but not questions about 'Dissenters'. In response one incumbent wrote, in terms

---

[10] Sermon held in the Northumberland County Records Office, Gosforth.
[11] *Clergy Visitation Returns*, 1810 and 1814, Auckland Castle Episcopal Records, held in the Department of Palaeography and Diplomatic, University of Durham.

similar to those of others, 'The special hindrance to ministerial success in all the Border Parishes is the lamentable extent of Presbyterian Dissent'. Indeed, throughout the second half of the nineteenth century Church of England clergy continued to write about the 'threat' of Presbyterianism. So, in 1891 the Bishop of Newcastle asked: 'What are the chief hindrances to the success of your Pastoral labours?' One incumbent responded bluntly: 'The struggle of Dissenters to keep their Ministers: dislike to Forms of Prayer: jealousy of Church: deep prejudice: neglect in the past.'

Ironically, Presbyterians in the area very seldom referred to 'Episcopalians', as they termed them. Instead their rivalries were chiefly with one another. Schisms within particular congregations went back at least to the eighteenth century. However, the Scottish Disruption of 1843 created enormous tension among local congregations, resulting in several new and rival churches being built in the decade following 1848. Normally prosaic session minutes became quite animated and, in one case, physical violence erupted within a congregation.

Catholic records, in turn, suggest that those in authority believed that they were bringing salvation to the area for the first time since the Dissolution. Records assiduously counted 'converts' and churches were described as 'missions'. In an area that already had very evident inter-church rivalries, Catholics and then Primitive Methodists brought more. The strength of these rivalries does seem to explain why they all continued to build in a context of depopulation, even when their own relative decline must have become apparent. Indeed, the mission halls built by Anglicans in the 1890s, far from being built because existing parish churches were full, were specifically designed to counter decline. They were built in the belief that one of the reasons for people not coming to church was that parish churches were sometimes too far away from the people. In reality, they must have drawn away even more people from parish churches which, from the evidence of clergy returns, were already experiencing declining congregations.

4

But did this happen elsewhere? To answer this question I examined the seating capacity of the churches and chapels for each Registration District in England and Wales, as given in the 1851 Religious Census,[12] against the population figures for the same Districts for 1901. Rather surprisingly this simple exercise reveals that in 84 Registration Districts (out of 623) the seating capacity of the churches in existence in 1851 would have exceeded the 1901 population. Such was the extent of rural depopulation in England and Wales (even allowing for extensive boundary changes between Districts) in the second half of the nineteenth century. Furthermore, in a total of 178 Districts there would have been room in 1901 for over 80 per cent of their populations. So, without allowing for any extra church building in rural areas after 1851 (despite abundant evidence that such building did

---

[12] See Horace Mann, *1851 Census of Great Britain: Report and Tables on Religious Worship England and Wales*, British Parliamentary Papers, Population 10, 1852–3 (reprinted by Irish University Press, Shannon, 1970).

take place), there would already have been a very considerable problem of over-capacity by the end of the century.

Obelkevich's otherwise useful study of South Lindsey[13] misses this crucial point. He does explore the rivalries between Methodists and Anglicans in the area and the degree to which both built in the context of depopulation. Yet he finally puzzles about why churches and chapels in South Lindsey were in decline by 1870. Had he examined the seating of the churches and chapels in the 1851 Religious Census against the 1901 population for Horncastle, Spilsby and Louth, he might have discovered why. In 1851 there was already an estimated overall seating capacity for 89.9 per cent of the total population of the three Districts. The Church of England alone could have accommodated 43.1 per cent of the population (its average nationally was 29.7 per cent). But by 1901, without any additional churches, the Church of England could have accommodated 52.0 per cent of the population and all denominations together 108.4 per cent of the same population. In such circumstances church and chapel debts and closures, shared ministers and persisting sparse congregations seem inescapable.

Most remarkably of all in England, the adjacent Registration Districts of Leyburn, Askrigg and Reeth in North Riding already had seating more than sufficient for their population in 1851. The estimates of seating given in Horace Mann's report of the 1851 Religious Census suggested that together churches and chapels could have accommodated 105.7 per cent of their total population. Even on my own estimates, made from the original returns with local additions,[14] they could have accommodated 92.8 per cent. On the basis of this more cautious estimate, by 1901 the same churches and chapels, without any additional building, could have accommodated 151.8 per cent of the population, and by 1971 a remarkable 197.7 per cent of the population. Not surprisingly, in 1851, although 35.2 per cent of the population were at the main service (calculated church by church), they occupied just 38.5 per cent of available seating. By 1901 an identical churchgoing rate would have filled only 23.7 per cent of the same seating – and this, it should be noted, denotes the rate at the best attended services.

These three Yorkshire Districts are particularly interesting because their total population reached its height in 1831. They thus represented a stage earlier than north Northumberland. They were also originally a part of the Chester Diocese, so Anglican churchgoing patterns in them can for once be traced back to 1821. And they provide abundant evidence of rival Free Church building accelerating despite depopulation.

A dramatic switch in the balance between the Church of England and the Free Churches seems to have occurred in the course of the first half of the nineteenth century. By going back to the original returns of the 1851 Religious Census, and calculating seating for each decade on the basis of the dates of dedication of the various churches and chapels given in them, it is possible to get some idea of this

---

[13] James Obelkevich, *Religion and Rural Society: South Lindsey 1825–1875*, Oxford University Press, Oxford, 1976; for a fuller critique see my *Competing Convictions*, Chapter 6.

[14] Three Church of England churches for Leyburn Registration District in the 1851 Religious Census do not specify seating: they have been supplied from *Clergy Visitation Returns*, 1821, Chester Record Office.

changing physical balance. Horace Mann pioneered this approach in his report. Of course it does not allow for church enlargements or chapels replacing older chapels. Yet, where it can be checked, it does not seem to be too misleading a method. So, for example, the figure of 33 per cent for the Church of England for 1821 calculated through this method compares closely with the figure of 35 per cent calculated from Chester clergy visitation returns for the same year.[15]

On this basis of calculation from the 1851 Religious Census, if the Church of England could have accommodated some 36 per cent of the population of these three Districts in 1801, the Free Churches could have accommodated some 21 per cent. By 1821 this balance had shifted somewhat to 33 per cent and 26 per cent respectively. With the population at its zenith in 1831, the balance shifted to 33 per cent and 30 per cent. Only after depopulation started did it tilt in favour of the Free Churches: in 1841 the Church of England had accommodation for 36 per cent and the Free Churches for 38 per cent, and in 1851 for 40 per cent and 52 per cent respectively.

Attendances too in the three Districts by at least 1851 were predominantly Free Church attendances. Of the 35.2 per cent of the population at the main service of the various churches and chapels in 1851, almost two-thirds were at the Free Churches: 12.9 per cent of the population attended the main Church of England service, or 16.5 per cent if Sunday schools are included. However, even in 1821 total Church of England 'attenders' in the same districts amounted to just 18.2 per cent of the population. If in 1821 all of these attenders had come to church for the same service, churches would still have been no more than 52 per cent full. By 1851 Church of England churches were on average only 33 per cent full at their main service (or 28 per cent if all services are counted). However, by then even the burgeoning Free Churches were only 44 per cent full.

Within the Free Churches, and again using the dedication dates supplied in 1851, another remarkable shift can be measured during the course of the first half of the nineteenth century. In 1801 some 45 per cent of the Free Church seating belonged to the Independent churches, but by 1851 they held only 19 per cent. It is seen in Chapter 4 that across urban areas Independent church attendances consistently declined during the nineteenth century. In contrast, Wesleyan Methodists mushroomed in these rural districts (and in many urban areas until the 1880s). By 1851 they had forty-two places of worship (including some house churches), against seventeen belonging to Independents. There were also fourteen Primitive Methodist places of worship, mostly built during the previous fifteen years. In contrast, there was just one Catholic church, built in 1836, serving the three Districts.

The 1851 Religious Census as a whole supplies abundant evidence of inter-church rivalry. In every Registration District throughout England and Wales several rival denominations were present. Indeed, the rate of church building was accelerating (only in part in response to the challenge of urbanization). On Horace Mann's calculations, between 1801 and 1811 1224 new churches and chapels were built; another 2002 were built by 1821; 3141 by 1831; 4866 by 1841; and 5594 by 1851.

---

[15] *Clergy Visitation Returns*, 1821, Chester Record Office.

5

Taken together, this research suggests that rural churches and chapels had a massive problem by 1901 – and one from which they are still trying to recover in the twenty-first century. Over-capacity, at least in part a product of inter-church rivalry in a context of rural depopulation, appears to have been widespread. For those congregations that lacked a substantial rural subsidy (i.e. the non-Anglican denominations) it seems to have been most damaging. The closure of Free Church chapels characterized much of rural England and Wales throughout the twentieth century. Even the Church of England has been forced to combine livings (as well as to close its rural mission halls) and, in effect, to return to the clerical pluralism of the eighteenth century.

Most denominations, with the instructive exception of the Roman Catholic Church, inherited the legacy of this problem throughout the twentieth century. For some it was more obvious than for others. Both English Methodists (especially after the Union) and the Church of Scotland have been aware of this legacy and have closed many buildings. English Methodists reduced from some 16 000 chapels that came together at the Union of 1932 to 6740 by 1989[16] (although, ominously, 51 per cent of the latter remained in rural areas). The Church of England, in contrast, has closed churches more reluctantly and continues to subsidize many parishes that would not otherwise be viable. In 1932 it had some 20 000 churches and mission halls; this increased to 21 913 in 1962.[17] By 1989 it had declined to 16 373 churches, of which 55 per cent remained in rural areas.

Herein lies a crucial physical difference between the Church of England and other denominations in this rural Northumberland case study. Throughout the period studied, the Church of England has acted as a subsidized church. Subsidy is ubiquitous, even if the pattern of this subsidy changes in each century.

In the eighteenth century, with few rivals, the rural Church of England was characterized by clerical pluralism and absenteeism, by churches that were frequently in a poor state of repair, and by congregations that were reputedly sparse. Branxton, for example, shared a priest with Cornhill-on-Tweed, and had a very poorly attended service once a month. The Church of England thus behaved as a monopoly church and the clergy as a privileged elite within it.

In the nineteenth century, in response to the vigorous challenge of the Free Churches, a considerable change took place in the Church of England. Bishops systematically combated absenteeism (frequently meeting clerical resistance) and attempted to establish a resident incumbent in every parish. Several parishes now had a resident incumbent for the first time since the Middle Ages. In the case of Alnham and Branxton, parish populations never reached 300 in either place, yet each had a resident incumbent and a substantial vicarage from the 1830s. They retained their incumbents until the 1960s, by which stage their populations were scarcely more

---

[16] See Peter Brierley (ed.), *Prospects for the Nineties: Trends and Tables from the English Church Census*, MARC Europe, 1991.

[17] The 1932 figure is estimated from seating capacities in *The Church of England Yearbook*, Church House, London, 1935; the 1962 figure is from *Facts and Figures About the Church of England*, Church Information Office, London, 1962; the 1989 figure is from Brierley, *Prospects for the Nineties*.

than 150. Rural tithes, a buoyant (even if fluctuating) agricultural economy, and, in several instances, vigorous litigation against landowners who failed to pay tithes, all made this possible. No longer a monopoly, the Church of England used the considerable subsidy afforded by rural tithes to change its structures and to respond to what must have appeared to be an ever-growing rural population.

By the late twentieth century the ratio of Anglican clergy to local population in north Northumberland had changed very little from the 1850s. Then it was 1097 people per priest; by 1989 it was 1178 people per priest. Of course, parish priests today have responsibility for a much wider area (albeit with the help of cars) and, whereas then there was approximately one priest per church, today there are three churches for every priest. In contrast, the ratio of non-Anglican ministers to population rose in the same period from 1351 to 1768 per minister. The crucial economic difference between these two patterns is that non-Anglican ministers have generally needed to be financially self-supporting, whereas (until very recently) Anglican clergy have not.

This key economic difference is also reflected in the different building curves of local Anglicans and Free Churches. The graph that characterizes the Church of England over the last 300 years might be described – like the local Cheviot – as a flat hill. Although Anglican parishes spent a good deal of money improving parish churches in the nineteenth century, they only slightly increased seating capacities (through the provision of galleries, mission halls and, occasionally, substantial chapels); they then gradually lost them in the twentieth century. In contrast, the Free Churches might be depicted as a mountain peak: vigorous building until 1900 and dramatic collapse ever since. They surpassed local Anglican seating capacity in about the 1790s, provided almost double the accommodation by 1900, and dropped beneath it in the 1980s.

Free Church and Catholic congregations have been required by their central administrations to be basically self-supporting. Each must raise sufficient resources from local people to ensure its continued presence in the area. In this task local Methodists have largely failed. Unable to establish a viable presence in this largely Presbyterian area (a pattern very characteristic of neighbouring Scotland), the nearest minister is now in Berwick-upon-Tweed. Presbyterians (in the form now of the United Reformed Church) do still have a resident minister and at least one viable congregation, but their presence is very much reduced from the 1850s. Catholics currently struggle to maintain two viable churches: in 1988 they still had two priests in the area, but today they have only one (with some 99 people going to Mass on a Sunday spread across three congregations). The Church of England alone retains five resident priests in the area, a situation made possible only by a considerable economic subsidy from the quotas of suburban parishes (and from the Church Commissioners to support pensions).

These differing economic relationships between denominations play an important role in the chapters that follow. For the moment it is sufficient to note that they were already writ large in my original rural case study.

3

Glan-llyn: A Rural Case Study

Does rural Wales offer a counter-example to the evidence set out in the last chapter about the effects of over-building on churchgoing? It apparently combined very high levels of church and chapel building (resulting in many areas in seating exceeding local populations) with high rates of churchgoing.

It has been seen that in north Northumberland churches and chapels were on average only half full when seating, in 1851, could have accommodated 63 per cent of the local population. By the turn of the century, as a result of vigorous building in a rapidly depopulating area, seating there could have accommodated 119 per cent of the local population. Very soon local chapels, church galleries, and then Anglican mission halls began to be closed, and remaining buildings would have struggled to be even a quarter full.

In parts of rural Wales, in contrast, there was already seating capacity exceeding local populations in 1851.[1] Yet churchgoing levels were high and chapel building continued. For example, the Registration District of Aberystwyth had seating for 101 per cent of its population in 1851 and that of Machynlleth 124 per cent. Yet an examination of dedication inscriptions on rural chapels in both areas soon reveals that building continued in the second half of the nineteenth century. Furthermore, both areas recorded remarkably high levels of churchgoing in 1851. Evening services in Aberystwyth were attended by 51.8 per cent of the population and in Machynlleth by 51.4 per cent. As a result, despite the abundance of churches and chapels in both districts, they were on average remarkably full in the evening: 61 per cent full in Aberystwyth and 46 per cent full in Machynlleth.

If an accurate assessment of this situation is to be made, longitudinal analysis is essential. This is seldom possible in rural areas. Most of the newspaper censuses, which will be reviewed in the next chapter, concentrated upon urban areas. A rare exception in 1881 is the census of the villages around Bath.[2] Unfortunately, its record of Free Church congregations in 1881 has crucial gaps and tends, in congregations of all denominations, to elide churchgoing and Sunday school statistics. Much more promising is the data from 1821 for Lancashire and parts of Cumbria. It does allow important urban/rural comparisons to be made. Chapter 5 will return to this in detail.

---

[1] See Horace Mann, *1851 Census Great Britain: Report and Tables on Religious Worship England and Wales*, British Parliamentary Papers, Population 10, 1852–3 (reprinted by Irish University Press, Shannon, 1970). Full details of individual returns are available in print for Wales alone, in I.G. Jones and D. Williams (eds), *The Religious Census of 1851: A Calendar of the Returns Relating to Wales*, 2 vols, University of Wales Press, Cardiff, 1976 and 1981.

[2] See *Keene's Bath Journal*, 26 November 1881.

However, one rural area that does allow very detailed longitudinal analysis is Glan-llyn. This highly Welsh-speaking, remote, rural area, bordering on the large lake of Bala in the heart of Meirionnydd, for once makes an extended case study possible. 'Chapel and Community in Glan-llyn, Merioneth' was the title of an unusual study made in about 1950 by Trefor M. Owen.[3] By comparing the data that he presented, first with that of the 1851 Religious Census (which he did not do himself), and then with data collected in 1990 and again in 2002,[4] a unique understanding of changes in rural Welsh churchgoing over a period of a century-and-a-half becomes possible. The theories developed in *Competing Convictions*, and outlined in the last chapter, can in this way be tested in a very specific rural context. Furthermore, this context makes observation possible of changes in churchgoing as they relate to the physical presence of local churches and chapels and to resident ordained ministers. It should also be possible to discover something about the economic factors underpinning the whole.

1

Today most of Meirionnydd, together with Anglesey and Caernarfon, is contained in the larger county of Gwynedd. This modern county remains Welsh-speaking, chapel-oriented and deeply rural. In the 1982 MARC Europe census,[5] Gwynedd was the only county in which a majority of adult churchgoers attended purely Welsh services and it had the highest adult churchgoing rate for any county in England or Wales – 19 per cent in contrast to the Welsh average of 13 per cent and the English average of 11 per cent. It is the only county in Wales in which Presbyterians are the largest denomination in terms of average adult attendance (36 per cent), and it is the only other county (in Clwyd Catholics have a larger proportion) in which the Church in Wales is not the largest (26 per cent). Furthermore, it is one of the few counties in Britain, together with Dyfed in Wales and the Highlands of Scotland, in which comparatively high levels of churchgoing persist without a strong Catholic presence (12 per cent of adult churchgoers in contrast to the Welsh Catholic average of 20 per cent). Even though, when measured in 1982, just less than one-fifth of the adult population of Gwynedd regularly attended church or chapel, two-fifths were still reckoned to be members. And of the latter, seven out of ten were chapel members.

---

[3] Trefor M. Owen, 'Chapel and Community in Glan-llyn, Merioneth', in Elwyn Davies and Alwyn D. Rees, (eds), *Welsh Rural Communities*, University of Wales Press, Cardiff, 1960, pp. 185–248.

[4] I am most grateful to the Revds Glyn Thomas of Bala and W.J. Edwards of Llanuwchllyn for their patience in answering my many questions about the situation in Glan-llyn in 1990 and to Glyn Thomas, again, and Dafydd Rees Roberts of Llanuwchllyn in 2002.

[5] Peter Brierley and Byron Evans (eds), *Prospects for Wales: Report of the 1982 Census of the Churches*, MARC Europe and Bible Society, 1983. For England, see Peter Brierley (ed.), *Prospects for the Eighties: From a Census of the Churches in 1979*, Bible Society, 1980. For Scotland, see Peter Brierley and Fergus MacDonald (eds), *Prospects for Scotland: Report of the 1984 Census of the Churches*, MARC Europe and the National Bible Society of Scotland, 1985 (all from Christian Research, Vision Building, 4 Footscray Road, London SE9 2TZ).

Between 1851 and 1901 the population of the district of Bala declined from 6736 to 5732. There were thirty-seven places of worship in 1851 with seating sufficient for 109 per cent of this population. Without any extra building this would have been sufficient for 128 per cent of the 1901 population. There were no Catholic churches in the whole of Meirionnydd in 1851. Rather there was an abundance of chapels. In the county as a whole in 1851, chapels provided 217 places of worship with seating for 79 per cent of the total population, and together with the fifty places of worship provided by Church in Wales, for 105 per cent. *The Royal Commission on the Church of England and Other Religious Bodies in Wales and Monmouthshire 1905–6*[6] suggested that the 273 chapels and their adjoining school-rooms in the county now had seating for 155 per cent of the population, and, together with the fifty-seven churches and seven mission halls of the Church in Wales, for some 185 per cent. Evidently churches and chapels continued to be built there, just as they were in north Northumberland, against a declining rural population in the second half of the nineteenth century.

Statistics between 1831 and 1906 for the Diocese of St Asaph,[7] in which Bala is situated, confirm this pattern of vigorous building. This predominantly rural diocese contained a few urban areas (notably Wrexham), yet its population grew only from 215 615 to 288 446 between these dates. However, its number of churches and mission halls more than doubled, from 151 to 326. Incumbents increased from 120 to 209, parsonages from 107 to 192, and curates from 40 to 89. Thus, whereas in 1831 one building would have served on average a population of 1428 and each clergyman a population of 1540, by 1906 each building on average was serving a population of only 885 and each clergyman 968. Clearly there were economic factors behind these dramatic changes that must be examined later.

What were the effects of this over-building? The survey evidence for Glan-llyn is especially relevant to this question. It represents very closely this whole area of Wales. It was and continues to be Welsh-speaking and chapel-oriented, with an abundance of chapels built since 1821 against an almost continuously declining rural population. Glan-llyn is mostly comprised of two thinly populated parishes, Llanuwchllyn and Llangywer. In 1801 the combined population of these two parishes was 1621. It reached its highest point in 1821 with a population of 1852, declining to 1631 by 1851. By 1871 it was down to 1493; by 1901 it was 1290; by 1931 it was 1045; by 1951 it was 887; and by 1981 it was just 808.

In 1801 there was a parish church in both parishes and a single Independent (or Congregational) chapel. The latter, known as Hen Gapel (Old Chapel), was first built in 1746, and was reputedly the oldest Independent chapel in Meirionnydd. The district around Bala had apparently been an important centre of Quakerism in the seventeenth century.[8] Under pressure from religious persecution, many had emigrated to America at the end of that century. However, pockets of disaffection with the Established Church remained in the area, responding to the visit to Llanuwchllyn of the Independent minister Lewis Rees in 1737. From 1745

---

[6] *Royal Commission of 1905–6*, Parliamentary Papers, 1911.

[7] See Summary D in *Royal Commission of 1905–6*.

[8] See Owen, 'Chapel and Community in Glan-llyn, Merioneth': his source is R.T. Jenkins, *Hanes Cynulleidfa Hen Gapel Llanuwchyllyn*, Bala, 1937.

Llanuwchllyn had its own Independent minister and it was he who built Hen Gapel in 1746, albeit that this was some distance from the village. Together these three buildings had seating for 850 people or 52 per cent of the 1801 population.

In 1805 the Welsh Calvinistic Methodists (or Presbyterians as they would usually be called today) built Pandy Chapel.[9] The Llanuwchllyn Methodist Society was first established in 1791, but it was able to expand more rapidly in the early nineteenth century as a result of schisms within Independent congregations in the area. And in 1810 the Independents rebuilt Hen Gapel, both buildings being at Llanuwchllyn. This meant that by 1811 there was sufficient seating for 64 per cent of the population. In 1813 the Calvinistic Methodists had also built a chapel at Llangywer, so that by 1821 with the population standing at 1852 there was now seating for 1234 (or 67 per cent of the population).

Just as in north Northumberland, it was precisely at the moment that rural depopulation started that the chapels became most active in their building campaign. In the decade following 1821 three chapels were built (one Independent and two Calvinist); in the decade following 1831 three further chapels were built (one Independent, one Calvinist, and Ainon Primitive Baptist Chapel); and in the next decade an additional Independent chapel. The result of this vigorous building against depopulation was that seating capacity exceeded the local population from 1831 right up to the present day. So by 1831 there were 1634 seats for a population of 1590 (103 per cent); by 1841 there were 1916 seats for a population of 1697 (113 per cent); and by 1851 there were 2016 seats for a population of 1631 (124 per cent).

What is particularly interesting is that, as in North Yorkshire, all of this took place by 1851. Since the local population in north Northumberland reached its peak in 1851, the suggested effects on churchgoing of radical building against depopulation were largely speculative. Here at Glan-llyn the 1851 Religious Census itself provides crucial evidence about these effects thirty years after depopulation started and at the very point when chapel building slowed down. Hen Gapel was completely rebuilt and doubled in size in 1871 and a Sunday School Hall was built by the Independents in the middle of Llanuwchllyn (in this part of Wales Sunday schools teach adults as well as children). Otherwise there was no substantial chapel building. But, of course, with all of these buildings there was by 1871 seating for some 2566. Put differently, there was by now room for 172 per cent of the population in the churches and chapels of Llanuwchllyn and Llangywer. Using the same measure of seating, this would have been sufficient for 199 per cent by 1901, for 246 per cent by 1931, and for 289 per cent by 1951.

Since all of the chapels were still functioning in the early 1950s, when Trefor Owen's study of Glan-llyn was made, a combination of the 1851 Religious Census and this study offers a unique insight over a hundred-year period of how a rural community struggled with this extraordinary excess of buildings. This case study represents *in extremis* a problem faced in the twentieth century throughout rural Britain. However, before examining how the same community still copes with the

---

[9] Information about the dedication of the chapels in Glan-llyn is given in the returns 1851 Religious Census reported in Jones and Williams (eds), *The Religious Census of 1851.*

only slightly reduced problem today, it is necessary first to compare these two earlier studies.

2

The 1851 Religious Census shows that each of the twelve churches and chapels had at least one service on the day of the census. Each of the ten chapels recorded an additional service for the Sunday school and three of these recorded a total of three services on that Sunday. Llanuwchllyn Parish Church alone had a single service. Neither of the parish churches had an evening service, but all of the chapels did. The total of 590 attenders at these evening services did not include Sunday schools (which met in the morning and/or afternoon) and represented 36 per cent of the total population, who occupied 39 per cent of the available seats. In 1851 45 per cent of the population of Bala Registration District was aged under 20. If this was the case also in Lanuwchllyn and Llangywer and if it was the older age group that was mainly present in the evening, then as much as two-thirds of the local adult population would have been at these chapel services.

Morning was the most popular time for Sunday schools. Eight chapels had a total of 409 Sunday school attendances. Again, if this basically involved the local population aged under 20 (even though adults were present, toddlers and babies presumably were not) and if local proportions were similar to those of the district, then over half of the young people (56 per cent) were present. Sunday school and churchgoing attendances in eleven churches/chapels (only a Calvinistic chapel in Llangywer had no morning service) amounted to 575. This would have involved 29 per cent of the seats being occupied.

Afternoon services were held in six chapels and one church. Three of the chapel services were for Sunday schools, with 127 attenders (the Baptist Ainon Chapel alone had Sunday schools in the morning and in the afternoon). These 127 Sunday school attenders, as well as the 590 afternoon churchgoers, taken together amounted to 44 per cent of the total population, occupying 57 per cent of available seats. However, two of the chapels, the Independent Hen Gapel and the Calvinistic Pandy Chapel, had the largest congregations of the day (300 and 211 respectively). Since Hen Gapel had seating for 350 and Pandy Chapel for 280, they were clearly fairly full. If later patterns are a guide, it is possible that churchgoers at these large afternoon services attended other, more local, chapels in the evening.

The four denominations represented in the 1851 Religious Census each had distinctive characteristics. These can be outlined as follows.

The two churches of the Church in Wales mentioned no Sunday school and shared an incumbent, Hugh Jones. He had held both livings since 1817.[10] The smaller Llangywer parish had a better income and a rectory. His income from there

---

[10] Information about Anglican clergy appointments and/or stipends that follows is taken from *Clergy Lists* 1847 and 1870, and then from *Crockford's Clerical Directory*, 1890, 1918–19 and 1963–4. These are not reliable sources of information for parish populations: all population figures quoted are taken directly from government census reports. The detailed information about the sources of stipend for 1851 are taken from returns reported in Jones and Williams, *The Religious Census of 1851.*

of £222 was provided mostly from tithes (£168) and from land and glebe. His income of £103 from Llanuwchllyn, in contrast, was provided only partly from tithes (£20), partly from land (£49) and partly from endowment (£34). Actual fees amounted to just £2.5s. By the 1860s there were separate incumbents in the two parishes and this remained the case for almost a hundred years. In 1958 Euros Bowen (a distinguished Welsh poet), who had been at Llangywer since 1939, was also appointed vicar of Llanuwchllyn. Back in 1851 the shared incumbent had a congregation of 49 in the morning at Llanuwchllyn (in a church seating 300) and of 27 and 14 in the morning and afternoon at Llangywer (in a church seating 200). The lack of congregations in these heavily subsidized churches was not the result of pew rents. Some 100 free seats were provided at Llanuwchllyn and 160 at Llangywer.

The Independents had four chapels, all of them in Llanuwchllyn, and a resident minister (Thomas Roberts). Altogether they recorded 576 attendances at services and 207 at Sunday schools. Amalgamated these attendances represented 48 per cent of the total population, but of course it should not be assumed that these were all different attenders. The congregation of 300 at Hen Gapel in the afternoon (when the three other chapels were closed) probably best represented the strength of Independents in the area. With all the qualifications mentioned earlier, this would have represented a third of the adult population of both parishes – a rather stronger presence than was usual for North Wales. On average, services were 44 per cent full. However, only four out of the nine services were more than half full.

The Calvinistic Methodists had five chapels (three in Llanuwchllyn) and a minister resident at Wernddu. They recorded a total of 660 attendances at services and 283 at Sunday schools. Again, these attendances (but not attenders) amalgamated would have represented 58 per cent of the total population. As in Gwynedd today, Calvinistic Methodists/Presbyterians were then the largest denomination in North Wales (in South Wales the Independents were larger).[11] In the Bala district in 1851, out of every ten attendances more than seven would have been Calvinists. At the evening services at the five chapels in Llanuwchllyn and Langywer there were 316 people present, again perhaps representing slightly more than a third of the adult population. On average the eleven services in the Calvinist chapels were 52 per cent full.

The Primitive Baptists had a single chapel seating 132 at Llanuwchllyn and a resident minister (Edward Humphreys). They had been attempting to establish themselves in the area, apparently with little success, since the 1780s.[12] Even by 1851 congregations were not large. In the morning and afternoon there were Sunday schools with 12 and 34 attendances respectively. In the evening there was a congregation of 20. The general congregation is stated to have averaged 45 over a period of twelve months. Clearly, this chapel did not expect to be much more than a third full throughout the year. Baptists were not particularly strong in North Wales in 1851; their strength, as today, was in South Wales. In Bala district in 1851 this was their only chapel, although by 1858 they had established a meeting house in Bala itself.

---

[11] See Brierley and Evans (eds), *Prospects for Wales*.
[12] See Owen, 'Chapel and Community in Glan-llyn, Merioneth'.

From these figures clear patterns emerge. The (then) Established Church had a financially secure position in the community, which it was to improve over the next two decades. By 1870 the income[13] for the now separate incumbency of Llanuwchllyn had risen from £103 in 1851 to £200, and by 1918 it was reported to be £243 net (the average for the diocese[14] in 1906 was £231). The income for Llangywer, which had risen from £136 in 1847 to £222 in 1851, was still reported to be £200 in 1880. However, by 1918 it was reported to be only £132 net (by which time there were less than 200 people living in the parish). Without being wealthy livings, and fluctuating somewhat like other rural livings with the changing fortunes of agriculture, they nevertheless provided relative financial security that was not dependent on the generosity, or even attendance, of parishioners.

In contrast, the Independents and Calvinists had the support of the bulk of the population. Between them it appears that some two-thirds of local adults attended their chapels on 30 March 1851. Both denominations built chapels vigorously, and perhaps in competition with each other, against a declining rural population in the thirty years up to 1851. Yet only the Independents appear to have had a resident minister. Most of the smaller chapels relied upon local deacons. Hen Gapel clearly acted as a focus for the Independents and, to a slightly less extent, Pandy Chapel for the Calvinists. While the former could claim the largest single congregation, there were already signs that Independent chapels were on average more empty than full. The Calvinists alone of all four denominations had chapels that were on average marginally more full than empty.

Finally, the Baptists were the last denomination to build in the area (1840) and did not seem to have established a sizeable presence. They did have a resident minister, but two of their three services were for Sunday schools. Not one of their services was even a third full on the day of the census. Measuring just 18 feet by 18 feet, but with provision for 132 seats, it was visibly empty.

3

One hundred years later a number of key differences were apparent, as well as some important continuities. Owen reported that almost the entire population was affiliated to one of the four denominations and that only a very small minority never went to any church or chapel. Owen noted that 'the relatively few English residents, who generally remain apart from the rest of the community, account for 19 per cent of the male and 27 per cent of the female absentees; and it is an interesting fact that Welsh-speaking inhabitants born elsewhere in Wales are also tardy in their support'.[15] Owen stressed the strong community nature and function of the chapels in his study and largely accounted for this absenteeism as a product of outsiders failing to integrate into these religious/social communities.

The Independents and Calvinists remained by far the largest denominations in Glan-llyn. However, their relative position had changed. Owen reported that

---

[13] See note 10.

[14] See Summary A in *Royal Commission 1905–6*.

[15] Owen, 'Chapel and Community in Glan-llyn, Merioneth', p. 195.

125 families were affiliated to the Independents (with a total membership of 356) and 106.5 to the Calvinistic Methodists. The Church in Wales had forty-four families and the Baptists just one-and-a-half families. He maintained that, 'the effect of the smallness of the Baptist congregation operates both ways: while it may deter any possible addition to its numbers, its members are exceptionally faithful because they feel that disloyalty on their part would mortally weaken the small congregation'.[16]

Because almost everyone was affiliated to a denomination, Owen detected few overt attempts to convert individuals to join a rival congregation. In any case, it was widely assumed that anyone who did so convert would not be accepted readily by the new congregation. Only on marriage did significant numbers of individuals convert – usually the wife joining her new husband's congregation. Of the 233 marriages that Owen investigated, 113 were endogamous. Of the rest eighty wives had changed to their husband's denomination and twenty-six husbands to that of their wives (usually men from outside the community). Only fourteen marriages persisted with differences: 'the ties which are a result of common worship and participation in the secular life of the chapel since childhood, are considered to be infinitely more important than any theological differences'.[17]

Owen's tabulation of the churchgoing rate in Glan-llyn is complicated and requires some interpretation if it is to be compared successfully with the 1851 Religious Census. He reported it as in the table that follows.[18]

Table 3.1 Attendance at a place of worship

	20 to 60 years old		*Over 60 years old*	
	Men (%)	*Women (%)*	*Men (%)*	*Women (%)*
Twice or more per Sunday	28.5	26.7	26.3	28.8
Once per Sunday	38.1	37.5	27.6	28.8
Once or twice per month	13.1	13.3	5.3	13.6
Once or so in three months	2.6	5.0	7.9	1.5
Less often	3.1	4.2	5.3	1.5
Not at all	14.6	13.3	27.6	25.8

Unfortunately, Owen did not report directly the numbers on which these calculations were based. Not even the total number of adults in Glan-llyn was given in the study (only the total population of 948: it covered an area slightly larger than that of the two parishes whose combined population in 1951 was 887). Furthermore, it is only possible at present to establish the age/gender distribution in 1951 for the wider area of Penllyn[19] – although from this it is clear that the 20–60 age groups

---

[16] Owen, 'Chapel and Community in Glan-llyn, Merioneth', p. 229.

[17] Owen, 'Chapel and Community in Glan-llyn, Merioneth', p. 228

[18] Owen, 'Chapel and Community in Glan-llyn, Merioneth', p. 194.

[19] Penllyn, with a population of 2830, is the smallest local unit showing age/gender distribution published in the 1951 population census.

were some three times larger than the over-60 groups and that adult males and females were fairly evenly balanced. So the percentage of the local population that was in church or chapel on a typical Sunday in 1950 can only be estimated within certain broad bands.

Nevertheless, these bands do suggest an extraordinarily high churchgoing rate in this part of rural Wales shortly after the Second World War. They also suggest that churchgoing remained about as strong in 1950 as it had been in 1851. In any of the age/gender groups recorded, the lowest churchgoing rate for attendance at least once on a Sunday was 53.9 per cent (i.e. for men aged over 60); in the much larger 20–60 age-groups it was some two-thirds. Furthermore, less than a third of the older groups, and less than a fifth of the younger groups, were recorded as attending seldom or never.

However, since all the churches and chapels in existence in 1851 were still functioning in 1950 (together with an enlarged Hen Gapel and an additional chapel/Sunday school in Llanuwchllyn), overall they would by now *have appeared* considerably emptier. The 1851 population of these two parishes was 1631, whereas by 1951 it had almost halved. As a result, a similar rate of churchgoing at the two dates would obviously have yielded a sharply different number of attendances. If in 1851 there were (excluding Sunday schools) 1346 attendances, in 1950 there would, without a drastic increase in the already-high overall churchgoing rate, have been barely 700.

On this basis, in 1851 a church or chapel could on average have expected 112 attendances on a Sunday, whereas by 1950 it could expect barely 58. It is difficult to resist the conclusion that churches and chapels, which struggled (and often failed) to be half full in 1851, would have struggled to be a quarter full in 1950. The irony is that this would have been the case despite persisting high churchgoing rates – indeed, despite rates well in excess of any of the contemporary English rates reported in Chapter 8.

Evidence of the effects of this radical change can be gleaned from Owen's study. He was inclined himself to attribute these changes to twentieth-century secularization. Once again, this all-encompassing, cultural explanation – so popular among academics at the time he was writing – may have served to mask much more mundane, physical factors.

First, Owen noted that Sunday schools and weekday prayer meetings were declining sharply. Despite the long-standing inclusion of adult classes in Sunday schools, he found that 57 per cent of the families had no representatives attending them. At the Calvinist chapel in Llanuwchllyn village, average annual attendance of the whole congregation at Sunday school fell from 41 per cent in 1939 to 28 per cent in 1949. Furthermore, less than a third of the households had any contact with the prayer or 'society' meetings that chapels held during the week. Some of the smaller chapels had even discontinued them altogether, 'and, as in other forms of religious observance, the older generation is more faithful in its attendance during the week'.[20]

Secondly, Owen noted a pervasive problem of leadership at services, especially in smaller chapels. It was the smaller chapels that tended to discontinue mid-week

---

[20] Owen, 'Chapel and Community in Glan-llyn, Merioneth', p. 196.

religious activities. In itself, since Hen Gapel acted as a focus for all of the Independent congregations, this may not have been too significant. However, Owen argued that the problem extended to Sunday worship as well:

> When no preacher is available, there should be present, ideally, sufficient members capable of conducting a prayer meeting between them. The success of such a meeting, in a purely superficial sense, depends on the presence of persons able and willing to come forward and 'take part'. Such persons are fewer than formerly, and this poses a problem which the chapels find difficult to solve. For example, out of over forty members in one of the smaller chapels, only two or three can 'take part' in a prayer meeting; at another chapel only two out of a congregation of fifteen. Conditions are similar in the larger chapels where there are only a dozen or so in congregations of between 100 and 150. Since the prayers uttered are sometimes barely audible throughout the whole chapel, and since they tend to become stereotyped in content and form, there is less variation in the prayer meeting than might be expected from the number of people taking part. The tendency is to look on the preaching meetings as the 'real' services and to regard the prayer meetings merely as stop-gaps.[21]

Thirdly, he noted that some smaller chapels had been forced to amalgamate their Sunday services. Despite sharp differentiations of denominational membership between families, the relative weakness of smaller chapels occasionally forced them into amalgamations:

> Instances of joint services held by congregations belonging to different connexions are few in number and arise out of the numerical weakness of one of the congregations. The Baptists and Independents ... attend services at each other's chapels during the Thanksgiving festival; Baptists also attend the Young People's Society of the Independents because they have none of their own. Occasionally the Young People's Societies of the Methodist and Independent chapels hold joint meetings (often debates on secular subjects between speakers from both societies) but such co-operation takes place on what is really the fringe of religious activities. In one neighbourhood two congregations have in recent years co-operated to the extent of holding joint Sunday services in each chapel alternately; but this arrangement again derives from the weakness of both.[22]

In each of these respects crucial changes were already taking place in the local chapels by 1950. In view of the radical drop in attendances (but not in the overall churchgoing rate), none of these changes is surprising. In terms of my overall argument, it is important to note that these changes occurred while up to two-thirds of the adult population appears still to have been regularly attending church or chapel. Here again is evidence that key aspects of what at the time might have seemed to be church decline (at least among Free Churches) first occurred *before* churchgoing rates actually did decline.

Sunday schools (despite the presence of some adults) would have been particularly affected by depopulation. In the Registration District at large, 45 per cent of the 1851 population was aged under 20; by 1951 it was only 29 per cent. In these circumstances, it is not difficult to envisage how it became progressively more

---

[21] Owen, 'Chapel and Community in Glan-llyn, Merioneth', pp. 193–4.
[22] Owen, 'Chapel and Community in Glan-llyn, Merioneth', p. 230.

difficult for smaller chapels to maintain viable Sunday schools. Leadership at services would also have been radically affected by depopulation. With less people to choose from, in an increasingly elderly community, leaders would have been at a premium. Owen supplied much evidence to show that, even by 1950, chapel leadership still carried with it high status in the community at large. This is hardly evidence of secularization. The effects of depopulation in an area stretched to the limit with an abundance of chapels seems to be a far more convincing explanation. And signs of co-operation between once rival chapels – again so often interpreted by sociologists as a product of secularization[23] – may more plausibly be explained in similar terms. Some of the older people in the area today remember such co-operation from their youth; so it may extend back even further than Owen realized.

4

By 1990 all of these changes had advanced further, but the churchgoing rate had by now also declined. There were 598 adults on the electoral register of the two parishes (76 of them at Llangywer) and an average Sunday might then expect to see about 106 of them, or 18 per cent, in church or chapel. The average churchgoing rate was thus slightly lower than the 19 per cent recorded for the whole of Gwynedd in the 1982 MARC Europe census.[24] However, in terms of denominational membership the two parishes were quite distinct from Gwynedd. The four denominations between them claimed 481 'members' (a concept for once that local Anglicans seem prepared to use), representing 80 per cent of the adult population. Membership in the county as a whole (a much more difficult notion here since, as explained earlier, it also includes Catholics), although the highest in England or Wales, was 41 per cent in 1982. The average for the whole of Wales was 24 per cent. Thus, from 1851 to 1990, the local population, unlike most of Britain, remained overwhelmingly connected by 'membership' (however interpreted) to its churches and chapels. Yet between 1950 and 1990 most of these members ceased to attend on a regular basis.

Perhaps the sharpest change was experienced by the Presbyterians (as the Calvinistic Methodists are now called) and the Congregationalists (as the Independents are more usually termed). They have long been rivals in Wales and especially, given the unusual local strength of Congregationalists, in this area. By 1990 they shared both a minister and their main service every Sunday. They still maintained separate membership records and, as in 1950, Congregationalists remained in this respect the strongest denomination. Their membership in 1990 stood at 218 (36 per cent of the adult population), whereas Presbyterian membership was 196 (33 per cent). However, attendances could no longer be easily differentiated. There was a shared afternoon or evening service, with an average attendance of 70, held alternately at the Presbyterian Pandy Chapel and the Congregational Ysgoldy chapel/Sunday school, and in the summer months at the

---

[23] See my *Competing Convictions*, SCM Press, London, 1989.
[24] See note 5; national 'membership' figures that follow are also from MARC Europe.

mother Congregational chapel, Hen Gapel. There was also a small separate service in one of the other chapels: one week at one and one week at another. Three chapels were now closed (one converted into a house), so the remaining four could expect only an occasional service. The average attendance at the latter was about 15. Since the community remained 85 per cent–90 per cent Welsh-speaking, all services were still held in Welsh.

The last separate Presbyterian minister to serve in the area left in 1982. The Congregationalist minister, who had lived in Llanuwchllyn since 1967, thus became the sole ordained minister living in the two parishes serving eight chapels (one of them outside the two parishes). Although Presbyterians and Congregationalists had not formally united in Wales as they had in England, they had *de facto* united in these two parishes. Doubtless, old rivalries and suspicions still persisted. And there was clear evidence that a shared service did not satisfy all more localized affections. Yet financial constraints and numerical weakness left the two local denominations with little alternative.

The sharpest change for the Anglican churches may have been the loss of any resident priest. In 1958 the two parishes were grouped under a single resident incumbent, thus returning to the position in the first half of the nineteenth century. In 1985, after a period of temporary arrangements, they were both formally placed under the charge of the new incumbent living at Bala. There was still an Anglican service every Sunday morning at Llanuwchllyn, with an average attendance of seventeen, but only a single afternoon service once a month at Llangywer, with an average attendance of six. All services were held in a mixture of English and Welsh.

The two parish churches remained a focus for some of the rites of passage in the community. It has been known for a chapel member to have a funeral service in them, but local custom dictates that there should still be some form of differentiation. The coffin of a chapel member would popularly be placed at the back of the churches. Only those of church members were expected to be placed in the chancel. Such occasional offices in both church and chapel, as in many rural areas, still involved a very high proportion of the local community. Again, like many other remote rural areas, most of the population would set foot in a local church or chapel for one reason or another in the course of a year. What most of them no longer did by 1990 was do this regularly.

Ainon Baptist Chapel still survived in Llanuwchllyn. However, it only had seven members in 1990 and its now infrequent services, usually held without a minister, expected an attendance of just four. It is perhaps remarkable that this chapel had survived at all, given its thin attendances in each of the three censuses. Few locally expected in 1990 that it would continue to survive for long into the future. Manifestly, it had now lost the 'vigour-due-to-smallness' noted by Owen forty years earlier.

The four decades between 1950 and 1990 apparently witnessed greater changes in the churches and chapels in the community than the previous century. Uniquely, chapels were closed, and few of the rest had regular Sunday services. The parish church in Llanuwchllyn was now the only building to have a service every Sunday, since the larger Congregationalist/Presbyterian service rotated. Also resident ministers and priests had not been replaced, and the churchgoing rate had declined more than threefold. Membership had stayed very high and most of the buildings remained (doubtless with their localized loyalties). Nevertheless, in *The Myth of the Empty Church* I predicted that radical declines would occur in both of these areas before the next census.

5

It is now possible to test these two predictions. A census that I conducted in 2002 confirms their accuracy. The adult population has risen slightly from 598 to 631 in the past twelve years, but overall church/chapel membership has declined from 481 to 386 and regular Sunday attendance from 106 to some 70. So, in contrast to the period 1950–1990, membership as well as attendance now shows a clear decline. Whereas previously membership represented 80 per cent of the adult population, it now represents 61 per cent. Of course the latter is still very high by national standards, but it is now losing its remarkable resilience. Meanwhile regular Sunday attendance has continued to decline, from some 18 per cent of the population to 11 per cent. This is still a rate much higher than the 8 per cent for Pentecost 2002 recorded in the previous chapter for north Northumberland, but the rate of decline is actually three times faster. As will be seen for Anglicans in *Table 18*, some remote rural areas have seen a very dramatic decline in regular churchgoing in recent decades.

The other prediction was rather easier. In 1990 there were already clear signs of a local community struggling to maintain historic chapels. By 2002 two more chapels have been closed and there are plans to close Pandy Chapel. In 1990 there were some doubts about whether the Presbyterians/Congregationalists would be able to replace their long-serving minister in Llanuwchllyn when he retired. In fact they did and there is now a resident Presbyterian minister serving the six remaining chapels (one of them still outside the two parishes). There have, however, been other changes. The small group of Baptists at Ainon Chapel have now joined the Presbyterians/Congregationalists and their chapel, alternating with Hen Gapel, is currently used for the main service (with an average attendance now of 50 – reduced from 70 in 1990) during the summer. There are only occasional services at the three remaining smaller chapels and, during the winter, all services are now held in the Hall in Llanuwchllyn. It is not difficult to predict that there are further rationalizations of buildings to come. The two Anglican churches are still served by the incumbent at Bala, albeit with congregations at Llanuwchllyn now reduced from about seventeen to thirteen.

6

Without resorting to explanations based upon some theory of secularization, is it possible to detect in this pattern of church decline the sort of explanatory factors identified in the last chapter? Specifically, can the five effects of empty churches/chapels isolated earlier (whatever cultural factors may also have contributed to decline) be detected here? There has been an abundance of empty churches and chapels in Glan-llyn since at least 1851. They preceded radical churchgoing decline in the area by a minimum of one hundred years. Thus they should provide a good test for my overall hypotheses.

The first effect suggests that empty churches or chapels, when unsubsidized, lead to their gradual closure. Elsewhere, closing churches/chapels is strongly associated with losses of membership and attendance.[25] Here in Glan-llyn there have indeed been closures, and more might be expected in the future. Even the Anglican Church may find difficulty in maintaining two historic buildings for so small a community. Both the Presbyterians and the Congregationalists face enormous building problems locally – and indeed nationally.

The 1982 MARC Europe census recorded that the Presbyterian Church of Wales had 1169 chapels, served by 220 ministers, with an average each of 32 adult attenders, and representing 1.7 per cent of the population. The Union of Welsh Independents and Congregationalists had 746 chapels, served by 210 ministers, with an average each of 35 adult attenders, and representing 1.2 per cent of the population. By contrast, Catholics in Wales had just 206 churches, served by 262 priests, with an average each of 322 adult attenders, and representing 2.6 per cent of the population. From these figures it is not difficult to see that the local problems faced by Presbyterians and Congregationalists in Glan-llyn are part of a national problem.

The second effect suggests that empty churches lead to financial problems. As early as the 1880s there was considerable discussion about chapel debt in Wales. The (admittedly biased) vicar of Carmarthen wrote to *The Times* in 1887 summarizing parts of this debt, and taking his statistics from the *Welsh Calvinistic Year-book*:

> The most remarkable fact recorded in the official year-book is the rapid growth of the debt on the chapels. In the year 1878 the chapel debt was £246 926; in 1881, £311 294; and in 1886, £323 118. The sum of money devoted to paying off the chapel debt in 1878 was £43 508, and this sum has been steadily decreasing until, in 1886, only £31 440 was given to this purpose – that is to say, that while the chapel debt has been increasing rapidly, the annual contributions towards its liquidation have decreased as rapidly.[26]

Of course this polemic ignored the huge subsidy from tithes that the Church in Wales received at the time – quite regardless of whether local people did or, as in Glan-llyn, did not frequent its churches. It was a polemic that continued fiercely in Wales and was recorded in detail in the *Royal Commission of 1905–6*.[27]

Throughout the century-and-a-half examined, the Free Churches in Glan-llyn struggled to pay for an effective ministry. With the abolition of tithes and the rapid inflation of the second half of the twentieth century, Anglicans have faced a similar problem. The financial difficulties faced by a small community today struggling to

---

[25] See J.N. Wolfe and M. Pickford, *The Church of Scotland: An Economic Survey*, Chapman, London, 1980, and my *Competing Convictions*.

[26] A.G. Edwards to *The Times*, 31 October 1887: reprinted in A.G. Edwards, *Facts and Figures about Church and Dissent in Wales*, Carmarthen, 1888.

[27] See note 6.

maintain the eight remaining churches and chapels are obvious. In 1801 there were 540 people of all ages in the community for every church or chapel; in 1851 there were 136; in 1901 there were 99; and today there are about 90. The five chapel closures have done little to remedy a long-standing and financially debilitating problem.

The third effect suggests that empty churches tend to share ordained ministers. Unsubsidized churches or chapels, if they are empty, inevitably face difficulties in recruiting, retaining and paying for ordained ministers. It should be clear by now that this has always been a problem for the Free Churches in Glan-llyn. The Baptists reported a resident ordained ministry only in the 1851 Religious Census. By 1950 they were struggling with lay leadership and by 1990 they were struggling to retain a separate membership at all. Presbyterians and Congregationalists clearly have had effective ordained ministries in the area. However, from the 1982 MARC Europe figures just cited it will be evident that, on average, Presbyterian ministers in Wales each care for five chapels and Congregationalists for four. Combining the two roles, the present minister in Glan-llyn's charge does not appear so exceptional. The Anglican incumbent at Bala cares for four churches (the national average is only two). Yet, however typical or atypical such multiple charges might be, it has already been seen that they are likely to have a depressing effect on local churchgoing.[28]

The fourth effect suggests that empty churches find it very difficult to integrate new attenders. It is not difficult to see how the marginal or occasional churchgoer might once have slipped into the back of a relatively full congregation in Glan-llyn. However, congregations of four or six may be far more difficult to penetrate. It has already been seen that Owen suggested that this was the case with the Baptists in 1950. Today only the rotating morning service of the Presbyterians/ Congregationalists offers a sizeable congregation in Glan-llyn on a regular basis. And, even then, it may occupy little more than 10 per cent of the seats in the summer at Hen Gapel. In effect, empty churches or chapels may serve to generate even emptier churches or chapels.

The fifth effect suggests that empty churches offer a major signal of secularization. While remaining sceptical of claims that the changes in churchgoing in Glan-llyn over 151 years are a direct product of secularization, their effect may be to reinforce or perhaps encourage secularization. Every generation will have remembered an earlier time when the chapels were stronger. There were many more Sunday attendances; each church and chapel used to have at least one, usually two, and sometime three, services on a Sunday; Sunday schools were active in every chapel; there were more chapel buildings; there were weekly prayer meetings and 'societies'; and there were resident ministers and priests. For the most part, these memories were probably accurate for every generation.

What are inaccurate are the memories of simultaneously full chapels and churches. What may also be inaccurate are many of the popular perceptions of why they 'failed'. And what have been largely ignored are the effects of vigorous chapel building against a rapidly declining rural population.

---

[28] See Leslie J. Francis, *Rural Anglicanism*, Collins, London, 1985.

4

Urban Churchgoing Decline

The main task of this book is to consider urban, rather than rural, churchgoing decline and it is to this task that I must now turn. Even if it is grudgingly admitted that over-building caused problems in many parts of rural Britain by the turn of the century, it is commonly supposed that it was under-building that characterized urban areas in the second half of the nineteenth century. So a revised version of the propositions set out in the Introduction might run as follows.

Several denominations throughout Britain built vigorously against declining rural populations in the nineteenth century. The evidence for this in England and Wales has already been set out, but it also happened in Scotland. Here it can be shown that whole counties had a very considerable excess of seating accommodation by 1901. If the seating capacity for counties, excluding major towns within them, is taken from the 1851 Religious Census (together with proportional estimates for missing returns)[1] and compared with 1901 populations, this becomes evident. Without any additional building, by 1901 Kinross would have had seating for 102 per cent of its rural population, Dumfries and Bute for 95 per cent, Orkney and Shetland for 94 per cent, Argyle for 87 per cent, and Berwickshire for 82 per cent. The Disruption of 1843 was thus already by 1851 producing excessive seating accommodation for a declining rural population. Since building continued vigorously over the next few decades, rural Scotland, like rural England and Wales, manifestly had a major problem by 1901. It is a problem that the Church of Scotland has been struggling with ever since its Union of 1929.[2]

Once this problem is observed across rural Britain, the five factors identified in the last two chapters become obvious: (1) many rural churches and chapels have been closed; (2) chronic debt typically preceded these closures; (3) ordained ministers of all denominations have progressively had charge of an increasing number of churches and chapels; (4) decreasing rural congregations find it difficult to integrate marginal churchgoers and become increasingly elderly; (5) largely empty churches and chapels finally become social signs of secularization. On this understanding, cultural factors such as 'secularization' are no longer identified as the primary agents of rural churchgoing decline. Physical factors seem to be more dominant, and secularization is instead seen as an end product.

---

[1] *Religious Worship and Education, Scotland, Report and Tables*, Eyre & Spottiswoode, 1854. The original returns for Scotland were destroyed, but the number of places of worship that gave no figures for seating is recorded for each county and major town. The overall mean of 488 seats per church for Scotland is used in my estimates for these missing figures.

[2] See J.N. Wolfe and M. Pickford, *The Church of Scotland: An Economic Survey*, Chapman, London, 1980.

However, in urban contexts it was secularization that appeared to be the cause of churchgoing decline. If anything, denominations under-provided for burgeoning urban, industrial populations. Significant sections of the urban working classes could not have gone to church because there was insufficient seating available for their use. There was both a shortage of buildings and a lack of 'free' accommodation; the latter because many churches and chapels financed themselves through pew rents that were beyond the resources of working people. Thus, the five factors identified in rural contexts apparently did not apply in urban contexts. In the latter it was progressive secularization – a product of secular thought and urban alienation – that was primarily responsible for the churchgoing decline evident since the First World War.

1

There are some obvious flaws in the urban part of this analysis. Anyone who walks around central Aberystwyth, York or Edinburgh today may soon notice a proliferation of churches and chapels, many still holding services but also quite a number that are now used for more secular purposes. One former church in Edinburgh in the 1980s displayed a sign reading 'Sweet Services' – which sadly was not an invitation to mellifluous acts of worship. Another, more notoriously, was a betting shop. Typically such former churches are in central urban areas that once supported far larger populations. Central urban depopulation, it will soon be observed, began, like rural depopulation, in the late nineteenth century. In the City of London it goes back to the early eighteenth century.

Another flaw lies in the assumption that excesses of seating over local populations occurred only in rural areas, and never in urban ones. Llanelli in South Wales and Caernarfon in North Wales provide startling counter examples. In 1851 Llanelli had seating[3] in its various churches and chapels for 85 per cent of its population of 8415, and Caernarfon for 81 per cent of its population of 9883. By 1881 the population of Llanelli had virtually doubled to 19 655, whereas that of Caernarfon has remained fairly static right up to the present day. However, in both places later newspaper censuses[4] estimated that total church and chapel seating had by then exceeded their local populations. In the case of Llanelli, seating by 1881 was estimated at some 103 per cent of its much enlarged population. In the case of Caernarfon, a population that had not grown at all by 1908 had none the less increased its churches and chapels from sixteen to twenty-two.

The Llanelli claim, and the newspaper commentary that accompanied it, caused considerable local controversy in 1881. The editorial of a rival newspaper, *The South Wales Press*, denounced it in the following revealing manner:

---

[3] Calculated from the original returns of the 1851 Religious Census reported in I.G. Jones and D. Williams, (eds), *The Religious Census of 1851: A Calendar of the Returns Relating to Wales*, vol. 1, University of Wales Press, Cardiff, 1976.

[4] Reported in *Western Mail*, 25 November 1881 and *Llanelly Guardian c.*17 November 1881; *Carnarvon and Denbigh Herald: North and South Wales Independent*, 31 January 1908 and 10 July 1908.

The writer says that no more chapels will be required 'for at least 15 or 20 years. For the present attendances the edifices are too numerous, and this is one reason why the debts are so heavy'. We presume if this writer had his own way every chapel and church would be closed at once. Noble philanthropist, to advise the churches 'to forget past little differences' when all his aim has been to bring religion into scorn and disrepute! It is a blessing that Nonconformity is not dependent on this miserable caviller. This is not an attack upon Church or Dissent, upon this sect or that, but upon 'religious Llanelly' as a whole, and we denounce the 'Census' and expose it as a deliberate and malicious attempt to sneer down the morality and religion of Llanelly as one of the foremost communities in Bible-loving God-fearing Wales.[5]

In the same edition of this newspaper, a letter from Canon Williams, vicar of Llanelli, disputed the seating estimates in ten of the churches and chapels in the town, on the basis of a census that he himself conducted eight years earlier. His estimates for these buildings showed a seating capacity some 30 per cent less than that given in the 1881 census. But, even on his estimates (which were, of course, eight years out of date – a long time given the speed of contemporary urban growth), there was still a remarkable amount of seating accommodation available in Llanelli. Furthermore, in the case of two of the churches for which he made estimates (his own and Capel Newydd), the seating given in the 1851 Religious Census was actually higher than his figures for the 1870s.

This example already provides indications of some of the factors identified in rural areas. Of course the population of Llanelli was growing, and growing very considerably. But evidently so were churches and chapels, and possibly they were growing faster than the population. Clearly there were considerable religious rivalries in the town and there was already mention of debt. If the 1881 census is to be trusted, Anglican churches, which were in 1851 on average 96 per cent full in the evening, were in 1881 just 40 per cent full; and Free Church chapels, which in 1851 were 74 per cent full, were 42 per cent full in 1881. Even allowing for possible exaggeration of seating in 1881, there were manifestly a great number of churches and chapels in Llanelli by then, which would have appeared on average distinctly emptier than they had been in the previous generation.

These claims are strongly reinforced by the local newspaper commentary following the Caernarfon census in 1908. The Sunday in January when the census was taken was very wet; a census taken subsequently on a fine day in July showed a slight improvement in morning attendances. Yet the overall January attendances were still high (51 per cent and, in July, 55 per cent) compared with most of those reviewed for the same period in Chapter 7 (in 1851 they were also high, at 63 per cent, compared with most other places).

Nevertheless, with the six extra churches and chapels by 1908 and a static population in Caernarfon, most denominations were evidently struggling for viability. Without these extra buildings the evening services in 1851 were on average 58 per cent full, but the morning services were only 37 per cent full. With the extra buildings most churches and chapels were clearly more empty than full, as the newspaper report in 1908 demonstrated:

---

[5] *The South Wales Press*, 1 December 1881.

Sectarianism, which is the curse of Wales, may be responsible for the multiplicity of chapels, not only in Carnarvon, but in other places. It cannot be gainsaid that the supply of chapels is greater than the demand, and we think it could be proved that the seating accommodation of all the places of worship in the town is greater than the whole population. We hear a great deal in these days about the union of Free Churches, but we are afraid it is a union in name only ... Notwithstanding that sectarianism is so often condemned, there are very few indications that it is dying out. It lies low, perhaps, during religious awakenings, but after these are over it flourishes quite as well as before. It is idle to hope for reform until the death warrant of this narrow sectarian spirit is signed.[6]

The quarter-century separating this report from that for Llanelli is crucial. In the earlier report evidence about over-building and the effects of over-building was mentioned but dismissed. In the later report evidence about over-building was accepted, some of its effects were noted and, most significantly of all, it was seen as a direct product of 'sectarianism'. This was a radical, albeit unusual, change of perception. Rivalries between Free Churches were now seen as mutually destructive. As in the countryside, such rivalries had apparently led to over-building to the point of saturation long before the First World War; and now a few contemporary commentators, who were certainly not hostile to organized Christianity, were beginning to observe this for themselves.

Since writing *The Myth of the Empty Church* I have discovered an even earlier report that did detect some of the physical features involved here.[7] The incumbent of a then new parish in Liverpool, Abraham Hume, made a careful statistical analysis of local churches in relation to population from the mid-seventeenth century until his own time of 1858. From this he concluded:

Now, since almost all our places of religious worship are supported on the voluntary principle, two facts are of constant occurrence. *First*, the Chapels of Protestant Dissenters, which have not necessarily any fixed position, are removed from time to time towards the outer margin of the town; thus keeping within the range of the paying population. *Second*, the churches of the town, which are consecrated to meet the wants of the people in a given area, retain their local position, many of them serving in succession for every grade of the population. Their resources are thus diminished, not only from generation to generation, but from year to year, until the congregations in some instances are scarcely able to support the expenses incidental to public worship.[8]

This remarkably perceptive analysis could apply equally to the churches in York today. It will be seen in Chapter 9 that it is a Baptist church which has relocated twice in the past twenty years that seems currently to have the largest congregation there. In contrast, city centre churches in York are struggling – even attendances at the Anglican St Michael le Belfrey and the Catholic St Wilfred have declined sharply within the past twelve years.

---

[6] *Carnarvon and Denbigh Herald: North and South Wales Independent*, 31 January 1908, p. 5.

[7] I am most grateful to Dr David Voas for calling my attention to this.

[8] A. Hume, 'Condition of Liverpool, Religious and Social; Including Notices of the State of Education, Morals, Pauperism, and Crime', privately circulated, Liverpool, 1858, p. 12.

Hume, although himself an enthusiast for providing more church accommodation in Liverpool, did warn his contemporaries about ill-conceived church building. His provided a rare, but largely unheeded, voice:

> Not infrequently the error in church building is multiplied. For example, a church is wanted to accommodate 800, and in such a neighbourhood that it should not cost more than £3 per sitting; and a church is built, to accommodate 1600, at a cost of £6 per sitting. It thus costs *four* times as much as was necessary. The additional seats which were not needed, and are not available there, are reckoned among the church accommodation of the town; and expense is entailed upon the congregation for keeping this larger and more costly fabric in repair.[9]

2

It has been so widely assumed that Victorians failed to keep pace with the rapid growth of urban populations in their provision of churches and chapels, that widespread evidence to the contrary has been persistently ignored. The Victorians themselves usually ignored it and so have twentieth-century social historians. However, in the chapters that follow I show that this assumption is mistaken. The finer details must await these later chapters. For the moment I will set out the broad outlines revealed by a careful examination of comparative longitudinal census data.

Specifically, I will argue that a careful analysis of London and Liverpool census data suggests that there has been a continuous process of declining Sunday attendances in the Church of England since the 1851 Religious Census. There has also been a continuous decline in the Free Churches since the 1880s. In both cases denominations continued to build new churches even when existing churches were only one third full on a typical Sunday. By 1902 all major denominations, except the Catholics, were characterized by empty churches. I will also argue that a major difference, in a wide variety of urban census data, emerges between the Free Churches and the Church of England; this may throw light on their mutual decline since the 1880s.

Even the five broad factors identified in rural areas are relevant to the urban data examined in this way. In Inner Greater London, for example, the Free Churches had 1512 chapels in 1903, but had reduced them to 1443 by 1914. By the turn of the century there was widespread discussion about the debts and sorry state of many chapels.[10] In contrast, the Church of England increased its churches in London from

---

[9] A. Hume, 'Condition of Liverpool, Religious and Social', pp. 34–5.

[10] For a full list of the churches and chapels in London in 1914, as well as an account of contemporary chapel debts there, see H. Wilson Harris and Margaret Bryant, *The Churches and London*, published by *The Daily News and Leader*, 1914. Chapel debts in London also feature in Charles Booth, *Life and Labour of the People in London: Third Series: Religious Influences*, (e.g. vol. 7, Ch. 3), Macmillan, 1902. Chapel debts in Wales were much discussed in the 1880s: see A.G. Edwards, letters written to *The Times* on 31 October 1887, 10 November 1887 and 3 January 1888; a report on the debts of South Wales Calvinist Methodists in *The Aberystwyth Observer*, 22 April 1882; and later reports in *The Royal Commission on the Church of England and other Religious Bodies in Wales and Monmouthshire 1905–6*, Parliamentary Papers, 1911.

1014 in 1903 to 1155 in 1914, despite thin attendances. There is even evidence, especially in the Church of England, of some city-centre churches sharing priests.

Too many church buildings inevitably mean emptier churches – in urban as well as rural Britain. And empty churches may act in both contexts as factors in an overall decline in churchgoing in two ways. As already argued, they provide an obvious signal at the grass-roots level of secularization. A great deal of newspaper attention has recently been given to the secularization of Britain; habitually this is primarily based upon declining urban church attendances and empty churches. Despite the very real sophistications of many more properly sociological understandings of secularization, I suspect that it is this signal that is the most socially influential.

The very social visibility of empty urban churches – or urban churches sold and used for more secular purposes – may shape and reinforce public perceptions of secularization. Empty or redundant rural churches may also reinforce this perception. But the decline of most public facilities is known to be widespread in the countryside. However, little used or redundant urban churches contrast sharply and unfavourably with urban pubs, discos, theme parks and shopping centres. Furthermore, when other urban voluntary associations cease to function – as undoubtedly they have during the twentieth century[11] – they generally leave few physical traces behind them. Redundant urban churches – preserved for ever as listed buildings – stubbornly remain as visible reminders of a once religious past.

And, of course, empty urban churches, like their rural counterparts, may also act as deterrents to marginal churchgoers. To attend a full church or chapel on an occasional basis may not be too difficult, but to attend a large urban church or chapel (they are characteristically far larger than those in the countryside) containing a small, predominantly female and probably elderly, congregation might be much more daunting.

But what, as I argued in *Competing Convictions*,[12] if churchgoing decline even within urban contexts is less a product of secularization than of churches competing to their mutual disadvantage? If this were the case, then decline might actually owe more to an excess of conviction and misplaced energy than to some supposed loss of faith. Almost without exception journalists (and many church people) seem to be convinced that it is loss of faith, liberalization and perhaps ecumenism that have 'caused' churchgoing decline. Sometimes they also mention the two world wars and the effects of television. Sociologists of religion have frequently concurred, but the census evidence on urban attendances suggests otherwise. From this, churchgoing decline seems to be much more long-standing than most people realize. It also appears to owe much to the physical factors already contained within census data.

It is interesting that even those involved in collecting census data in the late nineteenth and early twentieth centuries tended to explain declining attendances in very similar terms to present-day journalists. The otherwise excellent report of the London census of 1902/3 (which, unlike many other contemporary censuses,

---

[11] See Stephen Yeo, *Religious and Voluntary Organisations in Crisis*, Croom Helm, London, 1976.

[12] SCM Press, London, 1989.

provided data on the age and gender of churchgoers) wrongly saw decline as a feature only of the Church of England and attributed this to a lack of its commitment to evangelism.[13]

Arthur Black, too, in one of his reports to *The British Weekly* about the unique 1927/8 sample surveys of London churchgoing,[14] suggested a variety of factors responsible for church decline. All three of his samples (two working-class and one middle-class) showed a decline in average attendances at churches and chapels of at least a half from 1902/3. Yet it was the middle-class decline in what he described as 'a suburban area', in both the Church of England and the Free Churches, that he found particularly surprising.

The identity of this 'suburban area' has long puzzled scholars.[15] As is seen later, it was in fact Roehampton/Putney. It is particularly valuable because attendances there in 1886/7 and 1902/3 corresponded closely to the mean for Inner Greater London for those dates and provide rare inter-war census evidence. To explain decline in this area, Black suggested that it was 'partly due to causes beyond the control of the churches', namely the war, distractions provided by 'the gramophone, cinema, wireless' etc., improved social and travel conditions, 'and, last, the intellectual unsettlement, within the Church and outside, consequent upon modern Biblical scholarship and the new scientific explanations of man's place in the universe'.[16]

Yet, having offered such largely unmeasurable factors, elsewhere he noticed something quite different. Almost in passing he noted that Catholic churches, even in one of his working-class samples (which may have been Battersea), had not declined in the same way as other denominations. In the latter, 'no church or chapel, in view of its seating capacity, has an adequate attendance. The big chapel without exception is a burdensome problem'. But about the Catholics he remarked, 'How wise has been this Church in limiting the number of its centres, using them more fully, and concentrating strength in a few rather than dividing limited energies over many.'[17]

In his final report Black did not return to his unmeasurable factors. Instead, he saw co-operation between churches as a key factor, since 'to continue without change, with diminishing numbers and power is not business – is not Christianity. The resources of the churches in men, money and buildings are not used to full advantage.'[18]

---

[13] See Jane T. Stoddart, 'The Daily News Census of 1902–3 Compared with the British Weekly Census of 1886', in Richard Mudie-Smith (ed.), *The Religious Life of London*, Hodder, London, 1904. *The British Weekly*'s census of 1886–7 was published first in the journal itself and then as *The Religious Census of London*, Hodder, London, 1888.

[14] Arthur Black, 'London Church and Mission Attendances', *The British Weekly*, 23 February 1928, 1 March 1928, and 8 March 1928.

[15] e.g. C.E.M. Joad in *The Present and Future of Religion*, Benn, London, 1930; Michael Argyle in *Religious Behaviour*, Routledge & Kegan Paul, London, 1958; and Jeffrey Cox in *The English Churches in a Secular Society: Lambeth, 1870–1930*, Oxford University Press, Oxford, 1982.

[16] *The British Weekly*, 1 March 1928.

[17] *The British Weekly*, 22 February 1928.

[18] *The British Weekly*, 8 March 1928.

This crucial difference between urban Catholics and others has been largely ignored by subsequent commentators. Unfortunately Catholic attendance figures were frequently underestimated in religious censuses (including the 1851 Religious Census),[19] as a result of the tendency to count a single morning Mass when there were often several. Yet such figures as were given show that at every stage urban Catholics had more attendances on average than they had church accommodation. Even in 1989,[20] in contrast to the Church of England, Catholics in Tyne and Wear, Cleveland, Birmingham, Greater London, and the whole North-West Region, had more than twice as many churchgoers on an average Sunday, but about half the number of churches. In the whole of England, Catholics, Anglicans and the Free Churches were fairly evenly divided in attendances, yet Catholics had less than a tenth of all churches.

Even in Liverpool, with its high Catholic population, non-Catholics had proportionately more churches in relation to churchgoers than Catholics.[21] So in 1829 there were 4 Catholic churches (out of a total of 44 churches and chapels) in the town; in 1851 there were 16 Catholic churches (out of a total of 165 churches and chapels) in the borough; by 1912 there were 40 Catholic churches (out of a total of 415); by 1931 there were 50 Catholic churches (out of a total of 440). Yet at each date, with approximately a tenth of the churches, Catholics represented between a third and two-fifths of all churchgoers. By 1989[22] in the whole of Merseyside Catholics still had less than a quarter of the churches – 180 Catholic churches out of a total of 750 – but served two-thirds of all churchgoers. And, of course, Catholic churchgoing decline is far more recent. Irish immigration may not be the only measurable factor in this situation.

3

What emerges very clearly from the urban census data is that the Church of England expanded more slowly but for longer than the Free Churches. Yet it

---

[19] e.g. in the original 1851 returns for Chelsea – held at the Public Record Office, Kew – the Catholic morning attendances of 2300 (which must represent several Masses since the church seating was only 600) have been reduced subsequently in pencil to 700, and it is this second figure that appears in the census report; similarly, in the morning return for Marylebone figures have been reduced from 7300 to 5400, afternoon from 1950 to 900, and evening from 2750 to 1500. The problem of underestimating Catholic morning attendances is acknowledged in the London 1886/7 census and Liverpool censuses.

[20] Calculations based on data in Peter Brierley (ed.), *Prospects for the Nineties: Trends and Tables from the English Church Census*, MARC Europe 1991 (Christian Research, Vision Building, 4 Footscray Road, London SE9 2TZ).

[21] For the 1820s: Church of England statistics based on *Clergy Visitation Returns* 1821 and 1825, Chester Record Office (ms ERV 716); Catholic and Free Church statistics based on the survey of 'the Number of Places of Worship, not of the Church of England, in each Parish' for Lancashire, 1829, Preston Record Office (QDV 9). The 1881–1912 Liverpool newspaper censuses were all published by *The Liverpool Daily Post*, 15 November 1881, 24 November 1891, 11 November 1902 and 13 December 1912. For the 1930s, see C. Caradog Jones, *The Social Survey of Merseyside*, vol. 3, Hodder & Stoughton, London, 1934.

[22] See note 20.

continued (often to the present day) with churches that had tiny congregations and, in some cases, little surrounding population. The Free Churches expanded very vigorously, competing with each other and spreading attendances more and more thinly. They then collapsed dramatically. In some rural areas the Free Churches have all but disappeared and in many central urban areas their presence is much reduced. The interaction of these two patterns – subsidized persistence and free market expansion and collapse – seems to have been mutually destructive. And this, of course, is the same economic pattern that has already been observed in rural churches and chapels.

The evidence for these claims is drawn from three major sources, which are examined in greater detail in the chapters that follow: (1) Inner Greater London 1851, 1886/7 and 1902/3; (2) Liverpool for the 1820s, 1851, 1881, 1891, 1902 and 1912; and (3) groups of large towns compared first between the 1820s and 1851, next between the 1830s and 1851, then between 1851 and 1881, and finally between 1851 and 1902–4 – with occasional more intense data from places such as Newcastle upon Tyne. The size of these groups varies from ten towns for the Free Churches between 1829 and 1851 (with a total population in 1851 of 407 006), to three smaller towns between 1837–9 and 1851 (with a population of 58 220), to twenty-eight towns compared across denominations between 1851 (with a population of 946 553) and 1881, to eight towns between 1851 (with a population of 210 929) and 1902–4. An extended case study of York, for which, together with Hull, there is some of the most complete data for anywhere in Britain, will analyse the processes involved in greatest detail. There is also some additional corroboration from less complete data for Birmingham and Manchester.[23]

In each of the three major sources – with a combined population in 1851 representing about half of the urban population of England – the same broad pattern has emerged for the Free Churches:

1 Free Church attendances expanded or held steady between 1851 and the 1880s. Thus in Liverpool attendances increased from 10.7 per cent of the population to 12.7 per cent, in London from 11.3 per cent to 12.5 per cent and in the large towns they held steady at 20.6 per cent in 1851 and 20.4 per cent in 1881. However, it will be seen in a moment that their earlier expansion between 1829 and 1851 in Liverpool, Manchester and ten large towns was less vigorous than that of the Church of England between 1821 and 1851. And in the three small towns measured between 1837–9 and 1851, Free Church attendances (unlike those of the Church of England) actually dropped from a very high 30.6 per cent to 26.6 per cent.

2 Chapel seating in the Free Churches considerably increased between the 1820s and 1880s: in Liverpool from seating sufficient for 12.2 per cent in the town 1829 to 12.5 per cent of the population in the borough in 1851, and then to 15.5 per cent in 1881; in London from 11.0 per cent in 1851 to 16.1 per cent in 1887; and in the twenty-eight large towns from a striking 23.7 per cent in 1851

---

[23] For Birmingham, see *The Birmingham Daily Times*, 31 May 1887 (morning only) and *The Birmingham News*, 3 December 1892 (and the three following Saturdays). For Manchester for the 1820s, see sources for Liverpool in note 21.

to 25.6 per cent in 1881. In Manchester it increased from 13.6 per cent in the town in 1829 to 16.7 per cent in the borough in 1851. And in Birmingham, Free Church seating increased from sufficient for 14.2 per cent of the population in 1851 to 16.1 per cent in 1872. Only in the ten towns did it hold steady at 17.6 per cent in 1829 and 17.4 per cent in 1851; in contrast, in the three towns it rose from a very high 31.9 per cent in the late 1830s to 33.4 per cent in 1851.

3   In all three major sources, chapels were less full on average[24] in the 1880s than they were in 1851. So, if in London in 1851 chapels on average were 53.6 per cent full, by 1887 they were 43.1 per cent full, and by 1903 just 34.6 per cent full. In Liverpool they were 45.2 per cent in 1851, 43.6 per cent in 1881, 37.6 per cent in 1891, 37.1 per cent in 1902, and 31.9 per cent in 1912. And in the twenty-eight large towns they were 43.4 per cent full in 1851 and 39.8 per cent in 1881. In Birmingham too they were 44.4 per cent full in 1851 and 40.0 per cent in 1892. There is even tentative evidence of the same phenomenon occurring between 1829 and 1851. The Free Church attenders in 1829 in Liverpool, Manchester and the ten towns combined would have filled three-quarters of the available seats had they all gone to chapel at the same time. Had even half of them gone to chapel more than once on a Sunday, combined attendances would have exceeded total seating. In 1851 combined Free Church attendances – morning, afternoon, evening, and Sunday school – did not quite equal the total seating in the three areas. Certainly in the three towns measured in the late 1830s, chapels that were then 48.0 per cent full were only 39.8 per cent by 1851. Overall, then, *whether chapelgoing was increasing or decreasing, chapels generally looked and indeed were emptier.*

4   If the original larger Free Churches – Methodists, Congregationalists, Baptists and Presbyterians – are isolated, then the pattern of progressively empty chapels becomes clearer. The most remarkable pattern of decline was shown by Congregationalists/Independents. Although they held steady in the ten towns between 1829 and 1851, and probably increased slightly in Manchester, they declined rapidly in Liverpool and continued to decline in every subsequent census there to the present day. In the eight towns they declined sharper than all other denominations, with attendances of 4.1 per cent of the population in 1851 and only 1.6 per cent in 1902–4. Congregationalists and non-Wesleyan Methodists declined between 1851 and the 1880s in London and Liverpool, and Congregationalists, Wesleyan and non-Wesleyan Methodists, and Baptists in the twenty-eight large towns. By 1892 in Birmingham and by the early 1900s in London, Liverpool and the eight large towns, each of these denominations (with the minor exception of Presbyterians in the towns) had declined.

5   In contrast, new denominations such as the Salvation Army flourished briefly in the 1880s, but declined in any following census. So attendances at isolated congregations increased from 1.7 per cent of the population in 1851 to 4.6 per

---

[24] Calculations on how full on average churches and chapels are made by dividing amalgamated morning and evening attendances by the seating of the churches and chapels actually open for each service × 100.

cent in 1881 in the twenty-eight towns (against a mainstream Free Church decline from 18.9 per cent to 15.8 per cent). In Birmingham their increase was from 2.9 per cent in 1851 to 3.3 per cent in 1892 (against a mainstream decline from 9.6 per cent to 8.3 per cent). In London their increase was from 0.8 per cent in 1851 to 3.1 per cent in 1887 (against a mainstream decline from 10.5 per cent to 9.5 per cent). And in Liverpool their increase was from 1.2 per cent in 1851 to 2.2 per cent in 1881 (although in this case alone there was a mainstream increase from 9.5 per cent to 10.6 per cent, due mostly to an increase in Baptists). However, by the early 1900s the isolated congregations and Salvationists were themselves declining: to 1.7 per cent in Liverpool, 3.0 per cent in London, and 2.1 per cent in the eight towns. In Liverpool, where their individual fate can be measured in closest detail, the Salvation Army reached their strongest point in 1891, but had declined to a quarter of this strength by 1902, and had halved again by 1912.

6   In almost every case where it can be measured, overall Free Church attendances have declined since the 1880s/1890s. In Inner Greater London they declined from 12.5 per cent of the population in 1887 to 10.7 per cent in 1903. In 1979[25] Free Church attenders accounted for only 3.6 per cent. In 1989 the decline of the established Free Churches (Methodists, United Reformed Church, and Baptists) continued, with the adult rate dropping from 1.2 per cent to 0.9 per cent. Only the increase of Independent and Afro-Caribbean Churches raised the overall rate in 1989 (as it did generally in the South-East but not elsewhere) to 4.6 per cent. Free Churches in Putney/Roehampton declined from 12.0 per cent in 1887 to 10.8 per cent in 1903, and to 4.9 per cent in 1927. In Liverpool they declined from 12.7 per cent in 1881, to 11.9 per cent in 1891, to 10.8 per cent in 1902, and to 8.7 per cent in 1912. A sample for 1931 suggests attendance of no more than 7.3 per cent. By 1979, and again in 1989, adult Free Church attenders in the whole of Merseyside amounted to only 2.4 per cent. Established Free Churches there declined from 1.5 per cent in 1979 to 1.3 per cent in 1989. In the eight towns, Free Church attendances declined sharply from 23.0 per cent in 1851 to 14.2 per cent in 1902–4. And in South Shields and Wallsend they declined from 23.1 per cent in 1851 to 8.9 per cent in 1928.

The pattern for the Church of England is rather different:

1   Between 1821 and 1851 Anglican churchgoing seemed to increase faster than that of the Free Churches in Liverpool, Manchester and in the twelve towns. If in 1821 'attenders' represented 10.4 per cent of the population in these areas combined, in 1851 morning attendances alone (including Sunday school) represented 9.6 per cent of the population and the Index (i.e. all morning, afternoon, evening, and Sunday school attendances divided by population) was 18.4 per cent. In contrast, Free Church 'attenders' represented some 11.4 per cent in 1829, whereas morning attendances in 1851 represented only 7.6 per cent

---

[25] The 1979 figures are calculated from Peter Brierley (ed.), *Prospects for the Eighties*, MARC Europe, 1980, with corrections from *Prospects for the Nineties*.

and the Index 15.0 per cent. In the three towns Church of England attendances increased between 1837–9 and 1851 from 18.0 per cent to a very high 26.3 per cent (in contrast to the Free Church drop, just mentioned, from 30.6 per cent to 26.6 per cent).

2   After 1851 Anglican decline was the dominant feature of urban areas. In Liverpool and London, Church of England attendances declined between 1851 and the 1880s and, with only one exception, continued to decline thereafter. In Liverpool the decline was from 15.3 per cent of the population in 1851 to just 9.8 per cent in 1881. It rose slightly to 10.5 per cent in 1891, but then declined as follows: to 9.6 per cent in 1902; to 7.7 per cent by 1912; to no more than 4.9 per cent in the 1931 sample; to 4.6 per cent in the diocesan one-tenth sample for 1962;[26] to 2.5 per cent for Merseyside adults in 1979; and to 2.2 per cent in 1989. In Inner Greater London attendances dropped from 15.6 per cent in 1851, to 14.1 per cent in 1887, and then to 9.6 per cent by 1903. In Putney/ Roehampton the figure was 4.8 per cent in 1928; in the dioceses of London and Southwark sample for 1962 it was 3.7 per cent. Anglican adult attenders declined faster in London between 1979 and 1989 than in any other urban conurbation in England (the only counties to experience proportionate increases in relation to their adult populations were West Sussex and Staffordshire). Actual numbers declined by almost a quarter, from 44 000 to 33 400. This was a decline from 2.2 per cent of the adult population to 1.8 per cent (or, for all ages, from 2.5 per cent to 1.8 per cent). In the twenty-eight large towns it declined from 13.8 per cent in 1851 to 12.7 per cent in 1881; in Birmingham from 12.4 per cent in 1851 to 10.9 per cent in 1892; and in the eight towns from 17.9 per cent in 1851 to 9.5 per cent in 1902–4.

3   Church of England seating did not always keep pace with the rapid rise of most urban populations. In Liverpool it was sufficient for 16.8 per cent of the town in 1725, for 18.4 per cent in 1821, for 16.0 per cent of the borough in 1851, and then for 14.0 per cent in 1881. In London it was sufficient for 17.1 per cent in 1851 and for 16.5 per cent in 1887. In the twelve towns Church of England seating represented 21.0 per cent of the population in 1821 and 18.0 per cent in 1851; in the three towns it represented a very high 35.7 per cent in the late 1830s and 30.5 per cent in 1851; and in the twenty-eight large towns it represented 18.8 per cent in 1851 and 14.2 per cent in 1881. Only in Manchester did it rise significantly from 10.6 per cent for the town in 1821 to 12.6 per cent for the borough in 1851, and in Birmingham did it rise from 12.6 per cent in 1851, to 13.8 per cent in 1872, and then to 14.1 per cent in 1892. However, in London and Liverpool the next census showed a significant increase in church building there as well: 17.3 per cent in London in 1902/3[27] and 14.3 per cent in Liverpool in 1891.

4   In Liverpool, London and Birmingham, all but one census after 1851 showed Church of England churches to have been distinctly emptier on average. In

---

[26] Calculated from Leslie Paul, *The Deployment and Payment of the Clergy*, Church Information Office, London, 1964, but using 1961 census statistics for population given in the appendix rather than the clergy information used in the body of the report.

[27] I have calculated this from the 1886/7 census with allowances for the extra churches mentioned in 1902/3, since the latter does not estimate seating.

London they were 50.3 per cent full in 1851, 44.1 per cent in 1887, and 30.3 per cent in 1903. In Liverpool they were 54.1 per cent full in 1851, 36.1 per cent in 1881, 37.1 per cent in 1891, 36.3 per cent in 1902, and 29.6 per cent in 1912. And in Birmingham they were 50.7 per cent full in 1851 and 40.5 per cent in 1892. It was only in the towns that Church of England churches *appeared* fuller; in the three towns they increased from 25.2 per cent full in the late 1830s to 43.1 per cent in 1851, and in the twenty-eight large towns from 36.8 per cent in 1851 to 44.7 per cent in 1881 (the latter resulting from an increase in evening services).

5　On more detailed investigation this slightly surprising finding for the large towns is skewed. If the original churches in a large town are looked at separately, it transpires that they typically declined radically. It is the new churches that were most likely to have been full. So it can be seen in *Table 11* that in Newcastle upon Tyne[28] churchgoing rose from 12 703 attendances in 1851 to 18 973 in 1887 (a drop from 14.2 per cent of the population to 10.8 per cent). However churchgoing in the original ten churches there dropped from 12 703 to 9950. In Chelsea (*Table 14*) there were 10 200 attendances in 1851 and still 10 155 in 1887 (a drop from 19.0 per cent of the population to 13.9 per cent), but less than three-quarters of the latter were in the original 1851 churches. In Birmingham (*Table 15*) Church of England attendances rose from 29 217 in 1851 to 37 748 in 1892 – although, as already mentioned, this too represented a decline in relation to the rising population. But attendances in the original 1851 churches in Birmingham had declined to 20 674 by 1892. And attendances at the oldest churches in Hull almost halved between 1884 and 1912. Most of the original churches in the centre of Newcastle upon Tyne are still in use as churches, as is typical of many other urban centres – albeit for the most part without effective congregations or surrounding populations. Unlike the Free Churches, the heavily subsidized Church of England typically persists, and only closes churches very reluctantly.

4

These contrasting patterns seem to have been mutually damaging. Purely free market churches (as in the United States) or, less frequently,[29] largely uncontested established churches (as in Eire) can flourish even in an urbanized, and supposedly secular, environment. But can they flourish together?

Between the 1850s and the 1880s the Free Churches expanded faster and generally more successfully in urban areas than the Church of England. But then they seemed to encounter serious problems. The slow-moving Church of England expanded for longer and persisted with churches (in city centres as well as in the countryside) that had lost most of their populations. Together they presented by the turn of the century a picture of widespread and visible church decline.

---

[28] *Clergy Visitation Returns, Diocese of Newcastle* for 1887, Northumberland County Record Office, Gosforth.

[29] See David Martin, *A General Theory of Secularization*, Blackwell, Oxford, 1978.

By studying the churches in the City of London between 1700 and 1900 these twin processes can be observed more accurately. Fortunately it is possible to measure churches and populations during this period. If in 1700 the population (within the Walls) was about 139 000,[30] by 1801 it was down to 64 615, and then to just 10 640 by 1901. How did the various denominations respond to this drastic urban depopulation?

In 1700 the Church of England had seating in its churches for some 30 000 people. However, the Free Churches (mostly Independents) could seat some 33 000. Thus, taken together the City churches and chapels had sufficient seating for some 45 per cent of the population.[31] There had been a period of very active building of Free Church chapels following both the Restoration and the Great Fire. It has been estimated[32] that between 1640 and 1649 some 28 of the 108 City parishes had Independent ministers as incumbents at some point. With their exclusion from the Church of England alternative chapels were built instead.

By 1801 the Church of England still had some 29 500 seats (sufficient for 46 per cent of the population), whereas the Free Churches had reduced to some 21 000 (33 per cent). By 1901 the Free Churches had just three chapels left, with a seating capacity of 2100 (sufficient for 20 per cent). But the Church of England still had seats for 22 087 people ... provision for 208 per cent of the resident population. From contemporary records it appears that people were commuting back to the City on a Sunday.[33] In theory, the churchgoing rate in relation to the local population was going up. In practice, Church of England churches, which were on average 33 per cent full in 1851, were only 13 per cent full in 1902. And, perhaps not surprisingly, these City of London churches were seen by otherwise intelligent contemporary commentators as providing clear evidence that 'religion' was on the wane.[34]

Most dramatically, a church like St Andrew-by-the-Wardrobe had seating for 1020 and had a morning congregation in 1851 of 470 and an evening congregation of 691. By 1887 its congregations were reduced to 140 and 132 respectively and by 1902 they numbered just 57 and 56. St Mary Woolnoth, with seating for 704, had huge congregations of 1200 in the morning and 500 in the evening in 1851. In 1881 its morning congregation was only 65; in 1902, with its galleries removed, it had 47 present in the morning and 40 in the evening. Charles Booth reported on this church at the time: 'the congregation on the Sunday morning when we saw it, besides about twelve men and boys in the choir, consisted of twenty-seven adults and about twelve children with their parents, who might be of the shopkeeping or caretaker class'.[35]

St Swithin, Cannon Street, with seating for 400, had a morning congregation in 1851 of 130 and an evening congregation of 189. By 1881 its morning congregation

---

[30] The estimate made in the 1811 *Census of Population*.

[31] Estimates based on the information given in J.G. White, *The Churches and Chapels of Old London*, London, private circulation, 1901, and A.E. Daniell, *London City Churches*, Constable, 1895.

[32] See Alan Argent, 'Aspects of the Ecclesiastical History of the Parishes of the City of London, 1640–49', PhD London University, 1983.

[33] See White, *The Churches and Chapels of Old London*, and Daniell, *London City Churches*.

[34] e.g. Joad, *The Present and Future of Religion*.

[35] Booth, *Life and Labour of the People of London: Third Series*, vol. 3, p. 9.

of 43 consisted of 14 paid choristers, 10 officials and their families, and a general congregation of 7 men, 5 women and 7 children.[36] By 1902 its total attendances numbered 32 in the morning and 44 in the evening; by 1929 it was 'attended by seven or eight people'.[37]

Ironically, a Bill to dispose of nineteen City churches in 1926 was passed by the House of Lords but then thrown out by the House of Commons. The Bishop of London, speaking for the Bill in the Lords, regarded it as a 'scandal' that '£50 000 to £60 000 annually' was spent on the City churches when 'a dozen churches would suffice, and £23 000 a year would be saved'.[38] Meanwhile Anglican churches in the East End of London were often experiencing acute financial problems.[39] They could raise money from outside sources to build churches (a common pattern in the Church of England as is seen later), but found local resources scarce for maintaining them.

It was only after the Second World War that this century-old issue was partly, but certainly not wholly, resolved. With the formation of City churches as Guild churches they were no longer required by law to hold Sunday services. Thus, rather than being parish churches, they became and continue to be churches in search of alternative functions. Twenty-four of the fifty-nine churches within the City Walls in existence in 1851 were still functioning as churches in 1988[40] (only nine with regular Sunday services), employing twenty-five clergy. Both the manpower and the financial resources they use continue to the present day to be issues of contention within the London diocese – with consistory courts recently being used to resolve financial disputes between City churches and the diocese.[41] Altogether five separate commissions, the last in the 1990s, were held in the twentieth century attempting to establish a clear contemporary role for these historic churches.

Of course the City of London, with all those Wren churches, is unusual. However, the chapters that follow show that this general pattern can be found throughout England (with very similar patterns in Wales and Scotland as well). In response to population increases – urban or rural – the Free Churches expanded vigorously. When populations slowed down or contracted they collapsed. In contrast, the Church of England responded lethargically to population changes and continued to subsidize churches – again, urban as well as rural – whether or not they had active congregations or were serving viable populations. Furthermore, both continued to build new churches when existing churches were more empty than full.

The results of these differing patterns would have been obvious to all: empty churches and chapels throughout the countryside; chapels with mounting debts; central urban churches in search of a function; rural chapels closing everywhere;

---

[36] See 'Census of Congregations of the City Churches and Chapels', *Journal of the Statistical Society* (later Royal Statistical Society), vol. 44, September 1881, pp. 596–601.

[37] Joad, *The Present and Future of Religion*, p. 14.

[38] Joad, *The Present and Future of Religion*, p. 14.

[39] See Arthur Royall, 'Easier to Build than Maintain', *Church Times*, 22 March 1991.

[40] See Howard Willows (ed.), *A Guide to Worship in Central London*, London Central YMCA, 1988.

[41] 'Diocese Seeks £32 000 of Parish Windfall' in *Church Times*, 1 February 1991 (a story relating to St Andrew-by-the-Wardrobe).

rural and sometimes urban clergy having multiple charges. However, the physical factors behind them seem to have been more invisible. By concentrating more carefully upon these physical (and indeed measurable) factors scholars might avoid some of the less controllable speculations about secularization.

5

General Increase: 1821 to 1851

Among social historians it was until recently believed that little can be known about churchgoing patterns in England and Wales before the 1851 Religious Census. Whereas it is possible to plot membership patterns among the Free Churches and Easter or Christmas communicants in the Church of England before 1851, it was usually assumed that regular attendances at church or chapel were uniquely recorded only in 1851.

B.I. Coleman's scholarly 1980 analysis of the 1851 Religious Census provides a clear example of this belief. He pointed to Alan Gilbert's analysis of thirty Oxfordshire parishes,[1] in which showed a decline in Church of England communicants between 1738 and 1800, a numerical increase after 1800, but a proportional increase only after 1830. However, Coleman mentioned nothing at all about statistics of general churchgoing before 1851. He was aware of the newspaper censuses in the 1880s and of the Mudie-Smith study of London churchgoing 1902–3,[2] but even here he was sceptical about plotting longitudinal trends. In his conclusion he wrote about the Church of England:

> On the whole, though, the Church's own fortunes seem to have been rather happier in the century's second half than in the first. The prospect which some had seen in the 1830s of an almost total collapse of Anglican allegiance and practice had receded. Church extension and an improvement in pastoral zeal and efficiency had helped to stabilize the Church's position and to produce a long-term improvement in national figures of communicants and confirmations, though it is not clear whether church-going increased similarly. It seems likely, however, that most of the influences on Anglican practice after 1851 were beyond the Church's control and were similar to those that had operated before that date: demographic trends, migration and immigration, changes in residential patterns and class behaviour, the growth or decline of industries, changes in the character of employment and in labour relations in agriculture and industry. The Church 'revival' which some historians have detected in the century's second half probably owed more to these factors, the rapid growth of the suburbanized middle classes, than to anything else. The lack of a further official census of worship makes the changes in the social geography of religious practice hard to map.[3]

I have quoted this passage at length, both because it is a measured assessment of the then current state of historical knowledge about nineteenth-century church-going, and because the sets of data to be presented in this chapter and the two

---

[1] A.D. Gilbert, *Religion and Society in Industrial England*, Longman, Harlow, 1976.

[2] Richard Mudie-Smith (ed.), *The Religious Life of London*, Hodder, London, 1904.

[3] B.I. Coleman, *The Church of England in the Mid-Nineteenth Century: A Social Geography*, The Historical Association, London, 1980, p. 38.

following chapters suggest that it is wrong about this churchgoing at almost every point.

John Foster was one of the few social historians to have pointed out at the time that there is in fact statistical data on general churchgoing available before 1851. In an analysis of Oldham, in his radical study *Class Struggle and the Industrial Revolution*, he used the clergy visitation returns to the Bishop of Chester[4] for 1821 and 1825 and the statutory returns for Lancashire[5] about non-Anglicans made to Parliament in 1829. From these he compiled a profile of churchgoing in the 1820s in Oldham that he compared with the original returns for the 1851 Religious Census. On the basis of these three primary sources he argued as follows:

> Although church attendance always remained very much a minority activity among working people, probably never involving more than 10 per cent, there does seem to have been a definite increase between the 1820s and 1851. Comparing the returns for the two periods, the percentage of the adult population as a whole (including non-worker sections) seems to have risen from about 14 to 21 per cent. Still more interesting, the increase was very unevenly distributed. The Anglican Church received a disproportionately small share (of the seven churches put up in the 1840s three remained almost empty in 1851 and only two had secured congregations of a hundred or more). The 'old dissent' sects (Congregational, Baptists, Unitarians, Quakers) did only slightly better. The denomination which took the lion's share (over half the total increase) was the Methodists. And going by the censuses of 'sittings' or seating accommodation made in the decades after 1851, this trend appears to have been maintained till at least 1871.[6]

There are serious faults in Foster's methodology, but at least he was prepared to search for early statistics and then to compare them with the 1851 Religious Census. Unfortunately for his analysis, Oldham was an atypical town. It will soon be seen that the typical pattern in towns between the 1820s and 1851 seems to have been for the Church of England's attendances to fare rather better than those of the Free Churches. This is presumably either because there was a real increase of Church of England churchgoers in this period, or because those who already went to church once on a Sunday started to go twice.

Unfortunately such a pattern does not at all fit Foster's explicitly Marxist conclusion that, 'it was precisely those congregations in which the big employers no longer played a socially dominant role – those of the Methodists – which expanded fastest'.[7] Furthermore, there are serious problems in the way he compared the figures for the 1820s with those of 1851. The latter were for 'attendances', whereas the former were for 'attenders' on the Anglican side in 1821 and ambiguously for 'attenders' or for 'members' on the non-Anglican side in 1829. Aware of problems here, Foster used the doubtful methods of trying to estimate

---

[4] *Clergy Visitation Returns, Diocese of Chester*, Cheshire Record Office, Chester (ms. ERV 716). (I am most grateful to Dr Henry Rack for directing me to this invaluable evidence.)

[5] *Returns of the Number of Places of Worship, not of the Church of England, in the County of Lancaster*, Lancashire Record Office, Preston (ms. QDV 9).

[6] John Foster, *Class Struggle and the Industrial Revolution*, Methuen, London, 1974, p. 214.

[7] Foster, *Class Struggle*, p. 214.

1851 attenders 'by taking the total attendance at the largest and half that at the next largest'[8] services, and of arriving at a joint population for the two sets of figures for the 1820s.

Yet despite these methodological deficiencies, Foster was able to spot crucial shifts in Free Church attendance. He even noticed some of the changing physical presences of denominations, at a period for which most social historians believed that statistical evidence to be unavailable. As a result, he was able to show that the 1851 Religious Census can indeed be placed in a longitudinal context.

1

The Chester visitation returns (or clergy returns as they are sometimes called), together with a few others, such as those for Oxford in 1831 and an incomplete set for London and Canterbury in 1841, were unusual in that they contained questions about regular churchgoing before 1851. More typically these questions feature only in visitation returns for the second half of the nineteenth century. Consequently, Chester offers a rare opportunity for obtaining early longitudinal data. The Free Church returns for 1829 must be used with more circumspection, precisely because they did not always distinguish between members and attenders. Fortunately, where they did so the two do not appear to have been as different as they were a century later.

In addition, because of their different dates, Anglican and Free Church returns should not be combined too readily. Yet by studying them separately, and then by combining them cautiously only after this separate study, I hope to show that they can yield important comparative data. Since they reported attenders/members rather than attendances, the least contentious way to compare them with the 1851 Religious Census is with the latter's data for the best attended time of day (when, as argued earlier, attendances clearly represented separate attenders). In certain cases the 1851 Index (i.e. all morning, afternoon, evening, and Sunday attendances, divided by population) will also be relevant.

The southern part of Cumberland makes unusually detailed comparisons possible between rural and urban churchgoing in the nineteenth century. Because it formed part of the old Chester diocese it provides rare evidence about Church of England churchgoing in the 1820s – in an area, and at a period, when the non-urban Free Churches were still very small. In addition, it had a number of newspaper censuses in the 1880s and early 1900s, the latter including rare rural data across denominations. Taken together with the numerous (but not always statistical) clergy visitation returns to the Bishop of Carlisle[9] between 1858 and 1900, a very complete comparative picture emerges. This provides counter-intuitive insights at several points.

For comparative purposes the churchgoing data represented in *Table 1* have been divided into three groups examined at three key points – 1821, 1851 and 1902 –

---

[8] Foster, *Class Struggle*, footnote on p. 214.

[9] *Clergy Visitation Returns, Diocese of Carlisle, 1858–1900*, Bishop's study, Rose Castle, Carlisle.

with additional Anglican figures for 1861, 1900 and 1989.[10] The first group consists of eight deeply rural parishes: Bassenthwaite, Dean, Emmerdale, Haile, Loweswater, Lorton, Netherwasdale and St John's Beckermet. In each case the local population never exceeded 858 and declined between 1851 and 1901, having risen only slightly – or even declined – between 1821 and 1851. The second group consists of ten large villages or small towns: Arlecdon, Brigham, Clifton, Cockermouth, Cleator, Distington, Egremont, Harrington, Hensingham and Lamplugh. They varied in size between Brigham (961) and Cleator/Wath Brow (8120), both measured in 1901, but had in common the characteristic that they grew significantly between 1851 and 1902 (or, in the case of Cockermouth, that its population of 5355 was clearly that of a small town). The third group consists of two larger towns – Whitehaven and Workington – with independent information about Barrow-in-Furness. The churches in each group behaved very differently during the nineteenth century.

The rural group shows the pattern noted so often in earlier chapters – namely, over-building against a declining rural population actually to the point of exceeding this population by the turn of the century. By then there was seating for approximately 105 per cent for the local population in the various churches and chapels. The Church of England's seating increased slightly between 1821 and 1851, but not after 1851. Yet against depopulation it alone would have been sufficient for almost 80 per cent of the population of these eight rural parishes in 1901. The Free Churches expanded vigorously between 1821 and 1851 and added another hundred seats between 1851 and 1902 in what was already an over-churched area.

For once, though, it is possible to see the results of this rural over-building in terms of churchgoing. In 1821 the Church of England was strongest in the rural group, with 28.3 per cent of its population being 'attenders'. Yet with the Free Churches having more than three times as many seats in the larger towns, and with Catholic churches being present only in these larger towns, it seems probable that churchgoing across denominations was actually stronger in the most urban areas in 1821 than it was in the most rural areas. So, with estimates for non-Anglican churchgoers based upon seating patterns (estimating Free Church attendants as 62 per cent of their seating, as it was for the Church of England in the area, and estimating urban Catholic attendants as equal to Catholic seating), a speculative overall figure of 32.4 per cent for the rural group can be compared with one of 36.7 per cent for the large towns.

If this means of estimating Free Church and Catholic attendants is too conservative, then of course the gap between the groups would have been even wider. Indeed, if the relative balances between Free Church seating and attendants in 1829 shown in *Table 3* are used, then Free Church attendance in large towns represented 65 per cent of seating, whereas those in rural areas represented 21 per cent. Estimated on this basis, overall rural attendants would have represented 29.7 per cent of the population in 1821, whereas those in the larger towns would have represented 37.3 per cent. On either estimate, then, overall churchgoing was evidently stronger in Whitehaven and Workington in 1821 than it was in the surrounding countryside.

---

[10] The 1902 statistics from *The West Cumberland Times*, 20 December 1902; the 1861 and 1900 statistics from *Clergy Visitation Returns, Diocese of Carlisle*; the 1989 statistics from Church House, Carlisle.

In 1851 and 1902 the overall churchgoing rates were also higher in the larger towns than they were in the rural group of parishes. With the addition of Catholics in these west coast towns and the Free Churches, this may remain the case today. Furthermore, and perhaps most surprisingly, Church of England attendances were weaker in the rural group in 1851 than in either of the urban areas. Only the percentage of the population who were Anglican communicants remained consistently higher in rural areas than in urban ones in both 1861 and 1900. While the Church of England has always remained the dominant denomination in the rural areas, its rural churchgoing rate has not always been higher than that of the urban areas. So, contrary to long-standing beliefs, rural churchgoing (in this part of Cumberland at least) was in several respects actually weaker than urban churchgoing, particularly that of the larger towns.

The 1902 survey did encounter problems with the local December weather, which are discussed in Chapter 7. For the moment it is sufficient to note the comparative strengths of the different denominations within the survey (all of which presumably had the same weather). The Free Churches in rural areas, compared with those in urban areas, seemed to be near the point of collapse (as they were in rural Northumberland) by the turn of the century. They had expanded against a declining population and had a chapelgoing rate of only a fifth of that of the larger towns. On the evidence of 1902, chapels in the rural group were now barely 4 per cent full. Even if a good Sunday saw congregations two or three times larger (as the local newspaper that undertook the survey claimed), they would still have been ominously empty.

The small towns behaved differently again from the larger towns. In 1821 the Church of England had very comparable seating and attenders in both groups. However, the Free Churches were, in terms of their seating, more than three times as strong in the larger towns. By 1851 both the seating and the attendances of the Church of England were stronger in the larger towns (as were communicants in 1861), although in both cases churches on average were little more than a third full. In contrast, the Free Churches had come much closer to parity.

By 1902 this parity in attendances had begun to disappear. Once Catholics are added to the picture, the overall churchgoing rate (combining morning and evening services, but without Sunday school attendances) between the small towns and larger towns was quite distinct: 14.1 per cent for the former and 22.0 per cent for the latter. This difference was caused mostly by the non-Anglicans. Anglican communicants in the larger towns had by 1900 reduced to the level present in the small towns. The Anglican churchgoing rate was still slightly higher in the larger towns in 1902 (a difference that has largely disappeared today), but that of the Free Churches and especially that of the Catholic Church were very considerably higher. Whereas the Church of England had up to now been the dominant denomination in all three groups, in the larger towns by 1902 it represented little more than a quarter of all attendances.

A local survey covering only Whitehaven[11] shows that this pattern of Free Church dominance was already evident by 1881. In 1851 Church of England morning and

---

[11] *Whitehaven Free Press*, December 1881: also reported in *The West Cumberland Times*, 20 December 1902.

evening attendances in Whitehaven represented 27.4 per cent of the population, in contrast to Free Church attendances of 13.6 per cent. By 1881 the balance had already shifted to 11.3 per cent for the Church of England and to 17.2 per cent for the Free Churches. By 1902 it had widened still further to 4.5 per cent and 13.3 per cent respectively. The balance in seating at Whitehaven also confirms this crucial transformation between 1851 and 1881. In 1851 the Church of England there had seating for 32.0 per cent of the population and the Free Churches for 25.8 per cent. By 1881 the Church of England seating had declined in relative terms to 22.8 per cent, whereas that in the Free Churches had increased to a dominant 26.8 per cent.

This crucial transformation can be seen best in the remarkable evidence for Barrow-in-Furness. Between 1821 and 1851 it changed little in character. The population of the whole parish of Dalton-in-Furness grew from 2446 to 4683, but it remained a predominantly Anglican parish. In 1821 there was just a single Wesleyan Methodist chapel with 220 seats, which by 1829 still had only 24 members. In 1767 there were reported to be 22 'Papists'[12] in Dalton, together with a priest, but none were mentioned in 1829. The Church of England in 1821 had 700 attenders (representing 28.6 per cent of the population) in the three churches at Dalton, Rampside and Walney.

By 1851 an old barn (seating 70) was also being used by the Wesleyans. None the less, the parish remained overwhelmingly Anglican. The five places of worship belonging to the Church of England in 1851 had 1606 attendances (34.3 per cent of the population) in the morning and afternoon (there was no evening service) and 442 Sunday school attendances. The Wesleyans, the only other denomination reported, had just 196 attendances (4.2 per cent) and 109 in their Sunday schools.

However, by 1881 the population of Barrow-in-Furness, within the parish of Dalton, had mushroomed to an astonishing 47 276. In Chapter 6 I examine this radical change in some detail, since it offers a rare view of the effect upon the churches of this process of rapid urbanization. For the moment, it is sufficient to note that the overall churchgoing rate in Barrow in 1881 was little different from that of Dalton in 1851: 32.8 per cent for morning/evening attendances against the earlier 38.5 per cent for morning/afternoon attendances.[13] The main difference was that attendances were now overwhelmingly Free Church in character. Less than a third of the attendances (9.3 per cent of the population) were represented by the Church of England. Catholic attendances already represented 3.1 per cent of the population (and, in reality, probably nearer 6 per cent).[14]

---

[12] The 1767 statistics are printed in E.S. Worrall (ed.), *Returns of Papists: 1767 Diocese of Chester*, Catholic Record Society, London, 1980. These are transcribed from returns held in the archives of the House of Lords.

[13] *The Barrow Times*, 19 November 1881.

[14] David Voas has kindly pointed out a discrepancy in the data here. In the contemporary *Barrow-in-Furness: Its History, Development, Commerce, Industries and Institutions* (Barrow-in-Furness, published by J. Richardson, 1881) the Roman Catholic population there is given as 7000, yet *The Barrow Times* religious census recorded attendances at two masses of only 1448 (3 per cent total pop.). However, *The Barrow Times* (19 November 1881, p. 8) does admit that two earlier masses were not counted: hence my estimate of 6 per cent.

By 1979 another transformation of churchgoing had taken place in Cumbria.[15] In the county as a whole, 38 per cent of churchgoers were Catholic, 36 per cent Anglican, and only 26 per cent Free Church. The overall churchgoing rate at 16.3 per cent was one of the highest in England. By 1989 it had reduced to 13.9 per cent and by 1998 to 9.4 per cent – both figures well above the national levels of 9.9 per cent and 7.5 per cent respectively. The balance between the denominations had shifted again by 1998 with a more even distribution: Catholics now had 34 per cent of churchgoers, Anglicans 31 per cent and Free Church 35 per cent.

All of these changes since 1821 have been set in an overall context of churchgoing decline, with the sole exception of the increases in attendances that seem to have characterized the two urban groups between 1821 and 1851.

2

Urban, more than rural, churchgoing increase, at least on the Anglican side, is a dominant feature of the comparisons represented in *Table 2* and *Table 3*. The deeply rural District of Furness, or Ulverstone as it was later called, confirms the pattern of the rural group illustrated in *Table 1*.

Church of England attenders in Furness in 1821 (minus the town of Ulverstone itself) represented 29.5 per cent of the population. The 1851 morning attenders (plus Sunday school – as in all the 1851 morning comparisons that follow) represented 25.9 per cent. Here too the Catholic and Free Church presence was very small. In 1767, apart from the 22 Catholics in Dalton, there were only 12 reported to be in Ulverstone and 6 elsewhere in the District. In 1829 only 2 Catholics and 158 from the Free Churches were identified, representing less than 1 per cent of the population. In 1837 the Bishop of Chester reported that he had confirmed 1103 young people in Furness, representing an estimated 79 per cent of those aged between sixteen and nineteen in the District.[16] However, by 1851, with the addition of the barn at Dalton and a further two chapels and two house churches belonging to the Wesleyans and Baptists elsewhere, Free Church morning attendances had grown to 2.2 per cent and the Index to 4.1 per cent. If there were any Catholics in the District, they apparently had no church.

The relative strength of urban and rural Church of England churchgoing emerges clearly from *Table 2*.[17] In the four Rural Districts – Ulverstone, Leyburn, Garstang

---

[15] The 1979, 1989 and 1998 statistics are summarized in Peter Brierley (ed.), *UK Christian Handbook: Religious Trends*, No. 3 (2001) p. 12.9 (Christian Research, Vision Building, 4 Footscray Road, London SE9 2TZ).

[16] See John Bird Sumner, *Charges Addressed to the Clergy of the Diocese of Chester*, Hatchard & Son, London, 1841, 3.34.

[17] I have calculated many of the statistics in the tables that follow from the original returns held at the Public Records Office, Kew. However, some of those statistics that include Sunday school figures derive from Horace Mann's *1851 Census Great Britain: Report and Tables on Religious Worship England and Wales*, British Parliamentary Papers, Population 10, 1852–3 (reprinted by Irish University Press, Shannon, 1970), but always with denominationally proportional estimates for missing returns.

and Askrigg – Church of England attenders in 1821 represented 23.7 per cent of the population. Morning attenders in 1851 amounted to 20.6 per cent and the Index – which surely represented more than separate attenders here – was 35.4 per cent in 1851. In the twelve large towns – Lancaster, Whitehaven, Warrington, Burnley, Bolton, Chester, Rochdale, Stockport, Oldham, Macclesfield, Blackburn and Salford – the 1821 attenders represented 10.7 per cent of the population, whereas the morning attenders in 1851 represented 10.0 per cent, and the Index at 20.4 per cent was almost double the percentage of attenders in 1821. Even in the conurbations – Manchester and Liverpool – there appears to have been an increase between the two dates: from 10.1 per cent in 1821 to 9.4 per cent for the morning in 1851 and an Index of 17.0 per cent.

In contrast, the Free Churches in *Table 3* taken as a whole showed an unambiguous rise between 1829 and 1851 in the Rural Districts, but a more debatable rise in the more urban areas. The two Rural Districts – Ulverstone and Lancaster RD – rose from 1.1 per cent in 1829 to a morning figure of 2.9 per cent in 1851 and an Index of 5.9 per cent. However, the ten large towns – Lancaster, Warrington, Burnley, Bolton, Preston, Oldham, Blackburn, Bury, Wigan and Salford – recorded 11.5 per cent in 1829 and in 1851 a morning figure of 8.7 per cent and an Index of 18.0 per cent. The comparable figures for the conurbations – again Manchester and Liverpool – were 11.3 per cent in 1829 and 6.9 per cent and 13.2 per cent in 1851.

Whatever else this shows, it does suggest that Church of England attendances grew faster in urban areas between the 1820s and 1851 than the Free Churches taken as a whole, whereas the latter grew faster in rural areas (albeit from a much smaller base). At least some of these increases do seem to have resulted from more individuals going to church rather than from existing churchgoers simply going to more services.

However, a detailed examination of the relative positions of the various Free Church denominations in *Table 3* reveals a more complicated picture. In the large towns the non-Wesleyan Methodists and the Baptists showed an unambiguous increase. In both cases the percentage of morning attenders in 1851 exceeded the percentage of total attenders in 1829. In contrast, the two largest denominations, the Independents and especially the Wesleyans, were more static. In terms of seating, too, non-Wesleyan Methodists radically increased their physical presence in the towns, whereas the Independents showed a relative decrease.

Within the conurbations, the Independents apparently declined, since the percentage of attenders in 1829 exceeded the Index in 1851. This decline was more characteristic of Liverpool than of Manchester. In 1829 Independent attenders represented 2.5 per cent of the Liverpool town population. By 1851 morning attenders in the borough of Liverpool represented just under 1 per cent and the Index was only 1.9 per cent. This Independent decline was to continue in every subsequent Liverpool census. Morning and evening attendances combined represented 1.8 per cent in 1851, 1.4 per cent in 1881, 1.3 per cent in 1902, and just 1 per cent in 1912.

In complete contrast, the Catholic presence in Liverpool – the highest in Lancashire – grew from a reported population of 1743 (some 5 per cent of the total population) in 1767 to 45 000 in 1829 (some 27 per cent of the population). In

Chapter 7 it is seen that it was still reported that Catholics represented about a quarter of the Liverpool population at the beginning of the twentieth century. In Chapter 8 it is seen that Catholic churchgoers in 1989 represented 8.9 per cent of the adult population of Merseyside. If they in turn represented about a third of the Catholic population, then it would seem that the balance of Catholics to non-Catholics in Liverpool has changed very little over 150 years. What has changed dramatically is the denominational balance of churchgoers themselves. By 1851 Catholic morning and evening attendances in Liverpool (which in the case of Catholics probably did represent separate attenders) amounted to 13.9 per cent of the population, or just over a third of attendances across denominations. Today they represent two-thirds.

The relative physical presence of the Independents also decreased in Liverpool from seating for 2.8 per cent of the population in 1829 to 2.1 per cent in 1851 (although measured together with Manchester it held steady at about 3 per cent). However, by 1912 it was still 2.1 per cent. Clearly this must have resulted in extremely empty Independent chapels in the second half of the nineteenth century, as becomes more apparent in later chapters.

In areas in and around London, too, the Independents, who were physically dominant in the eighteenth century, became one group among several by the end of the nineteenth century. Their demise in the City of London has already been plotted in the previous chapter. In the county of Middlesex[18] beyond the City and Westminster, Independent chapels represented 47 per cent of all Free Church chapels in 1811. The only other groups to exceed 5 per cent were Wesleyan Methodists with 21 per cent of all chapels and Baptists with 15 per cent. By 1851 the Independents represented 32 per cent, against a Baptist total of 23 per cent and a Wesleyan total of 17 per cent. By 1903 Independents had just 17 per cent, against totals from the Baptists of 20 per cent, from the Wesleyans of 13 per cent, and now from the Brethren with 11 per cent, the Salvation Army with 8 per cent and the London City Mission with just over 5 per cent. Evidently the demise of the Independents was accompanied by increasing diffusion among the Free Churches. And, as is seen later, both of these processes were, by the end of the nineteenth century, set in an overall context of Free Church decline.

Table 3 also suggests that Baptists in the conurbations declined between 1829 and 1851, since the percentage of attenders in 1829 was little short of their Index in 1851. They also declined in terms of seating – a decline in this instance that occurred in both Manchester and Liverpool. However, the 1881 Liverpool census[19] shows that in the next thirty years they were to expand very vigorously, both in their physical presence and in terms of attendances. Unlike the Independents in Liverpool, their own long-term decline was not to become evident until 1891. Only the Methodists taken as a whole (they were not sufficiently differentiated in the earlier returns) showed clear signs of vitality in the conurbations between 1829 and 1851. In Liverpool they were to maintain their position between 1851 and 1881, but then they too started a long-term decline.

---

[18] See *The Victorian History of the Counties of England: Middlesex*, vol. 1, Oxford University Press, Oxford, 1969, p. 148.

[19] See Chapter 6 for the following Liverpool statistics.

Taken together, these relative changes in strength between the various urban denominations indicate the fluid nature of Victorian church attendances. Urban areas undergoing rapid shifts of population were experiencing rapid changes in differential strengths and weaknesses within and between denominations. Furthermore, some of the long-established denominations, such as the Independents and the more recent Wesleyans, were being surpassed in the towns by new separatist Methodist movements and by a variety of Baptist groups. Both of these Free Church patterns are also observed in much greater detail in the next two chapters. For the moment it is important to note that both patterns – diffusion and innovation – were already present in this earliest period.

3

At a broader level still, *Tables 2 and 3* suggest, perhaps surprisingly, that in the 1820s there was not a large difference in the overall churchgoing rates of rural and urban areas. Of course, the Church of England was thoroughly dominant in rural areas, whereas the Free Churches may have been slightly better attended than the Church of England in the urban areas. Some caution is necessary in making too fine distinctions in the urban balances, since the dates for measuring the Church of England and Free Churches were separated by a gap of eight years at a time of rapid population change. None the less, by crudely combining them it can be seen that an overall figure of 24.8 per cent for the rural areas does not contrast too sharply with a figure of 22.2 per cent for the large towns and 21.4 per cent for the conurbations. Comparable figures for 1851 suggest a slightly wider gap between the overall morning attendances of 23.5 per cent for the rural districts, 18.7 per cent for the large towns, and 16.3 per cent for the conurbations.

Despite the obvious crudity of these comparisons, they do perhaps suggest that claims about the inevitable secularizing features of urbanization, or of rural migration to urban areas, may require serious modification. Between the 1820s and 1851 it would seem that the Church of England did increase its urban attendances, just as the Baptists and non-Wesleyan Methodists did in the large towns and perhaps the Methodists as a whole in the conurbations. Chapter 6 shows that the Free Churches generally did the same between 1851 and the 1880s, although it was again the new groups such as the Salvation Army that were mainly responsible for this increase. And there are hints in the chapters that follow that urban Catholics did the same in the first half of the twentieth century. Even in the 1980s, Independent Churches experienced urban growth in some parts of England, albeit in many areas (with the important exception of London) in an overall context of Free Church decline.

Warrington and the Registration District surrounding it provide another urban/ rural contrast. In the town itself total attenders in the 1820s amounted to some 29.9 per cent of the population – crudely combining the Church of England figure of 15.8 per cent for 1821 and 14.1 per cent for the Free Churches for 1829. Morning and evening attendances combined for 1851 amounted to 32.6 per cent and for 1881 to 24.4 per cent. However, those in the rest of the Registration District of Warrington amounted only to 25.1 per cent for the 1820s, 26.9 per cent for 1851, and 25.6 per cent for a more select rural sample[20] for 1881. These comparisons lack the sophistication of the Cumbrian sample, since they do not allow a further distinction to be made between deeply rural and small town areas, but they point in a similar direction.

On the Church of England side, they suggest increases between 1821 and 1851 in both urban and more rural areas, but clear decreases in both between 1851 and 1881. So, in the more rural areas, attenders increased from 13.0 per cent in 1821 to morning attenders of 19.2 per cent in 1851, but between 1851 and 1881 morning and evening attendances declined from 19.2 per cent to 16.8 per cent. More ambiguously in the town, attenders in 1821 amounted to 15.8 per cent and morning attenders in 1851 to 12.3 per cent, but unambiguously morning and evening attendances declined from 18.5 per cent in 1851 to 10.3 per cent in 1881.

On the Free Church side, rural chapelgoing increased throughout: 2.1 per cent attenders in 1829 in contrast to 6.2 per cent morning attenders in 1851, and then 7.7 per cent morning and evening attendances in 1851 rising to 8.8 per cent in 1881. But in the town the Free Churches held steady at the figure of 14.1 per cent for attenders in 1829, and again 14.1 per cent for combined morning and evening attendances in both 1851 (morning plus Sunday school = 10.8 per cent) and 1881.

The pattern of church building in the first half of the nineteenth century supports the general picture of an overall increase in church attendances. Horace Mann in his report on the 1851 Religious Census[21] calculated that there had been an increase in church seating from sufficient for 50.8 per cent of the population of England and Wales in 1821 to 57.0 per cent in 1851. He made this calculation from the dates of dedication of buildings given in the 1851 returns. Furthermore, he calculated that the rise took place in both urban and rural areas. In the latter the rise was from 61.5 per cent to 70.0 per cent and in the former from 37.0 per cent to 44.7 per cent.

A study of Free Church chapels in Cheshire[22] showed that the first half of the nineteenth century was a particularly active time of building. In the fifty years between 1699 and 1748 a total of 437 chapels were built. In the next fifty years, 1749–98, only 164 chapels were built. However, in the fifty years 1799–1848, a remarkable 726 chapels were built in Cheshire.

Tables 2 and 3 suggest that there was a general increase in seating both in rural areas and in the conurbations. This characterized both the Church of England and especially the Free Churches. However, in the large towns the Free Church seating remained fairly steady, but the Church of England seating declined from sufficient for 21.0 per cent of the population to 18.0 per cent. Chapter 6 shows that a relative decline of seating in the large towns and in most conurbations particularly affected the Church of England in the period 1851–81, while Free Church seating continued to grow in all the main urban samples.

Because the figures for the 1820s are for attenders rather than attendances, and seldom give their relative distribution over different services, it is not possible to make accurate assessments of how full churches and chapels were at the time.

---

[20] See *The Examiner*, Warrington, 12 November 1881.

[21] Mann, *1851 Census Great Britain*, pp. cxxi–cxxii.

[22] See *The Victorian History of the Counties of England: Cheshire*, vol. 3, Oxford University Press, Oxford, 1980, p. 122.

Nevertheless, some useful comparisons can be made. On average, rural churches would seem to have been emptier than urban churches. In the Free Churches represented in *Table 3*, rural chapels would have been particularly empty, with total attenders representing barely 21 per cent of available Free Church seating.[23] Even in 1851, morning attendances in the Free Churches, together with Sunday school attendances, accounted for just 31 per cent of available seating.

In the urban areas chapels were likely to have been fuller than their rural counterparts at both dates. In 1829 Free attenders in the towns, as already mentioned, accounted for 65 per cent of available seats. In the conurbations they accounted for a very high 88 per cent. However, Baptist attenders in 1829 represented only 42 per cent of seating in the towns and 50 per cent in the conurbations. By 1851 morning attenders with Sunday schools accounted for only 50 per cent in the towns and for just 48 per cent in the conurbations. Chapter 6 supplies abundant evidence about urban Free Churches erecting more chapels between 1851 and 1881 than they could fill. In some denominations, at least, this may have been a problem that went back as far as the 1820s.

The pattern of Church of England churchgoing was rather different. In 1821 attenders accounted for only 51 per cent of available seats in the towns:[24] by 1851 morning and Sunday school attenders accounted for 55 per cent. In the conurbations the figure of 68 per cent for 1821 was also similar to that for 1851 of 62 per cent. In the countryside, too, it was higher than that for the Free Churches: 58 per cent for 1821 and 47 per cent for 1851.

Again, Chapter 6 shows that once Sunday schools are removed from these figures for 1851 (frequently they met at different times and even in different buildings to the morning worshippers), then in reality few denominations, rural or urban, with the major exception of Catholics, could expect their services to be even half full on a Sunday. Even on Horace Mann's calculations (which did include Sunday schools), morning service, which was generally the best-attended service in 1851, on average was only 40.1 per cent full in the rural areas of England and Wales and 53.4 per cent full in the urban ones. From the data presented in *Tables 2 and 3* there are already hints that even in the 1820s, outside the conurbations, there were empty churches and chapels of a Sunday.

4

By the 1830s another series of comparisons becomes possible. There was the Congregational Union survey[25] of some two hundred towns and villages in 1834, and

[23] The 1829 Free Church attenders/members are calculated from *Returns of the Number of Places of Worship, not of the Church of England, in the County of Lancaster*, Lancashire Record Office, Preston (ms. QDV 9). Since this source does not give Free Church seatings, these have been calculated from the dedication dates given in the original returns for the 1851 Religious Census.

[24] The 1821 Church of England attenders and seating are both taken from *Clergy Visitation Returns, Diocese of Chester*, Cheshire Record Office, Chester (ms. ERV 716).

[25] The Congregational Union survey is reported in, 'A Comparative View of the Hearers, Communicants, and Scholars Belonging to Churchmen, Dissenters, and Wesleyan Methodists in Two

there were individual censuses at Nottingham[26] in 1833 and at three quite similar smaller towns – York, Stockton and Penzance[27] – in 1837–9. Again they provide important information when set alongside the 1851 Religious Census, particularly since the individual censuses gave data about attendances rather than simply about general attenders (although only Penzance and York provide information about how these attendances were distributed over the morning and afternoon/evening).

As mentioned in Chapter 1, the Congregational Union survey does present severe methodological problems. It used the Free Church distinction between 'hearers' and 'communicants' to compare Catholics, Anglicans and the Free Churches alike. In the process it produced some figures that sit very awkwardly with other data. For instance, the 1821 clergy returns for Liverpool suggested that Church of England attenders amounted to a total of 14 100, or 11.9 per cent of the population. But the Congregational Union survey thirteen years later gave the broad figure of 45 000 for Church of England 'hearers', representing some 25.1 per cent of the population. The statutory returns for Liverpool in 1829 suggested that there were 18 230 Free Church attenders/members, or some 11.0 per cent of the population. Five years later the Congregational Union survey recorded 32 590 Free Church 'hearers', or some 18.2 per cent of the population. It is difficult to make much sense of such disparities. Only the Catholic figures seem comparable: in 1834 they were given as 50 000, comparing closely with the 1829 figure of 45 000. The 1821 and 1829 statistics refer only to the town of Liverpool, not to the borough. These Catholic figures seem to confirm that it was still the town, not the borough, that was being analysed in 1834. But even if a wider population base was being used in 1834, there still seems to be little correspondence between it and the 1821 and 1829 surveys. Indeed, it is difficult to know what population base was being used for a number of the places in the 1834 survey.

Clearly, considerable caution is needed here. However, *Table 4* suggests that at least part of the data from the 1834 survey can be used for broad comparisons. This table takes 1834 statistics for those eight towns – Bradford, Burnley, Coventry, Hull, Lancaster, Nottingham, Sheffield and York – that seem to correspond to other comparable data and for which population bases seem clearest. These are then compared with data from the 1851 Religious Census.

In broad terms, the results in *Table 4* do seem to accord with the thesis that, before 1851, Church of England attenders/attendances were increasing somewhat

---

Hundred and Three Towns and Villages', *The Supplement to the Congregational Magazine*, 1834. A seemingly independent survey of Hull for 1834, reported in *The Victorian History of the Counties of England: Yorkshire East Riding*, vol. 1, p. 315, is in fact identical to the Congregational Union survey.

[26] For Nottingham, see S.D. Chapman, 'The Evangelical Revival and Education in Nottingham', *Transactions of the Thoroton Society of Nottinghamshire*, vol. 66, 1962, pp. 40–1.

[27] For York, see J.R. Wood 'Tables Shewing the Attendances at Churches and Chapels in York', 19 December 1837, Archives Department, Manchester Central Library (ms. f310.6 M5 vol. 4); for Penzance, see R. Edmonds, 'A Statistical Account of the Parish of Madron, containing the Borough of Penzance, in Cornwall. Digested from the Replies to the First Series of Questions Circulated by the Statistical Society of London', *Journal of the Statistical Society*, vol. 2, 1839, pp. 198–233; for Stockton, see *The Dissenter*, published by William Robinson of Stockton, September 1836 (I am most grateful to the Revd Alex Whitehead for finding this survey).

faster in urban areas than those of the Free Churches. The gap between the two 1834 comparisons is distinctly wider than the gap between the four 1851 comparisons. For example, in 1834 there were more than twice as many Free Church 'hearers' and 'Sunday scholars' as there were in the Church of England in these eight towns (29.2 per cent of the population compared with 13.9 per cent). In 1851 the gap between morning attenders (including Sunday school) was less than half (12.4 per cent compared with 7.4 per cent) as was the Index (26.6 per cent compared with 15.1 per cent). The methodological problems of the 1834 survey preclude too fine an analysis, but at this broad level the data in *Table 4* seems to fit the overall pattern suggested by *Tables 2 and 3*.

The pattern in York, Stockton and Penzance, shown in *Table 5*, seems to provide additional confirmation. Together these three towns had church seating for a remarkable 67.6 per cent of their populations in the late 1830s and for 63.9 per cent in 1851. Of the larger towns, only Colchester (71.0 per cent) and Wakefield (67.2 per cent) in England provided more church seating in 1851. However, not withstanding a wealth of ancient Anglican churches (seating 35.7 per cent of the population), especially in York, it was Free Church attendances that predominated in the 1830s. Yet by 1851, despite Free Church seating actually surpassing Church of England seating, attendances at the latter had increased by almost half to reach virtual parity with Free Church attendances. In Chapter 9 I argue that this sharp change provides important clues about the mechanics of church growth.

The overall pattern, then, provided by these three towns does not differ from the bulk of the urban evidence for the 1820s. It was the Church of England that generally prospered better before 1851. Only in Nottingham, in 1833–51, did a Free Church attendance increase (22.4 per cent to 31.3 per cent) exceed an Anglican increase (11.6 per cent to 13.5 per cent), but Free Church attendances declined unusually early there (to 19.8 per cent by 1881). In the three towns, Anglican attendances rose from 18.0 per cent in the late 1830s to 26.3 per cent in 1851. In Chapter 6 it is seen that, after 1851, the predominant pattern was for Free Church attendances to prosper and Anglican attendances to decline in urban areas. What will be noted in a moment is that at this crucial early stage the leadership of the Church of England was engaged in a number of radical structural changes.

The Penzance survey also gave rare early evidence of another feature that is noted in later chapters. Churchgoers generally were disproportionately female even in the late 1830s. The ratio between males and females attending the parish church was estimated at three-to-five. That in the two Wesleyan chapels was estimated at four-to-five, and in the Independent chapel as ten-to-eleven. A straightforward 'excess of females' was also noted in the chapels belonging to the Baptists, the Catholic Apostolic Church, and the Wesleyan Association. The Quaker chapel was said to be 'equal' and only the chapels of the Jordan Baptist Church and the Primitive Methodists, and less surprisingly the tiny Jewish synagogue, recorded excesses of male over female attendances.

In a remarkable piece of longitudinal research, Clive Field[28] has shown that a male/female disparity has been characteristic of Free Churches for more than three

---

[28] Clive D. Field, 'Adam and Eve: Gender in English Free Church Constituency', *Journal of Ecclesiastical History*, vol. 44, no. 1, January/April, 1993, pp. 63–79.

hundred years. Examining 659 Baptist and Congregational lists for the years 1651–1950, he found that over the whole period there was a two-thirds majority of female members, and only in the second half of the eighteenth century did the proportion ever fall below three-fifths. In later chapters it is seen that a very similar disparity was evident in attendances for both London and York at the beginning of the twentieth century. Reviewing twenty-two churchgoing censuses for all denominations for the years 1901–68, Clive Field has also shown that attendances were predominantly female. In fact, he only found two surveys in which any denomination showed anything but a predominance of female attendances. The MARC Europe censuses[29] also suggest that female attenders have exceeded the national female population mean of 51 per cent in every English denomination in 1979 and 1989, with the sole exception of Independent Churches in 1989.

An 1841 survey in Pontypool[30] suggests a very considerable rise in Welsh industrial churchgoing over the following decade. The population of Trevethin changed little over the decade (17 196 in 1841 and 16 864 in 1851), yet both church seating and attendances increased dramatically. In 1841 there were seats in the twenty-eight churches and chapels for 60 per cent of the population: ten years later there were another nine buildings and seating for a remarkable 80 per cent. Attendances in 1841 accounted for 32.4 per cent and Sunday schools for a further 12.9 per cent. By 1851 evening attendances alone (the best attended services) accounted for 52.7 per cent and Sunday schools, measured at their main meetings, amounted to 23.6 per cent.

Amalgamated this would mean that in 1851 three-quarters of the population, young and old alike, went to a place of worship on the Sunday in question. But, as noted earlier, in Wales some caution is needed in making such amalgamations since adults as well as children attended Sunday school in the afternoon and may well have been in chapel again in the evening. None the less, church/chapel and Sunday school attenders in the evening alone accounted for almost 56 per cent of the total population. In England only Suffolk was capable of bettering such an attendance rate at a single point in the day – notably the Registration District of Risbridge with its remarkable church/Sunday school attendance of 58.1 per cent in the afternoon. Furthermore, on average the churches and chapels in Trevethin were two-thirds full at the evening service in 1851. So, as has been seen in Chapters 3 and 4, Welsh towns were capable, in 1851 at least, of sustaining both very high seating capacities and remarkably full churches and chapels.

This extraordinary increase was not entirely a Free Church phenomenon, although chapels predominated very considerably over churches in the town. Attendances at the parish church and two chapels of ease amounted to 5.2 per cent of the population in 1841. By 1851 a further two Anglican churches had been built

---

[29] See Peter Brierley (ed.), *Prospects for the Eighties*, MARC Europe 1980, and his *Prospects for the Nineties: Trends and Tables from the English Church Census*, MARC Europe 1991. A summary is given in *UK Christian Handbook: Religious Trends*, No. 2 (1999) p. 4.9 (Christian Research, Vision Building, 4 Footscray Road, London SE9 2TZ), but it does not include the 1998 census.

[30] See G.S. Kenrick, 'Statistics of the Population in the Parish of Trevethin (Pontypool) and at the Neighbouring Works of Blaenavon in Monmouthshire, chiefly employed in the Iron Trade, and inhabiting part of the District recently disturbed', *Journal of the Statistical Society*, vol. 3, 1841, pp. 366–75.

and a school seating 500 was also licensed for worship. As a result, attenders apparently more than doubled. Evening attenders alone accounted for 11 per cent of the population. Sunday school attendances in the Anglican churches showed an even sharper increase. In 1841 they amounted to 1.2 per cent of the population, whereas in 1851 the main meetings of the Sunday schools amounted to 4.3 per cent.

A very similar pattern of increase was experienced in the neighbouring community surrounding the iron works of Blaenavon. The population of this community increased slightly from 5115 in 1841 to 5855 in 1851. However, church and chapel attendances at least doubled from 22.2 per cent at six churches in 1841 to 42.8 per cent for the evening service alone at thirteen churches in 1851. Sunday school attendance increased from 10.7 per cent to 25.2 per cent. And the Anglicans increased from 2.9 per cent at church and 2.2 per cent at Sunday school at a single church building in 1841 to 6 per cent and 3.7 per cent respectively at two churches in 1851.

Do all these increases mean that individuals who never went to church or chapel in 1841 did so in 1851? Or do they instead mean that individuals who went irregularly in 1841 became more regular in 1851? The fact that only a single point in the day is used as a measure of 1851 attendance precludes a third possibility which has haunted much of the data in this chapter – namely, that individuals who already went in 1841 just went to more services in 1851 (a possibility, as Chapter 9 shows, that cannot be excluded altogether when analysing York statistics).

There is one piece of evidence provided in the survey that suggests that it may be the second possibility that should be taken most seriously here. In the survey of Blaenavon only 9.6 per cent of the population in 1841 were identified as 'persons who say they do not go to any place of worship', and in Trevethin the figure was 12.6 per cent. Even the overall amalgamation of 74 per cent of the joint populations being in church/chapel or Sunday school in 1851 is still consistent with these figures.

What is most remarkable about these statistics for Trevethin and Blaenavon is that they relate to working-class industrial populations. This is not a Welsh-speaking rural population such as that in Glan-llyn or even the rural Suffolk population of Risbridge. And it is not like the high levels of middle-class suburban churchgoing, noticed in subsequent chapters, in parts of London – such as Hampstead in 1851, Lewisham in 1887, or High Barnet in 1903. The report to the Statistical Society depicts the population of these two Welsh towns as 'consisting almost entirely of the working class employed in the Iron trade, of the shopkeepers who supply them with food and clothing, and of the few agriculturists who inhabit the cultivated portion of the district'.[31] The population had increased from 1200 at the turn of the century, largely as a result of the iron works. One fifth of the population in 1841 were lodgers, usually single men, and on average bedrooms had more than three people occupying them, sometimes in shifts. Over 11 per cent of the population apparently admitted to being 'drunkards'. Few sociologists or historians would identify this as fertile territory for chapel growth, let alone for growth of the Established Church.

---

[31] G.S. Kenrick, 'Statistics', p. 367.

5

One pattern of growth that this does reveal is that of the Sunday schools. As a result of a series of government and statistical enquiries, it is possible to plot the growth of Sunday schools nationally from 1818 in some considerable detail.[32]

In 1818 there were some 5463 Sunday schools in England and Wales with 477 225 scholars. By 1833 there were 16 828 Sunday schools and 1 548 890 scholars. By 1851 there were 2708 Sunday schools and 2 407 642 scholars. In relation to the total population, those belonging to Sunday schools had increased from 4.1 per cent to 10.8 per cent to 13.4 per cent. And whereas in 1818 there was one Sunday school for every 2131 people, by 1851 there was one for every 745. In contrast, the ratio of churches and chapels to people had widened very considerably. Despite rapid building there was approximately one church or chapel for every 770 people in 1801 (a rate little changed on some estimates from the 1720s), but only one for every 1273 people in 1851.[33]

Table 6 estimates the proportions of the population aged under 15 that these Sunday school figures might represent. Of course it cannot be assumed that all those enrolled at Sunday school (especially in Wales) were indeed aged under 15. And naturally, toddlers and babies are included in these estimations. Nevertheless, they do provide a rough indication of the relative strengths of the Sunday school movement at various periods. Specifically, they suggest that the movement continued to grow throughout the nineteenth century, reaching a peak of more than half of the eligible population somewhere between 1891 and 1911. They also suggest that there was a sharp rise, from 11.5 per cent to 30.3 per cent, between 1818 and 1833.

Relating the Sunday enrolment figures to the less speculative total population figures, it appears that by 1851 Lancashire and Cheshire were areas of high enrolment, with 15.6 per cent and 15.9 per cent respectively. Middlesex registered only 5.9 per cent, Surrey 6.5 per cent and Hereford 7.9 per cent. Of English counties, Bedford was highest at 19.8 per cent and Derby next at 18.0 per cent. Predominantly rural counties did not necessarily have high Sunday school rates and predominantly urban ones low rates. Indeed, some industrial towns had remarkably high rates. Oldham recorded 17.0 per cent, Leeds 16.9 per cent, and Manchester 14.0 per cent.

As with later churchgoing rates, there was a gradual shift away from the Church of England and towards the Free Churches for most of the nineteenth century. This again is evident in *Table 6*. In 1818 there was a rough parity between the Anglican and non-Anglican enrolments, but by 1851 almost two-thirds of enrolments belonged to non-Anglicans. However, as the twentieth century proceeded so the gap between the two began to narrow.

---

[32] Sunday school statistics 1818–51 calculated from the *Parliamentary Report: Census 1851 – Education: England and Wales*.

[33] The 1801 and 1851 estimates are based on Mann, *1851 Census Great Britain*. The estimates for the 1720s were often made on the basis of John Chamberlayne's *Magna Britanniae Notita*, London, 1735; for example, they were made on this basis by Frederick Martin, in a polemical pamphlet for the Society for the Liberation of Religion from State-Patronage and Control, entitled *The Property and Revenues of the English Church Establishment*, London, 1877.

6

Behind all of these changes in the first half of the nineteenth century lay an extraordinary burst of energy across denominations. It is widely reported by church historians that this was a time of theological revival stimulated by the growth of evangelicalism – first among the Free Churches and then within the Church of England. However, just as crucially it was a time of radical structural changes within denominations in response to rapidly increasing populations. In the first half of the nineteenth century, Chester had the fastest-growing population of any diocese in England. The counties of Cheshire and Lancashire grew from less than 87 000 people to almost two-and-a-half million. How did the Chester diocese cope with this population explosion?

Bishop (later Archbishop) John Sumner's *Charges Addressed to the Clergy of the Diocese of Chester*, between 1829 and 1841, provide remarkable primary evidence. That Church of England attendances (if not separate attenders) in urban areas in the diocese between 1821 and 1851 grew faster than the Free Churches, and possibly faster than this population explosion, has already been suggested from the data. That this apparent growth in attendances was planned and the result of well-thought-out structural changes in the Church of England becomes apparent from these Charges.

In his first Charge in 1829 the Bishop outlined some of the acute difficulties facing the Church of England in urban areas. He noted that there

> are many who imagine, that if the people are not in the established churches, they are in the dissenting chapels, and are therefore not destitute of religious instruction. The truth is not so ... The mass of the ADULT manufacturing population is, in point of fact, without religious instruction of any kind.

He was aware of some cases of 'crowded and attentive' congregations, but none the less maintained that 'the general state is one of total apathy: which can only be overcome gradually, by taking advantage of every favourable opportunity'.[34]

To remedy the situation he argued that there should be a number of radical structural changes, including systematic lay visitations, regular home instruction in Christian teaching, and the building of many more churches and schools to cater for the burgeoning urban populations. Then, having proposed these changes, he added pointedly in words that could equally apply today:

> You may suppose, that I am well aware of the difficulties which still intervene in our large towns, and obstruct a scheme of general superintendence; especially from the insufficiency of the church accommodation. It must not hinder our attempting all we can, that it is impossible to effect all we desire; that our population has outgrown our system; that our ecclesiastical divisions are imperfect and inconvenient. If we wait till all difficulties are smoothed, we shall wait till this world passes away. I am one of those who are inclined to expect much.[35]

---

[34] John Bird Sumner, *Charges Addressed to the Clergy of the Diocese of Chester*, Hatchard & Son, London, 1841, 1.96.

[35] Sumner, *Charges*, 1.29.

Twelve extremely busy years later, and in sharp contrast to the fifteen churches consecrated in the diocese earlier in the century, he was able to report:

> Our own diocese, Reverend Brethren, may well be cited to encourage our hopes, if encouragement were needed – to disperse our doubts, if doubts were entertained. It did present, some years ago, a specimen of religious destitution, which might well be deemed in every point of view appalling ... Since our first meeting, now twelve years since, the measures which had been already commenced for increasing the efficiency of the Church have come into fuller operation, and spread in new directions. The exertions used to provide for the wants of an overgrown and daily-increasing population, have prospered beyond our hopes. One hundred and seventy additional churches have opened their doors to receive a people, of whom the greater part were practically excluded from the benefits of the Establishment ... Numerous are the places, where, a few years ago hundreds, if not thousands, of families were congregated without any regular provision for their spiritual culture. The visitor of these districts now, will not only find the house set apart for the worship of God; but the minister, whose charge it is, permanently settled in his parsonage; the children collected in schools; the people systematically instructed; the general aspect of a christian community, where recently all was barren.[36]

Using Sumner's *Charges* as primary evidence, it is possible to reconstruct some of the most crucial structural changes that appeared to result in the proportional increase of urban Church of England attendances in this period. Interestingly, they differ little from present-day church growth techniques.

The most demanding was undoubtedly what would today be termed church planting. Because of the rapidly increasing urban population, the Bishop repeatedly stressed the need for more churches. As an example, he noted that Manchester, despite a population of some 200 000 people, was still a single parish. If the urban poor were to be encouraged to come back to the Church of England – either from 'dissenting' churches or from non-churchgoing – then he believed it was essential to provide many more places of worship.

In 1832 he argued that:

> [There] are two large towns in Lancashire, in which by efforts of this kind the church accommodation has been doubled within the last fifteen years, and church membership increased sixfold. In one of these towns, twelve years ago, the average congregations amounted together to about 850 persons, out of a population exceeding 20 000. They now amount to 5100: and there are one-third more communicants than there were then hearers. The children educated in connexion with the establishment, which in 1822 were 590, are now 3000.[37]

The town in question may well have been Blackburn. It had a population in 1821 of 21 940 and its single church, St John, had a morning congregation of 200 and an afternoon congregation of 800. Later that year St Peter was built, the Parish Church was rebuilt in 1826, and St Paul was built in 1829. Before 1851 another two churches were built to serve a population of 46 536. The result seems to have been a dramatic increase in attenders from 4.6 per cent of the population in 1821 to

---

[36] Sumner, *Charges*, 5.10–11.
[37] Sumner, *Charges*, 2.40.

morning attenders in 1851 representing 11.2 per cent of the population and an Index of 22.3 per cent. Perhaps not surprisingly, Free Church attenders/members in 1829 amounted to 10.8 per cent, but morning attenders in 1851 were only 8.7 per cent with an Index of 17.4 per cent. Evidently these structural changes did indeed increase the Anglican presence in Blackburn, and perhaps they even succeeded in Sumner's aim of abating the Free Church presence there.

Nevertheless, he argued (again in strangely modern tones) that church building was not the only way to promote growth. He believed that the school-room could sometimes be more effective. Specifically, he argued that it could be

> an important step between the indifference which is too general among the working classes, especially of a town population, and an established habit of church-going. It is at first a substitute for the church, to those who either could not enter one for want of seat-room, or would not, from long habit of neglect.[38]

Either because of having to work on a Sunday or because of long-established habits of Sunday leisure, the very act 'of attending the house of God requires in them something of an effort; and they are moreover continually and importunately tempted to withdraw themselves'.[39]

The Chester diocese was apparently less prone to clerical absenteeism than some other dioceses. Nevertheless, Sumner welcomed the Plurality of Benefices Act of 1838 and believed that it would benefit at least some of the 70 churches (out of the total of 580 for the diocese) that had absentee incumbents. More significant in the Bishop's view were the hundred new clergy that he saw added to the diocese by 1835. These, he argued, were essential to the Church of England's presence among the urban poor.

However, he did not believe that unaided the clergy could effectively reach all the urban unchurched. Long before present-day emphases upon lay ministry and house churches, he argued throughout his Charges that systematic lay visitations, accompanied by home instruction, were essential. By 1832 there were evidently critics of these ideas. Sumner responded at length to the accusation that Canon Law forbade preaching or the reading of prayers in private houses. In contrast, he maintained that a law to this effect was originally framed to restrain 'dissenters' not to curtail the work of the Church of England, and that in any case it was anachronistic. In his view, systematic visitations and instruction were important preludes to attracting the urban poor back to the Church of England.

Church schools and Sunday schools were also considered to be important. By 1837 he estimated that the whole parish of Blackburn, with a population of some 65 000, had 8254 children in Church of England Sunday schools (an above-average 12.7 per cent of the total population) and 1621 in its schools, compared to 4390 Free Church scholars. He was convinced that, even when education in general seemed to be the main object of much Sunday school teaching among the urban poor (itself important, he argued, for their future job prospects), 'gradually those who advance in age imbibe the principles of the religion which is the professed

---

[38] Sumner, *Charges*, 4.62.
[39] Sumner, *Charges*, 4.62.

object of their education, with a sincerity and earnestness which counteracts the dangers to which their circumstances expose them'.[40]

The extraordinary number of churches and schools built while Sumner was Bishop naturally involved raising huge sums of money. At several points in his *Charges* he argued that the cost ought still to be borne by the government, as some of it had been earlier in the century. In the event, most of the money was raised from public appeals. In 1841, for example, £53 000 was spent on church buildings and £11 500 on endowments to provide the incumbents' incomes. Of this money:

> £18 350 was derived from what may be termed public sources, though all, with the exception of £2700, originating in private benevolence: viz. Incorporation Society, £900. Her Majesty's Commissioners, £2700. Diocesan Society, £3550. Manchester and Eccles Church Building Society, £4700. Hyndman's Trust, £6500. The remaining £46 500 has been contributed by individuals locally or benevolently induced to provide the means of public worship and pastoral care for themselves and those around.[41]

If these calculations were at all typical, then as much as £1 000 000 would have been raised for church extensions in the diocese during Sumner's twenty years as Bishop. By present-day calculations, £100 000 000 might give a clearer indication of the enormous amount of money raised.

One final, and distinctly more negative, point can be drawn from his *Charges*. It gives flesh to the pattern of rural church building that has been seen in earlier chapters. In 1832, having cited the example of what appears to be Blackburn, he argued that the 'same system of church extension must be carried on in agricultural parishes no less than in crowded towns'.[42] He cited an imaginary parish of 1300 persons which also had a hamlet of 850 persons at a distance of two or three miles. If no Church of England building were placed in the latter, some thirty or forty of its inhabitants might go to the parish church, but 'a meeting-house would be erected, to which the great majority would be attached, not from preference or principle of any kind, but solely from convenience'.[43] This highly instructive comment fits well the thesis I offered in *Competing Convictions*[44] – namely, that rural church building in the nineteenth century owed more to inter-denominational rivalry, and perhaps also to mimicry of urban building, than to a distinctive need arising from burgeoning local populations.

The specific example that he gave to cement this argument is also instructive. Oddly, it was taken from north Northumberland. Duddo, in the border parish of Norham, adjacent to the parishes examined in *Competing Convictions*, was advanced as a model for others:

> The population 604; consisting of agricultural labourers and colliers, the great majority of whom previously to the opening of the chapel (in 1832) were in a state of complete alienation from the established church; indeed, they may be described as living 'without

---

[40] Sumner, *Charges*, 4.43.
[41] Sumner, *Charges*, 5.75.
[42] Sumner, *Charges*, 2.40.
[43] Sumner, *Charges*, 2.41.
[44] SCM Press, London, 1989.

God in the world' ... During a period of twelve years before the chapel was built, ten children only belonging to the district, and out of a population of six hundred, were brought to the clergyman of the parish for baptism. Within the last three years and a-half, the baptisms have been twenty-two, being an increase of seven for one. At the first celebration of the Lord's Supper the communicants were five, at the last thirty-four.[45]

Unfortunately the history of Duddo church (and parish, as it became in 1865) is more problematic than this early account might suggest. Seating 150 people, it was one of the first Anglican churches to be built in rural Northumberland in the nineteenth century. It has already been seen in Chapter 2, that in the second half of the nineteenth century there was an astonishing programme of church building in this area. In his Charge for 1871, the Archdeacon of Lindisfarne reported that, in the previous twenty-eight years, £160 500 had been spent in his area building fifteen new churches, restoring and enlarging forty-one others, and adding organs, stained glass windows and heating. With pride he concluded that, 'no better answer can be given to the envious enemies of our National Church, when they inquire, what the Established Church is doing for the people'.[46]

Sumner and others evidently regarded the building of churches such as that at Duddo as a crucial way to stop rural Free Church growth (in this area, Presbyterianism). Yet by 1851 Duddo had only a single service, in the morning, with a congregation of 35 and a Sunday school of 30. Despite being less than a quarter full, the church was rebuilt for a cost of £1200 after a public appeal (sponsored by the religious artist, Lady Waterford of neighbouring Ford) just outside Duddo in 1880 – anticipating a larger coal mining community that never arrived. With seating for an additional 28 people, it now had a regular congregation of only 30, just half of whom were communicants. By 1887 its congregation was still given as 30.[47]

Thus, in none of the records did Duddo's regular congregation amount to even 6 per cent of the local population. Eventually, after a century of depopulation, it ceased to have a separate incumbent, the vicarage next to the church was sold, and for many years it has had a single monthly service attended by a tiny and elderly congregation. Cited as a symbol of success by Bishop Sumner, it may act rather as a symbol at the end of this chapter of structural problems soon to emerge.

---

[45] Sumner, *Charges*, 2.42–4.

[46] George Hans Hamilton, *A Charge Delivered to the Clergy and Churchwardens of the Archdeaconry of Lindisfarne, at his Ordinary Visitation*, Whittaker, London, 1871.

[47] *Clergy Visitation Returns, Diocese of Newcastle*, 1887, Northumberland County Record Office, Gosforth. Those for 1866, 1874 and 1878 (all containing churchgoing statistics) are held in the Department of Palaeography and Diplomatic, University of Durham.

6

Free Church Increase and Anglican
Decline: 1851 to the 1880s

Deep structural problems affected both the Church of England and the Free
Churches in urban areas between 1851 and the 1880s. In the case of the Church of
England these structural problems were connected with churchgoing decline. In the
case of the Free Churches they were ironically connected with considerable
expansion – expansion everywhere of seating and usually of chapelgoing too. By
the 1880s problems that have persisted to the present day were already writ large in
both the Church of England and the Free Churches.

These problems were not identical. A fundamental problem for the Church of
England was that, as in the countryside, even when it responded to urban population
growth by erecting new churches and establishing new parishes, it characteristically
continued to subsidize older churches. It did this long after the bulk of
predominantly middle-class congregations in city centres had disappeared to the
new suburbs. A fundamental problem for the Free Churches was that they continued
to compete and to expand far beyond their capacity to fill chapels. Within both rural
and urban areas, neither the Church of England nor many long-established Free
Churches were adept at coping with large changes of population. It has already
been seen that, within rural areas, both expanded vigorously against depopulation.
Now it will be seen that urban population shifts, especially inner-city depopulation
and downward social mobility, proved to be equally problematic.

In economic terms, the Church of England started to suffer from the long-term
effects of what might now be identified as incremental budgeting and subsidized
inefficiency. The Free Churches suffered rather from chronic diffusion and
opportunistic expansion. These economic terms will become clearer later. For the
moment it is important to observe the quite distinct physical behaviour of the Church
of England and of the Free Churches. This emerges clearly from an enormous range
of data.

Indeed, the statistical evidence to be studied in this chapter is the fullest and
most intricate of that for all of the four periods. Only the three MARC Europe
surveys of England for 1979, 1989 and 1998 provide a more comprehensive
longitudinal comparison. Although invaluable, they do lack the congregation-by-
congregation comparisons that can usually be made elsewhere. The three major
sources of data for the 1851–1880s comparisons are for Liverpool, twenty-eight
large towns, and London.

The Liverpool evidence provides an important link with the previous chapter.
Because *The Liverpool Daily Post* was so assiduous and so methodologically
consistent in recording churchgoing between 1881 and 1912,[1] it forms a useful link

---

[1] *The Liverpool Daily Post*, 15 November 1881, 24 November 1891, 11 November 1902, and
13 December 1912.

to the next chapter as well. As it happens, the data for Liverpool is able to establish all of the major patterns that emerge from other sources.

The group of large towns to be studied in this chapter is considerably bigger than that in Chapter 5. It consists of towns with a combined population of almost one million in 1851 and of almost two million in 1881. The smallest is Widnes, with a population of 3217 in 1851 and 24919 in 1881. The largest is Sheffield, with a population rising from 135310 to 284410. A few towns that did have a census in 1881, but that were smaller than Widnes, have been excluded, as have those towns (such as Newcastle upon Tyne)[2] that only had a census in the morning, or those (such as Hastings)[3] that provided insufficient data on seating, or those (such as Bristol)[4] for which the original returns from the 1851 Religious Census have been lost. In every case the individual returns for 1851[5] have been consulted and Sunday school figures have been excluded to allow a proper comparison with the 1881 censuses. Proportional estimates have also been made for those few churches and chapels that provided no information on seating (and very occasionally on attendances). In one case (Bath)[6] figures have not been included in the group because the 1881 census amalgamated churchgoing and Sunday school figures.

In alphabetical order the twenty-eight large towns that form the group to be analysed are:[7] Barrow-in-Furness, Bolton, Bradford, Burnley, Burslem, Coventry, Darlington, Derby, Gloucester, Gosport, Hanley, Hull, Ipswich, Leicester, Longton, Newcastle-under-Lyme, Northampton, Nottingham, Peterborough, Portsmouth,

---

2   *The Newcastle Daily Chronicle*, 5 October 1881: this was the first of the 1881 newspaper censuses, carried out to mark the meeting of the Church Congress in Newcastle.

3   *Hastings and St Leonards Times*, November 1881. Most of the 1881 newspaper censuses were reported in Andrew Mearns, *The Statistics of Attendance at Public Worship, as Published in England, Wales and Scotland, by the Local Press, Between October 1881 and February 1882*, Hodder, 1882; and in *The Nonconformist and Independent*, 2 February 1882 and 23 February 1882. Where I specify the actual day of the particular report of a census, I have made calculations directly from the original newspaper.

4   Bristol, Halifax and a very few other original returns for 1851 are reported at the Public Record Office, Kew, as missing since 1955. Barnsley was also excluded from analysis because in 1851 only one out of three Anglican churches reported attendances.

5   Held at the Public Record Office, Kew (ref. HO 129).

6   *Keene's Bath Journal*, 12 November 1881.

7   *The Barrow Times*, 19 November 1881; *The Bolton Journal*, 10 December 1881; *The Bradford Observer*, 22 December 1881; *The Burnley Gazette*, December 1881; Burslem in *The Staffordshire Sentinel*, 24 December 1881; *The Coventry Herald and Free Press*, 9 December 1881; Darlington in *The Northern Echo*, December 1881; *The Derby and Derbyshire Gazette*, 23 December 1881; *The Gloucester Journal*, November 1881; Gosport in *Hampshire Telegraph and Sussex Chronicle*, 24 December 1881; *The Hull News*, 10 December 1881; Hanley as for Burslem; *The Ipswich Free Press*, 19 November 1881; *The Leicester Daily Mercury*, 23 November 1881; Longton and Newcastle-under-Lyme as for Burslem; *The Northamptonshire Guardian*, November 1881; *Nottingham and Midland Counties Daily Express*, 8 December 1881; *The Peterborough Advertiser*, December 1881; Portsmouth as for Gosport; Rotherham as for Sheffield; *The Scarborough Mercury*, December 1881; *The Sheffield Daily Telegraph*, 24 November 1881; Southampton in *The Hampshire Independent*, December 1881; Stoke as for Burslem; *The Warrington Examiner*, 12 November 1881; *The Whitehaven Free Press*, December 1881 (reported also in *The West Cumberland Times*, 20 December 1902); Widnes in *The Warrington Guardian*, November/December 1881.

Rotherham, Scarborough, Sheffield, Southampton, Stoke-upon-Trent, Warrington, Whitehaven, and Widnes. Together they provide a rich spread of, usually fast expanding, towns across urban England.

The third source of data is for London. *The British Weekly*[8] census of London churches and chapels in 1886, and of mission halls in 1887, allows for an immensely varied set of comparisons with the 1851 Religious Census. Precisely because access is now allowed to the original returns for 1851, it is possible to make the sort of detailed comparisons from which the Victorians themselves were precluded. The local newspaper censuses of 1881 often did reproduce charts from Mann's Report where these corresponded to their own data. But at the same time they frequently admitted that strict comparisons were impossible because of the earlier inclusion of Sunday school figures. In contrast, *The British Weekly* simply published the 1886–87 London statistics on their own, church by church and chapel by chapel, without longitudinal comparisons of any kind. Rather surprisingly, as is seen in Chapter 7, Mudie-Smith did only slightly better in 1904.[9]

1

Table 7 provides a mass of comparisons for Liverpool. It will be seen at once that the Church of England declined in three ways between 1851 and 1881. Its churchgoing rate (amalgamating morning and evening attendances, and of course excluding Sunday school attendances, as in all unspecified comparisons that follow) declined from 15.3 per cent to 9.8 per cent. Its church seating declined from sufficient for 16 per cent of the population to 14 per cent. And its churches on average (establishing a mean for the two services and allowing for buildings that were closed for one or the other) were 54.1 per cent full in 1851 and only 36.1 per cent full in 1881.

All of this provides a sharp contrast to the picture of the Church of England in *Table 2*. There, Anglican attenders in 1821 amounted to 11.9 per cent of the Liverpool town population. Morning attenders (with Sunday school) in 1851 alone amounted to 10.6 per cent of the borough population and the Index to 19.4 per cent. So, although seating did decline from 18.4 per cent to 16 per cent, attendances seem to have increased and the churches themselves were more than half full at their two main services in 1851. Given this decline in seating and apparent increase in attendances, services would (unless they became more frequent) have appeared fuller in 1851 than they were in 1821.

Why did this sharp change occur between 1821 and 1881? A clue may lie in a comparison of the congregations of the oldest churches. If the fourteen churches in existence in 1821 (represented in *Table 7*) are isolated from subsequent censuses, a very distinct pattern emerges. Arguably between 1821 and 1851 congregations over all were fairly static – with 14 100 attenders at the early date and 18 926 attendances at the later one. A few churches, however, were already showing signs of a pattern of decline that was to continue at subsequent census dates – notably, St Anne's, St George's and St Philip's.

---

[8] *The Religious Census of London*, Hodder, London, 1888.
[9] Richard Mudie-Smith (ed.), *The Religious Life of London*, Hodder, London, 1904.

But in every subsequent census there was a sharp overall decline in attendances – a loss of more than half by 1881 and of almost three-quarters by 1902. Elsewhere in Liverpool, Anglican attendances were still rising in absolute terms. Quite apart from any decline relative to the general population, these oldest churches were distinctly emptier than other Anglican churches in Liverpool at every point. By 1881 less than a fifth of their seats were occupied. And by 1902, even with four churches closed, less than a sixth of the seats in the remaining ten churches were occupied. In other words, after 1851 the occupancy rate of these oldest churches was less than half that of other Anglican churches in Liverpool. The observations (noted in Chapter 4) of Abraham Hume, a Liverpool incumbent in 1858, were remarkably accurate: in some town-centre Anglican churches resources were already 'diminished, not only from generation to generation, but from year to year'.[10]

Thus, like the churches in the City of London analysed in Chapter 4, old town-centre churches in Liverpool would have been visibly empty long before the turn of the century. Despite some flourishing churches in the suburbs – especially those recently built – the centre of Liverpool already presented a picture of Church of England decline.

In theory, the Free Churches presented a picture of considerable expansion. Attendances increased from 10.7 per cent to 12.7 per cent; seating increased from 12.5 per cent to 15.5 per cent; and chapels that were on average 45.2 per cent full in 1851 were still 43.6 per cent full in 1881. Viewed in these terms, the period 1851–81 seems to have been a much more successful one for the Free Churches than 1829–51. In the earlier period there may even have been a decline in Liverpool chapelgoing. The 11 per cent attenders/members in 1829 (represented in *Table 3*) were only matched by 5.8 per cent morning attenders and an Index of 12 per cent in 1851. Thus, if the earlier period was marked by the relative growth of the Church of England in Liverpool, the later period was characterized instead by the growth of the Free Churches.

In reality, this judgement is too facile. There are signs that by 1881 some of the larger Free Church denominations were already in considerable difficulties. The uninterrupted decline of the Independent/Congregationalists from 1821 to 1912 has already been noted in Chapter 5. By 1881, like the overall position of the Church of England in Liverpool, Independent chapels were on average only about a third full and by 1912 they were only a quarter full.

The most paradoxical pattern, which is to be found with slight variations in all three major sources, belongs to the Methodists. Taken as a whole, they managed to increase their attendances slightly, but they built chapels even faster; as a result, instead of being on average 51.1 per cent full as they were in 1851, they were only 45.1 per cent in 1881. They illustrate well the thesis that perceptual decline sometimes preceded actual decline. Empty chapels were not always the result of declining levels of attendance. Here they resulted instead from too vigorous a rate of expansion.

If the Free Churches are divided into two groups, with the older and larger denominations forming the first group and the newer and/or smaller denominations

---

[10] A. Hume, *Condition of Liverpool, Religious and Social; Including Notices of the State of Education, Morals, Pauperism, and Crime*, privately circulated, Liverpool, 1858, p. 12.

or sects forming the second, an important difference of behaviour emerges. In all three major sources the first group started to decline before the second. Here in Liverpool both groups increased attendances between 1851 and 1881, although the second almost doubled and the first had started to decline by 1891. In the large towns and London attendances in the first group were already in decline by the 1880s.

Furthermore, chapels in the first group in Liverpool were on average less full in 1881 than in 1851, dropping slightly from 45.3 per cent to 42.4 per cent. However, those in the second group actually increased from 44.4 per cent to 50.6 per cent. This increase was largely effected by the non-denominational chapels and by the new Salvation Army. Again, this is a difference in behaviour that will be noted in both of the other sources.

Thus, overall, the Free Churches contained a variety of patterns in tension. Older groups tended to decline, while new groups thrived. Chapter 7 shows that even the latter did not continue to thrive for long. Once again, the patterns of innovation and diffusion strongly characterized the urban Free Churches.

One important piece of information is missing from this analysis of churchgoing in Liverpool: data about Catholics. Given the size of the Catholic population in Liverpool (estimated in Chapter 5 as being about a quarter of the total population), this would be a very serious omission. The 1881–1912 censuses were generally themselves aware that Catholic attendances were substantially underestimated, as only a single morning Mass was counted. Exactly the same problem may have distorted some of the large towns in 1881 (although by no means all) and definitely did distort the London census of 1887.

However, enumerations made by the Catholic authorities in Liverpool between 1881 and 1912 – and also Catholic attendances given fully in the London 1902–3 census – allow for a more accurate assessment of the relative strength of urban Catholics. Chapter 7 will return to these in detail. For the moment, the 1881 returns of the Catholic authorities in Liverpool suggest that average Catholic attendances there represented some 10.4 per cent of the population (the newspaper census suggested only 4.3 per cent). The Index for Liverpool Catholics in 1851 was 15.3 per cent and morning and evening attendances, as noted earlier, and amounted to 13.9 per cent of the population. This does suggest a decline in Catholic attendances in Liverpool, but not quite as sharp a decline as in Anglican attendances. Using the smaller Catholic figure for 1851 and the larger one for 1881, attendances across denominations in Liverpool between these dates declined from some 39.9 per cent of the population to 32.9 per cent.

2

The broad patterns established from the Liverpool data are also evident in the mass of data for the large towns between 1851 and 1881. *Table 8* shows that the Church of England declined in terms of both attendances and seating and the Free Churches expanded their seating and held steady in their attendances. The older and larger Free Church denominations tended to decline, while the newer/smaller denominations prospered. And there is abundant evidence that town-centre Anglican congregations were declining faster than suburban congregations.

Again this offers a sharp contrast to the data for the large towns presented in *Tables 2* to *4*. Between the 1820s/1830s and 1851 urban Anglican attendances seemed to have increased faster than Free Church attendances. Between 1851 and 1881, as in Liverpool, this situation was reversed.

There are, however, some differences between the two sources. Free Church attendances in the large towns between 1851 and 1881 were almost double those of Liverpool or London, and very much larger than those of the Anglicans. Furthermore, although the Free Churches did increase their seating from that sufficient for a very substantial 23.7 per cent of the population to 25.6 per cent, their overall attendances did not actually increase; instead they held steady at just under 21 per cent. And the Anglican decline in attendances was very much less marked than that in Liverpool. But the most critical of all the differences was the fact that Anglican churches were considerably fuller in the evening in 1881 in the large towns than they had been in 1851. Previously, their best attended service was in the morning and their evening service was on average only a third full, but by 1881 their evening service was almost half full and was clearly better attended than the morning service (which held steady).

Overall, then, in the towns (as distinct from Liverpool or London) it was Anglican churches rather than Free Church chapels that may have given the appearance of growing congregations. And this despite the fact that their attendances were actually declining slightly in relation to the population at large. Thus, if perceptual decline in attendances preceded actual decline in the Free Churches taken as a whole, ironically in the Church of England perceived growth may have accompanied actual decline.

Once again it is necessary to enter some refinements to these initial conclusions. If the statistics for Sheffield are removed from *Table 8*, then the actual decline in Anglican attendances was rather sharper on average in the remaining towns. Instead of declining from 13.8 per cent to 12.7 per cent, they declined from 14.7 per cent to 12.9 per cent. In Chapter 1 it was shown that contemporary Sheffield sources[11] suggested that advanced publicity in 1881 enhanced attendances, as did an unusual combination of good weather and clergy returns (rather than independent enumerations). Unless there was a very localized rise in Anglican attendances there, *Table 9* seems to confirm this. Set alongside data for 1877 and 1884 from clergy visitation returns,[12] attendances at the older, central Anglican churches in Sheffield seem to have been particularly inflated (by as much as 3000 attendances). At nine of the twenty older churches, larger attendances were recorded in the 1881 census than in any of the other censuses.

In addition, by 1884 a difference appears between the Sheffield attendances of the original 1851 Anglican churches and those of the churches built subsequently. The latter were on average 46.9 per cent full, whereas the former were only 37.6 per cent full. So, according to the clergy visitation returns for 1884 – a source significantly not used by Wickham[13] – there was already an early indication in the 1880s of Anglican problems soon to emerge. Compared with the 1877 return,

---

11 See *The Nonconformist and Independent*, 2 February 1882, p. 112.
12 See *Clergy Visitation Returns, Diocese of York*, Borthwick Institute, York.
13 E.R. Wickham, *Church and People in an Industrial City*, Lutterworth, London, 1957.

several of the older churches – notably St Peter's, St Mary's, St Philip's, Christ Church Pitsmoor, Christ Church Attercliff – were already showing signs of decline. None of this is as dramatic as the Anglican decline – particularly of the oldest churches – in Liverpool. Yet it does point in a similar direction. Chapter 9 shows that by the turn of the century a very similar phenomenon was being noticed by newspapers in York. In addition, evidence from Hull continues the pattern apparently emerging in Sheffield in 1884.

It can be seen from *Table 10* that in Hull[14] there was no absolute decline in attendances by 1884 in the original 1851 Anglican churches. Yet, like Sheffield, there was already a slight difference in how full they were compared with post-1851 churches. By 1884 the latter were 47.1 per cent full, whereas the former were 41.9 per cent full. Furthermore, some of the older churches were already showing signs of decline. By 1912 the situation had radically changed; the Mariners' Church had been closed and attendances at the other 1851 churches had almost halved. On average the latter were now only 23.3 per cent full. In contrast, the post-1851 churches were 33.3 per cent full.

In other words, the older, central churches in Hull would have been visibly empty, albeit some twenty years later than churches in central Liverpool or the City of London. The pattern was similar, only the timing of their decline and the timing of the town-centre depopulation were different. A church by-church analysis of this pattern of decline is given in Chapter 9. It reveals the very nuts and bolts of Anglican urban church decline. For the moment, though, it should be noted just how widespread this pattern of decline was. It can be seen clearly in Birmingham (*Table 15*), Chelsea (*Table 14*), Hull (*Table 10*), Liverpool (*Table 7*), Newcastle upon Tyne (*Table 11*), Sheffield (*Table 9*), and York (*Table 19*). The pattern was so widespread that it can be predicted with some confidence that it will soon be found in local urban studies in many parts of Britain.

Again, appearance and reality did not always coincide in relation to the Free Churches in the large towns. Apparently Free Church attendances seemed to keep pace with the rapid population rises between 1851 and 1881, and seating, already generous, expanded further. Paradoxically, like Liverpool and London, chapels on average were slightly emptier in 1881 than they had been in 1851 – declining from 43.4 per cent full to 39.8 per cent. The sharpest decline seemed to be in the morning (although, unlike London and Liverpool, these are unadjusted percentages, taking no account of individual chapels that were closed in the morning).

In reality, the older and larger Free Church denominations in the towns did not expand chapel seating faster than population growth: they maintained seating for just under 21 per cent of the population. Free Church attendances did in fact decline from 18.9 per cent to 15.8 per cent and their chapels, which were on average 45.6 per cent full in 1851, were only 38.2 per cent full in 1881. In complete contrast, it was the newer/smaller denominations that expanded their seating, increased their attendances from 1.7 per cent to 4.6 per cent, and dramatically changed their ratio of empty to full seats. Their chapels, which on average were only 28.2 per cent full in 1851, were 46.2 per cent full by 1881. Unambiguously it

---

[14] See *Clergy Visitation Returns, Diocese of York*, Borthwick Institute, York.

was this second group that gave the overall appearance of Free Church growth in the towns.

The Independents/Congregationalists showed a particularly severe pattern of decline. Attendances dropped from 4.5 per cent of the population to 3.1 per cent and chapels that were 45.5 per cent full were now only 36.7 per cent full. Even their rate of adding extra seating was being outstripped by the expanding town populations. Wesleyan Methodists and Baptists also declined, albeit not so drastically. And non-Wesleyan Methodists, although they expanded their presence vigorously, declined slightly in attendances. As a result, their chapels, which in 1851 were almost half full, were now little more than a third full. As in Liverpool, it was this group of Methodists especially that expanded more rapidly than they could fill their chapels. It was only the tiny Presbyterian presence that increased slightly, although this did little to offset the losses of the larger denominations.

Another way of measuring the physical growth and decline of denominations in the large towns is by comparing buildings and the numerical size of congregations. It should be remembered that the population of the towns doubled. Anglican and Catholic churches slightly more than doubled, but Free Church chapels almost trebled. Against declining attendances, Anglican and mainstream Free Church congregations inevitably (and surely visibly) got smaller. In the newspaper censuses of 1881 there were already some complaints about the difficulty of filling larger churches and chapels. In the next period these complaints became more vociferous. *Table 8* indicates why this was so.

Wesleyans increased their chapels in the towns from 91 to 226, and attendances per chapel correspondingly decreased on average from 586 to 429. Non-Wesleyans increased from 101 chapels to 289, and their average attendances decreased from 437 to 299. Although waning, the Congregationalists still increased from 74 chapels to 154. Predictably, average attendances at these chapels also declined, from 581 to 392.

Even the apparently successful newer/smaller denominations experienced a slight decrease in average congregations from 201 to 195. On all other quantifiable measures they were very 'successful' in this period. They increased attendances from 1.7 per cent of the population to 2.4 per cent; they increased their seating at much the same level as the rise in population; and their chapels, which in 1851 were 28.2 per cent full, by 1881 were 37.7 per cent full. Yet they still managed to increase the sheer number of their chapels from 81 to 246, and with this increase average attendances fell.

Of course, this suggests that chapels generally were getting smaller. That in itself had economic implications. If a congregation was to support its own minister, then it obviously had to have a sufficient congregation (or a sufficient subsidy) to do so. Decreasing central congregations made large chapels themselves less viable, and increasing innovation and diffusion made smaller chapels abound. But smaller chapels, with ever smaller congregations, were financially precarious. Even when they half-filled their smaller chapels, and even when all their congregations added together constituted church growth, they were still precarious in financial terms.

Herein lies the 'Catch 22' of Free Church growth. The Church of England could tolerate levels of expansion and sparse congregations that would be difficult for others to emulate. Yet Methodists, in particular, did emulate the Church of England, both in urban areas and, amazingly, in rural areas too. Church growth seemed to require this. However, throughout the twentieth century this meant that Methodists had an abundance of financially precarious and little-used chapels. They stretched their stipendiary ministers over larger and larger circuits, relied upon an ageing lay leadership, and closed more than half of their chapels in England. But of course this contributed further to their decline.

All of this becomes clearer in Chapters 7 and 8. However, the basic pattern was already firmly established in this period. Chapels almost everywhere had become smaller and more numerous, and Free Church attendances had shrunk by an average of 87 per chapel. With the advent of the mission hall, Church of England attendances had also shrunk by as much, but their congregations were larger in the first place and their endowments were far more secure. Lacking comparable endowments and subsidies, smaller congregations were particularly hazardous for Free Churches.

Among the Free Churches, only the new Salvation Army was the major exception to this pattern. At this time they relied characteristically upon large halls and theatres for their generally packed meetings. Yet very soon, as will be seen in Chapter 7, they also started to build for themselves and then to rely upon an increasing number of ever smaller chapels. As a result, they too encountered the same dilemma and indeed started to decline quite rapidly.

At this stage it was the arrival of the Salvation Army that most dramatically transformed the Free Church situation in the towns. A repeated excuse in 1881 newspaper reports for low attendances in other Free Church congregations was the proximity of a Salvation Army mission in the area. With attendances at 2.2 per cent of the population, the Salvation Army presence in the towns was more than ten times larger than it was in Liverpool. And the Salvation Army already represented more than a tenth of all Free Church attendances in the towns. Chapter 9 presents evidence suggesting that this initial growth may have depended, at least in part, upon transfer growth from the Baptists.

3

A great deal of energy was spent by Victorians on the issue of urban church seating. Some of the polemical Free Church pamphlets that circulated in the decades following the 1851 Religious Census were particularly concerned about this issue. Prominent among them were the pamphlets of the London-based Society for the Liberation of Religion from State Patronage and Control. For example, a pamphlet produced by the Society in 1854 argued as follows:

> The first conclusion, and the most self-evident, is, that the Church of England, as a State-Church, has totally failed – not failed as a Christian organization formed for religious ministrations, but as a state appliance intended to maintain for the whole community means of religious instruction and edification, and to provide them in timely abundance, as new exigencies render them necessary ... Simply to have kept pace with a doubling of the population, in its own ratio to the total of all existing accommodation in 1801, the

Church of England should have had 8 179 254 sittings in 1851. But the total of its sittings in that year was 5 317 915.[15]

Instead, so the pamphlet argued on the basis of the 1851 Census, it was left to the 'voluntary spirit' of the Free Churches (and especially of the Methodists) to supply these 'missing sittings'. For the remainder of the century, the issue continued to be a matter of contention among the Free Churches, within Anglican dioceses, and even within parliamentary reports.

Obviously the huge growth of the urban population of Britain caused considerable difficulties for all denominations. But there was more to it than that. A comparison of the census data in the towns between 1851 and 1881 soon reveals that erecting urban churches and chapels did appear to be a successful way of increasing attendances. In most cases, proportional increases in overall church/ chapel seating were correlated with proportional increases in attendances. Occasionally (as happened at Coventry, Newcastle-under-Lyme and apparently Sheffield) Anglican attendances increased while their seating decreased relative to a rising population. More typically, proportional rises in attendance were correlated with proportional rises in seating. From this it can be seen why the later Victorians so fatally identified church growth with church building.

In the three largest towns in the group – each with a population in 1851 of more than 85 000 – this message was clear. In Hull the overall level of attendances held steady at about 40 per cent, but Church of England attendances and seating both dropped, whereas Free Church attendances and seating both rose (an unusual pattern of attendances for a town with bad weather in 1881). In Bradford both Anglican and Free Church seating increased (from 33 per cent to 41 per cent of the population) and so did overall attendances (from 25 per cent to 29 per cent). And in Sheffield, Free Church expansion meant that overall seating increased (from 31 per cent to 34 per cent) and attendances apparently did also (from 23 per cent to 29 per cent). All of these increases occurred despite the doubling of local populations.

It is often assumed that it was the sheer size or rapid growth of large towns that reduced attendances. Dense or rapid urbanization has frequently been identified as an agent of churchgoing decline.[16] But here it was some of the smaller towns that had the lowest overall attendance rates in 1881 – notably Widnes (13.7 per cent) and Hanley (17.4 per cent); these rates were both well below the rates for Hull, Bradford and Sheffield. Chapter 7 suggests that downward social mobility was much more troublesome for churchgoing than urbanization as such.

In the five towns with populations exceeding 40 000 a very similar pattern seemed to occur. In two of the towns, both Anglican and Free Church seating increased – in Bolton from 34 per cent to 39 per cent and in Portsmouth from 36 per cent to 40 per cent. Despite bad weather, overall attendances increased in Bolton from 20 per cent to 31 per cent and in Portsmouth from 37 per cent to 39 per cent. However, in the other three towns, seating did not increase in proportion to their

---

[15] *Voluntaryism in England and Wales*, Society for the Liberation of Religion from State Patronage and Control, London, 1854, pp. 52–3.

[16] Callum Brown documents and criticizes this assumption in his 'Did Urbanisation Secularise Britain?', *Urban History Yearbook*, University of Leicester, Leicester, 1988, pp. 1–14.

growing populations and proportional attendances dropped. Derby decreased seating from 48 per cent to 38 per cent and attendances dropped slightly from 38 per cent to 37 per cent; Leicester barely maintained seating at 40 per cent and had attendances declining from 44 per cent to 38 per cent; and Nottingham decreased seating from 45 per cent to 37 per cent and attendances fell from 45 per cent to 31 per cent (in this last instance these were mostly Free Church losses, albeit in bad weather).

In the five towns with populations exceeding 25 000, all but one place showed a similar pattern which appeared to link church building with an increase in churchgoing and a failure to build with a decline in churchgoing. Coventry increased its overall seating from 45 per cent to 47 per cent and its attendances rose from 28 per cent to 37 per cent. Northampton decreased its seating from 52 per cent to 37 per cent and its attendances dropped from 48 per cent to 39 per cent; Southampton decreased seating from 50 per cent to 37 per cent and attendances in bad weather fell from 49 per cent to 36 per cent; and Hanley decreased seating from 50 per cent to 32 per cent and attendances dropped from 20 per cent to 17 per cent. Only in Ipswich did the pattern fail to apply. There seating decreased from 48 per cent to 44 per cent, whereas attendances apparently increased from 42 per cent to 48 per cent. However, even this exception is more apparent than real. In 1851 it was unusually the afternoon service there that was better attended than the evening service. Since the afternoon service at Ipswich was also counted in 1881, it is for once possible to add it to overall attendances. On this basis, overall attendances declined between the two dates; from an overall 62 per cent to 59 per cent.

Even within the smallest towns, the pattern was for the most part similar. Attendances were more likely to be distorted in the very smallest towns by the Free Churches recruiting members from neighbouring villages. Nevertheless, the general experience was that, when seating did not keep pace with population growth, then overall attendances tended to decline. So the high 1851 seating in Burnley (70 per cent), Whitehaven (67 per cent), Gloucester (55 per cent), Burslem and Widnes (54 per cent), and Warrington (41 per cent) declined by 1881, as did attendances. In contrast, the seating in Darlington increased from 39 per cent to 51 per cent and attendances, despite bad weather, also increased from 33 per cent to 36 per cent. Only among some of the smallest towns in this group – Gosport, Longton, Newcastle-under-Lyme, Rotherham and Stoke-upon-Trent – did overall seating decrease and attendances apparently increase or hold steady.

Among these smallest towns, Scarborough seems to present the most startling evidence of the effectiveness of vigorous church building. Its population more than doubled from 12 158 to 30 484, yet its churches and chapels maintained a remarkable overall seating rate of some 74 per cent and attendances apparently held steady at a very high 63 per cent. Unusually in such a strongly Free Church town, Anglicans too built vigorously, increasing their churches from three to eight, and declined from a high Anglican attendance rate of 23 per cent to a still high 21 per cent (although this was a clergy-return census).

From all of this it is not difficult to see why Victorians were so convinced that building churches and chapels as vigorously as possible was essential to church growth. Experience in most of these towns would have convinced them that this was so. Of course, they occasionally also noticed that existing churches and chapels tended to be considerably under-used, but this second observation seldom deterred them from pressing for more church and chapel building.[17] And not just the Victorians. There are echoes of this conviction still in Wickham[18] in the 1950s, albeit in largely negative terms: the failure of the Church of England to reach the urban poor in Sheffield was attributed in part to a failure to build sufficient churches for them. In modern terms, church planting alone – rather than a judicious mixture of planting and pruning – has sometimes been identified as the key to increased churchgoing.

Horace Mann himself well illustrates this double focus. In earlier chapters it has already been pointed out that his report on the 1851 Religious Census provides abundant evidence of over-building in rural areas, as well as of churches and chapels being on average barely half full even at their main service. However, his guiding principle – namely, that seating for 58 per cent of the total population should be provided by churches and chapels in every area – led him to press for a considerable programme of building. For example, he concluded:

> To enable the Church of England to provide for all the population, an additional accommodation to the extent of 5 101 771 sittings would be requisite, nearly doubling the present supply; but, probably, considering the hold which several other churches, not extremely differing from the Church of England, have upon the affections of the people, few will advocate the present necessity of so extensive an addition. There exist, however, if the previous course of argument be accurate, as many as 1 644 734 persons wholly unprovided, by the agency of any church whatever, with the means of religious worship; and to this extent, at all events, there is an urgent claim upon the Church of England for augmented effort.[19]

The pressures at play here can be seen clearly in Barrow-in-Furness. In Chapter 5 it was noted how Dalton-in-Furness grew between 1821 and 1851 to a population of 4683. In 1851 it still remained an overwhelmingly Anglican parish, but by 1881 Barrow-in-Furness, with a population of 47 276, was predominantly a Free Church town. The Free Church newspaper, *The Nonconformist and Independent*, noted with pride in its contemporary commentary on the results of the 1881 census:

> It appears that the Established Church provides only 30 per cent. of the accommodation and 28 per cent. of the attendances. The growth of Barrow has been almost equal to that of the great American towns of the far West. In 1867 the population was 12 000; in 1877 38 000; and in 1881 it was 47 276. Thus in fourteen years it has nearly quadrupled. Nevertheless the provision for religious worship in Barrow has well nigh kept abreast of the population, and the supply has exceeded the demand, and is purely the natural action of voluntaryism in spiritual matters.[20]

---

[17] e.g. *The Nonconformist and Independent*, 2 February 1882, p. 106.

[18] Wickham, *Church and People in an Industrial City*.

[19] Horace Mann, *1851 Census Great Britain: Report and Tables on Religious Worship England and Wales*, British Parliamentary Papers, Population 10, 1852–3 (reprinted by Irish University Press, Shannon, 1970), p. cxxxviii.

[20] See *The Nonconformist and Independent*, 2 February 1882, p. 108.

The two Wesleyan chapels in the 1851 parish of Dalton had been supplemented by six Wesleyan chapels in Barrow alone by 1881, three Primitive Methodist chapels, and two each belonging to the Methodist New Connexion, the United Methodists Free Church, and the Congregationalists. There was a large Baptist chapel, and smaller chapels belonging to the Bible Christians, Plymouth Brethren, Christadelphians, Welsh Calvinists, Catholic Apostolic, and Spiritualists. In addition, a Salvation Army mission attracted a congregation of 1610 in the evening.

Faced with this formidable Free Church presence, it is not surprising that the once dominant Anglicans panicked. At first the Anglican response[21] was slow. A school-room, opened in 1852, led to the building of St James's in 1860 and St George's in 1861, both seating some 600. In 1861, with a population of 3500, St James's had only 56 Easter communicants (1.6 per cent), but at other services the 'Church is generally full'. If completely full at both morning and evening, this would have represented an attendance rate of 34 per cent.

By 1864 communicants at St James's had increased to 100, but since the population of the parish was now 8000 this represented 1.3 per cent. The incumbent mentioned in this return that 'practical infidelity is on the increase, in consequence of lack of Church accommodation'. Nevertheless, in 1872 neither incumbent thought that there were 'any peculiar obstacles in the way of attendance at Divine Service, such as want of room, or appropriation of pews'. By 1875 the incumbent of St George's for the first time mentioned a 'great want of Church accommodation'.

It was at this stage that panic became evident. The Anglican authorities took the extraordinary step of commissioning four identical new churches for Barrow.[22] They were built to the same design, each seating 520, named after the four Evangelists, and all consecrated on the same day: 26 September 1878. Each cost £6000. Instructively, the Duke of Devonshire donated £12 000, the Duke of Buccleugh £6000, and the shareholders in Furness Railway and Barrow Steelworks £4500. So, in sharp contrast to the vibrant Free Churches surrounding them, only a sixteenth of the cost of these four churches was raised directly from local individuals.

Within three years of being opened, only St Mark's had full congregations morning and evening. The other three churches were on average just 17 per cent full. St John's, in particular, had a morning congregation of 12 and an evening congregation of 30. Even Sunday schools, in all seven Anglican churches in Barrow, represented just 3.6 per cent of the total population in 1881.[23] The early Free Church advantage in building, and perhaps their more localized efforts in raising the money for this building, may have ensured that for the rest of the century Barrow was indeed a Free Church town.

It is perhaps not surprising, then, that by 1900 the clergy visitation returns showed signs of considerable unease. In response to the bishop's question, 'Is the attendance of your people at the Lord's Table satisfactory?', only two incumbents replied 'Fairly so'. The rest gave negative responses. By then, though, Easter communicants still represented only 3.5 per cent of the population of Barrow.

---

[21] For the clergy comments that follow, see *Clergy Visitation Returns, Diocese of Carlisle*, Rose Castle, Carlisle.

[22] See records kept on file in the Central Library, Barrow-in-Furness.

[23] See *Clergy Visitation Returns, Diocese of Carlisle*, Rose Castle, Carlisle.

The Anglican response to the extremely rapid growth of Barrow had at first been lethargic and then it had relied overwhelmingly upon outside subsidy. For once even new churches did not necessarily attract substantial congregations. Together with the two old chapels of Walney Island and Rampside, the nine Anglican churches were on average more empty than full. St George's had a large congregation in the evening, since it happened to be the final service of their incumbent. However, except for St Mark's, none of the other churches were even half full at any of their services on the census day in 1881.

The Free Church response had been immediate, localized and self-supporting, and of course it had transformed the character of local churchgoing. Yet it carried all the danger signs already noticed elsewhere. Only the Wesleyans and the Salvation Army had congregations filling more than half of the available seating. The seven non-Wesleyan chapels and the two Congregationalist chapels were on average less than a third full; and the Baptist chapel and the Presbyterian church were little more than a third full. Even the smaller, isolated chapels fared little better.

Catholics alone used their church seating to capacity. *The Barrow Times* admitted that two early services were not counted. As happened so often elsewhere, only one morning and one evening service were in fact counted. Yet in a church that could seat 750, this morning service had 700 attenders and the evening service 748. This physical difference between Catholics and others had already been established in this new town.

4

The London evidence also confirms the churchgoing and seating patterns established in Liverpool and the twenty-eight towns. In the context of an urban population that almost doubled, Anglican attendances and seating declined proportionately, while Free Church attendances and seating increased. Older Anglican churches fared worse than newer suburban churches. Both the Church of England and the Free Churches experienced a particular decline in their morning congregations. Despite their rise in attendances, on average (morning and evening) Free Church chapels were emptier in the late 1880s than they had been in 1851. Mainstream Free Churches fared worse than newer/smaller denominations. And Catholics maintained a ratio between attendances and seating quite distinct from any other denomination.

Anglican attendances in London were very similar to those in Liverpool and appreciably higher than those in the towns. However, the rate of decline in London – from 15.6 per cent attendances to 14.1 per cent and from 17.1 per cent seating to 16.5 per cent – was not nearly as pronounced as that in Liverpool between 1851 and 1881. As a result, the dominance of Free Church over Anglican attendances, which had already taken place in the towns by 1851 and in Liverpool by 1881, did not happen there until some time between 1887 and 1903. It is possible, though, that this might partly be a reflection of the slightly later date of the London 1887 census. In several urban areas Anglicans set in motion considerable programmes of fund-raising and building in the late 1880s and 1890s.

For example, in Newcastle upon Tyne[24] a special bishop's fund was established after the formation of the new diocese in 1882. In the following year it was planned to raise £66 000 for thirteen new parishes in the city. The results by 1887 can be seen in *Table 11*.[25] The addition of the new churches in Newcastle resulted in a numerical and even proportional rise in churchgoing, which was associated – as elsewhere – with a relative decline of the older central churches. In *Table 12* it can be seen that Anglican church seating did increase in London between 1887 and 1903, and in *Table 13* it can be seen that the number of Anglican churches, unlike Free Church chapels, was still growing in London up to the First World War.

As in Liverpool (but unlike the large towns), Anglican churches were distinctly emptier on average in the 1880s than they had been in 1851. But here too, perhaps for the same reasons, the difference was less dramatic. If the decline in Liverpool was from a mean of 54.1 per cent full to 36.1 per cent, in London it was from 50.3 per cent to 44.1 per cent. Morning congregations, dropping on average from 54.2 per cent full to 43.7 per cent, would surely have been visibly emptier.

More accurately, it was the older central churches that would have been most visibly empty. As mentioned in Chapter 4, the City churches were fast losing their congregations.[26] Morning attendances at churches within the City walls declined from 7750 in 1851, to 3417 in 1881, to 3234 in 1887, and then to 1815 in 1902. Evening attendances also declined, but not so fast: from 4723 in 1851, to 3828 in 1887, and to 2851 in 1902. So in the City, as elsewhere in London, morning congregations were dominant in 1851, but declined so fast that it was the evening congregations that were dominant by the 1880s.

This pattern of declining morning worship happened so swiftly in the City that it must have been obvious to the congregations themselves. Most older churchgoers in the 1880s would have been able to remember far larger morning congregations in the past. Indeed, of those present at the City morning services in 1881, two out of five people were officials, choristers or family of the clergy. Of the congregations proper, there was a three-to-two ratio of women to men. And churches that had on average been a third full in 1851, were barely a fifth full by 1887. The population factors behind these dramatic changes were discussed in Chapter 4. Here it is their sheer physicality that should be noted.

Of course this physicality was particularly stark in the fast depopulating City. However, it was also evident in parts of London that were still growing. Chelsea[27] can stand as a fairly representative area. Its population (minus the detached Kensal Newtown) grew from 53 725 in 1851 to 73 079 in 1881, and then declined slightly to 70 190 in 1901. As can be seen in *Table 14*, overall attendances there were very close to the mean for London in 1851, 1887 and 1903 – although generally

---

[24] See records kept on file in the Northumberland Country Record Office, Northumberland.

[25] Compiled from *Clergy Visitation Returns, Diocese of Durham*, Auckland Castle Episcopal Records, Department of Palaeography and Diplomatic, Durham University; and for 1887 from *Clergy Visitation Returns, Diocese of Newcastle*, Northumberland County Record Office, Gosforth.

[26] Sources for 1887 and 1902 as for notes 8 and 9; for 1881, see 'Census of Congregations of the City Churches and Chapels', *Journal of the Statistical Society*, vol. 44, 1881, pp. 596–601.

[27] See *Clergy Visitation Returns, Diocese of London*, Lambeth Palace Library.

Anglican attendances were slightly higher and Free Church attendances slightly lower than the mean.

In the late nineteenth century, Chelsea was still regarded as a 'suburban' area, and among London Districts it was ranked by Charles Booth in 1902 as coming thirty-second out fifty (one being the most socially deprived and fifty the least).[28] Booth considered that it contained only a moderate amount of outright poverty, but considerable overcrowding and a high death rate:

> In some way or another money enough is earned or obtained, but there are, nevertheless, all the signs of low life and filthy habits: broken and patched windows, open doors, drink-sodden women and dirty children. But these last, in spite of dirt, look fat and healthy, and the cats in these slums are sleek.[29]

Chelsea then was clearly different from its image today of affluence.

Anglican attendances declined sharply in Chelsea between 1851 and 1887 from a high 19 per cent to a near-average for London of 13.9 per cent. This decline mostly affected the morning services. *Table 14* shows that the total number of attendances in 1887 differed little from those in 1851. However, their distribution was quite different. Once again, if attendances at the seven oldest churches are considered on their own, then it can be seen that between 1851 and 1883 they almost halved. The independent enumeration of 1887 is surprisingly somewhat higher than the clergy returns for 1883. Yet even so, attendances in 1887 were still less than three-quarters of those in 1851. The extra attendances resulted rather from two new churches – St Simon and St John – and particularly from a series of Anglican missions. Individually, the older churches might sometimes prosper – for example, Chelsea Old Church had higher attendances in 1887 than in 1851 – but collectively they showed the pattern of decline already found elsewhere.

Mission halls, both Anglican and Free Church, were so numerous by the late 1880s that *The British Weekly* census[30] carried out a separate enumeration of them. Awkwardly this was done in 1887, whereas churches and chapels were enumerated in 1886. That apart, this census does give a unique insight into the tactics of denominations facing rapid rises in urban populations. These mission halls were frequently used for Sunday schools and for a single adult service, usually in the evening. They often provided free accommodation for the urban working classes. Yet, like their rural counterparts, they may also have drawn some churchgoers away from the older parish churches.

There were long-standing complaints from the clergy in Chelsea[31] about the non-churchgoing habits of the people. In 1810, with a population of about 16 000, there were two Anglican churches with combined seating for just over 1000, and '6 Chapels or Meeting Houses for Methodists or other dissenters which I understand will contain about two thousand five hundred persons'. In all, then, there was

28 Charles Booth, *Life and Labour of the People in London*, Final Volume, vol. 3, Macmillan, 1902, p. 17.

29 Booth, *Life and Labour*, p. 113.

30 *The Religious Census of London*, Hodder, London, 1888.

31 See *Clergy Visitation Returns, Diocese of London*, Lambeth Palace Library, London.

seating for little more than 22 per cent of the population. By 1842 Holy Trinity had been built, but the incumbent complained:

> A second Church or Chapel still required ... The want of Clergy impedes the progress of religion here, but it is hoped that want will soon be supplied as far as to have one minister for every 2000 souls. More stringent measures are wanted for enforcing better observance of the Sunday, which ought to be done by giving more power to the Churchwardens. The Churchwardens or guest men should be made officers of Police for that day to close all shops and prevent cries in the street, and so suppress the sale of profane and seditious publications. This impedes the progress of Religion here. Want of Church room for the poor is another cause, and the ignorance of the adult poor generally.

The Church of England in Chelsea never did reach a target of a clergyman/church for every 2000 people, yet it did build extensively. By 1851, despite a rapid growth of population, there was now seating across denominations for 29 per cent of the population. With seven Anglican churches, three of the incumbents in 1857 considered that their congregations bore a 'fair proportion of the population of the Parish'. The others were not so convinced. The incumbent at Chelsea Old Church argued that 'if the Church were larger I think perhaps the Congregation would be more in proportion to the population'. The incumbent at Christ Church blamed 'Popery, drunkenness, infidelity and the fact of several dissenting places of worship'. The incumbent at St Jude's made similar complaints. At Park Chapel the incumbent complained, in 1857 about 'many ... who I fear go nowhere', and in 1862 about the fact that, 'Many of the Congregation do not come from the District. Many in the District go nowhere, being attached to the Theatres and almost the whole District is constantly moving.'

By 1883 none of the incumbents wrote that their congregations represented a 'fair proportion' of the local population. The incumbent at St John's complained instead about 'the terrible indifference to religion existing amongst the people'. The incumbent at St Jude's also used the term 'indifference', and by 1900 three of the incumbents used the same term. And the incumbent at St Luke's wrote significantly in 1883 that 'a large proportion of this Parish consist a class who do not attend Church'.

In contrast, Free Church attendances rose from 8.1 per cent to 11.4 per cent between 1851 and 1887. *The Compton Census*[32] of 1676 suggested that there were only 10 'Nonconformists' in Chelsea as distinct from 590 'Conformists'. The 1810 report suggested a far greater presence, and by 1887 Free Church attendances in Chelsea were almost rivalling Anglican attendances.

Nevertheless, behind this overall growth lay a by-now familiar pattern of Free Church decline among older denominations. Wesleyans declined most dramatically from 4 per cent of the total population to 1 per cent, whereas non-denominational congregations, the Salvation Army, and Disciples of Christ had already reached 4 per cent by the 1880s. The only surprising feature of Free Church growth and decline in Chelsea was the rapid increase of the Independents/Congregationalists.

---

[32] Anne Whiteman (ed.), *The Compton Census of 1676: A Critical Edition*, Records of Social and Economic History, New Series X, The British Academy, Oxford University Press, Oxford, 1986.

Quite against the trend for the rest of London, they increased attendances in Chelsea from 0.8 per cent to 3.5 per cent. As it happens, this was a short-lived growth. By 1903 they had already declined to 2 per cent.

The general Free Church pattern for London fits very closely the patterns already established from the other urban data. *Table 13* shows the familiar pattern of older denominations almost doubling the number of their chapels; but, with their attendances diminishing, these chapels were appreciably emptier in the 1880s than they were in 1851. Whereas then they were on average 54.3 per cent full, now they were 42.5 per cent full. Even those older denominations that slightly increased their attendances – notably the Baptists, Wesleyans and Primitive Methodists – had chapels that were appreciably emptier in the 1880s than they were earlier.

In contrast, the newer/smaller Free Church denominations increased attendances from 0.8 per cent to 3.1 per cent of the population, while their chapels remained about 45 per cent full. They also increased the sheer number of these chapels from 113 to 527. Free Church growth in London as a whole clearly depended upon this group, and particularly upon the non-denominational missions and chapels rather than upon the mainstream denominations. It was only in the next period that they too were to show signs of decline.

All of the London patterns are studied in greater depth in Chapter 7 with the finer detail offered by the Mudie-Smith census[33] of 1902–3. Catholic attendances especially were distorted in the 1887 census, since – as mentioned earlier – only one morning Mass was counted. The figure of 2.1 per cent for Catholic attendances in *Table 12* is thus little more than a guess. However, the more accurate figures of 2.3 per cent for 1851 and 2.1 per cent for 1903 make it perhaps not too unreasonable a guess. Less fanciful is the number of Catholic churches in London in the late 1880s. As elsewhere, London Catholics increased their church accommodation very cautiously, expanding from 36 churches in 1851 to 68 (and then to 100 in 1902). Some entire Districts remained with just a single Catholic church. In contrast, the Free Churches expanded from 592 chapels to 1344. With almost 8 per cent of the overall attendances across denominations in 1851, Catholics had less than 3 per cent of overall seating. By the 1880s their seating still represented only 3.5 per cent of overall seating.

Another pattern that emerges more clearly in Chapter 7 is the relative shifts of churchgoing that occurred between Districts in the second half of the nineteenth century. Apart from the City (which was distorted because so many non-residents commuted back to it on a Sunday), the District with the highest overall level of attendances in 1851 was Hampstead at 54 per cent. By 1887 Hampstead had declined slightly to 49 per cent and Lewisham had risen from 35 per cent to 47 per cent. The only other Districts with attendances exceeding 40 per cent were Wandsworth, which declined from 49 per cent to 41 per cent, and Hackney, which declined from 48 per cent to 40 per cent. In contrast, at the lowest end of churchgoing, three working-class Districts had levels of attendance under 20 per cent in both 1851 and 1887. Only two of these Districts remained at this level: Shoreditch declining slightly from 14 per cent to 13 per cent and Bethnal Green

---

33 Richard Mudie-Smith (ed.), *The Religious Life of London*, Hodder, London, 1904.

from 19 per cent to 16 per cent. However, Poplar rose slightly from just under 20 per cent to 23 per cent, while Southwark declined sharply from 28 per cent to 18 per cent.

All of this suggests a great deal of social as well as physical mobility in London at the time. Middle-class churchgoers were moving out to the new suburbs such as Lewisham, and areas such as Southwark, even when their populations did not decline, were becoming poorer and less attached to the local churches. Chapter 7 supplements these statistical observations with contemporary comments on the processes behind them. For the moment it is sufficient to notice that even the population of the metropolis was highly mobile and that many mainstream denominations, and especially the Church of England, had great difficulty in coping with this mobility.

The failure of the cumbersome Church of England to cope with this radical social change, compared with the striking success of the newer/smaller Free Church denominations, was evident both in London and elsewhere in urban England during this period. In the 1890s the Church of England was to show some signs of change. Yet it was too little and too late. Meanwhile, the structural problems in the Free Churches, poised just beneath the surface throughout this chapter, were to erupt with a vengeance. The 'success' of the urban Free Churches was at an end.

General Decline: 1880s to 1919

The deep structural problems affecting churches and chapels continued between the 1880s and the end of the First World War. It was their outcome in the Free Churches that changed. By 1919 it should have been obvious to all but the most partisan that the urban Free Churches were in radical decline. Yet even at the turn of the century, some commentators who should have known better saw declining attendances as a purely Anglican phenomenon.[1] However, by the First World War, Free Church as well as Anglican attendances had visibly declined, chapels had begun to close, and churches and chapels everywhere were typically less than a third full.

Even in the 1880s there were those in the Free Church who saw serious problems emerging. Despite some more triumphalist comments noted earlier, *The Nonconformist and Independent* wrote candidly in its review of the 1881 newspaper censuses:

> Stated at the worst we may assume for the time being that the provision for public worship in our large towns is not much more than would accommodate one-third of the population, and that a large proportion of that is, on the average, unused ... the separated worshippers are estimated at 29.5 per cent, so that the standard estimate of 58 per cent worshipping at one time, or 70 per cent during the whole Sunday, is becoming more and more ideal, and the greatest benefit which has arisen from the publication of these local statistics has been to reveal the naked truth ... Whatever the reasons – and they are manifold – the masses of the population remain outside our places of worship, and the public ministrations of religion are, to a great extent, regarded by the working people in our towns as a matter which concerns the classes that are higher in social position, but has no particular relation to them. The church is, indeed, open to them, but its services are wearisome. The chapel is also nominally free to all sections of society, but our artisans regard it to a great extent as a middle class institution.[2]

In this quotation, *The Nonconformist and Independent* was harking back to the 1851 Religious Census. It was Horace Mann's ideal[3] that 70 per cent of the population should attend churches and chapels at some point on a Sunday, and to allow this to happen he urged a local seating capacity in churches and chapels of 58 per cent. Measured by their own high ideals, even the overall churchgoing rates characteristic of the period from 1851 to the 1880s constituted 'failure' for some Victorians.

---

[1] e.g. Jane T. Stoddart, 'The Daily News Census of 1902–3 Compared with the British Weekly Census of 1886', in Richard Mudie-Smith (ed.), *The Religious Life of London*, Hodder, London, 1904.

[2] *The Nonconformist and Independent*, 2 February 1882, p. 106.

[3] See Horace Mann, *1851 Census Great Britain: Report and Tables on Religious Worship England and Wales*, British Parliamentary Papers, Population 10, 1852–3 (reprinted by Irish University Press, Shannon, 1970), p. cxxi.

Twenty years ago Jeffrey Cox ably pointed out how present-day historians have themselves tended to be misled by Victorians' idealism; the latter's idealism has been taken far too literally. As a consequence, historians, he argued, 'are addicted to the language of inevitable and irreversible decline, decay, and failure, and explain that historical change with references to an underlying "process" of secularization'. In effect modern historians have bought the Victorian dream of 'the conversion of an entire city or an entire social class or an entire nation, a goal which could be achieved only by force of arms'.[4]

However, for once there was more to the gloomy conclusions of *The Nonconformist and Independent* than misplaced idealism. The journal was already beginning to notice empty churches and chapels from the census data. And, even at this early date, there was mention of urban over-building. None of this deterred the journal from pressing for more building, especially in the new suburbs: 'New neighbourhoods spring up, and the religious wants of the new populations need to be met, although there may be a surplus provision at the other end of the town.'[5] Planting was still deemed essential, but not as yet pruning.

Once chapels began to close and Free Church numbers began to decline in absolute terms, pessimistic reports became more frequent. Cox noted a spate of such reports occurring soon after the Nonconformist triumphs at the 1906 General Election. He explained this 'eclipse' of Nonconformity largely in cultural terms. He was dissatisfied with the explanations that most other historians tend to adopt – namely, secularization, urbanization and industrialization – and argued rather that Nonconformity was, at least in part, a victim of its own success. The philanthropic work of chapels was increasingly adopted by secular agencies and former chapel members used their Nonconformist training in predominantly political and civil roles. A shifting age structure in the population at large (particularly affecting Sunday schools) and a pattern of generational revolt added to this 'eclipse'.

Such cultural explanations may work quite well for individuals. Cox demonstrated this from several autobiographies of those brought up in a Nonconformity that they later abandoned. Yet such explanations hardly explain why chapels themselves declined. It is unclear why philanthropy should have improved chapel attendances, and it is just as unclear why a transfer of philanthropy to secular agencies should have fostered their decline.

In the light of the evidence set out in Chapter 6 about chronic Free Church over-building and individual congregations becoming smaller and smaller, it is possible that Cox misunderstood the causal relation between philanthropy and attendances. Precisely because Free Church congregations were becoming thinner and thinner (even while their overall attendances were still remaining high or even increasing), they may have found the sheer labour of philanthropy increasingly burdensome. Rather than chapelgoing decline being a product of the decline of Free Church philanthropy, the latter may well have been an effect of overstretched congregations. And a decline in chapel-based philanthropy (even if it was quite as pronounced as Cox maintained) may or may not itself have had any effect upon chapelgoing rates.

---

[4] Jeffrey Cox, *The English Churches in a Secular Society: Lambeth, 1870–1930*, Oxford University Press, Oxford, 1982, p. 265.

[5] *The Nonconformist and Independent*, 2 February 1882, p. 106.

Charles Booth was thoroughly convinced that philanthropy among churches and chapels could actually be counter-productive. For example, writing in 1902 about St Mary's, Haggerston, Booth observed:

> In this parish charitable relief takes its accustomed place in relation to parochial visitation, but is very carefully administered, so that it can hardly be called bribery. It is only an attempt, whether wisely conceived or not, to help the poor in their pinched lives and mitigate the hardships of their lot; and differs in no material way from the efforts of the evangelical missions or the Nonconformist churches. It certainly seems to have no result even on church attendance.[6]

Nearby there was an evangelical Congregationalist mission engaged in similar acts of philanthropy. Booth noted somewhat caustically:

> It is dole versus dole, and treat versus treat, a contest openly admitted on both sides; while the people, taking the gifts with either hand, explain how careful they must be, when attending a service, that the other side knows nothing of it. This atrocious system, based on the delusive claim of each party to a monopoly of religious truth, is injurious to both, as well as to the recipients of their demoralizing bounties.[7]

Chapter 9 will also review evidence, this time in York, of competitive philanthropy apparently uncorrelated with increased churchgoing. Similarly, Wilfred Rowland, in his survey of Liverpool in 1908, maintained that, 'few things are more demoralising than indiscriminate dole-giving. It injures those who give and those who take.'[8]

Instead of following Cox, this chapter will again focus upon structural factors that he only partly observed. Here too there is a wealth of statistical evidence for this period providing a very detailed picture of urban churchgoing. It also strongly reinforces the patterns identified in Chapter 6.

The sources of this data will again include both Liverpool and London.[9] A major census in 1892 allows for the inclusion of Birmingham as well. Since there is also partial evidence for Birmingham in 1872 and 1887, some very useful comparative evidence is provided by this new source.[10] It will soon become clear that it confirms very closely the patterns established in the other sources.

---

[6] Charles Booth, *Life and Labour of the People in London: Third Series: Religious Influences*, vol. 2, Macmillan, 1902, p. 91.

[7] Booth, *Life and Labour*, vol. 2, p. 95.

[8] Wilfred J. Rowland, *The Free Churches and the People: A Report of the Work of the Free Churches in Liverpool*, London and Liverpool, 1908, p. 92.

[9] For Liverpool, see *The Liverpool Daily Post*, 15 November 1881, 24 November 1891, 11 November 1902, and 13 December 1912; for London, see *The Religious Census of London*, Hodder, 1888, and Mudie-Smith, *The Religious Life of London*.

[10] *The Birmingham Daily Times*, 31 May 1887; *The Birmingham News*, 3 December 1892; 10 December 1892; 17 December 1892 (which includes an account of 1872 seating); 24 December 1892 (on Sunday schools); also for the same four dates, *Harbourne and West Birmingham News*, *Aston and East Birmingham News*, and *Handsworth Herald and North Birmingham News*.

The group of large towns studied in this chapter is considerably smaller than those of the two previous chapters. Only a few newspapers replicated the censuses of the 1880s in the early 1900s. None the less, the ones produced did provide useful data – albeit data, because of variant procedures of collation, lacking some of the refinements of the large town data of Chapter 6. However, once amalgamated, they too confirm the broad patterns of churchgoing established elsewhere.

The eight towns in this group are:[11] Chester, Hull, Lincoln, Middlesbrough, Wallasey, Whitehaven, Workington, and York. Added together, they had a combined population by the turn of the century in excess of half a million.

1

In the decade 1881–91, overall churchgoing in Liverpool (for the moment, excluding Catholics) changed little – from 22.5 per cent to 22.4 per cent. Yet the balance, shown in *Table 7*, did change. For once it was Anglican attendances that increased slightly (from 9.8 per cent to 10.5 per cent) and Free Church attendances that declined (from 12.7 per cent to 11.9 per cent). This Anglican change was to be very short-lived; the Free Church change was to continue to the present day.

In all four *Liverpool Daily Post* censuses[12] between 1881 and 1912, it was only in 1891 that Anglicans proportionately increased their seating and attendances. Up to 1902 the sheer number of Anglican seats and attendances continued to rise, and it was only in 1912 that attendances dropped in absolute terms. But, uniquely in 1891, both increased faster than the growth rate of the borough population.

Essentially these were suburban increases. If the original 1821 churches are analysed on their own, then the pattern of central decline noted in Chapter 6 clearly continued unabated. Attendances in them dropped by almost 900 between 1881 and 1891 and churches that on average were 18.8 per cent full were now only 16.8 per cent full. In contrast, Anglican churches elsewhere in Liverpool increased in number and were on average slightly fuller (41.5 per cent full to 43.1 per cent).

By 1902 these central churches were experiencing acute problems. Four of them had been closed and the rest were on average just 15.8 per cent full. Total attendances at them were now little more than a quarter of those recorded in 1851. Each generation of churchgoers in these central churches would have accurately remembered larger congregations, but now these churches were predominantly empty. And, although the other Anglican churches were on average more than twice as full, they too by 1902 were not quite as full as they had been (declining from 43.1 per cent to 39.1 per cent).

---

[11] For Chester, see *The Cheshire Observer*, 31 October 1903; *The Hull News*, 13 December 1903 to 17 February 1904 (I am most grateful to the Revd D. Stubley for finding this survey); for Lincoln, see *The Lincoln, Rutland and Stanford Mercury*, 31 January 1873, and *The Leader and County Advertiser*, 14 March 1903; for Middlesbrough, see *The Northern Daily Gazette*, 16 July 1904; *The Wallasey News*, 30 May 1903; for Whitehaven and Workington, see *The West Cumberland Times*, 20 December 1902; for York, see R. Seebohm Rowntree, *Poverty: A Study of Town Life*, Macmillan, 1901, pp. 345–9.

[12] 15 November 1881, 24 November 1891, 11 November 1902, and 13 December 1912.

Folk wisdom doubtless suggests that before the First World War churches and chapels were basically full. The 1912 Liverpool census suggests otherwise. On average, Anglican churches and Free Church chapels alike were by then less than a third full. With the minor exception of the Anglican rise in suburban attendances in 1891, churches and chapels had relentlessly become emptier from census to census between 1851 and 1912. Because this census evidence is so detailed and so consistent, it is extraordinarily valuable for any attempt to understand the phenomenon of the empty church.

Free Church seating continued to rise until 1891, but attendances reached a peak in 1881. In the newer/smaller denominations attendances held steady at 2.2 per cent between 1881 and 1891 and declined thereafter. The older/larger denominations in this same period saw a decline in attendances from 10.6 per cent to 9.7 per cent, and older/larger chapels became relentlessly emptier with every census after 1851. Only the smaller denominations remained volatile: sometimes building vigorously and maintaining or increasing attendances; sometimes declining proportionately in both seating and attendances. Furthermore, at every stage after 1851, their chapels were on average always fuller than those of the older/larger denominations.

Yet even in this more volatile, newer group problems were beginning to emerge. The Salvation Army expanded seating and attendances up to 1891, but declined relentlessly thereafter. Their services, which on average had been more than half full in 1881, by the next decade were less than a third full, and by 1912 were barely a fifth full. The Liverpool City Mission were by 1891 stronger in attendances and seating than the Salvation Army, and their services were more than 70 per cent full. Yet they too declined from that point onwards. By 1912 it was only the non-denominational chapels that still seemed capable of expanding.

Among the older Free Churches the picture was bleaker still. The continuous decline of the Independents from 1821 has been noted in previous chapters. From 1881 only the non-Wesleyan Methodists (excluding the Primitive Methodists) between 1881 and 1891, and the Wesleyans between 1891 and 1902, experienced a decade of increased attendances and of seating and chapels that were on average fuller. Baptists experienced uneven rises in the decade following 1891, but others experienced only decline. The predominant pattern was decline.

The Primitive Methodists in Liverpool clearly demonstrate these structural problems. Of all the Free Churches in the mid-nineteenth century, they had a particular reputation for being able to reach the urban working classes. Fiercely self-sufficient, they expanded where they could, in both urban and rural areas. In Liverpool they had almost doubled their presence proportionately between 1851 and 1881 and doubled their attendances from 0.25 per cent to 0.51 per cent. At the same time, their chapels were decidedly fuller (34.7 per cent full to 43.4 per cent). In the next decade their attendances declined faster than their seating, and by 1912 their attendances had returned to the same level they had been in 1851, whereas their seating declined very little. As a result, their chapels were now on average little more than a quarter full.

Indeed, predominantly empty chapels abounded in Liverpool by 1912. Congregationalists, Baptists and Primitive Methodists had chapels that were three-quarters empty. Chapels belonging to the Salvation Army, Bethel, and the Free Gospel movement were even emptier. Among older denominations, Wesleyan chapels were fullest, yet even they were almost two-thirds empty. And among others, it was only the Liverpool City Mission that was on average more than half full. Most chapels in Liverpool must have been visibly empty by the First World War.

This bleak picture of the Liverpool Free Churches, shortly before the First World War, is confirmed in a remarkable way by Wilfred Rowland's survey of 1908. He was commissioned to produce it by the Liverpool Free Church Council. The results of a self-return census of the Free Churches given in the report, made on a fine day in mid-June 1908, suggested an overall attendance rate in the city (with allowance for Unitarians who were excluded) of 9.1 per cent of the population. This fits closely with the pattern of Free Church attendances in the *Liverpool Daily Post* censuses shown in *Table 7* – namely, 10.8 per cent in 1902 and 8.7 per cent in 1912.

Rowland noted that chapels were already becoming ominously empty. From an independently enumerated census that he organized for Everton, he compared the fortunes of seventeen chapels between 1881 and 1908. Everton was specifically chosen because it was a working-class district that, unlike districts closer to the river, did not have a dominant Catholic population. What Rowland discovered was that, whereas some 40 per cent of the seats of these chapels were occupied at the morning service in 1881 and 58 per cent in the evening, by 1908 only 13 per cent were occupied in the morning and 28 per cent in the evening. Put another way, whereas in 1881 the average congregation in the morning was 274 and in the evening 392, by 1908 it had reduced to 85 in the morning and 190 in the evening.

Once again, decline must have been obvious to the chapels involved. Indeed, using a longer time scale than was possible for Rowland, the congregations of two of the largest chapels in Everton would surely have been only too aware of decline. In 1851 the morning congregation of Crescent Congregational Chapel was 574, but in 1912 it was 88. That in Great Homer Street Wesleyan Chapel was 700 in 1851, but just 85 in 1912. Taken together, their morning services were 61 per cent full in 1851, but only 8 per cent full in 1912. Even attendances at their evening services had declined almost threefold: from being 60 per cent full in 1851, they were just 21 per cent full in 1912.

Unlike the neighbouring working-class (and highly Catholic) districts of Scotland, Exchange and Abercromby, the population of Everton was still growing between 1881 and 1908 (from 108 812 to 123 952). In the same period, the number of chapels (not including mission halls) in Everton also increased from seventeen to twenty-two. But overall attendances at them almost halved, declining from 10.3 per cent of the population to 5.5 per cent. Rowland concluded that, 'the broad facts show that there has been a steady decline in church attendance since 1881, and this has coincided with the exodus of the middle class'.[13] He also noted that, of those who still went to chapel, about a third arrived late for the services: 'plenty of excuses may no doubt be found, but when all allowances are made there must remain many cases of sheer slackness'.[14] In short, he was not impressed by what he observed!

---

[13] Rowland, *The Free Churches and the People*, p. 21.
[14] Rowland, *The Free Churches and the People*, p. 20.

Rowland was already beginning to notice some of the physical factors associated with chapelgoing decline, arguing that there was a need for a joint advisory board serving the local Free Churches:

> [A board] would watch the rapid growth of new house property and note the needs of the population for places of worship. It would also seek to prevent over-lapping and thus competition between several struggling causes ... It is very depressing to ministers and office bearers to see a building sparsely attended week by week, and it is feared that sometimes a whole congregation may get into the grip of Giant Despair.[15]

There was also a recognition in Rowland's report of economic factors associated with chapelgoing decline:

> Often the diminution of a congregation is due to financial difficulties. The neighbourhood may become too poor to sustain the cause, and people are afraid to attend a church where there are constant appeals for money to which they feel themselves unable to respond ... The struggling Church proves a great tax upon poor members.[16]

Thus, six years before the outbreak of the First World War, there was already recognition that chapels in Liverpool were more empty than full, that there were physical factors associated with this situation, and that, if unchecked, this had worrying consequences for future chapelgoing. Just as Arthur Black (who wrote the foreword to this report) was to maintain twenty years later,[17] Rowland already held that:

> It ought to be possible for each denomination to review the position of all its churches which have diminishing numbers. There may be instances in which the neighbourhood is obviously overchurched where all the adherents come from a distance and where other churches continue to serve the neighbourhood.[18]

Without doubt, then, overall attendances in both the Church of England and the Free Churches in Liverpool showed clear signs of decline before the outbreak of the First World War. If, in 1851, their attendances together amounted to 26 per cent of the total population, by 1912 they represented only 16.4 per cent. In fact, the sheer number of Anglican attendances was little different in 1912 than it had been in 1851, despite a borough population that had all but doubled. Perhaps most dramatic of all, the Free Churches between 1902 and 1912 had lost more than 11 000 attendances.

The difficulties of assessing Catholic attendances in Liverpool were rehearsed in Chapter 6. Newspapers had a persistent habit of counting a single morning Mass when there were actually several. If Anglican early morning communicants were ignored, this perhaps mattered less. Where they were counted in this period, they

---

[15] Rowland, *The Free Churches and the People*, p. 29.

[16] Rowland, *The Free Churches and the People*, p. 30

[17] Arthur Black, 'London Church and Mission Attendances', *The British Weekly*, 23 February 1928, 1 March 1928, and 8 March 1928.

[18] Rowland, *The Free Churches and the People*, p. 32.

seldom added significantly to attendances,[19] and early communicants may well have also attended matins or evensong later in the day. But among Catholics, double attendance on a Sunday was not the norm and multiple Masses, where counted, did make a significant difference to attendances.

However, between 1881 and 1912 the Catholic authorities in Liverpool made their own counts of attendances.[20] In the 1851 Religious Census morning and evening Mass attendances amounted to 13.9 per cent of the population. Newspaper returns for a single morning Mass, together with evening Mass, amounted to 4.3 per cent in 1881, 3.8 per cent in 1891, 5.0 per cent in 1902, and 5.4 per cent in 1912. In contrast, the estimates supplied by the Catholic authorities, which took account of all Masses averaged over four consecutive Sundays, suggested a rather different and much increased pattern of attendances. They amounted to 10.4 per cent in 1881, 9.5 per cent in 1891, 9.0 per cent in 1902, and 10.2 per cent in 1912. The latter do suggest a Catholic decline in Liverpool from 1851, especially if the 1851 Index of 15.3 per cent is used (as well it might be for Catholics) – albeit with an increase in the last decade. Yet it was a decline considerably less than that experienced by the Church of England or the Free Churches. Instructively, it was also a decline carefully monitored by the Catholic authorities themselves.

If the figures of 13.9 per cent for 1851 and 10.2 per cent for 1912 are taken, then a series of comparisons can be made. Attendances across denominations declined from 39.9 per cent in 1851 to 26.6 per cent in 1912. However, the relative strengths of the denominations had totally changed. In 1851 Anglicans had 38 per cent of morning and evening attendances, Catholics 35 per cent and the Free Churches 27 per cent. By 1912 it was Catholics who now had the most attendances. They had 38 per cent, the Free Churches had 33 per cent, and Anglicans 29 per cent. Chapter 8 shows that this Catholic dominance in Liverpool continued (and increased very considerably) throughout the twentieth century.

Catholics, of course, were not immune from the effects of demographic factors. As early as 1891, *The Catholic Times* recognized that, 'it is well known that there has been a considerable migration during the past ten years amongst the Catholic working classes in Liverpool, numbers having left the centre of the city and moved northwards along the line of the docks, so that they might be nearer to their work'.[21] Yet, with their far greater control over church buildings than other denominations, such shifts of population may not perhaps have been so damaging.

The Catholic Times also foresaw difficulties, to be raised again a century later,[22] with the largely immigrant status of Liverpool Catholics: 'whilst the poor Catholics who came over from Ireland, with their strong faith, in a strange land, and

---

[19] e.g. Early Communion services for Southwark, Camberwell, St Marylebone, Lewisham, Hackney, Bethnal Green, Kensington and Stepney were all counted in 1902 or 1903 in Mudie-Smith, *The Religious Life of London*. They were highest in Kensington at 1.3 per cent of the population and lowest in Bethnal Green at 0.2 per cent.

[20] For 1881 and 1891 Catholic Mass attendances, see *The Catholic Times*, 30 October 1891; for 1902 and 1912, see *The Liverpool Daily Post*, 13 December 1912.

[21] *The Catholic Times*, 30 October 1891.

[22] Cf. Michael P. Hornsby-Smith, *Roman Catholics in England*, Cambridge University Press, Cambridge, 1987.

surrounded by poverty, made heroic efforts to hear Mass, many of their children who are in better circumstances and better educated do not attend Mass in the same way'.[23] For the moment, at least, these problems appeared not to be too acute. By 1912 *The Liverpool Daily Post* was praising Catholics, at the expense of other denominations, for their 'activity and faithfulness'.[24] Catholics alone had increased their church attendances in the city over the previous decade. Furthermore, if one uses Rowland's estimate of the Catholic population of Liverpool being about a quarter of the total population, then on the census day in 1912 some two-fifths of all Catholics would have been at Mass. In contrast, total Anglican and Free Church attendances represented little more than one-fifth of the remaining population (and separate attenders presumably less). So, even at this stage, Catholics in Liverpool were at least twice as assiduous as others in attending church.

2

The Birmingham census of 1892 for once included afternoon services and Sunday schools. As a result, very full comparisons (represented in *Table 15*) can be made with the 1851 census. To make the data still more comparable, the 1892 measurements that follow (unless stated otherwise) are for the same wards as for 1851 – that is, they ignore wards added later to the city. On this basis, the population of these wards in 1892 was almost 50 per cent greater than that in 1851.

In overall terms, the Birmingham Index increased whereas church attendances decreased. The Index increased from 35 per cent to 45 per cent, whereas morning and evening attendances declined from 27.6 per cent to 24.2 per cent. This seeming paradox was caused mainly by a very considerable increase in Sunday school attendances, alongside a familiar pattern of churchgoing decline.

Birmingham's morning and evening church attendances in the Church of England and Free Churches mirrored very closely the data from Liverpool. In Birmingham (1851–92) they declined from 24.8 per cent to 22.4 per cent; in Liverpool (1851–91) they declined from 26 per cent to 22.4 per cent. Even their seating was very similar. In Birmingham it increased from 26.8 per cent to 29.9 per cent; in Liverpool it increased from 28.5 per cent to 30.3 per cent. These similarities are all the more remarkable when it is remembered that Liverpool was such a Catholic city, whereas Birmingham had a reputation[25] at the time of being a Free Church city.

Sunday school attendances increased very considerably in Birmingham during the nineteenth century. By 1840[26] they represented just 2.3 per cent of the total population, but by 1851 they had almost doubled to 5.3 per cent, and by 1892 they had increased more than fivefold to 12.3 per cent. Represented as proportions of the estimated population under fifteen years, in 1840 some 7 per cent of the young

23 *The Catholic Times*, 30 October 1891.

24 *The Liverpool Daily Post*, 13 December 1912.

25 See *The Nonconformist and Independent*, 2 February 1882, p. 105.

26 'Report of the Birmingham Statistical Society on the State of Education in Birmingham', *Journal of the Statistical Society*, London, vol. 3, April 1840, p. 39.

people of Birmingham attended Sunday school, by 1851 this had risen to 15 per cent, and by 1892 to 35 per cent. Of course these figures are somewhat crude, since they include both those too young for Sunday school, as well as any fifteen-year-olds who still went to Sunday school.

The Birmingham News in 1892[27] attempted a more complicated calculation for the whole city (including the new suburbs), and concluded that, from an eligible population aged 5–14, some 63.2 per cent were enrolled in the various Sunday schools. Attendances at Sunday schools in Birmingham represented a very high 83 per cent of enrolments at the time. So, on this basis, slightly more than half of the city's children actually attended Sunday school on the census day itself.

Furthermore, since total church attendances in the morning and evening – which of course included those attending twice – amounted to less than a quarter of the population, there was clearly a considerable disparity already evident in Birmingham between congregations and Sunday schools. Even the fact that these are measured rather unevenly – on the congregation side by the total population and on the Sunday school side by the child population – does not remove this disparity. The London figures, to be discussed in a moment, show that children, quite apart from their presence in Sunday schools, also represented about a third of typical church congregations (approximately their proportion in the total population).

These Sunday school attendances and enrolments also allow comparisons to be made across denominations in Birmingham. In 1840 some 27 per cent enrolments were in the Church of England, 71 per cent in the Free Churches, and 2 per cent were Catholics. Wesleyan Methodists were the largest Free Church group, with almost a third of their enrolments. By 1851 the Church of England and the Free Churches had about 45 per cent of Sunday school attendances each and the Catholics had 10 per cent. By 1892 the Church of England had 39 per cent of the attendances, the Free Churches 58 per cent, and the Catholics were estimated at 4 per cent. In terms of enrolments, the Wesleyans were no longer the largest Free Church group. With a fifth of Free Church enrolments, they were now slightly behind the Baptists and Congregationalists. All in all this suggests considerable volatility.

This volatility also characterized the overall behaviour of the churches and chapels in Birmingham. With very few exceptions, the patterns already established elsewhere can be found here. By 1892 both the Church of England and the older Free Churches were clearly in decline. Only the newer/smaller denominations were still showing signs of growth.

The Church of England here differed in only one respect from other sources. Anglican seating in Birmingham grew from a low 12.6 per cent in 1851, to 13.8 per cent in 1872, and to a more characteristic urban level of 14.1 per cent in 1892. However, attendances still declined from 12.4 per cent in 1851 to 10.9 per cent in 1892. And churches, which were on average 50.7 per cent full at the earlier date, were now just 40.5 per cent full. The sharpest decline in attendances was again at the morning services, although evening services had already started to decline as well.

---

[27] *The Birmingham News*, 24 December 1892.

In addition, once again it was the older 1851 Anglican churches that showed the most critical levels of congregational decline. Morning congregations at these twenty-two churches can be measured in 1851, 1887 and 1892. From *Table 15* it can be seen that, at each stage, they showed clear numerical decline – losing, in all, almost 6000 attendances between them. And even the evening services had lost almost 2000 attenders over the whole period. St Bartholomew's showed the steepest decline. In 1851 it had congregations of 800 and 850; by 1892 its congregations were just 60 and 92. Even the celebrated St Martin in the centre of Birmingham, which once could muster huge congregations morning and evening, could do so now only in the evening.

The Free Churches characteristically increased their overall seating from 14.2 per cent in 1851 to 16.1 per cent in 1872. However, by 1892 their seating had declined slightly to 15.8 per cent, and their overall attendances had also declined to 11.5 per cent (from 12.4 per cent in 1851). These declines were confined entirely to the older denominations. It was their seating which declined from 12.7 per cent in 1871 to 10.8 per cent in 1892 and it was their attendances that declined from 9.6 per cent in 1851 to 8.3 per cent in 1892.

In contrast, the newer/smaller denominations increased attendances from 2.9 per cent in 1851 to 3.3 per cent in 1892 and seating from 3.6 per cent to 4.9 per cent. Here too it was the chapels of the older/larger denominations that changed most radically. In 1851 they were on average 46.5 per cent full, whereas in 1892 they were 40.5 per cent full. Nevertheless, as in Liverpool in the 1890s, the smaller group was also beginning to show slight signs of emptier chapels.

Among the older Free Churches, only the Wesleyans had chapels that were on average half full by 1892. The Congregationalists remained almost half full, but their attendances had declined and the typical size of their congregations had also declined by more than eighty. All other older/larger denominations showed a three-way pattern of decline: in their attendance rates, in the sheer size of their congregations, and in how full their chapels were. They were now on average almost two-thirds empty.

Catholics were not very strong in Birmingham in the nineteenth century. Today, in contrast, they have the largest number of churchgoers. Between 1851 and 1892 they declined from 2.8 per cent to 1.7 per cent (both censuses counted more than a single morning Mass). None the less, their churches typically remained better attended than any other denomination. In 1851 their four churches each had on average 1617 attendances. Even in 1892 the, by now six, Catholic churches serving Birmingham still had congregations of 1013. No other denomination built so cautiously.

In comparison, Anglican average attendances per church, which in 1851 had themselves been 1259, were just 532 by 1892. And chapel attendances were down from 475 to 333. As today, Catholic congregations were visibly different from those of any other denomination. Not for them the empty church.

In his studies of social class and churchgoing, Hugh McLeod[28] noticed huge disparities of attendance in 1892 between working-class and middle-class wards in

---

[28] Hugh McLeod, 'Class, Community and Region: The Religious Geography of Nineteenth-century England', in Michael Hill (ed.), *A Sociological Yearbook of Religion in Britain*, vol. 6, SCM Press, London, 1973; see also McLeod's *Class and Religion in the Late Victorian City*, Croom Helm, London, 1974, and *Religion and the People of Western Europe 1789–1970*, Oxford University Press, Oxford, 1981.

Birmingham. These matched very similar disparities to be found in other conurbations in the 1880s, such as London and Liverpool. In Birmingham (and indeed London) these disparities were already evident in 1851. Churchgoing was polarized at both stages, yet there were also distinct shifts, and as the middle classes progressively moved out to the suburbs so urban social segregation increased. Overall attendances at Ladywood increased between the two dates (from 26 per cent to 30 per cent), as did those at St Thomas (21 per cent to 31 per cent), Deritend (37 per cent to 40 per cent) and Duddeston (15 per cent to 21 per cent). But some of the inner-city areas showed clear signs of decline: St Martin decreased (from 31 per cent to 26 per cent), as did All Saints (16 per cent to 12 per cent). And by 1892, some of the now separate working-class wards had exceptionally low attendance rates: notably, St Stephen (13 per cent) and St Bartholomew (10 per cent); lowest of all was Saltley (9.5 per cent).

Nevertheless, some very high levels of churchgoing persisted in Birmingham. In 1851 St Philip had attendances of 63 per cent and St Peter of 52 per cent. By 1892, the comparable ward of Market Hall had a remarkably high level of 66 per cent. And in the new suburbs in 1892, Moseley and Kings Heath had attendances of 41 per cent. Significantly, on average the new suburbs had a higher attendance rate than the old city. As already seen, the overall attendance rate in the latter in 1892 was 24.2 per cent. However, in the suburbs it was 27.9 per cent. More striking still, churches and chapels in the suburbs were on average 60.3 per cent full. In sharp contrast to the old Anglican churches at the centre of Birmingham, evening services across denominations in the suburbs were three-quarters full.

From all of this it is clear that churchgoing was shifting in Birmingham in the second half of the nineteenth century. While it remained very high in some middle-class parts of the city, it was declining steeply in some of the old inner-city areas. It was also shifting to the new suburbs. There were still some very real contrasts to be found in the urban areas surrounding the old city, but average attendance rates in the suburbs were higher. Suburbanization, with pockets of central strength, was already affecting the churches in Birmingham.

3

Uneven rates of attendance also affected the eight large towns. *Table 16* shows an overall rate of decline that is by now very familiar. Reports on seating became more haphazard by the turn of the century, so the overall information that can be gleaned from these towns is more limited than usual. Nevertheless, attendances between 1851 and the early 1900s showed familiar patterns of decline. Yet within these patterns there are some surprises.

Anglican attendances at 17.9 per cent of the population were clearly higher in the eight towns in 1851 than those of the twenty-eight towns studied in Chapter 6. Free Church attendances were also slightly higher, but Catholic attendances were very similar. Within the Free Churches, the attendance rates of the Congregationalists, Presbyterians and isolated congregations were similar in the two sources. Wesleyans and non-Welseyan Methodists were higher in the eight towns and Baptists in the twenty-eight towns.

In both sources, Anglican attendances declined. In the earlier and larger source they declined from 13.8 per cent to 12.7 per cent (or, as noted in Chapter 6, somewhat more sharply if Sheffield is excluded). In the later source they declined from 17.9 per cent to 9.5 per cent. So if these eight towns started in 1851 at a higher level of attendance than Liverpool, London or the twenty-eight towns, by the early 1900s their attendance rate was remarkably close to the 9.6 per cent of both London and Liverpool.

Yet even within these overall similarities there were some surprising differences. As in pockets of Birmingham and London, there were some instances of resilient attendances. For example, in Lincoln and Chester, with their abundance of ancient churches, Anglican attendances actually rose between 1851 and the early 1900s. While Free Church attendances held fairly steady in both places, Anglican attendances in Lincoln rose from 14.2 per cent (or 17.6 per cent if afternoon attendances are counted in churches that still had no evening service) in 1851, to 16.8 per cent in 1873, and then to an adult attendance of 21.9 per cent in 1903; in Chester they rose from an estimated[29] 16.2 per cent in 1851 to 21.7 per cent in 1903.

Free Church attendances in the town sources contrasted very strikingly. In the earlier source they held steady between 1851 and 1881: at 20.6 per cent and 20.4 per cent respectively. In the later source they declined radically between 1851 and the 1900s: from 23.0 per cent to 14.2 per cent. Thus, starting in 1851 at more than twice the Free Church rate of London and Liverpool, by the 1900s they had declined to a position not far from the 10.8 per cent of Liverpool and the 10.7 per cent of London.

The collapse of Free Church attendances had been particularly dramatic in traditionally Nonconformist towns such as Middlesbrough and Hull. Free Church attendances in Middlesbrough in 1851 represented a dominant 26.7 per cent, in contrast to Anglican attendances of 8.0 per cent and Catholic attendances of 4.2 per cent. By 1903 Free Church attendances at 12.6 per cent had more than halved, Anglican attendances had declined to 5.8 per cent and Catholics had increased to 4.9 per cent. Soon Catholics would predominate.

In Hull it is possible to plot the Free Church decline in finer detail.[30] In 1834 Free Church 'hearers' were 25.8 per cent of the population (Anglicans 13.8 per cent); by 1851 attendances were 28.1 per cent; and by 1881 they were 30.8 per cent (Anglicans 8.9 per cent). However, between 1881 and 1904 they collapsed, declining to just 12.5 per cent (Anglicans 6.4 per cent). So, despite Hull having almost two-and-a-half times the Free Church rate of London and Liverpool in the 1880s, two decades later all three were remarkably similar.

Elsewhere, there were persisting pockets of stronger Free Church attendances in the early 1900s. Lincoln (27.4 per cent) was still outstanding (in 1873 it was 28.5 per cent), and Wallasey (17.1 per cent) and Chester (17.0 per cent) remained

---

[29] Half of the original returns for Chester are now lost. However, the ones remaining allow a basis for estimating the Sunday school component of the figures published in the Religious Census Report.

[30] For Hull statistics for 1834, see *The Victorian History of the Counties of England: Yorkshire East Riding*, vol. 1, Oxford University Press, Oxford, 1969, p. 315; for 1881, see *The Hull News*, 10 December 1881.

high. But they were becoming more difficult to find. As in the large conurbations, the dominant pattern was one of radical decline.

This pattern of decline was again particularly evident among the older Free Churches. In the later source it was once more the Congregationalists who experienced the most severe decline in attendances – declining by three-fifths between 1851 and the early 1900s. Non-Wesleyan Methodists halved their attendance rate, and Wesleyans declined by a third. In both sources it was only the small (and, following the disruption in Scotland, still volatile) presence of Presbyterians that was apparently growing.

In contrast, as elsewhere, it was the newer/smaller denominations that differed. However, the Salvation Army presence was very much smaller in these later towns than it had been in the earlier towns, and the isolated congregations without them were apparently declining. As in Liverpool and London, growth within this group as a whole would seem already to be at an end.

Evidence for Whitehaven and Workington is also contained in *Table 1* and this makes possible a number of interesting urban/rural contrasts. It should be noted again that the weather on the census day in 1902 was particularly bad in Cumbria and this might have suppressed attendances. This may have somewhat affected diachronic comparisons, but presumably not synchronic denominational comparisons. The latter reveal some important changes.

Perhaps the most important change was in the relative balances of urban and rural Anglican churchgoing. In 1821 the Anglican attendance rate[31] in the large towns (i.e. Whitehaven and Workington) was slightly higher than that in the small towns, although not as high as that in the rural parishes. By 1851 it was higher in the large towns than in both of the other areas. Indeed, including the Free Churches and the Catholics, the overall attendance rate in the large towns was 44.8 per cent, compared with a rural rate of 27.6 per cent. In 1902 the overall rate of the large towns was still much higher than the rural parishes (22 per cent compared with 15.2 per cent), but the specifically Anglican rate was less than half (5.8 per cent compared with 13.2 per cent). Today, as Douglas Davies, Charles Watkins and Michael Winter have established more widely,[32] urban Anglican attendances remain less than half the purely rural ones (2.3 per cent compared with 5.7 per cent).

In the two large towns, the only denomination consistently to increase attendances was the Catholic Church. It is not difficult to see how Catholics would eventually have the highest attendances in the whole of Cumbria. Anglicans apparently increased, as elsewhere, between 1821 and 1851, but decreased thereafter. Measured by attendances, Whitehaven had already become a Free Church town by 1881. By 1902 both Workington and Whitehaven were unambiguously Free Church towns, but they were already struggling (especially on a wet day) with chapels that were four-fifths empty and Anglican churches that

---

[31] Calculated from *Clergy Visitation Returns, Diocese of Chester*, Cheshire Record Office, Chester (ms. ERV 716), and *The Whitehaven Free Press*, December 1881 (also reported in *The West Cumberland Times*, 20 December 1902).

[32] Douglas Davies, Charles Watkins and Michael Winter, *Church and Religion in Rural England*, T. & T. Clark, Edinburgh, 1991.

were even emptier. In the rural areas (even allowing for the wet day!) more than nine out of ten seats in churches and chapels were empty. But by that time, as elsewhere in rural Britain, they already had more rural seats than they had rural population. Catholics alone (despite the wet day!!) had full churches.

Another way of measuring the comparative Anglican decline in the large towns is through Easter communicants.[33] In Chapter 1 I argued (against *Churches and Churchgoers*) that these should not be used as the primary means of assessing diachronic decline. There have been too many diachronic variations in popular attitudes towards Easter Communion. However, used synchronically they tell a much more interesting story.

In 1861 there was a difference between the overall rate of Easter communicants in rural areas and in the large towns, but it was not huge (10.9 per cent and 7 per cent respectively). What was much greater was the disparity between communicants and general churchgoers. In the countryside communicants represented almost two-thirds of general attendances. In the large towns they represented little more than a quarter.

By 1900 the overall rate of communicants had already widened very considerably between the countryside and large towns (to 10.7 per cent and 3 per cent), and by 1989 it had widened still further (to 15.4 per cent and 3 per cent). The ratios of communicants to attendances also remained distinct. In 1900 Easter communicants represented four-fifths of attendances in the countryside, and only about half in the large towns. In 1989 Easter communicants were more numerous than adult churchgoers in both the countryside and the large towns. Yet whereas there was a ratio of more than three-to-one in the countryside, it was one-and-a-half-to-one in the towns. In comparison, Sunday school rates were, until recently, much closer in the countryside and large towns: 8.8 per cent and 7.5 per cent in 1861; 8.7 per cent and 5.6 per cent in 1900; and 6.9 per cent and 2.5 per cent in 1989.

Once again this evidence suggests that generalizations about the inevitable affects of urbanization upon churchgoing should be treated with some caution. There are differences between rural and urban churchgoing – especially in Easter communication – but they are by no means static differences. Over time they have changed very considerably. And in this Cumbrian sample at least, churches and chapels in both rural and urban areas were evidently experiencing acute problems by the end of the nineteenth century.

Furthermore, both rural and urban areas were experiencing these problems despite their quite different clergy-to-laity ratios. In 1821 incumbents in the large towns had sixteen times as many parishioners as rural incumbents. By 1851, with new parishes formed in the towns, the ratio had been reduced to ten-to-one. However, by 1901, urbanization and rural depopulation had widened the ratio again to nineteen-to-one. This was a problem that affected the Church of England nationally (and indeed continues: the ratio in this area was still eight-to-one in 1990). The *Population Census 1901* shows that more than half of the ecclesiastical parishes in England and Wales (58 per cent) had populations of less than a thousand people.

---

[33] Calculated from *Clergy Visitation Returns, Diocese of Carlisle*, Rose Castle, Carlisle, and *Carlisle Diocesan Returns*.

This Cumbrian evidence does not suggest that such a striking imbalance ever had a commensurate benefit on rural churchgoing. At the height of the imbalance, not one of the rural incumbents reported their level of communicants as 'satisfactory'.[34] But then for them especially, occasional seasonal conformity (which still characterizes this area) was never a satisfactory substitute for Sunday by Sunday congregations. On any reckoning, the latter were already ominously thin – in the countryside as well as in the towns.

4

The very detailed *Daily News* census of London attendances in 1902–3, and a survey of church buildings[35] in 1914, add flesh to the urban side of these problems. As elsewhere, between 1851 and the early 1900s Anglican attendances consistently declined, whereas Free Church attendances rose until the 1880s and then declined. Churches and chapels were always emptier, whether attendances were declining or increasing. However, what becomes evident from the London data is that, even though Anglican churches were more than two-thirds empty in the early 1900s, the sheer number of them was still increasing in 1914. In contrast, Free Church chapels by 1914 were already beginning to close. Again, as elsewhere, only Catholics consistently had churches that were on average more full than empty. By the early 1900s most other denominations, small or large, had churches or chapels that were typically some two-thirds empty. However, more of the central churches in London appeared emptier than those in other urban areas. And by the early 1900s, as in Liverpool, even recently successful groups such as the Salvation Army were declining fast.

As in Chapter 6, Chelsea provides a microcosm of these changes. Only in Chelsea did the *Daily News* census make a careful count of attendances throughout the day, as well as at Sunday schools. Represented in *Table 14*, they show that, in contrast to Birmingham a decade earlier, the Index declined from 43.3 per cent on Mothering Sunday 1851 to just 34.7 per cent on a Sunday in mid-May 1903 (albeit a wet one). A slight rise in Sunday school attendances (from 5.4 per cent to 6 per cent) was outweighed by the sharp decline in church attendances. Morning and evening attendances in the Church of England had declined from 19 per cent to 11.7 per cent, and in the Free Churches, having risen from 8.1 per cent in 1851 to 11.4 per cent in 1887, they then declined to 7.7 per cent in 1903. Furthermore, the pattern of the oldest Anglican churches declining fastest was apparent in Chelsea as elsewhere. Between 1851 and 1883 attendances in these churches almost halved (as pointed out earlier, the self-return here for 1883 was significantly lower than the independent enumeration of 1887).

In *Table 14* the general decline of churches and chapels can be seen by dividing them into gains and losses. Only one church (the Catholic Apostolic) made gains in attendance, albeit modest ones, across all three censuses. Eight churches made some

---

[34] *Clergy Visitation Returns, Diocese of Carlisle*, 1900.
[35] H. Wilson Harris and Margaret Bryant, *The Churches and London*, carried out by *The Daily News and Leader*, London, 1914.

gains and most of them some losses as well. However, fourteen churches made only losses. In addition, among the older Free Churches, it was for once the Congregationalists who made the only gains in attendance between 1851 and 1887, and the Baptists between 1887 and 1903. The Wesleyans made continuous sharp losses throughout. And among the newer/smaller groups, a denomination that entered in one census had typically declined by the next. Furthermore, every census saw new groups entering the District. Diffusion and innovation were both well in evidence.

Yet more flesh is given to these patterns by the extraordinary coincidence that Charles Booth's *Life and Labour of the People in London* was completed in 1902. This immense survey of poverty reached its climax with a detailed account, in its final seven volumes, of religious institutions in London. Here is a first-hand account of churches and chapels at precisely the moment when churchgoing decline was at last becoming obvious; and it is an account, for once, not supplied by clergy writing to their superiors. It is also an account that has seldom been matched with the other statistical data for London.[36]

Anglican attendances in London, as can be seen from *Table 12* and *Table 13*, had declined from 15.6 per cent to 9.6 per cent between 1851 and 1903. Over the same period mainstream Free Church attendances had declined from 10.5 per cent to 7.7 per cent. Average attendances per Anglican church had almost halved, declining from 804 to 424. In the Free Churches, taken as a whole, average attendances per chapel had declined from 450 to 317. After half a century of energetic church and chapel building to meet the needs of a fast expanding population, places of worship abounded. However, their congregations, serving ever smaller local populations, were little more than half the size.

Only Sunday schools showed increases. In 1851 Anglican attendances in London represented 2.8 per cent of the population (and Sunday school attendances in all denominations 4.9 per cent). By 1890 enrolments at Anglican Sunday school[37] in London represented 4.5 per cent; by 1901 they had reached 6 per cent, but by 1910 they had already declined to 5.5 per cent. *Table 6* shows that national Sunday school enrolments across denominations confirm this pattern. Particularly when measured as a percentage of the population under fifteen, it was the period 1891–1911 that saw the zenith of the movement. Most of the generation of young men that fought in the First World War had evidently been to Sunday school, whether or not their parents still went to church.

Already in the 1880s there were signs of churches and chapels being emptier than they had been in 1851. Declining attendances then were mostly a feature of morning congregations, but by 1903 evening congregations had collapsed as well. In the Free Churches, especially, large evening congregations had for long been their mainstay. In 1851 they were on average 56.6 per cent full, but by 1903 they had declined to an estimated[38] 37.0 per cent full. And Anglican evening

---

[36] Although, for synchronic London comparisons, see McLeod, *Class and Religion in the Late Victorian City,* and for diachronic Lambeth comparisons, see Cox, *The English Churches in a Secular Society.*

[37] See *Summaries of the Church Work and Finance in the Diocese of London,* 1890 onwards, Guildhall Library, London.

[38] *The Daily News* census of 1903 (i.e. Mudie-Smith, *The Religious Life of London*) did not give seating, so I have calculated it proportionately for each District and Denomination from the 1887 census.

congregations had declined to a new low of an estimated 28.9 per cent full. As in 1851, morning congregations (albeit themselves much reduced) were again stronger. In reality most congregations at any time of day were now not full at all. They were predominantly empty.

Charles Booth repeatedly noticed that, in working-class areas especially, churches and chapels were typically empty. In such areas, he concluded in his summary, 'the vast majority attend no place of worship, and of those who attend somewhere the Nonconformist churches and the missions obtain their share'.[39] Nor was he always sanguine about Anglican churchgoing in wealthy areas. For example, in Westminster he found that 'fashionable dwellers in flats are seldom seen at church ... flat-dwellers are continually on the move in and out of town, and cannot be relied on to share in either the worship or work of the churches'.[40] In more qualitative terms, he observed:

> Yet, as a pervading spiritual force capable of uplifting the mass of its adherents, the Church of England fails even among the rich. Except as regards these chosen spirits, the Church does not get beyond recognition as the representative of religion. Among the churches of the rich, as between High and Low, Broad, essentially Individual, or markedly Parochial, I can find little difference in the numbers they attract or the influence they exert, and the choice among them, no less than the attendance, is mainly dictated by fashion. Eloquence invariably attracts crowds, but this, too, is largely a matter of fashion.[41]

Booth also supplied a very early account of the decline of the Salvation Army. Of the rise of this movement in the previous generation, he wrote that 'no religious phenomenon of our day is more remarkable than this development'.[42] But now things were quite different:

> Progress in any particular place has been slow or fitful, alternating with retrogression. The point is soon reached at which all that can be done has been done, and only with great difficulty is the work maintained at the highest level attained. As regards London the failure is palpable. Constant changes are made in the personnel, partly as a measure of discipline, no doubt, in order to maintain the feeling of dependence on headquarters, but also quite necessarily for the sake of vigour; fresh life having to be stirred up every nine months or so, by changing the officers in charge. But it is all in vain, and from year to year most of the corps lead a struggling existence.[43]

Even in the East End of London, where the Salvation Army first began, Booth found that it was 'now of little importance as a religious influence'.[44] *Table 13* shows that in London as a whole, as in Liverpool, Salvation Army attendances almost halved proportionately between the 1880s and 1900s; and their chapels,

---

[39] Booth, *Life and Labour*, Third Series, vol. 7, p. 4.
[40] Booth, *Life and Labour*, Third Series, vol. 3, p. 80.
[41] Booth, *Life and Labour*, Third Series, vol. 7, pp. 44–5.
[42] Booth, *Life and Labour*, Third Series, vol. 7, p. 323.
[43] Booth, *Life and Labour*, Third Series, vol. 7, pp. 326–7.
[44] Booth, *Life and Labour*, Third Series, vol. 2, p. 42.

which had on average been half-full, were now less than a sixth-full. Perhaps it was this that most disturbed Booth. Given his concern about poverty in London, he was impressed by the charitable work of the Salvation Army there. Yet he was unconvinced that it had contributed anything to its numerical strength.

Curiously, and against the trend for the rest of London, there was little change in the attendance rate in the Salvation Army in Shoreditch, Whitechapel, Stepney and Bethnal Green. In both 1887 and 1903 it was about 0.3 per cent of the population (in London as a whole, it declined from 0.8 per cent to 0.5 per cent). Unfortunately, though, the number of its missions there increased from four to thirteen. As a result, attendances per mission had shrunk, almost threefold: from 332 to just 122. Apparently, like the mainstream Free Churches almost everywhere, the Salvation Army too had over-built, and what Booth may have been observing were the early effects of this over-building. A similar pattern is seen in Chapter 9, but this time through the eyes of the other pioneer chronicler of poverty, Seebohm Rowntree of York.

As elsewhere, though, there were variations. Some churches were distinctly emptier than others, and while churchgoing rates generally declined, some Districts saw continuing high levels. Theoretically, at least, the City combined a rapidly increasing churchgoing rate with fast emptying churches. The churchgoing rate for the whole of the City increased from 35 per cent of its population in 1851, to 69 per cent in 1887, and to 86 per cent in 1903. But, as already observed, these rates in reality depended upon commuters, and the churches themselves were mostly empty. Booth wished these churches to be used for more secular purposes, since he admitted 'the comparative uselessness of almost all, and the absolute uselessness of many, if not most, of the City churches at present'.[45]

Less surrealistically, the highest churchgoing rates mostly moved out to the suburbs. The District with the highest London churchgoing rate in 1851 was Hampstead (54 per cent). In 1887 it was Hampstead (49 per cent) and Lewisham (47 per cent).[46] In 1903 it was High Barnet (60 per cent), followed by Ealing (51 per cent) and Woodford (50 per cent). As the middle classes moved progressively out of London, so strong churchgoing rates moved with them.

By 1903 Lewisham had already become more artisan. As Booth noted at the time, 'in Lewisham, more perhaps than anywhere else, we find a new population overwhelming the old. The rich have gone. Clerks and commercial travellers, themselves divided into several classes, have taken their place; and below them there is a great and growing population of wage-earners'.[47] So a District with a population doubling at each stage saw a sharp rise in attendances from 35 per cent to 47 per cent between 1851 and 1887, followed by an even sharper decline (despite a fine census day in mid-March) to 31 per cent by 1903. Amidst all the chaos of house-building that was taking place as he wrote, Booth groaned that, 'the future

---

[45] Booth, *Life and Labour*, Third Series, vol. 3, p. 49.

[46] Since the population of Lewisham was growing so fast, I have estimated the populations for 1887 and 1903. If the 1881 and 1901 population figures are used instead – as they are for other Districts – attendances would be 56 per cent for the 1880s and 33 per cent for the 1900s.

[47] Booth, *Life and Labour*, Third Series, vol. 6, p. 146.

lies on the knees of the gods'.[48] In order to greet the newcomers he noted that the Wesleyans, Congregationalists and Baptists (but not the Anglicans) were themselves building fast. The results can be seen in the 1887 and 1903 censuses. Anglican attendances collapsed from 30.4 per cent of Lewisham's population to 16.2 per cent: Wesleyan, Congregationalist and Baptist attendances combined declined only from 11 per cent to 9.2 per cent.

So those who moved fastest benefited the most, but all lost at least some ground. This example exposes a number of myths. Anglicans apparently could cope with rapid urbanization. In 1903 they were still coping much better in the suburbs than they were in Inner London. In the latter the Anglican attendance rate was 9.6 per cent and that of the Free Churches 10.7 per cent: in Greater London it was 13.3 per cent and 13.8 per cent respectively. Back in 1851, High Barnet was little more than a large village, with a population of 2380. The Anglican attendance rate there was 28.9 per cent. By 1903 the population had increased more than threefold, but Anglican attendances were unchanged at 28.8 per cent. At Ealing, with a much larger population in 1903 of 33 031, the Anglican attendance rate was 31.1 per cent. At Croydon, with a population larger again of 132 665, the Anglican attendance rate was still 18.4 per cent.

What most denominations found difficult was downward social mobility. Given an influx of their 'natural' supporters, Anglicans could cope. In Lewisham in 1851 their churchgoing rate had been 28.3 per cent. By 1887 they had increased this to 30.4 per cent and their churches from seventeen to thirty-two. But, given a loss of the middle classes and a huge influx of artisans, they built no extra churches in the next sixteen years and struggled with those they already had. And although Wesleyans, Baptists and Congregationalists coped better, they still declined.

In downwardly mobile Southwark overall attendances dropped from 28 per cent of the population to 18 per cent between 1851 and 1887, and in the once fashionable Greenwich from 33 per cent to 24 per cent. Between 1887 and 1903 there were declines in attendance associated with downward social mobility in Camberwell (37 per cent to 25 per cent), Kensington (39 per cent to 25 per cent), and Lambeth (36 per cent to 21 per cent). In some Districts there was a continuous process between 1851 and 1903 – notably in Hackney (48 per cent to 25 per cent), Hampstead (54 per cent to 26 per cent), Islington (36 per cent to 22 per cent), St Pancras (34 per cent to 18 per cent), and Wandsworth (49 per cent to 24 per cent). All of these rates of decline were faster than the mean rate for London as a whole. Only some were associated with wet weather in 1903, but none with very wet weather, and in Hackney the weather was fine.

In theory, again, Districts with the lowest churchgoing rates in 1851 seemed to change the least during the rest of the century. For example, Shoreditch had a churchgoing rate of 14 per cent in 1851, 13 per cent in 1887, and 15 per cent in 1903. The District with the next lowest rate, Bethnal Green, had a figure of 19 per cent in 1851, 16 per cent in 1887, and 16 per cent in 1903. None of these rates (both on a fine day in 1903) approached the lowest rate of 9.5 per cent recorded in Birmingham in 1892. In 1903 the lowest rate for anywhere in London, or Greater

---

[48] Booth, *Life and Labour*, Third Series, vol. 6, p. 151.

London, was at Fulham (13.5 per cent) – depicted by Booth as 'one of the dumping grounds of London'[49] – and the census there was on a 'very wet' day. So were the London working classes immune from further decline?

What this question ignores is another new feature noticed by Booth.[50] He claimed that whereas the working classes in London, if they went to church at all, went locally, the middle classes went eclectically. Furthermore, when he recorded large congregations in Anglican churches in the East End, he tended to claim that they depended, at least partly, upon middle-class outsiders. Added together, these observations suggest that the churchgoing rates of the actual residents of Districts such as Shoreditch and Bethnal Green may have been considerably lower than those recorded in 1903. Certainly eclecticism in middle-class urban churchgoing has remained a feature of the twentieth century. It may mean that middle-class areas of a city actually provide the bulk of churchgoers for the whole of that city.

Another feature to emerge strongly from both Booth and *The Daily News* census is that it was women and children who formed the largest part of most congregations. *Table 14* shows the extent of this disparity, already noted in earlier periods, in London in 1903. More than two-thirds of adult attendances were made by women. For once Booth excelled himself with a metaphor. Of the congregation of one Anglo-Catholic church, he wrote:

> The congregations, especially in the morning, are more numerous than those of other churches, but both morning and evening are almost entirely formed of women, and mostly young women, all very smartly dressed, so that, as seen from the pulpit, a church is said to resemble the flower-beds of Park Lane.[51]

If women predominated in congregations (especially in Anglican and Catholic congregations), then children came next. Some children were taken to church rather than sent to Sunday school, particularly in middle-class areas. So if these children are added to those already in Sunday school, then about half of the population under fifteen years in London may typically have been involved with a church or chapel on a Sunday. In contrast, adult female attendances (some of them representing individuals attending twice) represented little more than a quarter of the adult female population. Adult male attendances represented less than a fifth of the adult male population. Indeed, one East End parish conducted a survey, reported by Booth, which estimated that adult male churchgoers as just one-in-eighty of the local working-class adult male population.[52]

Why had these damaging disparities – social class, gender and age – developed? Booth offered several explanations, some cultural and some structural. They all seem surprisingly modern. At the cultural level he argued that, whereas among the middle classes there was a general expectation that all individuals belong to some church, among working-class men, especially, churchgoing would have appeared as exceedingly odd. The 'fashion' for these two groups was quite different. It was

---

[49] Booth, *Life and Labour*, Third Series, vol. 3, p. 171.
[50] Booth, *Life and Labour*, Third Series, vol. 7, p. 4.
[51] Booth, *Life and Labour*, Third Series, vol. 1, p. 36.
[52] Booth, *Life and Labour*, Third Series, vol. 2, p. 77 (the parish was St Matthew's, Bethnal Green).

expected that children should go to Sunday school, even among the working classes, but it was not expected that they should transfer when older to church:

> It is when school age is past that all denominations alike find their difficulty. The desire to put away childish things comes very early; much sooner than St Paul intended. Great efforts are made to retain some hold on the children at this time; everywhere the efforts are of the same kind and nowhere are they particularly successful.[53]

At the structural level, Booth was particularly critical of the Church of England. Interestingly, it was its economic base that attracted his fiercest criticisms. Anglican clergy were too protected and too protective. Compared with Free Church ministers, Anglican clergy were protected by freehold and were usually better paid. He estimated the average living in London to be £496, although there were huge variations – from £1211 to £180. In contrast, Salvation Army captains received less than £50 a year. And he noticed that, if there were insufficient local resources, 'they prefer to go without rather than become chargeable to the central fund'.[54] In contrast, Anglican incumbents received their income whether or not they were providing an effective ministry.

At several points Booth noted severe abuses among Anglican clergy. There were instances where:

> The fixed tenure of incumbencies works ill, and even at times scandalously; as when wits fail from senile decay or incipient insanity; or when there is drunkenness; or when the income of an absentee incumbent is sequestrated to pay his debts; or, still worse, when a man can even utilize his position in the Church to carry on a career of swindling.[55]

Booth was convinced that all of this made a system of compulsory retirement essential. Yet even for the assiduous, there were serious problems in London:

> The eclecticism of London church-goers and their frequent disregard of parish boundaries, render the position of those of the clergy and their co-workers, who struggle against the breakdown of these boundaries, very impracticable, and when the general failure of the Church of England to touch more than a fringe of the people is taken into account, the attitude of exclusiveness and the feelings of resentment at 'intrusion' which are often found become somewhat ridiculous.[56]

Nor was he convinced by the Anglican practice of supplying buildings and philanthropy from extra-parochial funds. He insisted that, 'our enquiry has already shown with sufficient clearness, and as we go on it becomes more and more manifest, that it is not by the use of outside funds in planting churches here and there, that the dormant religious sentiments of the people are to be roused or their spiritual needs met'.[57] As a result, he quickly dismissed the idea that City churches

---

[53] Booth, *Life and Labour*, Third Series, vol. 7, p. 15.
[54] Booth, *Life and Labour*, Second Series, vol. 4, p. 197.
[55] Booth, *Life and Labour*, Third Series, vol. 7, p. 27.
[56] Booth, *Life and Labour*, Third Series, vol. 7, pp. 4–5.
[57] Booth, *Life and Labour*, Third Series, vol. 3, p. 50.

should be sold off to allow for church planting elsewhere. In sharp contrast, he noted that Catholics everywhere tended to require even the poor to give to them.

Booth was finally unimpressed by Catholicism. He was convinced that it had contributed little to the 'moral character' of its members. These prejudices make his testimony to the economic base of London's Catholics all the more impressive:

> No buildings in London devoted to religious purposes are more fully used. The priests are accommodated at the presbytery, and receive a small allowance for expenses; the Sisters from some neighbouring convent take charge of the girl's school or help to visit the sick, and if charitable relief is needed for those in distress special assistance is forthcoming; but the necessary expenses of church and schools, apart from Government grants to the latter, are defrayed from the offerings of the congregation. The priests live as poor men among the poor. Their food is simple, their clothes are threadbare; they take few holidays.[58]

No admirer of their theology, Booth did approve of their self-sufficiency. Even in the poorest Districts of London, Catholics were required to donate a penny a week to their church. And Catholic congregations everywhere, unlike those of Anglicans or the Free Churches, were still thriving.

5

This picture of a widespread decay in urban churchgoing is confirmed by a unique survey undertaken by army chaplains at the end of the First World War. It allows for a very early comparison of popular religious beliefs and churchgoing. Taken together with the data presented in this chapter and the last, it surely destroys for ever the ten propositions with which I started this book.

The Army and Religion, subtitled 'An Enquiry and its Bearing upon the Religious Life of the Nation', was compiled from questionnaires channelled through army chaplains. Altogether some three hundred memoranda were received, 'resting on the evidence of many hundred witnesses ... from men of all ranks'.[59] It adds significant data in three areas: it attempted to estimate the percentage of men involved with the churches; it attempted to articulate their religious beliefs; and it listed their complaints about the churches.

On the first issue, the questionnaire asked, 'What percentage of the men, would you say, are in vital relationship with any of the Churches?' The authors were aware of the ambiguity of the question and of some of the answers received. Nevertheless, they estimated that, whereas four-fifths of the men had been to Sunday school, four-fifths of them did not subsequently go to church. More carefully, they calculated that only some 11.5 per cent of English and 20 per cent of Scottish troops were now 'in vital relationship' to a church. Given that the data for London as a whole for 1903 suggested adult male attendances of 18.5 per cent, then an English figure of 11.5 per cent attenders for 1918 does seem credible.

---

[58] Booth, *Life and Labour*, Third Series, vol. 7, p. 243.
[59] D.S. Cairns (ed.), *The Army and Religion*, Macmillan, London, 1919, p. vi.

Interestingly, the authors recorded a wide disparity in the returns from Catholic chaplains. In slightly patronizing terms it was decided that, 'allowing the claim of the Roman Catholic chaplains that *all* their men were vitally connected with their Church, the percentage of the whole in this regard should be set at thirty per cent. vitally related, seventy per cent. not so related'.[60] If anything, this calculation may have been somewhat conservative. Booth reported[61] that the Catholic population of London was about 200 000 and *The Daily News* census of 1903 recorded 93 572 Catholic attendances. Since, as argued earlier, most of the latter were probably separate attenders, it would appear that, as in Liverpool, at least two-fifths of the Catholic population of London were in church for the pre-war census. Chapter 8 suggests that, even by 1989, about a third of the Catholic population of England regularly attended Mass. But whether conservative or not, Catholic soldiers clearly attended church more regularly than non-Catholics.

Despite the general low level of non-Catholic churchgoing, the report maintained that most soldiers believed in God and in prayer. The authors reported poignantly:

It is very remarkable that the whole materialistic and anti-religious propaganda, which made so much noise, and apparently had so much vogue among our labouring classes a few years ago, seems to have simply withered away in the fires of the Line. The men of the British armies, however dim their faith may be, do in the hour of danger, at least, believe in God, 'the great and terrible God'. Most men we are told pray before they go over the parapet, or advance in the face of machine guns, and they thank God when they have come through the battle ... in the presence of the most terrific display of material force that human history has ever seen men believe that there is an Unseen Power, inaccessible to the senses, which is yet mightier than high explosives, which knows all and which hears prayer.[62]

Linked to these beliefs in God and in prayer was also a general belief in afterlife. Again the report concluded that, 'the marked drift of the evidence is that, taken as a whole, the men, though vaguely, believe in the life to come ... Whatever their present attitude to the Churches may be, they have in them the result of many centuries of Christian training and of the home life that springs up in such a soil.'[63] Nevertheless, the report was not convinced that surrounding beliefs were always specifically Christian. Prefiguring tensions that would sometimes be felt in Remembrance Day services, the report argued that, 'the idea of salvation by death in battle for one's country has been widely prevalent, and is one of those points in which the religion of the trenches has rather a Moslem than a Christian colour'.[64]

The third set of data that can be gleaned from this unique report concerns the complaints soldiers made about the contemporary churches. The authors of *The Army and Religion* admitted that largely non-churchgoing respondents were not best placed to make knowledgeable comments about churches: 'the great

---

[60] Cairns, *The Army and Religion*, p. 190.
[61] Booth, *Life and Labour*, Third Series, vol. 7, p. 250.
[62] Cairns, *The Army and Religion*, pp. 7–8.
[63] Cairns, *The Army and Religion*, p. 16.
[64] Cairns, *The Army and Religion*, p. 19.

preponderance of the evidence refers to men who, from their adolescence onwards, know practically nothing of the real life of the Churches from within'.[65] None the less, precisely because their voices were so seldom heard, the authors urged churchgoers to take them seriously.

One area of complaint concerned belief. The churches were felt to be 'lacking in the spirit of Reality'. More specifically, 'there is as yet not much indication of any reasoned unbelief; but the idea prevails that the Churches are afraid to face the whole truth'.[66] Intellectual difficulties were thought to be present, but not necessarily paramount: 'even more frequent than this complaint of want of reality in the teaching is the complaint that the services are unreal, that the preachers have no real contact with human life as the men know it'.[67] And there were constant references to a lack of correspondence between the beliefs of Christians and their actual behaviour.

It is this last complaint that recurred in several forms in the report. For the authors the point at issue was that, 'whether the charge be of the lack of fellowship within the Churches, or of their want of human sympathy with the disinherited classes, or of the divisions between different communions, it is an accusation of lack of love'.[68] In all of these areas there were widespread convictions that churches had failed. The authors of the report were evidently amazed at the prevalence and vehemence of these convictions, and they attempted to capture them as follows:

> To sum up a good deal of evidence we seem to have left the impression upon them that there is little or no life in the Church at all, that it is an antiquated and decaying institution, standing by dogmas expressed in archaic language, and utterly out of touch with modern thought and living experience ... they believe that the Churches are more and more governed by the middle-aged and the elderly; they think ministry professionalised and out of touch with the life of men, deferring unduly to wealth ... They say they do not see any real differences in the strength and purity of life between the people who go to church and the people who do not.[69]

Of course there were all sorts of qualitative judgements contained in these criticisms. Nevertheless, they clearly reflected a popular image of decline at considerable variance with present-day images of thriving pre-First World War churches and chapels. Furthermore, they confirm, and then add to, the statistical evidence presented in the last two chapters. By 1919 churches and chapels were predominantly empty, but religious beliefs – at least in a general form – persisted.

---

[65] Cairns, *The Army and Religion*, p. 192.
[66] Cairns, *The Army and Religion*, p. 196.
[67] Cairns, *The Army and Religion*, p. 202.
[68] Cairns, *The Army and Religion*, p. 204.
[69] Cairns, *The Army and Religion*, pp. 220–1.

8

Continuing Decline: 1920s to 2000

It is time to take stock. This is a book about the empty church, and it is also a book about some deeply ingrained myths. At the outset I listed ten widely held propositions that seem to explain why British churches are now empty. However, given the welter of data presented in the last three chapters, these propositions now seem highly questionable. Their mythological status should be apparent to all.

The first proposition held that before the First World War a majority of churches in Britain were full. Surely no further evidence is needed to show that this proposition is highly misleading. Long before 1914, empty churches and chapels predominated in both the rural and urban areas studied. Of course, there were still some middle-class pockets of high rates of churchgoing in the early 1900s – such as High Barnet, Ealing, Lincoln and Chester – and individual suburban churches might still be full, but these were pockets and not the norm.

The second proposition held that Victorians built extra churches because they needed them to meet the demands of rapidly expanding urban and rural populations. Doubtless, that is how many Victorian churchpeople themselves viewed their situation, but again it is highly misleading. In the second half of the nineteenth century, rural areas were radically depopulating while the Free Churches were building in such areas more vigorously than ever. In urban areas, the Free Churches persistently built chapels faster than the rate of urban population growth, and faster than they could fill them. And in both rural and urban areas, Anglicans built mission halls and church extensions while retaining little used older churches.

The third proposition held that competitive church building between denominations raised the general level of churchgoing throughout the nineteenth century. This may be accurate for the first half of the century, but not for the second. It also had the disastrous effect in the Free Churches of raising their overall attendance rate while making chapels themselves distinctly emptier.

The fourth proposition held that urban church building never quite kept pace with late nineteenth-century urban population growth and thus excluded significant sections of the urban working classes. In contrast, the Church of England's mission halls, and the newer chapels and mission halls of the Free Churches, were characteristically built for the urban poor. Yet neither the Church of England nor most Free Churches could fill them. In this respect, Wickham's pioneer study of Sheffield has been shown to be highly misleading.

The fifth proposition held that churchgoing started to decline generally in proportion to the population only after the First World War. In contrast again, most denominations had been declining proportionately in urban areas long before the First World War. Anglicans and Congregationalists had typically been declining for a good half century, and older Free Churches as a whole had been declining since the 1880s. And even newer groups, such as the Salvation Army, were showing clear signs of decline by the early 1900s. In short, there is abundant pre-1914 evidence of overall churchgoing decline in proportion to the population.

The sixth proposition held that disillusionment resulting from the war was a significant factor in causing this decline, especially among urban working-class men. But what *The Army and Religion* suggested was that, if anything, the First World War fostered among the fighting soldiers vestigial beliefs in God, in prayer and in afterlife. Typically, soldiers had been to Sunday school, but not to church. They had numerous complaints about the church, but little recent experience – that is, until they encountered army services. In turn, what the army chaplains seemed to encounter, apparently with some surprise, were the feelings of working-class men long separated from the churches. If the working-class soldiers were ignorant about the churches, the chaplains in turn found that they themselves knew little about the working classes.

Just after the Second World War Mass-Observation interviewed a random cross-section of 500 adults in 'a London semi-suburban borough'. Using evidence from this survey and from four earlier surveys made during the war, they concluded:

> War has produced a trend away from religion among those with no pronounced belief before. The proportion who feel they have *lost* their faith, however, is very small – between 1–4 per cent. in the samples studied. The indications are that major disillusionment with religion because of the war is confined almost entirely to those who never paid much more than lip-service to it before. In general the wartime trend is for those with a fairly deep faith to have had their belief strengthened.[1]

The seventh proposition held that secularization – the product of nineteenth-century developments in science and rational thought, spread in the twentieth century through better education – has proved to be the most abiding factor in church decline. At an early stage in the book I expressed considerable scepticism about some invisible hand of secularization being primarily responsible for church decline. In contrast, I have sought to show that there were more mundane, physical factors at work throughout much of the nineteenth century. By the turn of the century rural and urban churches and chapels were facing acute problems that were at least in part of their own making.

The eighth proposition held that urbanization – involving the breakdown of rural communities upon which churches thrive – has also contributed significantly to church decline. In contrast again, the urban churchgoing evidence for the period 1821–51 suggests that an increase in churchgoing was possible even in the context of rapid urbanization (as it was also in South Korea from the 1960s until the 1980s). Even at the end of the century there were pockets of strong urban churchgoing. Some forms of rapid urbanization – especially those involving downward social mobility – were indeed damaging to churchgoing, but by no means all forms of urbanization. In any case, the evidence examined suggests that rural/urban disparities are considerably more complex and varied than this proposition suggests.

---

[1] Mass-Observation, *Puzzled People: A Study of Popular Attitudes to Religion, Ethics, Progress and Politics in a London Borough*, Victor Gollancz, London, 1947, p. 23.

The ninth proposition held that twentieth-century leisure activities – cars, radios, televisions, etc. – have also contributed to church decline. Well, perhaps this is the case. But more to the point, once church decline became firmly established, almost anything could be blamed for its continuation. And doubtless almost anything would appear more attractive than empty churches and chapels. In any case, leisure activities (particularly drinking) were frequently mentioned early in the nineteenth century, when churchgoing was still rising. And they are not exactly unknown in the United States, where of course strong churchgoing persists.

The tenth proposition held that an accumulative result of these various external factors is that British churches – with the significant exception of competitive evangelical churches – have recently become secularized and increasingly empty. The word 'recently' will now have to go from this proposition. However, it also begs other questions about competitive evangelical churches, which will have to be examined more closely in this chapter and the next.

All of this suggests a radically different understanding of the empty church from the one dominant for so long among social historians. The empty church appears less a product of twentieth-century disillusionment and secularization than of structural problems endemic in the Church of England and the Free Churches facing huge shifts of population in the nineteenth century. It was exacerbated, among other things, by their long struggle for predominance. The empty church characterized most denominations in Britain throughout the twentieth century and continues now into the twenty-first century. And it may well have contributed to the gradual, but much later, decline in distinctively Christian belief.

With the empty church firmly established in urban areas, the five factors identified from rural areas again become relevant. Now one would expect to find the following in urban areas too: churches and especially chapels beginning to close; chronic financial problems typically preceding these closures; ordained ministers having single-handed charge of several churches/chapels; thinner and increasingly elderly congregations experiencing difficulties attracting new members; and predominantly empty churches and chapels being seen as signs of secularization.

If all of this is accurate, then predictions become possible. Despite the considerable rhetoric typically made by denominations about mission and evangelism, their deep-seated structural problems would have ensured that they continued to decline throughout the twentieth century. Both the heavily subsidized Church of England and the over-extended Free Churches, would – unless their structures were radically transformed – have continued to decline in an entirely predictable way.

Ex post facto predictions are seldom very impressive. The reader will be perfectly well aware from the title of this chapter that I already know that twentieth-century churchgoing continued to decline. So to term this decline 'predictable' may seem just too easy. Fortunately, two social scientists made real predictions a generation ago that can be tested today. Chapter 9 examines Seebohm Rowntree's predictions, made in the early 1950s, about churchgoing decline in York. The present chapter examines a very careful statistical prediction, made in the 1960s, about Methodist membership in Manchester (Chapter 9, again, applies the formula on which it is based to Methodist membership in York).

Both of these predictions by social scientists assume that churches now recruit almost entirely from the families of their existing members. Whatever denominations claimed in the past about evangelism, the reality is that their recruitment is basically endogenous. Declining churches find exogenous recruitment increasingly difficult and, as a result, they will continue to decline in a thoroughly predictable way. Strikingly, both of these predictions can now be shown as highly accurate.

This is crucial for understanding the empty church in the twentieth century. If the factors behind church decline lie to a significant degree in structural problems inherited from the nineteenth century, then, so long as these problems remained unresolved, twentieth-century decline would appear inevitable. A church that does not recruit from outside its own membership can survive only by giving birth to an abundance of new members. But, as birth rates decline, and as the children of remaining members look more and more isolated compared with their non-churchgoing peers, and feel less and less comfortable in sparse and elderly congregations, so the empty church finds sheer survival increasingly difficult. It no longer recruits from outside, nor does it retain sufficient children from within. At many levels the empty church feeds the empty church.

In this chapter I will review the evidence of this decline for the period from the 1920s to the present. I will take this evidence in two stages: first up to 1950 (the limited statistical evidence for this period confirms the overall picture of continuous decline); and then the second half of the twentieth century (when many denominations have once again become active in gathering churchgoing data). MARC Europe/Christian Research has also amassed an impressive amount of comparative denominational data in their three censuses of 1979, 1989 and 1998, and a variety of questionnaire surveys have added crucial longitudinal data on changing beliefs.

1

In London the five factors were already evident before the First World War. However, there were significant differences between Booth's account of the Free Churches in 1902 and that of *The Daily News and Leader* survey of 1914. Twelve years of empty chapels in London had apparently begun to take their toll.

As already seen, Booth did notice empty churches and chapels in London in the early 1900s. Furthermore (like Abraham Hume in the 1850s, as outlined in Chapter 4) he paid particular attention to their differing economic bases. Booth was also aware of chapel closures, of staffing problems, and of debts – especially among Methodists. For example, he noted that London Wesleyans benefited more than other Free Churches from immigration: 'amongst the new-comers in London, there is always some proportion of those of country parentage who have been born and bred in Wesleyanism'.[2] Yet at the same time there were problems. Because of

---

[2] Charles Booth, *Life and Labour of the People in London: Third Series: Religious Influences*, vol. 7, Macmillan, 1902, p. 133.

financial pressures within Methodist circuits, two ministers typically looked after three chapels. In addition:

> Wesleyans have suffered more than either Congregationalists or Baptists from chapels deserted and stranded owing to the removal of their supporters. The lack of individuality among their chapels, owing to the circuit system and the constant change of ministers, necessarily weakens the tie to any particular church.[3]

In a very remarkable passage, Booth summarized the effect of these various processes on Wesleyans, and then compared their fate with that of other denominations:

> Thus it came about that the new chapels filled, while the old ones fell empty. Of these many were sold. Except for a certain class, [Wesleyans] had never obtained support, and that class had moved away from them. So long as the chapels were filled the fact had not been so noticeable, but now the humiliating confession had to be made that the working classes and the poor were totally unmoved by the Gospel as it had been preached therein. The shame of this pressed heavily. The Church of England, entrenched in the parish system, could fall back on their patronage of the poor. The Congregationalists were eclectic and knew it ... as a rule, the fact of an unsympathetic social order which they could not penetrate was quietly accepted. Through such changes of population the Baptists maintained their numbers best, and could always count among their supporters a proportion of working men. They did not pander to the poor. Poverty, in their eyes, was too often a result of sin or self-indulgence, deserving reprobation more than pity; moreover, they could look forward steadfastly through the present gloom to the accomplishment of the elect and the speedy coming of the Lord.[4]

There were clearly problems, but they were not yet identified as 'secularization'. The churches themselves, with all their various rivalries, were mostly blamed for bringing these problems down upon their own heads.

In contrast, *The Daily News and Leader* explicitly referred to the 'secularisation of Sunday' and to now numerous chapel closures. As noted earlier, between 1903 and 1914 (see *Table 13*) there was, for the first time, a decline in the overall number of chapels in London (from 1512 to 1443).[5] It was no longer simply a matter of a chapel being closed in one impoverished area and then being replaced by others in more salubrious areas. There was now an overall and visible reduction.

Instead of going to church or chapel, people in working-class and now middle-class areas were occupying themselves in other ways:

> The secularisation of Sunday is not much worse in Walworth than in Belgravia, but it is more obtrusive. In the latter case golf links and river draw the population far from the churches they are deserting. (One minister specifies among the vices that lower his immediate neighbourhood 'Motoring, golf, cinema.') In the former the street market,

---

[3] Booth, *Life and Labour*, vol. 7, p. 132.
[4] Booth, *Life and Labour*, vol. 7, p. 133.
[5] Calculations made from Richard Mudie-Smith (ed.), *The Religious Life of London*, Hodder, London, 1904; and H. Wilson Harris and Margaret Bryant, *The Churches and London*, produced by *The Daily News and Leader*, London, 1914.

the cinema and the public-house are set full in the sight and in the path of the worshippers.[6]

Of course there was nothing particularly new about Sunday trading and entertainments in London, nor was there anything new about Free Church ministers denouncing them. The Scottish Congregationalist James Inches Hillocks[7] described and decried gin palaces, markets and prize-fights taking place on Sundays in London in the middle of the nineteenth century. What was relatively new in *The Daily News and Leader* was the specific link of chapel closures with 'the secularization of Sunday'.

The financial implications of these changes were also becoming increasingly obvious. *The Daily News and Leader* reported that 'both Established Church and Free Churches suffer from a serious shortage of money and workers'.[8] None the less, the authors detected a crucial difference between them:

> [The Church of England's] endowments, together with the support extended by such outside bodies as the East London Church Fund, the South London Church Fund, and the Bishop of London's Fund, are usually large enough to provide for the maintenance of a vicar and one or two curates, whereas the Nonconformist minister's stipend has generally to be raised by his congregation, and is usually the heaviest item in the annual balance sheet.[9]

These financial problems, allied to a decline in chapelgoing, were already having a very serious effect upon the Free Churches. Things had clearly deteriorated since Booth's time, as the following passage from the report shows:

> One by one Congregational chapels and Baptist, Wesleyan and Presbyterian, are being turned into workshops or picture palaces or furniture emporiums; not because their neighbourhood is over-churched, but because they cannot subsist on the meagre resources the district is capable of providing. A minister of long experience in the East End mentioned that within the area with which he was familiar, he had seen no fewer than thirty-six chapels closed. In one case a congregation, unable to raise its pastor's stipend, turned for assistance to a suburban church of the same denomination, able to pay its own minister over £1000 a year. The appeal met with no response, and the East End chapel had to close its doors and is now a cinematograph theatre.[10]

In 1927 Arthur Black made three surveys of attendances in London for *The British Weekly*.[11] The results of one of them, in an anonymous 'suburban area', are contained in *Table 12*. The area conformed very closely to the mean overall attendance rate for London in 1903 (21.5 per cent in the sample and 22.4 per cent in

---

[6] Harris and Bryant, *The Churches and London*, p. 40.

[7] James Inches Hillocks, *My Life and Labours in London*, William Freeman, London, 1865.

[8] Harris and Bryant, *The Churches and London*, p. 42.

[9] Harris and Bryant, *The Churches and London*, p. 42.

[10] Harris and Bryant, *The Churches and London*, p. 45.

[11] Arthur Black, 'London Church and Mission Attendances', *The British Weekly*, 23 February 1928, 1 March 1928, and 8 March 1928.

London). In the absence of any fuller data, it is possible that it indicates the way overall churchgoing patterns in London were changing.

While Catholic attendances persisted in this 'suburban area', Anglican and Free Church attendances had continued to decline sharply from 1903: Anglicans from 9.9 per cent to 4.8 per cent and the Free Churches from 10.8 per cent to 4.9 per cent. Average Anglican congregations declined drastically: in the morning from 380 to 169 and in the evening from 216 to 135. Among the Free Churches it was the congregations of the mainstream denominations that had declined most visibly: from a morning average of 189 to 114 and in the evening from 153 to 115. Churches and chapels that were already less than a third full in 1903 could now have been little more than a fifth full.

The identity of this area can be discovered through the oldest of the Catholic churches in the survey. In 1887[12] there were sixty-eight Catholic churches in London, and the only one to have attendances of 342 (the attendances given by Black) was St Joseph's, Roehampton. Once this is discovered, the other attendances given by Black for the Anglicans and Nonconformists for 1887 and 1903 can also be seen to fit Roehampton/Putney. A long-standing puzzle is solved.

Since Black's commentary on this sample has already been discussed in Chapter 4, it is unnecessary to rehearse it in full here. Sometimes he blamed cultural factors for the evident decline revealed by these figures (gramophone, cinema, travel, intellectual ferment, etc.), whereas at other times he noticed some of the more structural problems. However, in the present context, what his evidence confirms is that the decline in middle-class churchgoing that was noted just before the war had indeed continued after the war. As Black himself expressed the issue: 'the old ease with which suburban churches and chapels could be regularly filled has disappeared'.[13]

Attendances in the working-class areas surveyed by Black had also declined. Overall attendances in one had declined from 17.5 per cent in 1887, to 15 per cent in 1903, to just 7.1 per cent in 1927 (and, if this was Battersea, to about 2 per cent in 1965[14]). In both working-class areas taken together, Black concluded that attendances had dropped by a half in twenty-five years and by two-thirds over forty years. After what was evidently a very dispiriting visit to morning services in one area, Black asked: 'What is one to think of organised Christianity after a two-hour round like that?'. He concluded bleakly that, 'if the population became vitally concerned with religion, more and better accommodation would be needed. But increasingly, the problem thrusting itself forward is how to keep in use some almost deserted buildings.'[15] It was thus no longer just churchgoing that was seen as the problem. Ironically, the buildings themselves had become the problem.

Another familiar feature that emerges from Black's reports is the pattern of persisting diffusion and innovation within the more sectarian groups. In words that could almost as well reflect the situation in London in today (albeit now with Black Pentecostal and charismatic congregations), he reported:

---

[12] See *The Religious Census of London*, Hodder, 1888.
[13] *The British Weekly*, 1 March 1928.
[14] See Leslie Paul, *A Church by Daylight*, Chapman, London, 1973, p. 178.
[15] *The British Weekly*, 23 February 1928.

'The number of independents seem to grow with the failure of the regular churches. One has only to name some of them to illustrate the point:- Faith healers; Four-Square Gospellers; Seventh Day Adventists; Bible Student Association; and amongst the better class, the Christian Science Church, the British Israel party and the Spiritualists.[16]

Black's reports provide unambiguous evidence of the five factors associated with the empty church. He reported that: 'the big chapel without exception is a burdensome problem'; all denominations in poor areas lacked sufficient funds; 'Anglicans are seriously hindered by the shortage of clergy, and they do not use lay help very freely';[17] churches 'with their small bodies of worshippers, seemed very little fitted to withstand' the attractions of the cinema and other forms of Sunday leisure; and finally, 'these lessened attendances ... have an intimate bearing upon such problems as the presentation of the Christian message'.[18]

Mass-Observation's pioneer surveys in the late 1940s makes it possible to complete this picture of London churchgoing (or, rather, lack of churchgoing) in the first half of the twentieth century. In early 1949 *The British Weekly* ran a series of articles based upon evidence from these surveys. By now the author of the article took it for granted that, although there 'still remain a few possessed of vigorous life and as full as they were in the most intense days of religious interest', there are also 'hundreds of churches that are half-filled or less than half-filled'.[19] Granted that most churches were not, and were unlikely to be, full, one possible way of reducing the problem was to change the internal layout of church buildings. On the basis of interviews with laypeople and ministers in London, the author found that:

> one point that clearly emerged was the necessity for buildings to be the right size. Thus a Nonconformist minister, who has special charge of evangelical work, insisted that building was by far the most important problem facing his church, not because present buildings were too old, but because they were too big. But what he required was not new buildings but temporarily converted old ones. Thus he pointed out that a church capable of holding 1000 and only having 50 in the congregation was a certain handicap. What was needed was the fencing off of a space for 200, or so, so that vast emptiness is avoided and an intimate atmosphere created. When the 200 seats were full a new reconversion should be made so that the space to be used is capable of holding 400, and so the expansion would go on.[20]

Evidently empty churches were now clearly recognized, not just as a financial problem, but as a problem for the very 'atmosphere' of churchgoing.

16 *The British Weekly*, 8 March 1928.
17 *The British Weekly*, 23 February 1928.
18 *The British Weekly*, 8 March 1928.
19 *The British Weekly*, 3 February 1949.
20 *The British Weekly*, 27 January 1949.

2

A similar pattern of decline can be plotted in a number of places that had churchgoing censuses between the wars. A survey of South Shields and Wallsend[21] revealed a situation little better than that in Roehampton/Putney. Even with a greatly increased Catholic presence, overall attendances there declined from 33.4 per cent in 1851 to 19.2 per cent in 1928. It was shown in Chapter 4, using a sample for 1931, that in Liverpool, Anglican and Free Church attendances declined from 20.4 per cent in 1902, to 16.4 per cent in 1912, and to no more than 12.2 per cent in 1931. Chapter 9 also shows that in York overall adult attendances declined from 35.5 per cent in 1901 to 17.7 per cent in 1935.[22]

However, a survey of Ipswich[23] in 1924 suggested an inter-war churchgoing rate at least 50 per cent higher than any of these. A rather undifferentiated census, after a large mission there in 1921, gave overall attendances as some 30 per cent of the population (14.1 per cent in the morning and 15.9 per cent in the afternoon or evening). It also claimed that 'on a very good Sunday' attendances could reach nearer 40 per cent. Sunday school enrolments also represented 12.7 per cent of the total population, or about half of the population aged under 15. Even what were termed 'communicant members' apparently represented 11.9 per cent of the total population.

Yet set in a longitudinal context, these high rates in Ipswich also represented very considerable decline. In Chapter 6 it was seen that attendances at all services there in 1851 (including afternoon, since this was the best attended time of day) amounted to 62 per cent of the population. By 1881 this had dropped slightly to 58.8 per cent. This decline had happened most dramatically in the afternoon adult service – which by 1881 was the worst attended time of day. By the 1920s, only in the Social Settlement was there a sizeable afternoon service, and attendances over all had halved. Even the Sunday schools had apparently declined. In 1851 morning and afternoon Sunday school attendances amounted to 8.9 per cent of the total population (morning being strongest at 5.3 per cent). By 1881 these attendances had increased to 18.4 per cent of the population (afternoon being strongest then at 12.4 per cent). Children at afternoon Sunday school alone would have amounted to some half of the population aged under 15 years and all attendances to some two-thirds. And these, it should be noted, were attendances not enrolments.

The South Shields/Wallsend survey illustrates this process of decline in considerably more detail. In contrast to the data for the large towns between 1851 and the 1880s, the sharpest decline was in the Free Churches. Although they remained the dominant group, between 1851 and 1928 their attendances declined from 23.1 per cent to 8.9 per cent of the population. Meanwhile, Catholics increased from 1.1 per cent to 5.5 per cent.

---

[21] Henry A. Mess, *Industrial Tyneside: A Social Survey*, Ernest Benn, London, 1928.

[22] For Liverpool, see, D. Caradog Jones (ed.), *The Social Survey of Merseyside*, vol. 3, Liverpool University and Hodder & Stoughton, London, 1934; and for York, see B. Seebohm Rowntree, *Poverty and Progress: A Second Social Study of York*, Longmans Green, London, 1941.

[23] *Ipswich: A Survey of the Town*, COPEC, Ipswich, 1924.

In the final decades of the twentieth century, relative balances between denominations in the whole county of Tyne and Wear continued to shift.[24] By 1979 Catholics had become by far the largest churchgoing denomination. Their attendances still represented 5.2 per cent of the population, whereas the Free Churches had declined to 3.0 per cent and Anglicans to 1.9 per cent. By 1998 Catholics had declined faster than others, with attendances halved in two decades and now representing 2.7 per cent of the slightly reduced total population. Anglican attendances had also declined sharply, albeit not quite so sharply, to 1.3 per cent of this population and the Free Churches showed comparative resilience at 2.7 per cent. This last figure represents a by-now-familiar pattern that characterized the Free Churches a hundred years earlier; namely, of comparative (albeit temporary) resilience set in an overall context of decline across denominations (from 10.2 per cent in 1979 to 6.7 per cent in 1998), with the sharpest rise being in new, independent congregations and the sharpest decline among long-established Methodists.

Among the Free Churches, Methodists have for long predominated here. This was a region of strong Methodist rivalries – in the mid-nineteenth century between Wesleyans, Primitive Methodists, Methodist New Connexion and Wesleyan Methodist Association. Their overall pattern of decline has been startling. In 1851,[25] all Methodist attendances represented 39 per cent of total church and chapel attendances in South Shields/Wallsend, but by 1928 they represented 23 per cent of total attendances. By 1998 Methodist attendances represented only 19 per cent of the much-reduced total attendances in Tyne and Wear. Indeed, between 1979 and 1998 their numbers dropped from 22 300 to 14 400. In an overall context of decline, Methodists here have consistently declined faster than other Free Church denominations. But then, compared with others in this area, they have long had an abundance of empty chapels inherited from their nineteenth-century rivalries.

The 1928 survey was conducted by Henry Mess as part of a large social survey of industrial Tyneside. It provides evidence of the effects of empty churches and chapels that is remarkably similar to that for London. Evidently, Methodists in Tyneside – very soon to become part of a single Church – already had considerable problems staffing all of their various chapels. For example, Mess reported that there were sixty chapels and mission halls on Tyneside belonging to the United Methodists and just seventeen ordained ministers to serve them. The Wesleyan ratio was little better. They had seventy-two chapels and mission halls and twenty-six ordained ministers serving them.

If anything, the situation in the smaller denominations was even worse. Of Baptists and Congregationalists in the area, Mess noted that:

quite a number of their churches were in 1926 without ministers, and their membership was very small. It seems likely that this is due to the polity of these denominations; their

[24] Peter Brierley (ed.), *UK Christian Handbook: Religious Trends*, No. 3, 2001, p. 12.29 (Christian Research, Vision Building, 4 Footscray Road, London SE9 2TZ).

[25] Calculated from the original returns of the *1851 Religious Census*, held at the Public Records Office, Kew (ref. HO 129).

churches are strong where the middle-classes are strong and can finance them well, but in the poorer towns there are not the resources necessary for a strong church life.[26]

He also noticed that in Wallsend (as in Liverpool at the time)[27] female attendances predominated over male attendances by a ratio of three-to-two, and that children represented a fifth of those present at church services. In short, the long-standing disparities of class, gender and age persisted.

Unlike most other social analysts in the twentieth century, Mess was not given to talk about secularization. Instead he believed that 'a majority of those outside the churches are not opposed to religion ... it is indifference, and not intellectual rejection, which keeps them away'.[28] Rather than blaming cultural factors for empty churches, he tended to identify structural problems within the churches themselves. In words that could again apply with equal force today, he argued:

> It is common for those who care about organised religion to say that what is most needed at the present time is a great spiritual revival. Doubtless we need a spiritual revival. But to the writer of this report it seems that we need at least as much an overhauling of the machinery of the churches.[29]

The specific example he gave to demonstrate the need for this overhaul was as follows:

> There is a lamentable waste of resources involved in the maintenance of a number of small separate causes. To take a concrete example: in one of the Tyneside towns the Baptist Chapel, the Congregational Chapel, and the Presbyterian Chapel are all within a mile of each other. The form and tone of their services are very similar, the differences of doctrine and of practice are not such as to constitute a high barrier between their members or their ministries. Yet every Sunday all three are kept opened, three chapel keepers and three organists are kept busy, and three ministers have the disheartening experience of addressing a small number of persons in a building too large for the audience ... If the three congregations had amalgamated and had met in the largest of the three chapels, less than 40 per cent of its seating accommodation would have been used in the morning and about 70 per cent in the evening.[30]

Of course, the point here is not whether the solution offered by Mess would have worked. Methodists were soon to discover that attempts to bring together congregations that had for long been rivals were problematic, to say the least. In theory, a multiplicity of small chapels may well raise the overall chapelgoing rate in an area. In reality, a multiplicity of chapels means predominantly empty chapels, and empty chapels are basically unattractive. And unattractive chapels do not recruit (and nor, of course do closed chapels). So if they are kept open, chapelgoing declines, and if they are closed, chapelgoing also declines. Throughout the

---

[26] Mess, *Industrial Tyneside*, p. 139.
[27] See Caradog Jones, *The Social Survey of Merseyside*.
[28] Mess, *Industrial Tyneside*, p. 138.
[29] Mess, *Industrial Tyneside*, p. 140.
[30] Mess, *Industrial Tyneside*, p. 139.

twentieth century British Methodists were caught with empty chapels and with chapels forced to close. Their drastic decline in Tyneside, especially, reflects this painful 'Catch 22'.

The point is rather that, by 1927–8, Mess in Tyneside and Black in London were observing very similar phenomena. Apparently the empty church was beginning to bite.

Anglicans were better protected financially than others in Tyneside, but their attendances always remained thinner. *Table 10* demonstrates that in a similar town, Kingston upon Hull,[31] Anglican attendances continued to decline between the two wars. As in Tyneside, Free Churches attendances in Hull were considerably stronger than those in the Church of England. But, as was seen in Chapter 7, it was the Free Churches that collapsed most dramatically after the 1880s (from 30.2 per cent in 1881 to 12.5 per cent in 1904). Anglicans there declined more gradually from 9.7 per cent in 1884, to 6.4 per cent in 1904, and to 5 per cent in 1912. Their decline to 3.9 per cent in 1931 does not suggest that the First World War made any appreciable difference to attendances. They had declined to 1.7 per cent by 1947, to 1 per cent in 1969, and then to an exceedingly low 0.7 per cent by 1990. Anglican decline may have been slower than that of the Free Churches, but it has been distinctly more relentless.

Yet, despite their thin attendances, Anglicans still had the nominal allegiance of the bulk of the population in Tyneside. Mess calculated that in 1925 more than 70 per cent of babies there were baptised in the Church of England. Furthermore, given the weakness of the Anglican churchgoing rate, both Sunday school enrolments and numbers coming for confirmation were surprisingly strong. Some 17.7 per cent of the population aged under 15 years were enrolled in Anglican Sunday schools in Tyneside (the national average, shown in *Table 6*, for Anglicans in 1921 was 19.1 per cent) and about a fifth of all adolescents were confirmed. As might be expected in an urban area, Easter communicants at 4.1 per cent of the total population were lower than the national average of 7.1 per cent.

Herein lay another problem for the Free Churches. Anglicans still retained the nominal allegiance of the bulk of the population, even in an area where non-Anglican churchgoers were so much more numerous. Being financially secure, the Church of England demanded little from this population. As Mess pointed out, most people did not go to church, but 'they like to be married at church, they bring their babies to be baptised, they send their children to Sunday Schools'.[32] And in the Church of England they could achieve all of these things very cheaply. In contrast, Free Churches demanded a great deal. Without the financial support of active members they perished. Belonging to a Free Church was a comparatively expensive business. Tynesiders were not fools.

Mess surveyed an urban population that 'believed' far more than it 'belonged'. Peter Forster's survey[33] of residents in Longhill in 1986 – what he terms a

[31] Hull statistics are derived from *The Hull News*, 10 December 1881, and 13 December 1903 to 17 February 1904; and *Clergy Visitation Returns, Diocese of York*, Borthwick Institute, York.

[32] Mess, *Industrial Tyneside*, p. 138.

[33] Peter G. Forster, *Church and People on Longhill Estate*, Department of Sociology and Social Anthropology, University of Hull, Occasional paper 5, Hull, 1989.

'respectable' Hull council estate – might just as easily represent Tynesiders today. The weekly churchgoing rate claimed by the respondents was low at 4.9 per cent, although together with monthly attenders it was 6.9 per cent. The mean of 6.8 per cent for the whole of Humberside, in the 1989 MARC Europe census, was the lowest in England. Two-thirds of the respondents at Longhill stated that they never went to church at any point in the year – not even at Christmas. In contrast, in the two European Value Systems Study Group surveys (to be examined in a moment), non-attenders represented just less than half of those sampled.

Yet almost half considered themselves to be 'religious', two-thirds thought 'there is a God' and still claimed to pray privately, and three-quarters did not believe in horoscopes or fortune-telling. On the other hand, in sharp contrast to the findings of *The Army and Religion*[34] earlier in the century, little more than a third believed in 'life after death' and just over a fifth in reincarnation. Given the option of being identified in (say) hospital as an 'atheist/agnostic', 'none', or as some form of Christian, most people opted for the latter. More than three-quarters identified themselves as 'Church of England'. Furthermore, four-out-of-five people believed that non-churchgoers had a right to marry in church and even more to have their children baptised. In summary: most people wanted to use churches for rites of passage, but they did not attend them for regular worship; they still prayed privately and had some theistic beliefs, but they were sceptical about after-life and were only loosely affiliated to any church; and, in the final resort, their affiliation rested with the Church of England.

3

The second half of the twentieth century has seen a continuing overall decline in attendances. It has also seen four areas of very considerable change. First, and most dramatically, Sunday schools have collapsed. Second, there is now longitudinal evidence suggesting a shift away from specifically Christian beliefs. Third, Catholic attendances have declined. And fourth, suburban areas that were still showing remarkable resilience at the beginning of the twentieth century had radically declined by the end of the century. All of these changes are new. Less new is the chronic decline of older Free Churches and of the Church of England. However, verifiable predictions about their decline are new. Finally, increases in newer/smaller Free Churches are certainly not new, but their present forms in house churches, charismatic groups and ethnic churches are new.

Table 6 shows the decline of Sunday schools. Between the wars the pattern established in the second half of the nineteenth century basically persisted. Most children went to Sunday school, but most of their parents did not go to church. After the Second World War this pattern changed significantly: most children did not go to Sunday school, nor did their parents go to church.

By the end of the 1970s, child involvement with churches, in any measurable form, was lower than it had been since the early nineteenth century. If Sunday

---

[34] D.S. Cairns (ed.), *The Army and Religion*, Macmillan, London, 1919.

school enrolments in 1818[35] measured some 11.5 per cent of the population aged under 15 years, by 1979 across denominations they measured an estimated 10.5 per cent. Free Church and Anglican Sunday school attenders in 1989 amounted to just 6.7 per cent. If child churchgoers in the past could be added, the present situation may be even worse. In Chapter 7 it was seen that in London in 1903, in addition to high Sunday school attendances, children constituted a third of typical church congregations. In 1989 there was still a difference between the attendance rates of adults and children, but the gap was narrow (9.5 per cent and 13.7 per cent). MARC Europe predicted at the time that by 2000 this gap would be even narrower (9 per cent and 11 per cent). In reality their 1998 census showed that the gap between adults and children had disappeared altogether; both had attendance rates of just 7.5 per cent.[36]

This collapse of child involvement with churches in the second half of the twentieth century may account, directly or indirectly, for most of the rapid decline in churchgoing to be mapped out more fully in a moment. The three MARC Europe/Christian Research censuses of 1979, 1989 and 1989 show clearly just how this collapse has affected the age profile of congregations. As can be seen, those in the oldest age-group increased from representing 18 per cent of all churchgoers in 1979 to 25 per cent in 1998, whereas those in the youngest decreased from 26 per cent to 19 per cent. The population at large also became more elderly (the oldest group rising from 15 per cent to 16 per cent) and the proportion of children declined (21 per cent to 19 per cent), but the rises and falls among churchgoers were obviously sharper. So, if there were 100 people of all ages in church in 1979 there were 64 in 1998, yet in the youngest age-group there would have been 26 in 1979 but only 12 in 1998, whereas in the oldest group 18 reduced to 16. The pattern of increasingly elderly congregations is evident across cohorts:

Table 8.1 Age profile of churchgoers

Age group	1979 (%)	1989 (%)	1998 (%)
<15	26	25	19
15–19	9	7	6
20–29	11	10	9
30–44	16	17	17
45–64	20	22	24
65+	18	19	25

Source: MARC Europe/Christian Research

---

[35] The 1818 Sunday school statistics have been calculated from *Parliamentary Report: Census 1851 – Education: England and Wales.*

[36] Calculated from Peter Brierley (ed.), *Prospects for the Eighties*, MARC Europe, 1980, *Prospects for the Nineties: Trends and Tables from the English Church Census*, MARC Europe, 1991, and *UK Christian Handbook: Religious Trends*, No. 3, 2001 (Christian Research, Vision Building, 4 Footscray Road, London SE9 2TZ).

In *Churchgoing and Christian Ethics*[37] I identify other evidence pointing in the same direction. Questionnaire-surveys that ask people about their religious affiliation usually include a 'no religion' group. Much depends upon the wording of the initial question. Polls that ask bluntly 'What is your religious denomination?', tend to minimize this group (it is perhaps a question expecting an affirmative answer). Others are less directive, notably the invaluable 1950 survey of Geoffrey Gorer,[38] asking 'Would you describe yourself as being of any religion or denomination?', and more recently *British Social Attitudes*,[39] asking 'Do you regard yourself as belonging to any particular religion?'. Those responding negatively to either of these very similar questions constitute the 'no religion' group here:

Table 8.2 'No religion' compared

Age-group (as % pop)	Gorer 1950 n = 4983	BSA 1983–4 n = 3280	BSA 1994 n = 3315
18–24	22	61	66
25–34	22	44	54
35–44	24	35	49
45–54	22*	25	31
55–64	22*	22	26
65+	24	15	21
All	23	33	39

Note: * Groups combined

In 1950, at a time when most people living in England had at least been to Sunday school, there was very little difference across the 'no religion' age-groups. However, by the 1980s there were already wide differences between young and old – differences that deepened a decade later. More than that, the differences between the 1980s and 1990s suggest that these were cohort changes – the 'no religion' groups in the 1980s carried their diminished affiliation into the 1990s. Given the very sharp decline in Sunday school attendances in the second half of the twentieth century, it is not difficult to see how such cohort changes would have radically affected overall churchgoing rates. With the oldest generation gradually dying and the younger generations increasingly disaffiliated, the 36 per cent decline in churchgoing mapped by MARC Europe/Christian Research between 1979 and 1998 becomes understandable.

---

[37] Cambridge University Press, Cambridge, 1999.

[38] Geoffrey Gorer, *Exploring English Character*, Cresset Press, London, 1955.

[39] The data used here from *British Social Attitudes* were made available through Data Archive. The data were originally collected by the ESRC Research Centre on Micro-social Change at the University of Essex. Neither the original collectors of the data nor the Archive bear any responsibility for the analyses or interpretations presented here.

4

In *The Myth of the Empty Church* I tentatively mapped out evidence of changing patterns of belief in the second half of the twentieth century. Joint research with C. Kirk Hadaway and Penny Long Marler subsequently provided a much more substantial basis for studying these changes. The results can be seen in *Table 20*. The longitudinal evidence summarized there suggests that there have been three overall patterns of change over a period of half-a-century: specifically Christian beliefs have declined in the general population; disbelief has increased; and minority non-traditional religious beliefs have persisted or even slightly increased. I review these changes at length in *Churchgoing and Christian Ethics* so it is not necessary to review them again here.

By definition, beliefs measured in this crude way lack nuance. None the less this evidence is consonant with other data presented in *The Myth*. The latter suggested that – following the lengthy decline in churchgoing mapped out in every chapter except Chapter 5 and especially following the more recent collapse in Sunday school attendance – it does appear that specifically Christian belief is also in decline.

For example, a survey conducted on students at Sheffield University[40] in 1961 and again in 1972 suggested that decline in religious practice had been faster than decline in belief, but none the less, both had declined. So whereas there was a decline in attendance at church from 46 per cent to 25 per cent, in being an active church member from 38 per cent to 16 per cent, and in saying private prayers daily from 31 per cent to 16 per cent, what the authors termed 'religious belief' had declined less sharply from 73 per cent to 53 per cent. In both surveys, female students were always more inclined to actual practice and to belief itself than male students, but none the less their rate declined also.

Another example is supplied by the two Independent Television surveys of 1968 and 1987, reported in *Godwatching: Viewers, Religion and Television*.[41] The percentage of people switching on television to watch a religious programme had declined, from 34 per cent to 29 per cent, although it was still very much higher than the percentage of those who went to church. However, the proportion of those who specifically switched off, or changed channel, when a religious programme came on had increased more decisively from 16 per cent to 27 per cent. Furthermore, in every area of belief measured, there was a shift away from Christian beliefs. So, in response to the statement 'God created the universe', 80 per cent thought it true in 1968 and only 62 per cent in 1987. Examples of other shifts were as follows: 'Jesus Christ is the Son of God' (85 per cent down to 74 per cent); 'The miracles of the Bible really happened' (70 per cent to 54 per cent); 'People who believe in Jesus as the Son of God can expect salvation' (66 per cent to 47 per

---

[40] G.W. Pilkington, P.K. Poppleton, J.B. Gould and M.M. McCourt, 'Changes in Religious Beliefs, Practices and Attitudes Among University Students Over an Eleven-Year Period in Relation to Sex Differences, Denominational Differences and Differences Between Faculties and Years of Study', *British Journal of Social and Clinical Psychology*, vol. 15, 1976, pp. 1–9.

[41] Independent Television Authority, *Religion in Britain and Northern Ireland*, 1970, and *Godwatching: Viewers, Religion and Television*, Independent Television Publications, London, 1988.

cent); 'Without belief in God, life is meaningless' (68 per cent to 44 per cent); 'To lead a good life it is necessary to have some religious belief' (69 per cent to 48 per cent).

In *Churchgoing and Christian Ethics* I also present evidence that conventional Christian belief is declining faster among the young than in any other age group. Even in 1947 Mass-Observation reported that:

> both in regard to formal observances and general attitude, the younger generation show a much more critical outlook, and much less interest. Two young people (under forty) express doubt about the existence of God for every older person who does so. It is mostly the younger generation who dismiss religion with apparent disinterest.[42]

The European Value Systems Study Group surveys of the early 1980s and 1990 in ten European countries also established such differences across age-groups. Just taking the two British EVSSG surveys,[43] the 1990 survey found that only 31 per cent of the 18–24 age-group reported that they had been 'brought up religiously at home', compared with 58 per cent of the 35–44 age-group and 82 per cent of the 65-and-over age-group. The sharpest declines in Christian belief were noted between the 1981 and 1990 surveys in the youngest age-group: belief in God declining from 59 per cent to 45 per cent, in a personal God from 23 per cent to 18 per cent, in life after death from 44 per cent to 36 per cent, in heaven from 46 per cent to 41 per cent, and in sin from 58 per cent to 49 per cent. Disbelief also increased sharply in this age-group: professed atheism rising from 28 per cent to 38 per cent and disbelief in life after death from 39 per cent to 52 per cent. So, although levels of belief in most of these areas were still higher than the 31 per cent level of those 'brought up religiously at home', Christian belief among the young did seem to be declining sharply and disbelief growing. Indeed, amongst those over 55 years-old in 1990, some of these beliefs remained relatively strong: 83 per cent believed in God, 48 per cent in life after death, 62 per cent in heaven and 70 per cent in sin. Among this older group there was not a considerable difference from those levels of belief in the oldest age-group recorded three or four decades earlier.

This sharp decline in Christian belief among the young is also what Leslie Francis' twenty-year study[44] of religious attitudes amongst 11–15-year-olds helps to establish. Testing attitudes on twenty-four questions on six samples of school-children between 1974 and 1994 he shows changes in all but one area. Some of the changes are very sharp indeed. For example, the statement 'I know that Jesus helps me' was supported by 42 per cent in 1974 but only by 22 per cent in 1994; support for the statement 'God is very real to me' fell from 41 per cent to 25 per cent; support for 'The idea of God means much to me' fell from 40 per cent to 24 per

---

[42] Mass-Observation, *Puzzled People*, p. 157.

[43] See Mark Abrams, David Gerard and Noel Timms (eds), *Values and Social Change in Britain: Studies in the Contemporary Values of Modern Society*, Macmillan, London, 1985, and Noel Timms, *Family and Citizenship: Values in Contemporary Britain*, Dartmouth, Ashgate, 1992.

[44] Reported in William K. Kay and Leslie J. Francis, *Drift from the Churches: Attitude Toward Christianity During Childhood and Adolescence*, University of Wales Press, Cardiff, 1996.

cent; for 'God helps me to live a better life' fell from 39 per cent to 22 per cent; for 'Prayer helps me a lot' fell from 36 per cent to 20 per cent; and for 'I know that God helps me' fell from 42 per cent to 25 per cent. The mean score for each year-group declined over the twenty-year period.

Another important source of evidence used increasingly by historians and social scientists is drawn from oral-history archives. This evidence too suggests that the twentieth century has seen a sharp move away from conventional Christian belief and practice, especially among the young. Callum Brown summarizes the evidence for the period 1900–40 as follows:

> Interviews show that Sunday school attendance was widespread. Amongst the Stirling archive of 76 female Protestant interviewees, 73 per cent claimed to have attended Sunday school, 45 per cent attended weekday meetings of teetotal organisations (the Band of Hope, the White Ribboners or Good Templars), 13 per cent were in church-affiliated uniformed youth organisations, and 14 per cent were in church choirs. Most of those who didn't attend Sunday school or uniformed organisations lived in rural areas where either these organisations did not exist or travel to church was extremely difficult. The sheer weight of testimony towards children's patronage of church organisations is compelling. If the level of child association was extraordinarily high, the *intensity* of their connection was remarkable. The researcher in an oral-history archive comes away overloaded with accounts of entire Sundays, and two or three weekday evenings, devoted to religious meetings.[45]

He contrasts this sharply with those brought up since 1958, when he believes churches were at their zenith (he bases this claim largely on membership statistics). Although I have argued elsewhere[46] that he exaggerates the extent of churchgoing decline in the late twentieth century (seeing it as a product of cultural changes in the 1960s, but ignoring the mass of earlier evidence of churchgoing decline presented in *The Myth of the Empty Church* which he lists in his own bibliography), his use of oral evidence does support the claim that the specific collapse of children's involvement in churches did largely happen in the second half of the twentieth century.

Of course, there is never an easy way of encapsulating belief, let alone 'religiosity', in a form that will satisfy both the complexities of faith and the simplicities of quantitative, or even qualitative, questionnaires. Yet questionnaires and oral interviews do suggest that, in the absence of both churchgoing and Sunday schools, a broad spectrum of Christian beliefs in any recognizable form is unlikely to persist in the general population. *The Army and Religion* noted that a number of key beliefs – in God, in prayer, and in some form of afterlife – were still predominant among soldiers during the First World War. Yet, even then, Christocentric beliefs were distinctly less common. Most soldiers had been to Sunday school as children but few to church as adults. By 1947 the Mass-Observation survey suggested that (in a London borough at least) a majority still believed in God but not in afterlife and that about two-thirds of the adults 'never, or practically never, go to Church'. At the beginning of the twenty-first century, the bulk of a generation that has been

[45] Callum G. Brown, *The Death of Christian Britain*, Routledge, London, 2001, p. 140.
[46] See my *Changing Worlds*, Continuum, London, 2002, Chapter 6.

neither to Sunday school nor to church has even less contact with Christian beliefs – however they are defined.

None of this is to assume an absence of religious belief. It suggests mainly a shift away from specifically Christian beliefs, as *Table 20* suggests (albeit also with increasing scepticism or, at least, a squeezing out of the 'don't knows'). Recently there has been considerable discussion by sociologists of religion about forms of 'common', 'implicit', 'folk' or 'unofficial' religion that may still persist in British society.[47] Again, this is not the place to discuss this complex issue. A shift from Christian beliefs (however defined) does not necessarily imply a shift towards secularism. Forster concluded from his study that, ironically, today 'religious commitment' and 'anti-religious commitment' are both 'seen as suspect on Longhill Estate'.[48]

Two longitudinal surveys of religion in British newspapers that I conducted also suggest there has been a shift away from conventional Christianity. The religious content of all the national daily newspapers was measured, first in August 1969 and then in July 1990. The results are given in *Table 17*. A purely conventional definition of 'religious content' was adopted: 'items referring explicitly to religious institutions, their functionaries, or their central transcendent beliefs'. This religious content was measured as a percentage of mean total space in each newspaper for the full month in each case. A perceptual definition of the notion of 'deemed hostile' was adopted: 'items which mainstream religious institutions might themselves deem to be hostile – e.g. reports about clergy or their families involved in sex scandals or crime'. And the 'peak religious content' was measured on 1–2 August 1969 (the historic Peace Mission to Uganda of Pope Paul VI) and on 26 July 1990 (the first announcement that George Carey was to become Archbishop of Canterbury).

From *Table 17* it will be seen that the relative proportion of space given to religious items in national newspapers has declined overall and in all newspapers except *The Daily Telegraph*. However, material perceived as 'hostile' has also declined over all. Only *The Daily Mail* and *The Sun* were now noticeably hostile. In those papers that still publish general letters from readers (i.e. non-tabloids), there is always a far higher religious content than in the paper as a whole. In the tabloids (including *The Daily Express* and *The Daily Mail*) the space given to horoscopes in 1969 was approximately equal to that given to religious items. In 1990 it was half as much again.

In so far as newspapers reflect popular sentiments, then a shift away from mainstream religious institutions, but with little outright hostility, is again apparent. Nevertheless, letter writers throughout would appear decidedly more interested in these institutions than the newspapers themselves.

---

[47] See Edward Bailey (ed.), *A Workshop in Popular Religion*, Partners Publication, London, 1996 and 'Implicit Religion: A Bibliographical Introduction', *Social Compass*, vol. 37, 1990, pp. 499–509; see also P.H. Vrijhof and J. Waardenburg, *Official and Popular Religion: Analysis of a Theme for Religious Studies*, Mouton, Netherlands, 1979.

[48] Forster, *Church and People on Longhill Estate*, p. 125.

5

The third major change since the Second World War concerns Catholic attendances. For most of the period studied in this book, the persistence of Catholic churchgoing, compared to the Church of England or the Free Churches, is one of the most remarkable features. At every measurable point it has been noted that Catholics are quite distinct from any other denomination. Their ratio of church seats to attendances has always been strikingly different. And even while the attendances of others have decreased, Catholic rates have, until recently, held steady or even increased.

In 1851 total Catholic attendances in England represented just 3.8 per cent of all church attendances; in 1989 they represented 35.2 per cent. In 1851 all their attendances (including Sunday school) represented 2.1 per cent of the total population; by 1989 they represented 3.6 per cent. Since the Catholic population of England was estimated in the mid-1980s at about 11 per cent of the whole,[49] it would seem that about a third of all Catholics typically went to church then on a Sunday. Again, in 1851 Catholics had 641 attendances of all ages on average per church; by 1989 they still had very sizeable attendances, estimated[50] at 463. No other denomination can remotely match these figures.

Furthermore, churchgoing in England's major conurbations would be extremely thin today without Catholics. In London, Catholics in 1989 represented 38 per cent of adult church attendances, in Birmingham 48 per cent, in Manchester 51 per cent, and in Liverpool 66 per cent.

This dominant position in Liverpool has been achieved thoroughly against the trend in other denominations. In Chapter 7 it was shown that morning and evening Catholic attendances there amounted to 13.9 per cent of the population in 1851, when non-Catholic attendances (Church of England and Free Church combined) amounted to 26.0 per cent. By 1912 they were still 10.2 per cent, when non-Catholic attendances had declined to 16.4 per cent. Catholic attendances in Merseyside as a whole amounted to 14.6 per cent in 1979, whereas non-Catholic attendances were just 5.4 per cent. Even though Catholic adult attendances in Merseyside apparently declined rather faster than non-Catholic attendances by 1989 – to 12.2 per cent and 5.0 per cent respectively – and again in 1998 – to 8.2 per cent and 3.9 per cent – they do still represent two-thirds of all attendances (albeit in the more ominous context of an attendance across denominations that has dropped from 20.0 per cent in 1979 to 12.1 per cent in 1998).

This difference between Catholics and others in Liverpool is well illustrated by a survey of four districts in 1964.[51] The four districts surveyed – South Scotland,

[49] Michael P. Hornsby-Smith, *Roman Catholics in England*, Cambridge University Press, Cambridge, 1987, his *The Changing Parish: A Study of Parishes, Priests, and Parishioners After Vatican II*, Routledge, London, 1989, and his *Roman Catholic Beliefs in England: Customary Catholicism and Transformations of Religious Authority*, Cambridge University Press, Cambridge, 1991.

[50] Estimate based on the Catholic weekly adult attendances given in Brierley, *Prospects for the Nineties*, p. 45, together with average child attenders; Hornsby-Smith, in *The Changing Parish*, estimates average Mass attendances in 1985 as 540.

[51] W.D. Shannon, 'A Geography of Organised Religion in Liverpool', University of Liverpool, BA dissertation, 1965.

Abercromby, Childwall and Speite – undoubtedly had a combined higher Catholic population than Liverpool as a whole. None the less, the physical patterns evident in all of the earlier Liverpool censuses occurred again here. Catholic churches alone were full on a Sunday. So the overall attendance rate in 1964 was 17.5 per cent of the population of these districts; Catholic attendances amounted to 14.2 per cent of this population and non-Catholics to just 3.3 per cent. The survey was conducted in the summer, but also estimated average attendances throughout the year. On this second basis, Catholics increased to 17.1 per cent and non-Catholics to 4.6 per cent. Yet despite having four-fifths of attendances on either estimate, Catholics had less church seating than non-Catholics. Together all denominations had seating for 17.5 per cent of the population, but non-Catholics had 9.5 per cent and Catholics 8.0 per cent.

Inevitably, Catholic churches in these districts were once again full and non-Catholic churches decidedly empty. On the basis of the summer figures, Anglican churches were on average 19.1 per cent full and Free Church chapels just 12.2 per cent full. If Catholics had only a single Mass in the morning and evening (some of them evidently had more), then they were on average 106.6 per cent full.

In Scotland the position of Catholics[52] is even more dominant than in England. In 1851 total Catholic attendances represented 4.3 per cent of all church attendances in Scotland; by 1984, despite having only 14.9 per cent of the churches in Scotland, their share of churchgoers had increased to 43.5 per cent. In contrast, the Church of Scotland in 1984 had 44.1 per cent of the churches, but only 40.3 per cent of the churchgoers. Catholics in 1984 had on average 474 adults per church and the Church of Scotland 148. In Glasgow the contrast was even greater; in 1851 all Catholic attendances represented 6.5 per cent of the population and 14.5 per cent of total church attendances, and by 1984 Catholic adult and child churchgoers amounted to 11.9 per cent of the population and 61 per cent of all churchgoers. And in Wales, too, total Catholic attendances rose from representing 0.5 per cent of all church attendances in 1851 to 19 per cent in 1982.[53]

Michael Hornsby-Smith largely explains these astonishing differences between Catholics and others in terms of their predominantly immigrant culture. Yet, returning to the late nineteenth-century point noted in Chapter 7, he argues that English Catholics are now losing this distinctive culture and becoming increasingly middle class. He believes that in the process they are being gradually assimilated into the non-churchgoing habits of the bulk of the population. For example, he points out that 72 per cent of Catholics in the late 1930s married other Catholics, whereas by the late 1970s only 31 per cent of them did. Furthermore, 59 per cent of Catholics in the 1930s had other Catholics as the majority of their friends; forty years later it was only 39 per cent.

Hornsby-Smith concludes that, 'Catholics have in the post-war years diffused throughout British society as a result of their increasing participation in the

---

[52] Calculated from *Census of Great Britain, 1851: Religious Worship and Education: Scotland: Report and Tables*, Eyre & Spottiswoode, London, 1854; and Peter Brierley and Fergus McDonald (eds), *Prospects for Scotland: From a Census of the Churches in 1984*, MARC Europe, 1985.

[53] Calculated from Peter Brierley and Byron Evans (eds), *Prospects for Wales: From a Census of the Churches in 1982*, MARC Europe, 1983.

processes of social mobility facilitated by educational expansion and the general economic prosperity.'[54] At many levels, including that of churchgoing, Catholics form less and less of a distinctive culture.

Even in *The Myth of the Empty Church* I warned that there were signs that Catholics were showing signs of decline. For example, there was evidence that the 'success' of Catholics among the urban working classes was probably changing. In 1934 *The Social Survey of Merseyside* found that, 'in the Protestant churches ... manual workers as a class seem to go to church considerably less than the average; in the Roman Church, rather more ... Catholics are much more like the general population, but the numbers of the unskilled are appreciably more, and of the skilled distinctly less, than the average'.[55] In sharp contrast, Horsnby-Smith argued that, 'the alienation of the working class has ... become more apparent with the ending of large-scale immigration from Ireland; this had always given the Catholic Church the misleading appearance of being able to retain the allegiance of the working class'.[56] He also noted that, although the sheer number of Mass attendances in England and Wales changed little between 1960 and 1970, they then declined sharply from 1 934 853 to 1 461 074 in 1985. In addition, between 1965 and 1985 adult converts halved and 'the number of child baptisms, confirmations and marriages declined by over two-fifths'.[57]

Over the last decade evidence of Catholic decline has become more obvious. Today few would deny that attendances at Mass are declining rapidly throughout Britain. In the MARC Europe/Christian Research censuses, English Catholic churchgoers represented 37 per cent of all churchgoers in 1979. However, in 1989 they had declined to 36 per cent and in 1998 to 33 per cent. In a context of overall decline, then, their decline was sharper than that of Anglicans or the Free Churches. In London they were the dominant denomination in 1979, but a decade later they had been overtaken by the Free Churches. Catholic congregations remain far larger than those of any other denomination, but they are generally declining (in England average attendances per church have declined sharply from 542 in 1979 to 326 in 1998). It is clear that the prevalent British habit of non-churchgoing is now affecting Catholics as well.

6

Few denominations have been able to resist churchgoing decline for long and none for ever. It is easy to see how such a predictable change was so easily confused by social historians with cultural secularization. Such a seemingly ineluctable pattern of decline has all the hallmarks of a major social process. And, being intellectuals, historians quite understandably looked for the roots of such a major social process in some earlier, profound, cognitive transformation. The intellectual debates about religion and the triumphs of empirical reasoning in the nineteenth century had

---

54 Hornsby-Smith, *The Changing Parish*, p. 39.
55 Caradog Jones, *The Social Survey of Merseyside*, pp. 338–9.
56 Hornsby-Smith, *Roman Catholics in England*, p. 211.
57 Hornsby-Smith, *The Changing Parish*, p. 207.

ineluctably led to the demise of religious institutions in the twentieth century. It all fitted so neatly.

Just how predictable it has all become is shown by a unique set of studies and predictions made by and about Methodists in the 1960s.[58] It has already been mentioned at several points that Methodists faced a particularly acute problem after their Union. In comparison, the problems now facing the United Reformed Church are quite modest. The sheer number of empty chapels that resulted from the Methodist Union faced its members with an immense problem. Given the mass of data about attendances at these chapels presented in the last few chapters, it will be obvious that many of them did not have a long-term future. In 1851 Methodists of all denominations had just over 11 000 places of worship in England and Wales. In theory, they almost matched the Established Church's 14 000 churches – although in practice a fifth of the Methodist places were little more than rooms. By 1901 Wesleyans[59] alone had over 8000 places of worship and Primitive Methodists over 5000. At the Union of 1932, the Methodist Connexion had inherited some 16 000 chapels. By the early 1960s they had already reduced them to 11 000 and today to little more than 6000.

Correlated with these extensive chapel closures was a relentless decline of the membership of the new Connexion. At the Union the English membership was 769 101. Eleven years later it had dropped below 700 000 and by the end of the 1960s it had dropped below 600 000. In the 1970s it dropped below 500 000 and today it is set to drop below 300 000. Associated with these membership declines is a declining ability to attract new members. Whereas at the time of Union the Connexion could expect to enrol almost 40 000 new members each year, by 1970 this had dropped to less than 12 000, and by 1989 to less than 9000. And Sunday school enrolments, which first dropped below one million in 1939, had declined to less than half a million by the mid-1960s, and then to a tenth of a million by 1989.

Of course members are not necessarily attenders and there has for long been an argument within Methodism about the meaning of their membership statistics. Over time their relationship to attendances has undoubtedly changed. Today, however, the correspondence is much closer – morning and evening attendances combined represented 84 per cent of membership by 1972 and 94 per cent by 1989. Since 1972 it has been possible to measure average attendances as well as membership. They too show a similar pattern of numerical, and of course proportional, decline. Using the Methodist Church's own statistics: in 1972 morning and evening attendances in England amounted to 476 429, or some 1.3 per cent of the adult population, but by 1989 they had declined to 380 620, or 1 per cent of the adult population. These losses occurred particularly in the evening services, which had more than halved over the seventeen years. Evening congregations have become visibly depleted up and down the country. Using

---

[58] All of these are held in the Methodist archives in the John Rylands Library, University of Manchester.

[59] Calculations that follow are from *Minutes of the Methodist Conference*; Robert Currie, Alan Gilbert and Lee Horsley, *Churches and Churchgoers*, Cambridge University Press, Cambridge, 1977; and recent data kindly supplied by the Division of Ministries, the Methodist Church.

MARC Europe/Christian Research statistics:[60] in 1979 there were 621 000 attendances of all ages representing 1.3 per cent of the general population, but by 1998 they had almost halved to 379 700 representing just 0.8 per cent of the general population.

Because of the visible nature of Methodist decline, there have been a series of internal studies of it since the early 1960s. In a study of Methodism in Wales over the previous decade, W.J. Roberts was already reporting in 1960 that 'the restricted nature of our Methodist membership, both in numbers and quality, makes it difficult to provide suitable leaders'. He related this decline to external factors such as depopulation and the emigration of young people looking for work. But he was also aware of more internal factors, including, it should be noted, 'the weakness of the Free Church witness through the multiplication of small and ineffective units', and 'the closure of churches' which he was convinced 'had an adverse effect upon Church membership'. Frank T. Pagden also concluded from a study of the Liverpool District in 1966 (just as Abraham Hume had a century earlier), that 'larger churches in cities are finding the going tough'. He was, though, still convinced that 'smaller societies can thrive'.

Some ministers undertook questionnaire-surveys. Among the more adventurous was one by Arthur H. Bird, who surveyed some 1200 people in pubs, bingo halls and clubs in the Rhondda Valley in 1966. From this he uncovered a by now familiar pattern. Whereas only 21 per cent of his sample went to church, 81 per cent had been to Sunday school. Interestingly, though, none made any mention of disbelief. He concluded that 'there is not quite the apathy or indifference to the Christian Church which we have been led to expect'.

Two other questionnaires in the early 1960s looked at 'lapsed members'. The first of these was sent out to ministers in 1962, asking them to identify why people lapsed from membership. Significantly, of the 357 case studies made, only two gave 'loss of faith' as the reason for lapsing. Instead, the most frequent response was 'I seem to have lost interest' and complaints of difficulties of assimilating into new congregations. Almost a third let their membership lapse when they moved from one area to another and then failed to join a new congregation. The second questionnaire, by the social scientist John Butler, concluded from a study made in 1964 that those most involved in leadership functions in their congregation were the least likely to lapse. However, over all 'the impression is formed that the decisions involved in becoming what is termed a "lapsed member" are rarely clear and precise decisions'.[61]

It is interesting to note that these two Methodist studies of 'lapsed members' fit the broad pattern discovered in the late 1940s, Mass-Observations surveys (albeit neither they, nor I when I wrote The Myth of the Empty Church, were aware of this). On the basis of these surveys, The British Weekly argued that people stop going to church because they move house, lose interest, or change life-style, rather than because they lose faith. Indeed, 'comparatively few churchgoers maintain the

---

[60] Peter Brierley (ed.), UK Christian Handbook: Religious Trends, No. 2, 1999, p. 12.3 (Christian Research, Vision Building, 4 Footscray Road, London SE9 2TZ).

[61] John R. Butler, 'A Sociological Study of Lapsed Membership', The London Quarterly and Holborn Review, July 1966, p. 243.

practice unbroken throughout their lives … people who return to church are generally won back as a result of personal contact, and as least as often by personal friends or lay visitors as by ministers'.[62] The empirical work of John Finney[63] and then of Philip Richter and Leslie Francis[64] in the 1990s has confirmed this broad picture.

The most impressive piece of Methodist research was the one again conducted by John Butler, but this time with Bernard Jones in 1967. They analysed Methodist membership in the Manchester/Stockport District, making a series of predictions about its rate of decline over the next thirty years. They have proved astonishingly accurate. In 1966–7 there were 31 088 members in the District. Almost a third of these were aged over 60. Butler and Jones predicted that in twenty years time membership would have declined to 18 748. In reality, it was 18 678 in 1986. By 1996–7 they predicted that it would decline to 14 564 and that two-fifths of the membership would then consist of those aged over 60. In reality, again, it was 14 824 in 1996 and 14 456 in 1997.

Clearly, their central prediction that membership would more than halve in three decades was not simply based upon guesswork. Nor, in contrast to Callum Brown and especially to Steve Bruce who often uses Methodist decline in Britain as a prime example,[65] was it premised upon some invisible but ineluctable process of secularization. Rather, it was based upon four careful assumptions. The first was that, with such an elderly membership, 2 per cent a year would be lost through death. The second was that lapsed members (mainly through transfer) would amount to 3 per cent a year in the 21–60 age group. The third was that new members would amount to 2.5 per cent per year: half of them under 20, a quarter aged 21–30, and a quarter aged 31–45. The fourth assumption was that 'within any group the number of members is the same at each single age'.

In other words, they assumed at every point that nothing went radically wrong among the membership. It merely declined through deaths in an increasingly elderly membership, through transfer losses, and through failure to recruit outsiders. Furthermore, they accurately predicted a correlation with church closures: 'if Methodism continues as a separate denomination it will need only half the number of churches'. This final prediction prompted them to prescribe that, 'instead of waiting for churches of various denominations to close one by one in a particular area the churches should plan together for future needs'.

These predictions are all the more persuasive because they did not match the official mood of Methodism in the intervening years. Bernard Jones was well aware of a dichotomy here. There was a spate of documents[66] suggesting how growth had been achieved in Methodism in the 1970s and early 1980s. In a then confidential

---

[62] *The British Weekly*, 13 January 1949.

[63] John Finney, *Finding Faith Today*, British and Foreign Bible Society, Swindon, 1992.

[64] Philip Richter and Leslie J. Francis, *Gone But Not Forgotten: Church Leaving and Returning*, Darton, Longman and Todd, London, 1998.

[65] See Steve Bruce, *God is Dead: Secularization in the West*, Blackwell, Oxford, 2002.

[66] Jeffrey W. Harris, *A Profile of Methodism*, The Methodist Church, Home Mission Division, London, 1982, and David Bridge, *The Missionary Shape of the Congregation: A Study of Methodism's Growing Churches*, The Methodist Church, Home Mission Division, London, 1986.

memorandum[67] prepared in 1980 on 'Likely Trends in Church Membership', Jones wrote somewhat defensively:

> Of course we cannot forecast what precisely the Holy Spirit may achieve against the odds of human expectation either in the ministry or membership, but as the report (on future trends) attempts to assess the ministerial needs it is only right that we should do the same with the information we have about membership. Publicly, as Church Membership Secretary, I have deliberately emphasised the signs of hope and there have been many, but it would be wrong to shut our eyes to some of the more disturbing facts.

The exasperation here is obvious. Of course a whole list of extenuating circumstances and qualifications could be made. The decline in evening congregations may reflect a drop in double attendances and a more elderly group hesitant about going out after dark. The decline in membership may partly reflect a membership roll that is more tightly kept (to avoid excessive local quotas). The decline in young members and the increase in older members may partly reflect changes in the population at large. Some apparent declines are not actually churchgoing losses but rather transfers to house churches. And so forth ...

Yet underlying the predictions of Butler and Jones was a simple assumption that could apply equally to many other denominations today; namely, that the Methodist Church no longer recruits sufficient members to replace those who are lost, for whatever reason. In short, it is a denomination in remorseless decline.

7

And so is the Church of England. Despite periodic bursts of optimism, the evidence of long-term decline is overwhelming.[68] Indeed, it has been so continuous and so predictable that it is perhaps not surprising that it has regularly been cited as evidence of secularization. In the late 1920s it was primarily Anglican statistics that C.E.M. Joad used to illustrate what he termed 'the drift from the churches'.[69] Forty years later it was still Anglican statistics that Bryan Wilson used to illustrate a thoroughgoing model of secularization.[70] Throughout the twentieth century the Church of England has appeared as an icon of religious decline.

Apart from the data on declining urban attendances analysed in the last three chapters, some of the most long-term evidence of institutional decline relates to the clergy. Despite a population in England that has almost tripled, there are now about three-fifths of the number of full-time Anglican clergy than there were in 1851.

---

[67] Kindly supplied by the author.

[68] Calculations that follow are from *Facts and Figures about the Church of England*, Church Information Office, London, 1962; *The Church of England Year Books*; *Church Statistics: Some Facts and Figures about the Church of England*, The Central Board of Finance of the Church of England 1991–1996, London, and *Church Statistics: Parochial Membership and Finance Statistics January to December 1999*, Archbishop's Council, Church House, London, 2001.

[69] C.E.M. Joad, *The Present and Future of Religion*, Ernest Benn, London, 1930.

[70] Bryan Wilson, *Religion in Secular Society*, Watts, London, 1966.

At that time there were an estimated 16 194 clergy, each one serving on average 1043 people. The sheer number of Anglican clergy reached a peak in 1901 of 23 670, but they were by now each serving on average 1295 people (and, as was seen earlier, the disparity between urban and rural parishes had become wider). By 1951 they had declined to 18 196, each serving on average 2111 people, and by 1999 they had almost halved to 9648 (now, of course, male and female) full-time clergy, each serving some 5182 people. In addition, after 1851 clergy became progressively older. Then almost a third were aged under 30, but a hundred years later it was just a tenth.

In the early 1900s the Sunday school movement across denominations reached its peak. In 1910 there were some 2 437 000 on the registers in Anglican Sunday schools, representing an estimated 29.8 per cent of the population aged 3–14. By 1931 the sheer number had dropped by a quarter, but, since the birth rate had also dropped sharply, this still represented an estimated 24.8 per cent of the population aged 3–14. However, by 1958 enrolments had dropped to 1 161 000 representing just 14.9 per cent. By 1989 Sunday school attenders[71] amounted to just 2.5 per cent of the population aged under 15.

Since 1968 usual Sunday attendances in the Church of England have been collated centrally. Six years earlier Leslie Paul was the first to survey attendances across dioceses, using a one-tenth sample, in his celebrated report *The Deployment and Payment of the Clergy.*[72] However, considerable caution must be taken about using the percentages he gave in the body of the report, since they were worked out on the basis of clergy estimates of the populations of their parishes. Too late in the day, Leslie Paul discovered that these were seldom accurate and were sometimes double the populations measured in the 1961 population census. Even when Leslie Paul's percentages are worked out afresh from the data he supplied in an appendix to his report (suggesting an overall rate of 5.9 per cent), his sampling technique seems to have exaggerated churchgoing rates considerably in rural dioceses.[73] This may unfortunately have led him to identify churchgoing decline as a purely urban phenomenon.

Using centrally collated Anglican statistics, *Table 18* shows that usual Sunday attendances have almost halved in three decades, declining from 3.5 per cent of the population in 1968 to 1.9 per cent in 1999. MARC Europe/Christian Research suggests an even sharper decline, from 3.6 per cent in 1979 to 2.0 per cent in 1998.

Table 18 also shows that some of the most dramatic declines in attendances were in rural dioceses. In thirty-one years Worcester experienced a 59 per cent decline, Sodor and Man 58 per cent, Exeter 57 per cent and Norwich 56 per cent. In contrast, Derby had a decline of 32 per cent, Sheffield 33 per cent, London 34 per

---

[71] This calculation is based on MARC Europe figures.

[72] Church Information Office, London, 1964.

[73] Recalculations from Leslie Paul can be made by dividing his average population per living (estimated by the clergy) by percentage average attendance: this figure is then calculated as a percentage of census-based average population per living. Diocesan figures (and national) are then calculated individually on the basis of this second percentage. But on this basis Hereford had a rate in 1962 of 13.2 per cent (presumably because the sample contained only purely rural parishes), whereas Birmingham's rate was 3.1 per cent – a disparity of more than four-to-one.

cent and Coventry 35 per cent. The gap between rural and urban rates of Anglican churchgoing is clearly narrowing.

These findings are highly revealing. If the five factors identified earlier are accurate, then this is exactly what one would predict. It is the most rural dioceses that have experienced a plethora of empty churches; and of course it is in these areas especially that churches have been closed, that priests single-handedly look after more and more churches, and that sparse and elderly congregations struggle for survival.[74]

All three of these declines – in clergy, Sunday school enrolments, and average attendances – would have affected parishes Sunday by Sunday. They have also been endemic throughout most of the twentieth century. Declines in churchgoing at major festivals and in rites of passage are more recent, particularly in rural areas. For several decades people who were not regular churchgoers, continued to have their babies baptised and, to a lesser extent, encouraged their young people to be confirmed. Some of them also continued to communicate at Easter. But since the Second World War these more occasional practices have begun to decline sharply.

Communions on Easter Day represented 8.4 per cent of the population aged over 15 in 1885. They reached their highest point in 1911 at 9.8 per cent. A slightly wider category of 'Easter Communicants' was adopted from the 1920s, which included communions made in Easter Week. On this basis, in 1928 the rate was still 9 per cent (or 8.5 per cent on the original basis). It had already declined to 6.5 per cent by 1960, to 4.6 per cent by 1970, to 4.2 per cent by 1980, to 3.5 per cent by 1990, and to 3.0 per cent by 1999.

The number of those being confirmed also declined sharply after 1960. In 1872 there were almost 121 000 people confirmed, representing an estimated 28 per cent of the population aged 15. They too reached their highest point in 1911, with some 244 000 representing 38 per cent of those aged 15. By 1960 there were still 190 000 people confirmed representing some 32 per cent. But after this point, and despite confirmands being drawn from a much wider age range, the sheer numbers dropped sharply to 113 000 by 1970, to 98 000 by 1980, to 60 000 by 1990, and to 37 000 by 1999.

Finally, baptisms declined sharply at about the same point as confirmations. In 1900 Anglican baptisms represented 65 per cent of live births, and in 1950 they still represented 67 per cent. They declined to 55 per cent in 1960, to 47 per cent in 1970, to 37 per cent in 1980, to 28 per cent in 1990, and to 19 per cent in 2000.

These patterns of decline are so consistent that it is hardly surprising that they should now be regarded as predictable. At every point, the Church of England appears to be an organization in chronic decline. The decline certainly started very much earlier than Callum Brown claims. None the less, the confirmation and baptism statistics do support his thesis about a radical decline in church involvement by young people since 1960. This factor ensures that, like those of British Methodists, Anglican losses consistently exceed gains. Furthermore, this

---

[74] See Leslie Francis, *Rural Anglicanism*, Collins, London, 1985; my *Beyond Decline*, SCM Press, London, 1988; Douglas Davies, Charles Watkins and Michael Winter, *Church and Religion in Rural England*, T. & T. Clark, Edinburgh, 1991.

pattern of decline is mirrored very closely by the Church of Scotland.[75] Communicant membership at the turn of the century represented some 46 per cent of the population aged over 19. By 1941 this had declined to 38 per cent; by 1961 it was still some 37 per cent, but by 1989 it had declined to 21 per cent. Sunday school children had declined from 54 per cent of school-age children in 1901, to 31 per cent in 1941, and to just 11 per cent in 1989. Baptisms too declined from 50 per cent in 1961 to 28 per cent in 1988.

The *Church of Scotland Year-Book* for 1991 pithily expressed the central problem facing all of these denominations: 'From the above it is clear that the fall in membership is due mainly to failure to enrol new members to replace the deaths'.[76]

8

There is one recent pattern of church attendances that seems quite different. After the 1989 MARC Europe census Peter Brierley predicted 'explosive growth' of independent churches within the next decade.[77]

In *The Myth of the Empty* Church I expressed some reservations about this judgement. Firstly, I argued that the historical data presented in the last three chapters showed a persistent pattern, within an overall context of Free Church decline, of only short-term growth in newer/smaller Free Church denominations. Secondly, one of the reasons why newer/smaller groups seemed to find growth difficult to sustain was that their initial growth typically depended, at least in part, upon transfers from other denominations. And thirdly, newer/smaller groups tend to expand to the point of collapse – a pattern apparent already in Afro-Caribbean churches. In the MARC Europe censuses adult attenders in these churches increased from 66 000 in 1979 to 68 500 in 1989 (although, more ominously, child attenders declined from 41 000 to 35 600). However, many new Afro-Caribbean churches were also opened, increasing their number from 822 to 949. As a result, adults per church decreased from 80 to 72, and children from 46 to 38. Ironically, by taking over so many redundant church buildings from other denominations, they may have inherited their long-standing structural (and indeed architectural) problems. With the benefit of hindsight, who was actually right?

MARC Europe bravely made some predictions in *Prospects for the Nineties*[78] that can now be tested. In their data the numerical gains of independent churches and Pentecostals (and, to a lesser extent, Afro-Caribbean churches) were alone responsible for ensuring that Free Church adult attendances held steady between 1979 and 1989. In a few urban areas – notably in Greater London – they actually

---

[75] Calculations from *Church of Scotland Year-Book*, The General Assembly, Committee on Life and Work, Edinburgh, 1991 (figures before the Union of 1929 amalgamate Free Church and Established Church statistics).

[76] *Church of Scotland Year-Book*, 1991, p. 332.

[77] Peter Brierley, *'Christian' England: What the English Church Census Reveals*, MARC Europe, 1991, p. 37.

[78] Peter Brierley (ed.), *Prospects for the Nineties*, MARC Europe, 1991, p. 24.

raised Free Church attendances over all. Nationally, independent churches increased their adult attendances from 206 000 to 292 800 and Pentecostals from 88 000 to 95 200. On this basis, MARC Europe predicted that, by the year 2000, independent churches would have reached 397 000 and the Pentecostals 119 000. With these increases, overall Free Church attendances would by then, despite mainstream losses, be appreciably larger than those of Catholics or Anglicans.

The last of these predictions was confirmed by the 1998 census. Free Church attendances across age groups now represented two-fifths of all churchgoers. Yet the specific predictions about 'explosive growth' among independent churches and Pentecostals did not happen. Not surprisingly it has proved very difficult to maintain categories consistently from one census to the next. Not the least of the problems is that local congregations may change their self-identification from 'Independent', to 'Pentecostal', to 'Charismatic', to 'New', or to whatever. Yet amalgamating all the Free Church groups, but excluding the Baptists, Methodists and United Reformed Church, in 1979 there were 668 000 attendances of all ages, representing 1.44 per cent of the total population, whereas in 1998 there were 699 800, representing 1.41 per cent. Average attendances per church had dropped slightly from 100 to 97. Among specifically Pentecostal churches average attendances per church had dropped more sharply from 127 to 101. Like Pentecostals elsewhere in the world[79] local congregations have tended to be fissiparous.

So, in the event, we were both about half right. It was not exactly 'explosive growth' but it was sufficiently resilient to boost the Free Church share of overall attendances in England between 1989 and 1998. MARC Europe had predicted that the growth of the newer Free Church congregations would ensure that overall attendances across denominations would only decline from 10 per cent of adult and 14 per cent of child populations in 1989 to 9 per cent of adult and 11 per cent of child populations in 2000. In the event, as already seen, both adult and child attendances had declined to 7.5 per cent by 1998. However, without the resilience of the newer Free Church congregations this 7.5 per cent might instead have been 7.1 per cent.

9

The final area of decline in the twentieth century has been in affluent suburban areas. In Chapter 7 it was noted that in the early 1900s there were still pockets of resilient high attendances in places such as Lincoln and Chester and in the more affluent suburbs of London and Birmingham. Since completing *The Myth of the Empty Church* a study of churchgoing in Bromley has shown that this particular resilience did not last throughout the twentieth century.

In 1851 morning and evening attendances combined (excluding Sunday school) across denominations in the parish of Bromley amounted to 37.4 per cent of the

---

[79] See David Martin, *Pentecostalism: The World Their Parish*, Blackwell, Oxford, 2002 and André Corten and Ruth Marshall-Fratani (eds) *Between Babel and Pentecost: Transnational Pentecostalism in Africa and Latin America*, Hurst, London, 2001.

local population of 4127. With a much larger population of 27 292 in 1903, morning and evening attendances (again without Sunday school attendances which were unrecorded) combined still amounted to 37.9 per cent. The independently enumerated 1903 census of churchgoing in Bromley[80] on October 11 was made on a wet day. By a fortunate coincidence the incumbent at Bromley Parish Church also complained in 1851 that 'Sunday 30 March was very wet and the attendance considerably below average'.[81] If morning attendances alone are taken, 22.2 per cent of the population were present in Bromley churches and chapels in 1851 but only 19.0 per cent in 1903. Evening attendances, as elsewhere, rose in contrast from 15.2 per cent to 18.8 per cent. So, compared with most other urban areas studied in Chapter 7, Bromley was evidently a place of fairly high churchgoing in 1903.

The population of old Bromley[82] rose again by 1993, reaching 44 146. However, churchgoing declined sharply in both proportional and absolute terms. The relative absence of evening services in many churches today makes it more difficult to compare churchgoing on the same basis as 1851/1903. However, using the 1903 estimate of Greater London 'twicers', it is possible to produce some broad comparisons. Keeping in mind the three factors of weather, enumeration and Sunday schools, on this basis 31 per cent of the Bromley population were in church in 1903 but only 10.5 per cent by 1993. Thus a threefold decline, and perhaps in reality a fourfold decline, seems to have taken place in these ninety years. Or, to express this differently, there were some 8472 attenders on that Sunday in 1903 but only 4631 on an average Sunday in 1993 despite a greatly increased population.

Stated so baldly, these figures disguise some more subtle changes between denominations in Bromley during the twentieth century. The Roman Catholic Church, at least until recently, has increased both proportionately and absolutely, whereas the United Reformed Church has literally been decimated. Anglicans and Methodists have both declined sharply, whereas Baptists have increased in absolute but not in proportionate terms. The Salvation Army now has one of its strongest congregations in Greater London at Bromley. There is also considerable fluidity between House Churches and the evangelical congregations of the Baptists and the Anglicans. So, although Bromley churchgoing during this century is down by at least two-thirds, relative balances here as elsewhere between denominations are still shifting.

The Anglican churches also suggest that balances are still shifting within denominations. In 1903 the 4620 estimated attenders represented 16.9 per cent of the Bromley population. The 1312 attenders in 1993 represented just 3 per cent. This 3 per cent is still higher than the 2.5 per cent for the Rochester Diocese as a whole in 1994 and higher still than the national 2.2 per cent (see *Table 18*). In 1903 the Parish Church of St Peter and St Paul had congregations more than twice the size of most other local churches (619 in the morning and 898 in the evening),

[80] Richard Mudie-Smith (ed.), *The Religious Life of London*, Hodder, London, 1904.

[81] Margaret Roake (ed.), *Religious Worship in Kent: The Census of 1851*, vol. XXVI, Kent Archaeological Society, The Museum, St Faith's Street, Maidstone, Kent, 1999, p. 39.

[82] As defined in the 1903 survey by the Anglican parishes of St Peter and St Paul, St Mark, St John, Holy Trinity, St George, Christ Church and St Mary. I am most grateful to the Revd Richard Freeman for supplying me with their population figures.

St Luke's Church had the next largest congregations and Christ Church the smallest (80 morning and 67 evening). By 1993 the Parish Church remained strong, but the evangelical Christ Church was now the strongest and St Luke's the weakest.

In 1903 there was a single Roman Catholic church in Bromley with 177 attenders (0.6 per cent of the population), whereas by 1993 there were two churches with a combined 1450 attenders (3.3 per cent of the population). Catholics in Bromley are now the most numerous regular worshippers. St Joseph's Church in 1993 had six masses of a Sunday drawing people from a wide radius. Two Catholic churches served the same area but had slightly more worshippers than the eight Anglican churches. Not surprisingly, all the Anglican churches, except Christ Church and St Peter and Paul's, appeared thinly attended in comparison. Ironically, in 1903 it was only Christ Church that had a thinner congregation than St Joseph's.

Baptists in Bromley have shown remarkable resilience in the twentieth century. In 1903 they had four churches with an estimate of 748 attenders. By 1993 there were five Baptist churches in Bromley (one of them Strict Baptist) with a total of 926 attenders. The earlier figure represented 2.7 per cent of the local population and the later 2.1 per cent. The central Baptist Church in 1993 had much the largest congregations, with 350 adults and 70 children typically present in the morning and 200 adults in the evening (half of the latter having already attended in the morning). It is hardly surprising that some of the smaller evangelical congregations have felt the draught both from this congregation and from that at Christ Church. One chapel, with an attendance in 1993 of just fifteen adults, reported that until a few years ago it had a congregation of one hundred which had now been largely 'fed' to other churches. Churchgoers with young children not surprisingly found the central Baptist Church more appealing than this thinly attended chapel with an entirely adult congregation. As happened at the turn of the century in some towns when the Salvation Army became popular at the expense of local Baptists, and in the previous century when Primitive Methodists benefited from defecting Wesleyan Methodists, so in the 1990s a similar process apparently continues in Bromley. This time around, such transfers benefit the Baptists.

Finally, Bromley Methodists, Congregationalists and Presbyterians have all experienced severe decline. In 1903 there were five Methodist chapels and missions with an estimated 1244 attenders, representing 4.6 per cent of the Bromley population (they had grown from having just two small chapels with attendances representing 3.2 per cent of the population in 1851). By 1993 there were three chapels, but now with only 245 attenders, representing 0.6 per cent of the local population. Congregationalists and Presbyterians, each with their own church (now a part of the United Reformed Church) had congregations representing 4.0 per cent of the local population in 1903 (Independent attendances in 1851 represented 5.8 per cent of the population). Ninety years later their two congregations represented just 0.4 per cent. Like most of the Anglican churches, they have found it difficult to recruit new members in an area with an array of active Baptist and evangelical churches. Alongside these established Free Churches, there is also a small Society of Friends. It too makes little numerical impact upon local churchgoing.

The institutional weakness of many of the churches in Bromley by 1993 is underlined by the relative absence of children within them. In the Anglican churches only 252 children were recorded as usual Sunday attendances in 1993. In contrast, in 1903 there were 878 children present in the morning service alone (and, of course, at least twice that number might be expected to attend Sunday school in the afternoon). It does seem, then, that this suburb shares the national pattern already outlined of a sharper decline in attendance among children than among adults. It will be seen in the next chapter that, in Rowntree's surveys of churchgoing in York,[83] a relative absence of children proved to be a crucial criterion in his accurate predictions about the future of particular denominations. Even Catholic attendances of young people in Bromley in 1993 were little better. Within the Methodist and United Reformed Church attendances of young people were considerably worse.

Old Bromley represents in microcosm a pattern of decline and change evident elsewhere in suburbia. Measured by MARC Europe/Christian Research[84] fourteen (out of thirty-three) districts of Greater London had attendances across denominations of 10 per cent or more of the local population in 1989 but only eleven in 1998. Bromley as a whole (some seven times larger than the area studied) had reduced from 10.7 per cent to 8.1 per cent, Richmond-upon-Thames from 10.8 per cent to 7.8 per cent, and Redbridge from 10.0 per cent to 8.0 per cent. Excluding the Cities of London and Westminster (doubtless inflated by tourists), there were still some areas of remarkably high churchgoing in 1998 – notably Brent at 15.8 per cent, Kensington and Chelsea at 14.8 per cent, and Enfield at 14.0 per cent – but they were getting fewer and were in any case well down on the 1903 highest districts noted in the previous chapter – notably, High Barnet at 60 per cent, Ealing at 51 per cent and Woodford at 50 per cent.

10

The complex evidence about churchgoing in the twentieth century, set out in this chapter and the last, can be presented in summary form:

- *By 1900* urban adult Anglican and Free Church churchgoing was already in decline.
- However, there were still pockets of suburban and rural resilience.
- Sunday schools were still very strong.
- However, rural churches were already facing radical problems of overbuilding and depopulation.
- *By 1918* most soldiers in the First World War had been as children to Sunday school, had residual Christian beliefs, but had not been regular churchgoers at home.
- Chapels and mission halls in rural and central urban areas were already closing.

---

[83] B. Seebohm Rowntree, *Poverty: A Study of Town Life*, Macmillan, London, 1901, *Poverty and Progress: A Second Social Study of York*, Longmans Green, London, 1941 and *English Life and Leisure: A Social Study*, Longmans Green, London, 1951: written with G.R. Lavers.

[84] Peter Brierley (ed.), *UK Christian Handbook: Religious Trends*, No. 3, 2001, p. 12.36 (Christian Research, Vision Building, 4 Footscray Road, London SE9 2TZ).

- *By 1950* Catholics had become a major force among churchgoers.
- Sunday school attendances and confirmations were still relatively high, albeit declining.
- There were still pockets of resilient churchgoing in some deeply rural areas.
- There was a slight rise in churchgoing in middle-class suburban areas
- Generalized Christian belief was still relatively strong.
- But otherwise decline continued.
- *By 1970* Catholic decline had started.
- Sunday school attendances and confirmations were declining fast.
- Christian belief had started to decline.
- Independent Free Churches were growing in urban areas.
- But older Free Churches were declining fast in rural and urban areas.
- *By 1999* there were no longer any pockets of rural or urban resilience.
- Overall decline was ubiquitous.

9

York: An Urban Case Study

In this book I have deliberately focused on what I have termed 'physical' factors that may have been responsible for churchgoing decline. Unlike most other theorists, I have tended to avoid cultural explanations of churchgoing decline and especially explanations based upon some theory of secularization. It is not, of course, that I am unaware of cultural explanations. Quite the contrary, I have traced some of these cultural explanations back to the beginning of the century and I am well aware how much they have abounded until recently in the academic world. However, I have gradually become convinced that such explanations have served to hide other factors, and particularly those factors that can be gleaned from the mass of census data that I have just discussed.

An obvious question remains, though. Given a detailed instance of long-term churchgoing decline, can physical variables alone account for this decline? Of course, even if they could, that of itself would not prove that they alone have been responsible for churchgoing decline. Frankly there can be no question of 'proof' in an area such as this. Long-term human processes inevitably defy 'proof', if for no other reason than that we cannot return to the mid-nineteenth century and re-run things differently.

Forgetting about 'proof', we can still search for explanations that are more or less convincing in terms of the available data. Better still, we can look for explanations that are susceptible to some form of control. As I said at the outset, my difficulty is not that I have lacked helpful suggestions from others about why churchgoing has declined, for almost everyone seems to have their own pet theory. The problem is not so much a lack of theories as a serious lack of control over them.

For a considerable period scholars were broadly convinced by various theories of secularization, and while this was the case, evidence of churchgoing decline seemed to need little further explanation. But now that they are not so convinced (albeit for other reasons), alternative explanations for churchgoing decline are required. So the question inevitably arises, just how convincing are the sort of physical explanations offered in the previous chapters?

This chapter will offer an extended urban case study precisely to respond to this question. Of all the cities and large towns in England, York provides some of the most complete churchgoing census data. For this reason it can be used as an extended and finely tuned case study of the mass of urban churchgoing data already presented. For once it is possible to trace urban church decline in considerable detail across denominations and over a very long period of time (as well as updating data that I first collected in 1989). Very fortunately York, as the *locus classicus* of recent evangelical Anglican revival, is also a place of considerable interest today. In fact, the data is so rich in York that it is even possible to make predictions about the future of churches there. As will be seen, such predictions have been made successfully in the past. Although ignored at the time, they do suggest that long-term patterns can be predicted with some degree of accuracy and, what is more, that they can be predicted on the basis of measurable and controllable variables.

Although York had no 1880s, newspaper census, it did, as has already been seen, have one of the rare censuses for the 1830s.[1] Longitudinal analysis for Catholic and Quaker attendances in York can even start as far back as 1764.[2] Furthermore, there is uniquely detailed data for the first half of the twentieth century. Seebohm Rowntree's celebrated studies of social conditions in York provide comparative denominational data on adult church attendances for 1901, 1935 and 1948.[3] Once this is set alongside data that I collected myself in 1989 and again in 2001–2, an unusually complete picture emerges. Finally, Church of England clergy returns to the Archbishop provide an exceptionally long run of average Sunday attendance estimates from 1865 through to 1969.[4]

As a result of all of this, there are eight points between 1764 and 2002 at which denominations can be compared, with full church attendance statistics for six of them. There are also a further nine points at which Church of England congregations can be compared in detail with one another.

Owen Chadwick cautions that, 'York was neither a typical town nor a typical cathedral town of the smaller kind, for it contained a larger colony of Irish than was usual in such a town, and the railway and cocoa and brewing offered more industrial employment than was common in a small cathedral town.'[5] It should also be added that it had an unusually large amount of church/chapel seating. Of other large towns in 1851,[6] only Colchester and Wakefield had a slightly higher level of total church/chapel seating. The centre of York, like the City of London, had a profusion of Church of England churches in the early nineteenth century that had little relation to population needs. Again, of other large towns in 1851, only Bath (which, because it did have a newspaper census in 1881,[7] can act as a useful comparator) and Worcester had slightly higher levels of Church of England seating. Also, like the City of London, York still has many of these city-centre churches today, most of which are in search of alternative functions. Finally, in both contexts, a large cathedral, probably sufficient itself for local churchgoing, is surrounded by parish churches.

---

[1] J.R. Wood, *Tables Shewing the Attendance at Churches and Chapels in York 1837*, Manchester City Central Library, Archives Department. MS f 310.6 M5 vol. 4.

[2] *Clergy Visitation Returns 1764*, Borthwick Institute, University of York, York.

[3] See B. Seebohm Rowntree, *Poverty: A Study of Town Life*, Macmillan, London, 1901, pp. 345–9; B. Seebohm Rowntree, *Poverty and Progress: A Second Social Study of York*, Longmans Green, London, 1941, pp. 417–28; and B. Seebohm Rowntree and G.R. Lavers, *English Life and Leisure: A Social Study*, Longmans Green, London, 1951, pp. 339–74.

[4] *Clergy Visitation Returns 1865, 1868, 1877, 1884, 1912, 1931, 1947, 1953 and 1969*, Borthwick Institute, University of York, York, are the clergy returns giving statistics on average Sunday attendances.

[5] Owen Chadwick, *The Victorian Church*, vol. 2, A. & C. Black, 1972, pp. 231–2.

[6] Calculations based on Horace Mann's 1851 *Census Great Britain: Report and Tables on Religious Worship: England and Wales*, British Parliamentary Papers, Population 10, 1852–3 (reprinted by Irish University Press, Shannon, 1970).

[7] The Bath census is to be found in *Keene's Bath Journal*, 12 November 1881, p. 6.

Without claiming that York has always been a 'typical town', it will soon become apparent that it does illustrate clearly (and in greater detail) the various patterns of churchgoing that have been found elsewhere. Furthermore, it illustrates in unusual detail the physical variables already observed elsewhere. The differing patterns of growth and decline that have already been observed between the heavily subsidized Church of England and the opportunistic Free Churches are as apparent here as elsewhere. So is the crucial difference between Catholics and others in their far tighter control over church buildings. In addition, precisely because York had one of the highest levels of urban church seating in the early nineteenth century, it serves as an excellent case study for analysing the possible effects of this seating on factors themselves affecting attendances.

All in all, York provides an obvious challenge to my theoretical position. How far can physical variables account adequately for the churchgoing decline that has characterized York for a hundred or more years?

1

In 1764 the Church of England dominated York. With the Minster and its twenty-three parish churches it easily had sufficient space for the entire population to attend worship at a single point in the day. The twenty-four parishes (in one the church had been demolished) recorded a population of 2709 families. The somewhat elusive concept of 'families' was soon replaced in census data by that of 'households'. However, in 1811 this concept was still in use – a 'family' in York then representing on average of 4.6 people.[8] This would suggest a 1764 population of some 12 461; by 1811 it had grown to 19 099.

Calculated on this basis, there were according to the clergy returns of 1764 some 297 Catholics, 130 Presbyterians/Unitarians, 115 Quakers and 28 Methodists. So, in theory at least, 95 per cent of the population, or just under 12 000 people, were members of the Church of England. In reality, this calculation probably overestimates the strength of the Established Church relative to other denominations. The *Recusant Returns* for 1767[9] estimated (it allowed for five people per family) that there were 642 Catholics in York, and the size of Methodist chapels at that time suggests a far larger Methodist following than 28. Since, for some time to come, individuals continued to go both to services in the Church of England as well as to services in the Methodist chapels, the comparative strength of Methodism was doubtless difficult to assess.

It is difficult also to give an accurate figure for the seating of the twenty-four Church of England buildings in 1764, since by 1851 several had been radically reconstructed. For example, between 1820 and 1851 two churches (St Mary Castlegate and St Lawrence) doubled their seating capacity. Nevertheless, the total Church of England seating for 1851 of some 12 766 would, even in a somewhat reduced capacity, have far exceeded the needs of the 1764 population. In 1851 this would have been sufficient seating for 35 per cent of the population of York. In

---

8 Calculated for York from the 1811 *Census Report*.
9 *Recusant Returns 1767*, Borthwick Institute, University of York, York.

1764 it would have been sufficient for everyone – from newborn babies through to centenarians.

How did the churches cope with this extraordinary over-capacity? In the City of London this problem was not to occur for another hundred years, and then, as seen in Chapter 4, it was set in the context of a rapidly declining inner-city population. In York, in contrast, this over-capacity was fortuitously set in the context of a rapidly increasing population. It was only in the second half of the nineteenth century that inner-city depopulation radically affected its central churches. Nevertheless, in 1764 there was evidence of considerable strain. No church had more than a single service on a Sunday and two (St John and St Lawrence) had services less frequently than that. Several congregations shared a priest, who took a morning service in one church and an afternoon service in another. Altogether there were twelve resident, three partly resident and two absentee incumbents. In contrast, by 1845 there were sixteen resident and five non-resident incumbents.[10]

Only five of the parishes reported the presence of 'dissenting meeting houses'. Catholics already had a convent in one parish and an active church, with a congregation of about 170, in the parish of St Michael le Belfrey. Quakers had a single meeting house, with a congregation of 30, in the parish of St Mary Castlegate.[11] St Saviours had Presbyterian and Methodist chapels and St Sampson had Moravian and Sandemanian chapels.

But how well attended were the Church of England services? If they were all even half full, a sizeable proportion of the Church of England population would have been in church. In the absence of statistical information it is not possible to form a reliable judgement. However, by the turn of the century there is anecdotal evidence that suggests that some churches at least were far from being half full. In the 1851 Religious Census there is a remarkable statement in the return from the old Vicar of St Helen:

> In 1815 I first received the appointment to the vicarage of St Helens – the first time I did duty the congregation consisted only of 7 persons. Having got the church repewed, in a short time every sitting was occupied. I then commenced an Evening Lecture – this also became the same till about 1846. My voice then having failed me, and two adjoining Churches, which before then had only afternoon service, being required to have morning service also, about half of my congregation consisting of persons belonging to these two parishes gradually left and took their place in their own Churches. These – my advanced years – the failure of my voice – and several other evening Lectures having since been commenced in different parts of the City – and one very near where there is a popular preacher – were the chief causes why my congregations are hereto so much reduced.[12]

This quotation contains within it several clues that may help to explain the remarkable increase in Church of England attendances that occurred between 1837 and 1851 and that may already have occurred before 1837. The vicar, John Acaster,

---

10 Calculated from *Report on the State of the Rural Deanery of the City and Ainsty of York*, December 1845, Borthwick Institute, University of York, York.

11 Catholic and Quaker figures are given in *Clergy Visitation Returns* 1764, Borthwick Institute, University of York, York.

12 From the returns of the *1851 Religious Census*, Public Record Office, Kew.

was an evangelical who had been a curate of one of the Richardson brothers. The latter, together with John Graham at St Saviours (the best attended of all the churches in 1837), were strong supporters of the evangelical revival of the first half of the nineteenth century.[13] Together with their former curates, they had a major influence upon the York churches. Certainly the evangelical stress upon preaching is evident in this quotation.

Yet there is more than that. There are hints of more physical factors too: that vigour and church reconstruction contributed to church growth, and that loss of vigour and greater competition from other churches contributed to decline. Acaster repewed his church and introduced an additional service, raising his congregation from 7 in 1815 to 110 in the morning and 130 in the evening (it seated 400) in 1837. The three surrounding churches in 1837 had a single service each. There were afternoon services at St Martin Coney Street with 60 present in a church that seated 620 and at St Michael le Belfrey (despite its reputation as an evangelical stronghold under the Richardsons) with 280 present in a church that seated 1000. St Sampson had a morning service with 220 present.

By 1851, just as Acaster had reported, the situation had changed. By now he had a congregation in the morning of just 45 and an evening congregation of 110. St Michael le Belfrey, on the other hand, had an afternoon congregation of 475 (with an additional 160 in Sunday school) and a new morning service of 420 (with a further 160 in Sunday school). St Martin had changed its service to the morning and had increased attendance to 150. And St Sampson had introduced an evening service or 'lecture' with an attendance of 210, in addition to its morning attendance of 150.

From all of this it is clear that churches at this time were exceedingly changeable. Congregations could move from one church to another within a period of fourteen years. Times of services were changed and extra services were introduced. The single service in 1764, frequently in the afternoon, still characterized thirteen of the twenty-three churches in 1837. But in 1851 only seven churches still conformed to this pattern: a morning service followed by an afternoon or evening service was by now the norm.

The situation at St Helen continued to change in the next decade. With a new incumbent in 1865 it reported a morning service of 150 and an evening service of 250. However, by this time St Michael le Belfrey reported that it was 'decreasing' with a total attendance of 650 and St Sampson recorded a morning attendance of just 55 and an evening attendance of 165. Only St Martin reported that it was still 'increasing': it had two services like the other churches with attendances of 100 and 140. By 1868, however, it too reported that it was 'decreasing', with a total attendance of 140. Unfortunately St Helen also reported a loss in 1868 of 50 attendances from its evening service, and St Michael reported a decline in its total attendances to 350. St Sampson alone was now 'increasing', with an extra 60 people attending its evening service.

By 1877 it was St Sampson, together with St Helen, that reported decreased attendances. In contrast, St Michael reported a slight increase in 1877 and a very

---

[13] See Edward Royle, *The Victorian Church in York*, Borthwick Paper No. 64, University of York, 1983.

substantial increase in 1884. St Martin reported a substantial increase in 1877, but a large decrease in 1884.

It is difficult to escape the conclusion that individual congregations did tend to prosper at the expense of their neighbours. Complete records for these four adjacent churches are available from 1837 through to 1877. Competing for congregations and all clustered near the Minster, they recorded total attendances of 800 in 1837 and 1560 in 1851. But then they started to decline – to 1510 in 1865, to 1365 in 1868, and to 1105 in 1877.

By setting the census data for each congregation alongside the statistical information on average attendances supplied in the clergy returns to the Archbishop, a remarkably complete picture emerges of the early growth and long-term decline of the Church of England in York. *Table 19* gives the results. Where figures are missing or are too vague in the original returns, the nearest figure (indicated by an arrow) has usually been inserted to complete the data.[14] Furthermore, as was seen earlier in the context of Chelsea, independent enumerations here do not suggest that clergy returns of attendances were particularly prone to exaggeration. Any differences are certainly no larger than those detailed in *Table 8*. The figures for 1901, 1935 and 1948 were independently enumerated by Seebohm Rowntree,[15] but still fit the overall pattern of the figures given in the clergy returns. This again confirms that clergy returns, despite some gaps, can provide reliable synchronic and diachronic evidence.

Since afternoon services were once the norm in York, it would be misleading simply to compare morning and evening attendances across different censuses. In any case this expedient, essential in most comparisons (since, as noted earlier, afternoon attendances were not counted in most of the newspaper censuses of the 1880s), is unnecessary in York. Both the 1837 and the 1851 censuses give a full record of morning, afternoon and evening services and it is an amalgamation of all of these that is represented by the attendances in *Table 19*. If attendances at the Minster are also included, then in 1837 there were a total of 5763 attendances representing 20.6 per cent of the population, whereas in 1851 there were 10 117 attendances representing 27.9 per cent of the population. Sunday school attendances, recorded separately in 1837, have been removed from the 1851 figures.

As in Penzance and Stockton, this remarkable increase must be set alongside a corresponding decline in Free Church attendances from 30.9 per cent in 1837 to 25.7 per cent in 1851. There was also an increase among Catholics from 3.4 per cent to 5.7 per cent. What physical factors might be suggested for this Church of England increase?

Several have already been mentioned: church rebuilding, an increase in resident incumbents, vigorous evangelical ministries. As noted earlier in the Chester diocese, a great deal of money and energy was spent in the early nineteenth century on repewing, restoring and sometimes totally rebuilding urban churches. St Michael, Spurriegate (1820) and Holy Trinity, King's Court (1829) had already been extensively restored. But the period between 1837 and 1851 saw one of the busiest

---

14 Only in the returns for St Olave are there two gaps together, and even here, as will be seen later, there are verbal indications of numbers present.

15 See note 3.

rebuilding times in the century. St Saviour (1844), St Sampson (1848) and St Margaret (1851) were all rebuilt. In every case, despite the fact that it was the populations of less central parishes that were growing most rapidly, larger attendances were recorded by 1851. Similarly, larger attendances following rebuilding were seen in 1865 at St Paul and St Thomas, in 1877 at St Clement and St Mary, Castlegate, and in 1884 at St Lawrence and St Maurice.

Furthermore, church extensions in the 'suburbs' proved fairly effective, and a new church in the fast growing area of Holgate was started. *The Yorkshire Gazette* in 1848 announced that, 'The population in the immediate neighbourhood of the schoolroom, and for whose benefit it has been chiefly opened, consists for the most part of families connected with the railway. It is confidently hoped that they will gladly avail themselves of the great privilege thus afforded them.'[16] Still described as a 'schoolroom' in the parish of St Mary Bishophill Junior in the 1851 Census, it could seat 250 and it was, as 'confidently hoped', completely full morning and evening. Four years later a church seating 500 – St Paul – was built to replace it and in 1856 it became a separate parish. The entire parish of St Mary (including an area in the countryside) had a population in 1851 of 4392. In the 1840s it had already increased by 72 per cent. By 1911 St Paul alone had a parish population of 9221.

A further schoolroom, seating 150, was used for two services in 1851 in the fast-growing, suburban parish of St Olave. This too was replaced with a church building, St Thomas, four years later. Not surprisingly perhaps, *Table 19* shows that throughout their history both have continued to be relatively strong churches – albeit with congregations representing only a very small proportion of their surrounding populations.

Livings in York in the nineteenth century were not particularly prosperous, so there was always a tendency to combine those in the city centre. Edward Royle argues:

> The major cause of local pluralism was, and long remained, the poverty of the livings, very few of which could support a clergyman in anything like the style appropriate to his class. In 1840 the average value of the York livings was only £131 a year – and eight of them fell below £100. The majority of the York clergy seems to have managed to reside in the city either by holding more than one benefice or curacy in York itself or surrounding villages, or by virtue of some office in the Cathedral ... The consequent arrangements, however, were workable only on the assumption of a low level of parochial activity.[17]

Nevertheless, a reduction in absenteeism and an increase in curates does seem to have characterized the 1840s. By 1849 there were twenty-one incumbents and fourteen curates in York[18] and it was more widely accepted that incumbents should have pastoral duties beyond a minimal single service on a Sunday. The strongly evangelical character of many of the York clergy meant that by 1851 eighteenth-century styles of ministry were an increasing rarity. By then the absentee rector of

---

[16] *The Yorkshire Gazette*, 10 September 1848.
[17] Royle, *The Victorian Church in York*, p. 7.
[18] Calculated by Royle in *The Victorian Church in York*.

Holy Trinity, King's Court, Richard Inman, who held the living from 1808 until 1866 while living near Rotherham, was already unusual. His church up to 1865, under a succession of poorly paid curates, had mean attendances of only 72. In 1845 the rural dean reported that even the curate was also a pluralist and that 'the only service in this Church is on the Sunday afternoon, which is very thinly attended'.[19] With a resident incumbent attendances considerably increased. Against the trend in most other churches, from 1868 to 1884 the mean more than doubled to 177.

The rural dean of York's report of 1845 marks a very similar crucial point of transition in the Church of England to Bishop Sumner's Charges in Chester. The rural dean was determined to make structural changes: fighting against absenteeism, providing adequate local parsonages, restoring church buildings (some of which were very dilapidated) for public worship, and generally responding vigorously to the challenge offered by 'Dissenters'. He was convinced that 'the Church interest is ... very weak in York', but could with effort be improved:

> To obviate this, every Church should have its Minister, whether Rector or Curate is not very material. But the Benefices being very small and the Churches contiguous, it is often thought advisable to give two to the same person. For instance the Rector of St Mary Castlegate is most desirous of succeeding the Rector of All Saints, Pavement now in his 93rd year, and he hopes to be recommended by the Archbishop to the Chancellor on the ground that the two Parishes adjoin and both benefices would make up but a small living. This is on many obvious accounts the worst sort of plurality ... As it is, the Vicar of Poppleton 4 miles from York holds the curacy of All Saints and he is looking forward to the vacancy. This would be greatly objectionable, unless he had an assistant. The maxim never to be lost sight of is, Where a Church is, there should be a Clergyman.[20]

Can these physical factors alone account for the sharp rise in Church of England attendances between 1837 and 1851? Certainly a new incumbent at All Saints Pavement seemed to have a startling impact on church attendances there. In 1837 there was just a single morning service with 130 people present; in 1845 a single morning service was still the norm, albeit now taken by the popular incumbent of Nether Poppleton; by 1851 the morning service had 275 present and the evening service 343. In the context of a corresponding decline in Free Church attendances, it is plausible to argue that a revivified Church of England was able to attract back part of a population that it once virtually monopolized. A combination of an increase in resident priests, vigorous evangelical preaching, pastoral activity and church rebuilding was able temporarily to regain lost ground.

This explanation would, of course, fit well with the account given in Chapter 5 of the Chester diocese. Nevertheless, it overlooks a more prosaic factor. If in 1837 a total of 5763 attendances (including those at the Minster) represented 20.6 per cent of the then population, in 1851 the same proportion of the new population would have meant 7478 attendances. However, it should be remembered that these are attendances and not necessarily separate attenders. In the 1840s there was a

---

[19] See *Report* in note 10.
[20] See *Report* in note 10.

vigorous attempt to ensure that every church in York moved from having one service on a Sunday to having two. But did this increase in services increase attendances or attenders? Suppose, for a moment, that it was simply the former. In 1837 there were thirty-one Sunday services, whereas in 1851 there were forty-one in the same churches. Calculated on this basis, the 7478 attendances now become 9890[21] – just 227 short of the actual attendances recorded in 1851. Thus what appears to have been a significant rise in Church of England attenders might have been rather a slightly increased proportion of attenders who were simply going to church more often.

This seems, as seen earlier in the context of Chelsea, to have been a trend in the Church of England that continued throughout the nineteenth century. As overall attendances decreased, so the number of services increased. Royle calculates that by 1901 there were sixty-eight Sunday services in the York churches:

> Weekday services also multiplied, mainly towards the end of the century. In 1865, five churches each held one weekday evening service. By 1892 there were thirty-eight weekday services in York, and by 1901 over a hundred. In the decade preceding the First World War, six churches were each providing an average of two or more services every day ... By 1914, Sunday services were being said more than twice in ten churches, and twice in thirteen, while seventeen had some form of regular worship on one or more occasions during the week.[22]

The Free Churches, in contrast, already had at least two Sunday services each in 1837, and only the tiny Swedenborgian chapel had a single service. The new evening services were not universally approved of at the time. In 1838 *The Yorkshire Gazette*, although itself a Free Church newspaper, complained that:

> reading of the Bible and religious books in the family circle and edifying, yet cheerful, conversation, and family prayer. These ought to be the Sabbath evening occupation of every God-fearing household ... The simpler and more wholesome habits of our forefathers inclined to public prayers in the early hours of the morning, rather than after nightfall.[23]

Perhaps it was fears of the secular consequences of gas turning 'night into day', as much as religious conservatism, which prompted these misgivings.

Whatever the internal misgivings, fear of the challenge presented by the Free Churches seems to have been an important factor in prompting the Church of England to provide two Sunday services in every church. Again, reporting on the situation in York in 1845, the rural dean wrote:

> One of the great objects of the Ecclesiastical Authorities should be, to have a double Service every Sunday Morning and Afternoon, which last is in most cases much better than the Evening. In this case every family has its appropriate place of worship and minister – but when the Parish Church is only opened once on the Sunday it is with many

---

[21] The figure of 9890 is calculated by dividing 7478 by 31 and multiplying by 41.
[22] Royle, *The Victorian Church in York*, p. 20.
[23] *The Yorkshire Gazette*, 29 September 1838.

the practice to seek out some other church, where they are probably considered as Intruders, which encourages the habit of wandering from Church to Church, and in very many instances to the Dissenting Chapels. Nothing can be worse than the accommodation for a Congregation in many of the Churches of York, and having only one Service, the number attending is inconceivably small when compared with the Population; and the Church Interest is, as a result, greatly consequent upon this state of things, very weak in York.[24]

When this quotation is compared with that cited earlier from the Vicar of St Helen, the importance of making a clear distinction between attendances and actual attenders becomes obvious. The rural dean in effect provides evidence that extra services were intended to encourage those, who already went to their parish church for one service, from attending a second service elsewhere. The Vicar of St Helen was also aware that *his* congregation at his two services had been partly dependent upon individuals from other parishes. In these circumstances this more prosaic interpretation of the 'increase' between 1837 and 1851 seems to gain some credence.

Of course this explanation need not be adopted quite so rigorously. There is clear evidence in *Table 19* that rebuilding was associated with increased attendances at every stage. The church extensions of St Paul and St Thomas also seem to have attracted additional attendances. The presence of resident incumbents at Holy Trinity, King's Court (together with rebuilding) and All Saints Pavement seem to have been similarly effective. And it is not difficult to imagine that vigorous resident incumbents elsewhere and more numerous curates would have increased attendances. Yet so would an increase in double attendances on a Sunday, and as a result, the dramatic increase in the Church of England may have been as much apparent as actual. Churches were undoubtedly fuller. If on average they were 29 per cent full in 1837, by 1851 they were on average 47 per cent full. But they were still not full. And were they fuller as a result of churches generating new churchgoers or rather recycling existing ones? It is usual for social historians to assume the former. The evangelical revival that undoubtedly transformed the Church of England in York in the first half of the nineteenth century at first seems to corroborate this assumption. Deeper inspection makes it appear more tendentious.

2

After 1851 unambiguous churchgoing decline in the Church of England is evident. Within forty years from 1837 the proportion of attendances to population had returned to their old levels and by 1931 had reached single figures. *Table 19* provides clear evidence that Church of England churchgoing in York has been steadily declining for at least 125 years.

It is a pattern of decline that would have become increasingly obvious to churchgoers themselves. Churches by 1901, which fifty years earlier had been on

---

[24] *Report* as in note 10.

average almost half-full, were now some 35 per cent full. Five years later *The Yorkshire Gazette* noted that, 'vacant seats seem highly fashionable in nearly all the city places of worship'.[25] If in 1851 mean attendances per church were 384, by 1865 this had declined to 349 and by 1877 to 305. The relative distribution of these attendances improved somewhat between 1851 and 1868, with the median rising from 215 to 350. But by 1877 the median too had declined to 250, and by 1931 the mean had declined to 212. By 1989 a mean of 148 and by 2001 one of 104 show continuing decline in attendances and medians of 96 and 71 respectively show that these attendances are also ill distributed. In other words, as has been noticed so often elsewhere, every generation of Church of England churchgoers would accurately have been able to remember fuller churches. Things really were better in the days of old.

There was one important exception to this. As elsewhere in England, Sunday schools in York continued to grow long after Sunday congregations had started to decline. It has already been seen that in Birmingham, for example, church attendances declined by an eighth relative to the population between 1851 and 1892, whereas Sunday school attendances more than doubled. In 1837 Church of England Sunday schools in York had 1708 members, representing some 18 per cent of young people there.[26] In 1851 there were 2117 Sunday school attendances in the Church of England in York, again representing some 18 per cent of young people. Since this was attendances rather than just membership it probably indicated an overall rise. By 1880 there had been a very evident rise in membership to 3850, now representing some 22 per cent of young people.[27] However, by 1935 there had been a decline in attendances to 2973, although this still represented some 17 per cent of young people in York.[28]

If young people in church but not in Sunday school are also included, then Anglican Sunday attendances of young people in 1935 amounted to 4560 or 26 per cent – more than three times the adult attendance rate then of 7.5 per cent. As was seen earlier (*Table 6*), Sunday schools nationally reached their peak (total membership across denominations amounting to over half of all young people) between 1891 and 1910 and were already in decline by the 1930s. The York evidence is consistent with this. By 1948 Seebohm Rowntree reported a further (but unquantified) drop in Sunday school attendances and some of the difficulties that the movement faced:

> Most of the children in Anglican Sunday schools come from the lower middle-class. Parents of a higher class do not often send their children, nor do those of the working-class, unless almost the whole of a parish belongs to that class ... In Anglican Sunday

---

[25] *The Yorkshire Gazette*, 28 April 1906, and 2 and 23 June 1906.

[26] *Report of a Committee of the Manchester Statistical Society, on the State of Education in the City of York*, London, 1837.

[27] W. Sessions, *York and its Associations with the Early History of the Sunday School Movement*, 1882: quoted in Edward Royle, 'Religion in York, 1831–1981', in C.H. Feinstein (ed.), *York 1831–1981*, Sessions, York, 1981.

[28] From Rowntree, *Poverty and Progress*. His other two studies of York churchgoing did not include Sunday school attendances.

schools teachers are difficult to obtain and are recruited mainly from the same class as the children, often beginning to teach as early as 14 years of age ... We were informed that very few children continue in Church membership after they reach an age when they are able to break away from the Sunday school.[29]

By 1989 this situation had changed again.[30] Instead of 4560 attendances of young people at an Anglican church or Sunday school (a distinction that is no longer made in Anglican returns), there were 625. And instead of this representing 26 per cent of young people in York as in 1935, it now represented 3.2 per cent. The drop in adult attendances during this same period of time – from 5395 or 7.5 per cent to 2989 or 3.8 per cent – is serious, but far less pronounced. Two churches now reported that they had no young people attending regularly in any capacity, and nine churches each had less than ten. Just three churches had more than fifty young people attending regularly. Thus, if by the beginning of the twentieth century Anglican churches in York, as elsewhere, were characteristically more empty than full (albeit with thriving Sunday schools), towards the end of the century they were typified also by a relative lack of young people. Now at the beginning of the twenty-first century this situation has deteriorated still further. By 2001 average attendances of young people have fallen to just 345. I shall argue later that this latest change has serious implications for the future of the Anglican Church in York.

Another way of illustrating this change is by looking at baptism and confirmation figures. In 1845 the rural dean of York reported figures both for York itself and for some rural parishes around York. Most babies, he found, were still baptised by the Church of England despite the relative strength of the Free Churches: 'Since there has been a civil Registration Baptisms are said to have decreased, but by inquiring I do not find, that the Dissenters baptise many, nor do the Baptisms appear to me, as yet, to be very much below the number of births'.[31] In the York diocese in 1985 they represented just 38 per cent of live births.

Confirmation rates provide further evidence of Anglican decline. Here the rural dean in 1845 was less sanguine. He concluded that, 'I have been struck in many instances with the very small numbers confirmed when compared with the population.' Calculating that 8 per cent of a given population would be between the ages of 14 and 18, he argued that Tadcaster had only a sixth of this age group coming forward for confirmation and York parishes just a third. Furthermore, in every case that he quoted, there were always more females than males. If the rural dean's method of calculation were still used, then at the turn of the century only 7 per cent of the relevant age group were coming forward for confirmation, and today just 2 per cent.

Of course, such calculations do not take into consideration changing age balances in the population at large; or the wider age band presenting for confirmation today; or, in the case of baptisms, changes in local church policy. Yet they do illustrate the long-standing problem for the Anglican Church noted in Chapter 8. In 1845 the rural dean was worried about the relative lack of communicants in churches. Of

---

[29] Rowntree and Lavers, *English Life and Leisure*, pp. 360–1.
[30] Information based on Church of England returns for 1989.
[31] See *Report* as in note 10.

the York churches that he itemized, communicants at festivals represented less than 5 per cent of local populations and less than a fifth of general church attendances in York in 1851 (clear evidence again that Easter communions are an unreliable indicator of church decline). His problem was to know how to persuade general attenders to become communicants: 'So with regard to the number of Communicants, one half at least are of a proper age, say that one fourth of a Parish attend the Church – How many of that one fourth ever think of communicating?' Today, with Family Communion services being the norm in many Anglican churches, the very small proportion of the population that comes forward for confirmation is far more critical. In contrast to 1845, there is no longer a quarter of any of the parishes in York regularly attending non-sacramental services.

Yet another way of illustrating the long-term decline of the Church of England in York is through a series of hundred-year comparisons. The very rich data available here makes this possible. Between the 1830s and the 1930s attendances relative to the total population halved. Between the 1850s and the 1950s attendances dropped from representing more than a quarter to less than one twentieth of the population; and the sheer number of attendances almost halved. Between the 1860s and the 1960s attendances dropped from a fifth of the population to almost a thirtieth; and the sheer number of attendances was now considerably less than half. Between the 1880s and the 1980s there was a fivefold decline in attendances relative to the population. And, using data that will emerge at the end of this chapter, Anglican adult attendances between 1901 and 2001 in York declined by more than threefold in numerical terms and by some fivefold relative to the population. This final comparison is particularly interesting since it matches so closely the pattern of twentieth-century decline mapped out in the previous chapter for Bromley (with attendances across denominations of 34 per cent of the population for York in 1901 and 31 per cent for Bromley in 1903 they also had similar initial bases).

In 1937 a number of suburban areas in York were officially added to the city. To make comparisons clearer, *Table 19* adds them to the attendances from the 1931 clergy returns onwards (some of those for 1931 were not actually completed until 1936). Some of the churches in these areas certainly benefited from an influx of population. The church at Acomb, for example, reported increased attendances from 330 in 1931, to 450 in 1947, and to 470 in 1953. *Table 19* suggests that there was a slight rise in the attendances at the suburban churches between 1948 and 1953, although not in the more central churches. A similar rise in the early 1950s has been noted by others examining national church membership statistics. It was also a period of renewed church building in suburban areas. However, this rise in suburban attendances in York was not sustained in the 1960s, despite the building of two new churches (St Aidan and St Stephen Acomb).

Even with some growth in the suburbs, by the 1930s the clergy themselves were apparently well aware of overall decline. The responses in 1931 of the York clergy to Archbishop William Temple's question, 'What do you consider the chief evils in your own parish against which the energy of the Church should be directed?',[32]

---

[32] *Clergy Visitation Returns 1931*, Borthwick Institute, University of York, York.

show clear perceptions of this decline. If Temple had hoped that the clergy would talk about the social conditions of their parishioners, he would have been disappointed. The incumbent at St Denys specifically mentioned 'overcrowding in bad houses', but most referred instead to 'indifference' towards the Church. The incumbent at St Lawrence reported more typically: 'Indifference is perhaps what one is chiefly up against. It surprises me that so many parishioners seem thoroughly well disposed to both Church and Clergy yet do not come to Church as regular worshippers.'

As seen earlier, 'Dissenters' in the nineteenth century were frequently regarded as 'the hindrance'.[33] In the twentieth century the hindrance was rather 'indifference' – a term used here by eight of the incumbents in their replies. The incumbent at the new parish of St Luke reported the presence of a Primitive Methodist chapel seating 300 which had 'moderate attendance'. It was no longer identified as a direct threat. His own church also seated 300, but it too was only a third full. Rather, the threat was perceived to lie elsewhere: 'There is much modern paganism together with ignorance and indifference to spiritual things. The neglect of the Lord's Day is particularly bad in the summer months when even good people cease to come.'

But perhaps a more accurate term would have been 'disillusionment'. If an analysis in more physical terms is again adopted, then the Church of England in York, despite its apparent strength in 1851, already contained the seeds of its own demise. It was already facing several crucial structural problems. It had an abundance of city-centre churches which, despite hefty financial subsidies, it could not afford to maintain and also to meet the needs of an increasingly suburban population. And it could not contain a sustained challenge, followed by rapid decline, of the Free Churches. Given the characteristically slow response of subsidized institutions to rapid social changes, the gradual demise of the Church of England in York, with its expanding and mobile population, followed naturally.

That the Church of England had too many city-centre churches in York is again confirmed by *Table 19*. The difficulties faced by the churches surrounding St Helen in sustaining mutual growth can be seen to have been a general rather than a purely local problem. At almost every point, a different set of churches was strong and the high point of 1851 was never repeated. By focusing on the city-centre churches that recorded attendances of 600 or more, the following pattern emerges.

In 1837 just two churches, St Cuthbert and St Saviour had large attendances. The first of these was never again to be so strong and the second (after rebuilding) only in the subsequent census. In 1851 seven churches had large attendances: All Saints Pavement, Holy Trinity Micklegate, St John, St Margaret, St Michael le Belfrey, St Olave, and St Saviour. In 1865 just three of these, together with the new church out at Holgate, remained strong: St John, St Michael le Belfrey, and St Olave (although the figure given is an estimate, the return says that there were 500 present in the morning and 'less' in the evening). In 1868 it was only St John and St Olave (this return merely states that the church, which seated 675, was 'full' in the morning and 'not full' in the evening) that remained strong. By 1877 every one of

---

[33] For examples, see my *Competing Convictions*, SCM Press, London, 1989, Chapter 5.

these churches recorded attendances of less than 600: St John in particular had collapsed from 600 to 65 in nine years. Instead, it was the new church across the river, St Clement, that was strong. A slight revival of attendances by 1884 (in the decade between 1881 and 1891 the population of York grew by over one-third – the sharpest rise since accurate records began) meant that there were four churches, together with the church at Holgate, with strong attendances: St Clement again, together with St Lawrence (rebuilt in 1883), St Mary Castlegate (rebuilt in 1870), and St Michael le Belfrey. By 1912 just two churches, St Clement and St Olave, had attendances exceeding 600, and by 1931 just one, St Clement. At the subsequent dates, 1947, 1953 and 1969, no single church reached this level of attendance. However, in 1989 St Michael le Belfrey did.

Set in this context, the remarkable (by present-day standards) attendances at St Michael le Belfrey can be seen to conform to a long-term pattern. Individual city-centre churches might flourish for a while – and St Michael has flourished more often than others – but they never appeared capable of flourishing together or even of sustaining their own strength for very long (by 2001 even St Michael has declined by a third since 1989). Indeed, it seems that they could only flourish separately and temporarily at the relative expense of their immediate neighbours.

Some of the city-centre clergy themselves recognized this physical problem. The incumbent at All Saints Pavement complained in the 1860s about the counter-attraction of the Minster and of 'the excessive number of parishes which fritter away the parochial principle'.[34] At the same time the incumbent at St Mary, Bishophill Junior, suggested the building of a new church outside the walls and the closure of some of the city-centre churches. And in 1894 the incumbent at St Clement wrote that the major hindrance to his work was 'the existence in York of several large churches with small populations. These in the struggle for existence find themselves compelled to prey upon their neighbours for money and congregation.'[35]

Similar points were made in relation to the dramatic increase in attendances first at St Cuthbert and then at St Michael le Belfrey in the 1970s. The clergy return of 1969 for St Cuthbert of 370 attendances already gives an indication of this. In a church with 200 seats, there were regular morning congregations of 170 and evening congregations of 200. By November 1969 *The Yorkshire Evening Press*[36] was reporting an evening attendance of 350; this filled the church itself and had to be relayed to St Anthony's Hall next door. It also reported that in July 1965 the congregations there consisted of 4 in the morning and 7 in the evening. St Michael was at this time virtually unused for regular services, and was scheduled for redundancy in 1971. However, in January 1973 the still growing congregation moved to that larger church (now seating 700) instead and St Cuthbert became the administrative offices for the parish.

Five years later criticisms from other churches became public. *The Yorkshire Evening Press*[37] reported that the congregation at St Michael le Belfrey was

---

[34] *Clergy Visitation Returns 1865*, Borthwick Institute, University of York, York.
[35] *Clergy Visitation Returns 1894*, Borthwick Institute, University of York, York.
[36] 5 November 1969.
[37] 29 September 1978.

disproportionately middle class and depended upon members drawn from other parishes. Given that it had little population in its own parish, it is perhaps hardly surprising that this criticism arose. However, what will be more apparent by now is that this was an issue endemic in York for more than one hundred years. Given such a plethora of churches in the city, any 'successful' church risked suspicions of 'poaching' from neighbouring churches. Even worse, it risked accusations that it was depriving other churches of potential lay leadership.

But why did this promote overall decline? American churches seem to have flourished on such mutual competition[38] – as one church declines, so another grows. Arguably the process encourages individual congregations to try harder, to attract new churchgoers and to retain existing ones. For the present it seems to be some of the independent, evangelical mega-churches, seating several thousand and set on the edges of large towns, that are flourishing in the United States, while long-established, liberal congregations decline. In the future it may be something else, and in the past it has certainly been something else. Growth and decline do not seem to be mutually destructive processes. So why were they in York?

A key difference here may be an economic one. Church of England churches in York, unlike churches in America, survived whether they were growing or declining. Unlike the Free Churches, their economic viability, and especially the payment of clergy, were not directly dependent on their congregations. As has been observed so often already, city-centre and rural churches could continue to survive even when they had lost effective congregations and local populations, precisely because they were subsidized. In York this subsidy was relatively poor, so there was a constant tendency to combine city-centre livings. Yet, until recently, the churches themselves still remained. Even in 1989, fourteen of the pre-First World War city churches, with thirteen parochial clergy serving them, remained (in addition to the Minster) for a total of 1845 attenders of all ages. What is more, two-fifths of these 1845 attenders went to St Michael le Belfrey.

It could, of course, be argued that it is the large congregation at St Michael that ensured that the overall Anglican churchgoing rate in York declined so little between 1969 and 1989 (from 3.5 per cent to 3.4 per cent). In contrast, the figures presented in *Table 18* suggest a national decline from 3.5 per cent in 1968 to 2.4 per cent in 1989. Supposing the congregation at St Michael conformed instead to the 1989 mean for York of 148 attendances, the churchgoing rate in York would appear as 2.8 per cent rather than as 3.4 per cent.

There are obvious difficulties in this supposition. For example, it assumes that the entire congregation at St Michael in 1989 came from the city boundaries (when

38 See Laurence R. Iannaccone, 'The Consequences of Religious Market Regulation', *Rationality and Society*, 3, 1991, pp. 156–177. An important debate about the effects of religious pluralism on 'participation' is to be found in Roger Finke and Rodney Stark, 'Religious Economies and Sacred Canopies', *American Sociological Review*, vol. 53, 1988, pp. 41–9; and Kevin D. Breault, 'New Evidence on Religious Pluralism, Urbanism and Religious Participation', *American Sociological Review*, vol. 54, 1989, pp. 1048–59. Unfortunately this debate is marred by using 'adherence' and not 'attendance' as the key variable for 'participation'. It is just this deficiency that mars Kevin J. Christiano's *Religious Diversity and Social Change: American Cities, 1890–1906*, Cambridge University Press, Cambridge and New York, 1987, as well as a very limited longitudinal range.

in fact some travelled from a considerable distance) and it also assumes that the members of the congregation who did come from York would not otherwise have gone to church. Yet even so, the strong possibility remains that St Michael was at least partially responsible for the relative stability of overall Anglican churchgoing in York between 1969 and 1989. Furthermore, since the number of Anglican churches has been reduced from twenty-eight to twenty-three, mean attendances increased in this period from 125 per church to 148. However, what had decreased was the median; from 125 to 96. In other words, attendances were now more skewed than they were twenty years earlier. By 2001 St Michael's congregation still remains much larger than those of other Anglicans churches in York, yet it has indeed declined in thirteen years from some 600 usual adult attendances to 400 and from 150 children to 100 (significantly, the nearby central Catholic church of St Wilfred has experienced a comparable decline in usual mass attendances from 750 to 475 in the same period).

In a subsidized context, internal competitiveness may have been mutually destructive. One congregation flourished at the expense of its neighbours, but they all remained in existence. So in 1851, for every 'successful' congregation there were at least three comparative 'failures'. And as the 'successes' became fewer, so the 'failures' increased, and the gap between the two widened. In 1851 the strongest church had attendances twenty-three times larger than the weakest; by 2001 the strongest church had thirty-nine times the attenders of the weakest. With a stress upon expository preaching in nineteenth-century evangelicalism, the notions of 'success' and 'failure' readily transferred to the clergy as well as to their churches. This is clearly present in the honest but defensive statement of the Vicar of St Helen cited earlier. His own vigour and preaching had, in this perception, contributed to his 'success' over his neighbours, and his infirmity had resulted in decline and gradual 'failure'. The very notion of the 'successful priest', so irresistible within competing churches and so heartening in a context of general decline, naturally implies that others are comparative 'failures'. Yet in a subsidized denomination all the clergy remain in their posts – 'successes' and 'failures' alike. And as 'successes' become rarer, so 'failures' become the common currency.

Here we arrive at the nuts and bolts of such physical accounts of churchgoing decline. The notion of the 'successful' church or priest may help to generate or sustain a series of myths. 'If others would only be more like X they could all succeed'. The 'if only' may involve expository preaching, it may involve liturgical experimentation, or church rebuilding, or pastoral counselling, or action in the community, or 'true' belief, or ... Whatever the 'if only', it involves a similar model. A few are identified as exemplars who, if the many would only copy them, could bring the unchurched back to church and return congregations to the halcyon days of 1851. Predominantly empty churches could once again become predominantly full.

There are a number of myths implicit in these claims that may actually have contributed to a widespread disillusionment with existing churches. Through these myths a majority of clergy and churches were thereby deemed to have 'failed'. Yet all were subsidized, or protected by the possibility of subsidy, and the subsidy remained almost whatever. So, despite having 'failed', clergy remained in their parishes and churches remained open but empty.

Of course these myths ignore the structural problems inherent in persisting with too many churches against all the evidence of population shifts. They may even have served to perpetuate rather than resolve the long-term decline of the York churches. Despite many heroic attempts in York to reverse decline and to create 'successful' churches, the latter have remained elusive and have become rarer in the twentieth century than they ever were in the nineteenth century. And popular disillusionment has slowly become more and more apparent.

Evidence of widespread popular dillusionment is strikingly present in the third and last of Seebohm Rowntree's reports. The Quaker Rowntree was scarcely a neutral observer of religion in York, and the final report in particular contains a number of prescriptive comments directed against Catholics and sometimes Anglicans. Yet he was an invaluable recorder of both statistics and anecdotes. Among the latter for 1948 were the following:

> We have come across many ... examples of this distrust of the motives of the clergy of which we quote three as typical:
> (a) A working-class man in early middle age. 'Nobody believes all the nonsense they read out in church. The parsons just do it to earn their living.'
> (b) A middle-class man in middle age describes the attitude of both church-goers and clergy as a 'mixture of superstition, sentimentality, hypocrisy and – in the case of the parsons – pure chicanery'.
> (c) A working-class widow in late middle-age. 'Don't talk to me about parsons! They've got a pretty soft job, if you ask me. Telling decent working folk how to behave! What do they know about it? Never done an honest day's work in their life, most of them.'
> Besides their anti-clericalism, non-church-goers not infrequently express a dislike for people in general who do go to church. Often this goes no further than some such sneer as, 'Fat lot of good it'll do them', but in a good many cases charges are made by the non-church-goers that churchmen do not live up to their principles.[39]

This anecdotal evidence is not particularly useful in trying to establish a theory of churchgoing decline. There is no reason to believe that people then had any better idea than people today. Rather, it is useful in suggesting that 'disillusionment' is a more apt term to depict popular sentiment at the time than the clergy's own term of 'indifference'. It is understandable that clergy should themselves have preferred the term 'indifference'. Largely unaware of the Church of England's structural deficiencies and their own place within them, the resistance of adults in York to clergy efforts to persuade them to come to church would more comfortably have been interpreted by them as 'indifference' rather than as 'disillusionment'. But the adults themselves, like the troops surveyed in *The Army and Religion*, were still familiar with churches and chapels from their childhood experiences of Sunday schools, and might well have felt disillusioned about the empty churches that they observed and into which they had never been integrated by their Sunday schools.

With Church of England churches at the turn of the century barely more than one-third full, disproportionately middle-class and almost two-thirds female,[40] it is

---

39 Rowntree and Lavers, *English Life and Leisure*, p. 346.

40 See Rowntree, *Poverty*, for the male/female imbalance. On a rather crude measure he did not detect a social class imbalance at this stage, but later reports suggest that he did. For extensive research on this

not difficult to see how the adult working-class male in York would have felt distinctly out of place in church. Unwittingly, it may have been the churches' own inattention to structures and to the needs of a radically changing population that contributed to this sense of disillusionment. Given a spiral of diminishing returns, rivalries both between churches and perhaps also between churches and Sunday schools became increasingly likely – and increasingly damaging.

3

But did competitiveness between the Free Churches and the Church of England in York contribute to their mutual decline? There are several levels at which this question can be approached. At the most general, an overview is required of the balance between these two forms of churchmanship since 1764. A more intermediate level involves examining ways in which they may have influenced each other's policies in directions that eventually proved mutually damaging. And the most proximate, but perhaps finally undiscoverable, level involves an analysis of the extent to which they may over the years have recycled each other's churchgoers.

The three-quarters of a century between 1764 and 1837 witnessed a very sharp rise in the Free Churches in York. On the basis of the calculations given earlier, in 1764 the clergy reported that some 95 per cent of the population were, at least nominally, Anglican. Even if this is an over-estimation of actual Anglican strength, it at least gives an indication of the perception of the Church of England clergy themselves. By 1837 Free Church attendances exceeded those in the Church of England and represented some 31 per cent of the population. Even allowing for multiple attendances at the later date – reducing the 31 per cent attendances drastically to, say, 16 per cent attenders – and even allowing for a certain vagueness about Free Church membership at the earlier date, this does seem to indicate a sharp rise.

It is still, of course, quite possible that the bulk of the population remained nominal members of the Church of England. And it is even possible that the Free Churches gained their new strength from the immigrants who helped to more than double the population of York between these dates. The Districts to the east and south of York were particularly strong for the Free Churches and especially the Methodists. In 1851 the Districts of Malton, Pocklington, Howden and Selby all had more seating and higher attendances in the Free Churches than in the Church of England.[41] In all of these, except Malton, the Wesleyan Methodists alone had more attendances than the Church of England. It was only in the Districts to the north and west of York – Easingwold, Knaresborough and Tadcaster – that the Church of England had more seating and attendances than the Free Churches combined.

In York, too, Methodists were, and indeed still are, by far the strongest of the Free Churches. In 1764 a single Methodist chapel is mentioned, but by 1837 there

---

second imbalance at the turn of the century, see Hugh McLeod, *Class and Religion in the Late Victorian City*, Croom Helm, London, 1974.
[41] Calculated from Mann, *1851 Census Great Britain.*

were five chapels and by 1851 there were eight chapels with sufficient seating for some 18 per cent of the population. The largest of these chapels, the Centenary Chapel, was built in 1840 in the centre of York to accommodate 1469 people. With six huge pillars supporting its façade, it remains a most impressive, and of course listed, building. Over the next fifty years Methodists built or entirely rebuilt a further twenty chapels: nine of these being built by the Wesleyans, seven by the Primitive Methodists, two by the New Connexion, and two by the United Methodist Free Church. By 1935, just three years after the Methodist Union, there were twenty-two Methodist chapels serving York.[42] Alongside them there were just six Congregationalist chapels (only two of which were substantial buildings), three Salvation Army Halls, and five other chapels.

In the early nineteenth century a number of the evangelical incumbents in York would have been sympathetic to Methodism. Thus the relationship between the two denominations was by no means one of clear-cut antagonism. Edward Royle argues:

> The chapel in Aldwark held morning service at 8am, so as not to conflict with the Church; indeed, even after Aldwark was replaced by a larger chapel in New Street in 1805, the practice was continued and the York Welseyans did not avail themselves of the opportunity (granted by the Connexion in 1795) of holding their own Holy Communion services until 1815. It was a common sight to see Methodists walking up Aldwark from their services to those of William Richardson at St Michael le Belfrey where some leading Methodists experienced their conversions. Contrary to the general assumption, that Methodism grew out of the weakness of the Church, in York it grew out of the strength of the revival within a Church which was unable to contain it.[43]

Interestingly, one of the stronger Methodist congregations in 1989 serving York (albeit just outside the city boundary) was at Heslington. Ministering to the university community,[44] it was a local ecumenical project shared with Anglicans and had a total of 237 attendances at its services and 49 at its Sunday school. It is frequently assumed by sociologists that ecumenism contributes to church decline.[45] Once again this may be a myth in need of further inspection.

However, it seems likely that rather stronger rivalries were more characteristic of the second half of the nineteenth century. Primitive Methodists first established themselves in York in 1820, and by 1837 their chapel in Grape Lane, with seating for 500, had an evening attendance of 350 and by 1851 of 500. Their vigorous building over the next fifty years was very typical of the strong rivalries within Methodism that have been noted in other urban areas.

By 1837 all five Methodist chapels had at least two Sunday services. They had a combined attendance of 5240, representing some 19 per cent of the York population; and on average services were 66 per cent full at these chapels. The evening services, with a total of 2830 people present, were slightly stronger than the morning services, with 2210 present. These were now self-sufficient congregations;

---

42 See Rowntree, *Poverty and Progress*.
43 Edward Royle, *Nonconformity in Nineteenth-century York*, Borthwick Papers No. 68, University of York, York, 1985, p. 7.
44 Information from Methodist central returns, 1989.
45 See my *Competing Convictions*, SCM Press, London, 1989.

they no longer seemed to make provision for additional attendances at the Church of England.

By 1851 there were already signs of strain beginning to appear. Total attendances at the now eight Methodist chapels (four of them Wesleyan) amounted to 6471, representing 18 per cent of the York population. Unlike the Church of England, they could not increase attendances by providing a second Sunday service. Rather, their services now were on average only 46 per cent full. The familiar pattern of competitive diffusion was already evident. So among the largest body of Methodists in York, the Wesleyans, total attendances appeared to have dropped slightly in numerical terms – from 3360 in 1837 to 3227 in 1851 – despite a very sharp rise in York's population. The new and enormous Centenary Chapel was on average 59 per cent full at its two services, with a total of 1740 attendances, but New Street Chapel (built in 1805) and Albion Chapel (built in 1816) were both significantly emptier than they were in 1837. At that time they were 78 per cent full, whereas in 1851 they were only 37 per cent full at the same four services. St George, Walmgate (built in 1826) had two services with a total of 460 attendances in 1837, but by 1851 it had reverted to being a school chapel, with only 'occasional services'. The relative strength of the Centenary Chapel had apparently been at the expense of the older chapels.

It is possible also that other Methodist groups had encroached on Wesleyan attendances. The Primitive Methodists at Grape Lane declined slightly in attendances from 800 at three services in 1837 to 701 in 1851. However, later that year they moved out to a new chapel in Little Stonegate. By 1853 there were reports of a group of Wesleyans joining them.[46] Other Methodists in York seem to have increased their attendances in 1837 from 1080 to 2543 in 1851. However, this apparent increase at the expense of Wesleyans may be somewhat misleading. In 1851 a very large group of Methodists (885 in the morning and 1317 in the evening) were meeting in the Festival Concert Room, describing themselves as only temporarily estranged from the Wesleyans. Whatever their actual allegiance, local Methodist attendances were clearly volatile during this period of both rapid social change and considerable controversy within national Methodism.

Rowntree's report for 1901 shows that at some point during the previous fifty years Methodists in York must have declined very significantly. If total Free Church attendances amounted to 31 per cent of the total population in 1837 and 26 per cent in 1851, in 1901 adult attendances amounted to just 13 per cent of the adult population. In 1935 the 4329 attendances of all ages at Free Church chapels (two-thirds of them Methodist) represented only 5 per cent of the total population. Despite a population now almost three times larger, these attendances were actually less than the 4953 attendances of 1851. Adult attendances in 1948 had declined: from 5 per cent of the adult population in 1935 to 4 per cent at the later date. By 1989 they stood at about 3 per cent.

Although it is not possible to extract specifically Methodist attendances from these figures for the first half of the twentieth century, it is clear that they must have been quite different from those of the first half of the nineteenth century. The most

---

[46] See Royle, *Nonconformity in Nineteenth-century York*, p. 14.

vigorous period of Methodist building in York was in the second half of the nineteenth century, yet Methodist attendances at the end of that period were weaker than they had been even in 1851. Once again, the sheer number of chapels or even an aggregate of their membership are poor indicators of their real strength. Rowntree's data confirms that, at least by the beginning of the twentieth century, Methodists in York, as elsewhere, had far too many chapels for their regular attenders.

Can anything more be said about the gap between 1851 and 1901? In the absence of a newspaper census in the 1880s, Royle is sceptical. Yet he does provide evidence of one of the physical factors noted so often already; some of the smaller Methodist denominations were experiencing serious financial and membership problems:

> The New Connexion in particular found the going as hard as did the Baptists later. Trinity chapel cost £3072, of which half remained as chapel debt at the opening (in 1856), and circuit membership rapidly declined from over 200 in the 1850s to under 100 by 1872. A small school-chapel, opened in the suburbs near the cemetery in 1856, failed for lack of money and preachers in 1872 and was handed over to the Wesleyans. The United Methodists were more numerous with over 500 members in the circuit in 1861, but these numbers too had fallen to half by the mid-1880s.[47]

So the familiar problems of chapel debt and competition for members apparently did affect York, as in other urban areas, during this crucial period.

Perhaps Bath provides a further clue. Unlike most other newspaper censuses in the 1880s, that for Bath included Sunday school attendances.[48] For once, then, the 1851 figures that follow also include Sunday school attendances. Of a similar size in the 1880s to York, Bath too had a plethora of churches and chapels. For a population of 51 790 in 1881 it had no less than seventy, with seating sufficient for 68 per cent of the population (in York there were sufficient seats in 1851 for 66 per cent). It even had four more Church of England churches than York. Against a population that had declined very slightly by some 2500 over the previous thirty years, the Free Churches had continued to build, increasing from seating sufficient for 22 per cent of the total population to 25 per cent.

Some of the denominations – such as the Independents, the Primitive Methodists and the Brethren – had expanded vigorously, and the Salvation Army had entered Bath anew. But in terms of attendances, several of the Free Churches experienced very considerable decline, especially the Wesleyan Reformers, Lady Huntingdon's Connnexion and a number of isolated congregations. Salvation Army attendances, in contrast, now accounted for some 11 per cent of Free Church attendances. Overall, Free Church attendances declined from 27 per cent of the population to 24 per cent and their chapels declined on average from being 62 per cent full to 50 per cent.

In Bath, then, an increase in chapels, in a town that already had an abundance of churches and chapels, did not result in an increase in attendances between 1851 and 1881. On the contrary, a smaller proportion of the population attended than thirty years before, and chapels in general were distinctly emptier than they had been. And all of this in spite of the fact that the 1881 Bath census included Sunday school

---

[47] Royle, *Nonconformity in Nineteenth-century York*, pp. 14–15.

[48] See note 7.

attendances. If Bath followed the same pattern as elsewhere, Sunday school attendances would of course still have been increasing in the 1880s. As a result, adult attendances there would have been declining even more sharply than these figures indicate.

Most dramatically, the Independents (one of the strongest denominations in York) had seating sufficient for 2.6 per cent of the Bath population in 1851, but for 4.5 per cent in 1881. Attendances declined slightly from 4.9 per cent of the population to 4.1 per cent, but the services, which in 1851 were on average 92 per cent full, were in 1881 only 46 per cent full. Out of thirteen Free Church denominations present in Bath in 1851, services in nine of them were on average emptier in 1881.

The two towns were not identical. Bath had yet to experience the same suburban development as York. However, there were sufficient similarities to make their comparison interesting and possibly instructive. In Bath the decline in the Church of England between 1851 and 1881 was not as pronounced as that in the Free Churches. With exaggeration probably caused by including Sunday school attendances, total attendances appeared to remain stable at just over 41 per cent of the population. But in both contexts it was the Free Churches rather than the Church of England that were currently adding new church buildings. Competitive diffusion was predominantly a Free Church feature.

Again in both contexts, as has been seen in all other urban areas, there was a switch to evening services in the Church of England as well as in the Free Churches. The introduction of gas lighting doubtless had much to do with this. Urban morning services in the Church of England became significantly emptier: in Bath they were on average 67 per cent full in 1851, but only 51 per cent full in 1881. Since this was the prime time for Church of England Sunday schools to meet, adult morning attendances must have appeared visibly thinner to those attending them. Here again, perceived decline probably preceded actual decline.

In both Bath and York the Salvation Army were active from the1880s. As was seen earlier, London and Liverpool data suggests that the Salvation Army made a significant impact in the 1880s, expanded vigorously, but then was already declining in attendances by the early 1900s. If in 1881 Salvation Army attendances represented some 11 per cent of all Free Church attendances in Bath, in 1901 they also represented 11 per cent of Free Church adult attendances in York. Sharing the same level of decline as other Free Churches, they still had 11 per cent in 1935 in York, but had increased their physical presence from two halls to three. However, by 1948 they had declined even faster, now having slightly less than 7 per cent of Free Church adult attendances in York and having closed one of the halls. By 1989 the Salvation Army in York had returned to a single hall – at Gillygate from where it first started in 1881 – and attendances there represented some 6 per cent of Free Church attendances.

The churchgoing decline of the Salvation Army can thus be assessed in three different ways.[49] From 1901 it shared the general decline of the Free Churches in

---

[49] Salvation Army statistics 1901–48 are in Rowntree and Lavers, *English Life and Leisure*; present-day statistics have been kindly supplied by the local corps in York (85 morning attendances and 70 in the evening for 1989 and 95 and 65 respectively in 2002).

York. After 1935 it declined even in relation to other Free Churches. And at each census until the most recent the sheer number of adult attendances declined: in 1901 there were 800, in 1935 there were 503, in 1948 there were 249, and in 1989 there were 155 (only today has it risen slightly to 160). Here is some of the clearest evidence of competitive diffusion followed by decline.

There is even a further refinement that might be suggested from other towns. It is consonant with Royle's observations about the relative decline of Baptists in York. If Free Church congregations are compared in those towns measured in 1881 where the Salvation Army was strongest, then it was the Baptists that appear to have been most affected. So, in Wrexham the Salvation Army represented 23 per cent of all church attendances (and a remarkable 15.6 per cent of the population), in Runcorn 22 per cent, in Barnsley 20 per cent, in Hull 18 per cent, and in Scarborough 17 per cent.[50] In the five towns taken together, Salvation Army attendances in 1881 represented 8.4 per cent of their populations: in contrast, the mean in *Table 8* was 2.2 per cent. What is more, the Salvation Army in these towns had seating provision for 5.4 per cent of the populations and these seats were on average 79 per cent full; in contrast, again, mean averages in *Table 8* were 1.8 per cent and 61.5 per cent respectively.

Attendances, seating provision, and seat occupation for other denominations (except the Baptists) differed little between these five towns and towns generally in 1881. However, in the case of the Baptists there was a marked disparity. In the five towns Baptist attendances represented just 1.0 per cent of their populations, their seats 1.7 per cent, and these seats were on average only 29 per cent full. Whereas in *Table 8*, Baptist attendances represented 3.1 per cent of populations, their seats represented 3.7 per cent, and these seats were 41.3 per cent full. It seems possible, then, that it was Baptists who lost out most to a vigorous Salvation Army presence.

Whether Free Church decline in York is seen as a continuous process starting soon after 1837 (as the additional Bath data would suggest), or as a process of decline to 1851, rise to the 1880s, and decline to 1901, is a matter of speculation. From 1901 to 1948 Rowntree's data provides unambiguous evidence of decline. And this despite the physical growth of Free Churches (excluding missions) from eighteen chapels in 1901 to thirty-five in 1935, declining to thirty-three in 1948. Since there was a dramatic decline in the actual number of adult attendances during this period – from 6447 to 3883 to 3514 – these chapels must have been visibly emptier. Their gradual collapse and closure in the late twentieth century followed naturally.

Today less than half of the Methodist chapels from the 1930s survive, although the enormous Centenary Chapel still exists. In contrast to its morning attendance of 703, evening attendance of 1037 and Sunday school attendance of 236 in 1851, in 1989 it had a morning attendance of 88, an evening attendance of 44 and a Sunday school attendance of 13. The other very large central Wesleyan Chapel at Priory Street (built in 1856) was bought in the mid-1980s by the Pentecostal Assembly of

---

[50] For these 1881 statistics, see Andrew Mearns, *The Statistics of Attendance at Public Worship: As Published in England, Wales and Scotland by the Local Press, Between October 1881 and February 1882*, Hodder, 1882 (a copy is in the Bodleian Library, Oxford) and *The Nonconformist and Independent*, Supplement, 2 February 1882.

God. A generation earlier the Wesleyan Central Mission at Swinegate (built 1910) had been bought by the Elim Pentecostal Church. Altogether, the twelve Methodist chapels in 1989 (excluding Heslington) had an average of 1264 adult Sunday attendances and 272 Sunday school attendances between them, representing together some 1.6 per cent of the population. The decline from the 18 per cent of 1851 is obvious.

In the case of the city chapels in the south circuit it is possible to measure their decline between 1967 and 1989 in some detail. A survey[51] of the seven Methodist chapels involved (Acomb, Albany, Holgate, Lidgett Grove, Southlands, Wesley Priory Street, and West Thorpe) in 1967 showed that they had a total membership of 1160. This membership was carefully analysed in terms of sex and age ratios, and showed a disproportionately female and elderly membership similar to Manchester (in both cases, females outnumbered males by two-to-one and a majority of the members were aged over 45). Calculated on the basis of the Butler/ Jones formula used in Chapter 8, these chapels would have had a membership in 1989 of 665. In reality, the five remaining chapels in 1989 had a membership of 650. Here too the decline in Methodist membership appears to have been remarkably predictable.

It is clear from the 1967 survey that these chapels were already struggling. Only a third of members were described as 'regular' chapelgoers and almost a third were depicted as attending 'rarely'. With 372 attendances in the morning and 537 in the evening and with 3004 seats available in these chapels, they were at best 18 per cent full. By 1989 attendances were still 392 in the morning, but had declined sharply in the evening to 197. These evening services were now only 12 per cent full. In contrast, morning services, with the reduced seating, were now 23 per cent full. So the national pattern for Methodists noted in the previous chapter also characterized these York chapels. Both membership and attendance at evening services had declined drastically; only morning services appeared resilient. However, comparing the combined statistics for the York North and South Circuits in the period 1989–2001, Methodist decline now seems to cover all services. In this period membership has declined by 15 per cent, morning attendance by 11 per cent, evening attendance by 25 per cent, and Sunday school attendance by 46 per cent.

To gain a more complete picture of Free Church attendance in York 1989, a further fifteen chapels needed to be added.[52] There were two churches belonging to the United Reformed Church (with an average total of 178 attendances). One of these is a former Presbyterian church, built in 1879 to minister to a largely Scottish congregation. The other is the last surviving of the six Congregational chapels mentioned in the 1930s. Quakers retain a stronger presence in York than in many other cities. Tending to thrive in university towns, there were in 1989 two Quaker Meeting Houses (148 attendances) in the city itself and a third small one on the edge of York. The two Baptist churches (some 200 adult attendances and perhaps 50 at Sunday school), one in the centre at Priory Street and one out at Acomb, were

[51] 'Review of the York Wesley Methodist Circuit', 1967, held in the Methodist archives in the John Rylands Library, University of Manchester.

[52] All the statistics that follow have been kindly supplied by members of local churches; only the very smallest chapels proved elusive (a problem that Rowntree admitted at times!).

in a state of flux in 1989. Representing somewhat different traditions, some of the older members were transferring to one congregation, leaving the younger members at the other. Twelve years later Baptists are still changing, with the younger congregation now located closer to the University and claiming the largest non-Catholic congregation in York. In 1989 there was also a Pentecostal Church at Priory Street (some 170 adult attendances and 30 at Sunday school), an ancient chapel bought in the 1920s by the Brethren (some 100 attendances with a Sunday school of 20), and the one remaining Salvation Army Hall at Gillygate (155 attendances and 30 at Sunday school). By 2002 the adult attendances at this Salvation Army Hall have increased slightly to 160 but the Sunday school has halved to 15. Added together, these estimated attendances, together with those of the Methodists, amounted in total to 2617 in 1989, representing 2.6 per cent of the York population. Some allowance must also be made for approximately six further small independent chapels or House Church groups (including a seventeenth-century Unitarian chapel and a small Elim Pentecostal chapel). Free Church attendances in York could scarcely have exceeded 3 per cent of the population in 1989 (and almost certainly are less than 3 per cent today) – ten times less than their total attendance rate in 1837.

In terms of their visible presence in the population of York the Free Churches seem now to have come full circle from the 1760s. If their population as identified by the clergy in 1764 was something between 2 per cent and 3 per cent (excluding Catholics), today their regular attendances are little different. If the Quaker congregation in 1764 amounted to 30, by 1989 Quaker attendances amounted to 148 for a population more than eight times larger. If in 1764 there was one chapel for approximately every 2500 people, by 1989 there was a chapel for approximately every 3500 people. It is almost as if the evangelical revival of the early nineteenth century had never happened.

As in the Church of England, Sunday school attendances in the Free Churches[53] seem to have declined much later than adult attendances. Free Church Sunday schools in York in 1837 had 1655 members, representing just under 18 per cent of the young people and slightly less than those in the Church of England. By 1851 Methodists alone had 755 Sunday school attendances and Independents a further 317, representing altogether some 9 per cent of young people. However, by 1880 Wesleyans now had 2850 members. The Free Churches taken together had 6230 members – many more than the Church of England and representing some 38 per cent of young people. Combined Free Church and Church of England Sunday school membership in 1880 amounted to some 62 per cent of young people in York – a figure little different from that for Birmingham for 1892. With national Sunday school membership rates (as shown in *Table 6*) for 1891 of 51.4 per cent, the relative strength of the movement in the late nineteenth century in specifically urban areas is evident.

Drastic twentieth-century Sunday school decline is also evident in the York Free Churches. By 1935[54] there were 2736 Free Church Sunday school attendances, representing some 16 per cent of young people. The 272 recorded in 1989 for the

---

[53] For 1837 Free Church Sunday school attendances, see note 26; for 1880 see note 27.
[54] See Rowntree, *Poverty and Progress*.

Methodists represents 1.4 per cent of young people in York. All but one of the Methodist chapels by 1989 still had a Sunday school. In this respect they differed significantly from the Church of England. However, like the Church of England, few of their Sunday schools were strong – only two of them catered for as many as fifty young people. Perhaps predictably, by 2001 the number of Sunday schools in the combined York North and South Circuits had halved. Of the other Free Churches in York in 1989, the largest Sunday schools were at the Pentecostal church and at one of the Baptist chapels. Yet even they could muster only some thirty young people each.

4

But did these contrasting patterns of decline between the Church of England and the Free Churches mutually damage one another? It might by now be accepted that the subsidized persistence of the Church of England, with city-centre churches competing with one another for a diminishing group of churchgoers, contributed to its own decline. It might also be thought that the competitive diffusion of the Free Churches contributed to their gradual decline. But did these contrasting patterns contribute to each other's decline?

At an explanatory level, a notion of mutual destructiveness may provide a missing link. Competitive diffusion of itself may not lead to decline. At least, that seems to have been the experience in the United States. New denominations or extensions of old denominations enter an area, supplanting long-established denominations without necessarily contributing to overall decline. Overlapping patterns of growth and decline apparently subsist in a context of persisting high levels of church membership and attendance. However, even here, slight caution is necessary. It has often been assumed that churchgoing in the United States is remarkably resilient and shows nothing of the tendency towards decline apparent elsewhere in the Western world. In the next chapter I will point to some statistical evidence that suggests otherwise. Nevertheless, even if this evidence of some recent decline is accepted, the general pattern here is different from that in Britain. The main difference is that the experience of competitive diffusion in Britain has been set in a context of national churches which persist in both rural and city-centre areas whether buildings are used or not.

Perhaps it is this that explains the Methodist attempt in the centre of York to provide enormous chapels to match the Church of England, and then to persist with them long after they had lost effective congregations. The Centenary Chapel was already causing problems for its Wesleyan neighbours in 1851. By the time of the Union, Methodists in York had twenty-two chapels, with thirty churches belonging to the Church of England. Given the history of Methodism, and despite all the internal rivalries within it, some rivalry with the Church of England was only to be expected. But it was a dangerous rivalry. The Church of England had the economic power to persist far longer than most of its rivals. By 1989 Anglicans still had twenty-four churches in York, but Methodists had just twelve chapels left.

Visual evidence of this past rivalry is most startlingly manifest in York's Priory Street. At either end of this short street were ancient Anglican churches. In the

1850s land in between them became available for building – one of the last substantial building sites left within the city walls. So over the next two decades three large chapels were built facing one another, belonging to the Wesleyans, the Baptists and finally the Presbyterians. Within a stone's throw, a Primitive Methodist chapel was also built and a Catholic church.

That the Church of England thought of itself in relation to other denominations is still apparent in the 1930s. In the return to the Archbishop for 1931, the incumbent at St Martin, Coney Street and St Helen wrote:

> Many of our evening congregations are people very loosely attached to the Church. Probably many of them (are) Non-Conformists who 'like Church better than Chapel'. They are loathe to take any steps which definitely end their Non-Conformist allegiance – often family reasons.[55]

There are echoes here, albeit in a more modern voice, of the rural dean's comments of 1845 cited earlier, when there were fears that Established Church members might be tempted to attend Free Church services unless adequate provision was made for them. By the 1930s the fear had been reversed; Free Church members were now believed to be attending Anglican services, albeit without finally severing their Free Church ties. In both cases, cross-attendances were thought to reduce individual commitment. Here again is a pattern familiar from Charles Booth's London data. Individuals, wittingly or unwittingly, were believed to play off one denomination against another while sitting loosely in both.

In the same clergy returns for the 1930s, the incumbent at St Saviour also provided evidence of continuing rivalries between denominations:

> This is the poorest parish in the City – I have no one I could ask for five shillings for any cause. I never ask for money in the Church, as I would not have any body kept away, because they had nothing to give. The whole parish, within the next two years will be changed, by Housing Authorities. At present I get about 60 of the poorest to Church and they look to the Church in anything they need. There are 7 different places of worship in one Street, but I do not find any of them doing any visiting – they may be Nonconformists when they are well, but are parishioners when they are ill. The work is very hard, but very encouraging. Only last week I gave away 120 bags of coal, and every case had to be enquired into, and rarely any were under 60 years of age. The offertories do not average about 7s 6d a Sunday, out of which to pay Organist, Caretaker, lighting, heating and incidental expenses – but I have a fund which will help for the next two or three years.

So, as in the East End of London at the turn of the century, provision for the poor in York itself became a point of rivalry between denominations. Even if less than a third of those attending his church services were poor themselves, philanthropic activities on their behalf dominated the incumbent's ministry. All of these activities were subsidized. For him, unlike his rivals, there was no question of raising funds from the poor, or even perhaps from the rest of his congregation. And he was clearly conscious of the local presence of other denominations – 'I do not find any of them doing any visiting'.

---

[55] *Clergy Visitation Returns 1931*, Borthwick Institute, University of York, York.

On issues of church policy it seems difficult for one denomination to ignore all others. It has already been seen how the Church of England in the 1840s increased the number of its services in response to the Free Church challenge. But policies about a whole range of physical factors – church building, provision of ordained ministers, establishing of schools and Sunday schools, welfare action in the community, membership requirements, together with baptism and marriage policies – are all likely to be influenced by the presence of other denominations. And several of these factors seem to be crucial in understanding the long-term demise of the churches and chapels in York.

Although it is probably impossible to discover just how many people crossed over from one denomination to another in the competing denominational situation of York, there does seem to be sufficient evidence about the damaging effects of this overall situation. A mixture of internal rivalries and cross-denominational rivalries between the overabundant churches and chapels of York appears to have weakened all but a small handful. Of course other, more cultural, factors may also have been responsible for churchgoing decline in York. They can never be finally excluded, but neither can they be adequately controlled. In any case, what do they actually add to our understanding of the existing data for York?

5

One last piece of the jigsaw puzzle remains: the situation of the Catholics in York. It was mentioned at the outset that Catholics were more numerous in York than in most other English towns of this size. Nevertheless, their response to population changes over 225 years gives an unusually complete picture that confirms patterns already discovered elsewhere.

In 1764 there was a convent, which had operated as a girls' boarding school since 1686, in the parish of Holy Trinity, Micklegate, and a Catholic church, opened in 1760, in that of St Michael le Belfrey. According to the incumbent's return, the latter had 'a congregation of about 170'. If the clergy's own calculations are followed, the Catholic population of York at this time was about 297, representing some 2.4 per cent of the total population. If this figure is correct, then some 57 per cent of York Catholics attended this church. But of course such a calculation ignores both any congregation at the convent and the much higher Catholic population estimate of 1767.

From the church's baptismal records, Royle calculates[56] that the Catholic population remained steady until the end of the century and then began to accelerate. Twenty baptisms a year became thirty, then fifty in the 1820s, and sixty in the 1830s. By 1837 the convent recorded attendances of 100 both morning and afternoon and the church (rebuilt in 1802 to seat 490 and dedicated to St Wilfred) had 160 in the morning, 350 in the afternoon and 250 in the evening. The combined attendances of 960 now represented some 3.4 per cent of the York population.

---

[56] Royle, *Nonconformity in Nineteenth-century York*.

By 1851 there were two Catholic churches in York: St Wilfred and the new St George (seating 500). St Wilfred, with a morning attendance of 861 and Sunday school of 130, clearly now had more than one service on a Sunday morning. Together with afternoon and evening services, it had a total of 1293 church attendances and 311 in Sunday school. St George had a morning attendance of 359 and an evening attendance of 418. The total attendances of 2381 now represented 6.6 per cent of the York population. If Sunday school and afternoon attendances are excluded to make effective comparisons, then Catholic attendances in York in 1851 represented 5.5 per cent of the population. It was thus considerably higher than the 2.8 per cent of *Table 8*, but nothing like Liverpool's 13.9 per cent.

Now any other denomination faced with this scale of increase in attendances would instantly have built new churches. It has been seen repeatedly that the Free Churches did not even need to have full chapels to build new chapels in the second half of the nineteenth century. Furthermore, the Church of England persisted with thinly attended city-centre churches at the same time as it was opening new suburban churches. However, the Catholics in York built no new church until 1889, when they opened English Martyrs in Blossom Street. The most that they did was rebuild St Wilfred in 1864. Indeed, the British (and Irish) Catholic pattern of providing less accommodation in churches than is needed even for regular attenders, and of having multiple Masses instead, is as characteristic of York as elsewhere. Thus in 1837, when there were thirty-five churches and chapels of all denominations, Catholics had a single church and convent chapel; in 1851, when there were forty-one, Catholics had two churches; in 1901, when there were fifty-one, Catholics had three; in 1935, when there were seventy, Catholics had four; in 1948, when there were sixty-nine, Catholics had five; and in 1989, when there were about sixty, Catholics had seven. As noted so often in earlier chapters, Catholics have built far more cautiously than other denominations, but have until their recent decline in churchgoers continued to build even when other denominations started to contract.

As a result of this more cautious policy, Catholic services in York, as elsewhere, have been more consistently full than those in other denominations. In 1837 services at St Wilfred were on average 52 per cent full. In 1851 they were on average 88 per cent full and those at St George were 78 per cent full. No other denomination in 1851 could match such figures. By 1901 the three Catholic churches had a total of 2360 adult attendances, representing some 4.9 per cent of the adult population; and by 1935 four churches had a total of 2989 adult attendances, representing 4.1 per cent of the adult population. Including children, the total attendances in 1935 were 4568 or 5.1 per cent of the total population. Since the Catholic population of York depended so heavily upon such groups as Irish railway workers, it is difficult to be sure whether these decreasing percentages represented a decline in attendances or simply fluctuations in Catholic population. Whichever is the case, the churches themselves remained well attended. In 1851 there was a mean of 1191 attendances of all ages per church; in 1935 there was still a mean of 1142 attendances per church.

By 1948 adult attendances, at the now five churches, had increased numerically to 3073, although this represented a slight decline to some 3.9 per cent of the adult population of York. By 1989 the now seven churches together had an average Sunday attendance of all ages of about 3950, representing some 4.1 per cent of the total population.[57] However, by 2002 this had declined to 3175 (and the number of priests serving these seven churches had also declined from twelve to just seven). Attendances per church had certainly declined from 1935; by 1989 there was a mean of 594 attendances of all ages per church and by 2002 it has reduced further to 454. Yet no other denomination can remotely approach such an average (for example, the Methodist mean was 128 in 1989 and the Anglican mean, as noted earlier, was only 104 in 2001). Furthermore, in the Rowntree reports Catholics were the only denomination to show a numerical (even if not percentage) increase in both 1935 and 1948. This was also the case in 1989, although for the first time Catholic attendances now exceeded those of any other denomination. If estimates of adult attendances for 1989 and 2001–2 are added to Seebohm Rowntree's final table, it now appears as follows:[58]

Table 9.1 Statistics of adult attendance in York

	1901	*1935*	*1948*	*1989*	*2001*
Anglican	7,453	5,395	3,384	2,989	2,248
Free Church	6,447	3,883	3,514	2,180	1,853
Salvation Army	800	503	249	155	160
Roman Catholic	2,360	2,989	3,073	3,160	2,540
Totals	17,060	12,770	10,220	8,484	6,801

From all of this it is obvious that the relative strength of Catholic attendances compared with those of other denominations in York (as in England as a whole) has until recently increased with every census. In 1837 Catholic attendances represented 6 per cent of all church attendances and by 1851 this had increased to 10 per cent. By 1901 Catholic adult attendances represented 14 per cent of all adult attendances; by 1935 this had increased to 23 per cent: by 1948 to 30 per cent, by 1989 to 37 per cent and by 2001 it was still 37 per cent.

Rowntree also recorded other indications of this relative strength. In earlier reports he had found little difference between Catholics and others in their preponderance of female attendances (59 per cent in 1901 and 62 per cent in 1935, against a mean of 58 per cent and 61 per cent respectively). By 1948 Catholic attendances were only 56 per cent female, whereas no other denomination was less than 60 per cent. And Catholic attendances were distinctly more youthful than those of others: 77 per cent were aged under 50, as distinct from 64 per cent of Anglican, 67 per cent of Salvation Army and 55 per cent of Free Church attendances. He concluded with a remarkable prediction:

---

[57] Catholic statistics for 1989 and 2002 were kindly supplied locally.

[58] For 1901–48 see Rowntree and Lavers, *English Life and Leisure*; for 1989 and 2001, Anglican figures are derived from official returns, with an estimate of 200 local attendances for the Minster; Free Church figures in 1989 assume adult attendances representing 3 per cent of the adult population and a proportional decline of 15 per cent (in line with Methodist returns) in 2001; and Catholic figures are based on those quoted in the text, minus 20 per cent for those aged under 16 (as per York population in 1981).

It follows from these figures that the Roman Catholics have an excellent chance of maintaining a vigorous and expanding congregation for some decades, because the proportion of younger adults attending their churches is substantially higher than the proportion in the nation as a whole. No particular change in attendances is to be expected in the Anglican Church and Salvation Army arising solely from the distribution in age groups of their attendances, but the long term prospect for the Nonconformists in York appears to be distinctly bleak, for these figures indicate that they are not attracting sufficient of the younger age groups.[59]

Catholics becoming relatively stronger and the Free Churches becoming relatively weaker is exactly what happened in York, albeit with a clear decline among Catholics in recent years. The smallness of the Salvation Army alone may have misled him about their prospects. That apart, this offers a very rare and remarkable demonstration of largely substantiated predictions, based upon physical not cultural criteria, and resulting from the careful accumulation of longitudinal census data.

Compared to Anglicans, Catholics in York display a number of physical differences. Their churches are fewer in number and are on average far better attended. Most commentators notice the second of these differences but not the first. As a result, they quickly conclude that Catholic churches are better attended solely because far more Catholics go to church than Anglicans.

In York more Catholics apparently *do* now go to church on an average Sunday than Anglicans. If some 3950 Catholics of all ages were in church on a typical Sunday in 1989, there were at the same time some 3614 Anglicans. This last figure contains an estimate of 200 local adults who regularly attend the Minster,[60] although even on this point it is necessary to add a slight note of caution. The presence of the Minster, which has not always been included in parochial statistics, may somewhat disrupt too fine a set of calculations of Anglican churchgoing in any census. In the past, clergy frequently complained about the propensity of the Minster to encourage eclectic churchgoing. Even today, it is difficult to know how best to measure the Minster's varying constituency. Nevertheless, if York is like the rest of England, baptised Catholics do seem to have been significantly more assiduous in going to church than baptised Anglicans and, despite very similar rates of decline over the past twelve years, this remains the case today.

However, the fact that Anglicans in York have more than three times as many church buildings as Catholics makes the difference between them *appear* far sharper than it is in reality. What was evident in 1989 was that four of the seven Catholic churches still claimed usual attendances in excess of 600. In contrast, just one of the twenty-three Anglican parish churches regularly had such attendances, and not one of the Free Church chapels had even half that number unless it was a special occasion. Twelve years later there is now an independent Baptist church (albeit just outside the city area) claiming a congregation approaching this size, but only one Catholic and no Anglican church in York today that claims such a regular congregation.

Furthermore, this difference, which seems to have persisted throughout the twentieth century, was achieved with fewer Catholic than Anglican priests. If

---

[59] Rowntree and Lavers, *English Life and Leisure*, pp. 344–5.

[60] This estimate was kindly supplied by a member of the chapter at York Minster.

Anglicans in 1989 had some twenty-four purely parochial priests working in York (excluding those connected with the Minster or in full-time diocesan appointments), Catholics had just twelve. So on average an Anglican parochial priest ministered to 142 people of all ages on a Sunday, while his Catholic counterpart ministered to 329. In this respect the Catholic priest in 1989 most closely resembled the Church of England priest in 1851 (the ratio of Anglican priest to parochial attendances then was 330). In 2002 the situation has changed again. Now there are only seven Catholic priests serving York – one for each church – and there are reports that they are struggling, with declining attendances and an increased ratio of 454.

Despite all the qualifications that have been made about York not being typical of other towns because of its higher than average Catholic population, it is really not that atypical today. In the 1989 MARC Europe census[61] 35 per cent of adult church attendances in England were Catholic, representing 3.4 per cent of the adult population. The 1989 York estimates for adult Catholics of 37 per cent and 4.1 per cent respectively *are* somewhat higher, but they are not all that different. In contrast, the Greater London adult Catholic attendances in 1989 of 4.1 per cent of the adult population represented 45 per cent of total adult attendances there. The Church of England adult attendances in York in 1989 of 35 per cent and 3.8 per cent respectively are also somewhat higher than the MARC Europe 1989 figures of 31 per cent and 2.9 per cent, and are appreciably higher than the Greater London figures of 18 per cent and 1.6 per cent. Only the Free Churches are low in York at some 28 per cent and 3 per cent respectively in 1989, compared with the 1989 national means of 34 per cent and 3.2 per cent.

From all of this it follows that the total adult church and chapel attendance rate in York in 1989 of 10.9 per cent is somewhat higher than the national rate in the same year of 9.5 per cent. However, if attendances of all ages are counted, then the rate in York is much closer. For York the rate in 1989 was 10.8 per cent, whereas the national rate was 10.3 per cent.

This last comparison may suggest that York can act as a fairly representative barometer today. However, it does point to a very ominous feature of present-day churchgoing. In the 1989 MARC Europe census, young people were apparently better attenders than adults. If 9.5 per cent was the rate of adult attendance nationally, 13.7 per cent was the child attendance rate. In York this ratio in some denominations would seem to be reversed. Anglican adult attendances in 1989 accounted for 3.8 per cent of the adult population of York, but child attendances accounted for only 3.2 per cent of the population aged under 16 (national averages are 3.2 per cent and 3.9 per cent respectively). Similarly, among Methodists in York, adults represented 1.6 per cent, but children only 1.4 per cent (national averages are 1.0 per cent and 1.3 per cent). If it is children who represent the future of churches, then on this basis their future looks bleak – and the recent Sunday school statistics quoted earlier makes it look still bleaker.

Although York still has considerably more space in churches and chapels than it actually uses, its ratio of buildings to population today is no longer particularly unusual. In 1989 it had a church or chapel for 1621 people. The MARC Europe

---

[61] See Peter Brierley (ed.), *Prospects for the Nineties: Trends and Tables from the English Church Census*, MARC Europe, 1991.

census for 1989 suggested a figure of 1284 for the region of Yorkshire and Humberside as a whole. In rural areas the ratio is very considerably less than in urban areas. So in Northumberland there in 1989 there was one church/chapel for 844 people, in Norfolk for 645, in Cumbria for 641, in North Yorkshire for 625, and in Cornwall for 527. The highest ratio was recorded in the West Midlands with one for 2101 people. Merseyside had one for 1931 people, Greater London one for 1898, and Tyne and Wear one for 1806. York remains a large town and not a major conurbation and its 1989 ratio reflects this.

6

By paying closer attention than is usual to the physical characteristics of denominations over a period of 225 years, I have argued that it is possible to learn more about church growth and decline. York supplies abundant evidence that there have been major differences of behaviour between the Church of England, the Free Churches and the Catholic Church for many years. These differences have been largely invisible to the Churches themselves. Yet I have argued that they have had a major effect upon their changing levels of churchgoing. Left unchecked there are already clear signs about what the future holds for the different denominations in York. Following Rowntree, my own prediction is that both the Church of England and the Free Churches will face further decline over the next decades, despite the relative strength of a few of their evangelical congregations. From the present-day Sunday school figures it is already clear that both the Church of England and the Free Churches lack the active support of most young people. Even Catholics in York, despite a more prudent use of church buildings, are now showing clear signs of general disaffection. Perhaps they are not helped by a shortage of priests to serve them. Several of the smaller Anglican and Free Church congregations can expect to face closure over the next few decades.

Of course these predictions assume that existing structures and long-established patterns of behaviour continue unchanged. They assume that the Anglican Church will continue with its pattern of subsidized persistence, the Free Churches with their pattern of competitive diffusion, and the Catholics with their pattern of diminishing numbers of (celibate) parish priests. All three national patterns are strongly characteristic of York today. Periodic attempts at religious revival in York, as elsewhere, may have failed in the past to promote effective numerical growth precisely because these patterns remained unchallenged and unchecked. In between completing the research for my original *Myth of the Empty Church* and this present book the churches in Britain engaged in a 'Decade of Evangelism'. Inspired by a new Archbishop of Canterbury, the hope was that a major initiative on evangelism across denominations could reverse widespread decline in churchgoing. This initiative has now finished and a new Archbishop is in office. The evidence presented here suggests that, whatever else it might have achieved, the 'Decade of Evangelism' did not stem this decline. Sadly it was based upon words and rhetoric and not upon identifying clearly and then changing long-established patterns of behaviour.

If churches are to grow again in the future, they might do well to examine carefully the York evidence now.

10

The Future of the Churches

It would be far too simplistic to claim that the empty church was the one and only cause of churchgoing decline in Britain. I have stressed throughout this book that monocausal explanations of long-standing social processes are unlikely to be convincing. Social processes are inevitably complex because the actors within them are complex, and human behaviour can rarely be encapsulated convincingly in simplistic paradigms. More modestly, this book has been concerned to investigate the extent to which the empty church has played a pivotal, but often unnoticed, role in British churchgoing decline.

A variety of factors have been suggested for empty churches – paradoxically, only some of them are to do with declining attendances. In the countryside, vigorous building against radical depopulation led to empty churches. In urban areas rapid suburbanization left city-centre churches stranded without effective congregations – either because city centres too had depopulated or because they now lacked the churchgoing middle classes. However, once established, empty churches seem to have had a number of predictable effects; and it is the latter that would appear to have been important in initiating British churchgoing decline.

It is quite remarkable how little these factors were understood at the time. What contemporary commentators repeatedly noticed were churches that were getting emptier and emptier. The demographic, economic and structural factors behind these empty churches were seldom noticed. Instead, cultural explanations predominated. For example, one Free Church writer, who should have known better, argued in 1901:

> In the Church we have witnessed, to say the least, a very considerable collapse of what I may call conventional religion – that is, public opinion does much less to enforce church attendance and church communion. The change began in Scotland, perhaps thirty years ago. I remember the time when churches were fully attended twice a day, when in many places non-churchgoers were quite exceptional. This is no longer the case. Many are content with occasional attendances, and, in spite of all the efforts of the churches, the number of outsiders is very great, and is constantly increasing. I question, in this respect, whether Scotland is not in a worse position than England.[1]

Note that there is not a word here about the explosion of church buildings that characterized Scotland in the second half of the nineteenth century. By 1901 even a very small town like Coldstream had three brands of Presbyterian church serving its declining population of less than 2000 – quite apart from Baptists and Episcopalians. This is a pattern that can be found throughout Scotland. If Methodist

---

[1] *The British Weekly*, 24 December 1901.

rivalries contributed to over-building in England, Presbyterian rivalries in Scotland were even sharper. The Scottish Disruption of 1843 led to an astonishing duplication of parish churches, both in the fast-growing cities and, ironically, in the fast depopulating countryside. Since its Union of 1929 the Church of Scotland has, as was observed earlier, been continuously trying to reduce their number. But all that the writer in 1901 could notice were empty churches; and it was 'the collapse of conventional religion' that he saw as their cause.

Yet by placing the empty church in a pivotal position, I am not positing anything so foolish as a monocausal explanation of church decline, or even a total elimination of theories of secularization. Demographic factors have been seen throughout this book to be linked to churchgoing decline, and declining Christian belief has been seen to be one of the most recent cultural features of church decline. As the twentieth century has unfolded, a variety of factors seem to have exacerbated churchgoing decline.

Not least of these is the fact that most denominations in Britain today seldom recruit from outside their existing churchgoers and their immediate families. The Jones/Butler formula for predicting membership decline in the Methodist Church proved so accurate precisely because it assumed that recruitment was basically endogenous. Whatever claims were made about mission within Methodism, and whatever hopes were expressed in the 1980s about numerical growth, the reality was that membership and attendances declined in remarkably predictable ways. Even when particular congregations have shown remarkable growth, the overall effect may have been to produce more, not less, 'failures' elsewhere. Thus Chapter 9 suggested that the median for average Anglican attendances has drastically deteriorated in York since the startling numerical growth of St Michael le Belfrey, even though the mean has declined less than the national rate. Most of the surrounding Anglican congregations seem to have experienced a rather sharper decline than might otherwise have been the case. Clustering churchgoers in 'successful' churches may have as an ironic side-effect a larger number of declining churches.

As a majority of churches have slowly declined in the course of this century, so the perceptions of most people will surely have been affected. Despite isolated strong congregations in predominantly middle-class areas, most non-Catholics in Britain today will have known only struggling churches. Some will also have seen rural areas surrounding cities, as well as relatively affluent suburban areas, gradually being replaced by populations that have long since ceased to be churchgoers. A lengthy process of attrition, rather than recent sharp decline, is evident from the mass of data analysed in the previous chapters.

However, my aim in *The Myth of the Empty Church* was also to offer suggestions for structural change to British churches. This was explicitly a piece of action-research following the precedent of Leslie Paul's *The Deployment and Payment of the Clergy*[2] in believing that suggestions for structural change should always be preceded by a rigorous empirical analysis that is capable of sustaining inspection from other scholars. It also followed Leslie Paul in believing that, whatever

---

[2] Leslie Paul, *The Deployment and Payment of the Clergy*, Church Information Office, London, 1964.

refinements and qualifications other scholars may add, the previous chapters have already raised sufficient evidence about structural defects in British churches to require radical attention. Since I have set out these suggestions for structural change more fully since writing *The Myth* I will not repeat them again here.[3] Instead, I will first outline Leslie Paul's earlier attempt to address the decline of the Church of England and then set this decline into a wider context of Western churches.

1

In the early 1960s Leslie Paul made a careful study of the Church of England. Even then he was well aware of its numerical and social decline, plotting this in some detail using the, then recently published, *Facts and Figures about the Church of England*.[4] At the very beginning of his report he noted that, 'whether we base membership most broadly on infant baptism or more narrowly upon confirmation figures, there is in both cases serious evidence of decline'.[5] Furthermore, as noted in Chapter 8, he was the first analyst in recent times to try to measure average Anglican Sunday attendances nationally and to compare them diocese by diocese.

Having set out his data at considerable length, Paul introduced his proposals for change with these words:

> There is no doubt that what the evidence urges upon us is a reform of the ministerial structure and of the pastoral machinery of the Church, or rather not one single reform, but an interlocking series of reforms; in fact, an operation of the utmost delicacy and complexity. Though the difficulties stare us in the face, the alternatives are chilling – to do nothing, which means to abandon the nation to its religious decline and the clergy to their isolation, or to attempt a few piecemeal reforms which may save face but leave the central missionary problem to the conurbations unresolved. The crux of the whole problem of deployment seems to me this – though short of manpower the Church cannot use the clergy it has as effectively as it ought to: it is bad stewardship. It needs more clergy, but it has no moral right to ask for them unless it can deploy them effectively ... Considered as a corporate body, the Church needs the same control over its organisational life as it is beginning to insist it must have over its liturgical life. Conceived as a total corporation, not just the clergy, it must, if it can, bring the laity into a joint ministry with the clergy. The clergy and the laity together form a minority over against a society which has largely abandoned regular Christian practice.[6]

If this was the situation of decline four decades ago, it is even more so today. Surely it is unnecessary to rehearse again the data showing that Anglican churchgoing, Sunday schools, festival attendances, baptisms, confirmations, and the number of parochial clergy have all declined sharply since Leslie Paul wrote these words. Decline in almost every measurable form has characterized the Church of

---

[3] See my *A Vision for Growth*, SPCK, London, 1994 and (with Derek Burke) *Strategic Church Leadership*, SPCK, London, 1996.

[4] *Facts and Figures about the Church of England*, Church Information Office, London, 1962.

[5] Paul, *Deployment*, p. 17.

[6] Paul, *Deployment*, p. 171.

England in the past forty years. But has this decline occurred despite Anglicans making the radical structural changes that Paul proposed?

As its title indicated, the two issues that predominated in Leslie Paul's report were clerical payment and clerical deployment. None the less, he was clearly conscious, as a layman himself, of the role of the laity and, as a sociologist, of the need for new diocesan structures. With synodical government becoming a reality a decade later and a continuing emphasis on the role of the laity in most churches, his briefer proposals in these two important areas are now less pertinent.

By the time he wrote, the very considerable discrepancies in clergy stipends that were still in place at the beginning of the century had already largely disappeared. Leslie Paul noted that in 1906 the average clerical income was £150, whereas some incumbents received £1500 or more, the Dean of Durham £3000, and the Archbishop of Canterbury £15 000. However, by the early 1960s inflation had greatly eroded such discrepancies and dioceses had policies of minimum stipends. The latter varied between £750 and £950 or more, yet £800–£849 was the most common rate. At the highest end of the range, only sixty-one livings had stipends of £2000 or more (half a per cent of all livings). Paul observed that 'the number of "plums" is not as great as rumour would have it'.[7]

Nevertheless, he still saw the need for a number of reforms – most of which have now taken place. He argued that benefice funds should be pooled for general stipends; that there should be no distinction in payment between beneficed and unbeneficed clergy; that there should be a common stipend on a national scale; and that pension differences should be resolved. Continuing inflation, as well as conscious policies to equalize stipends and to improve pensions, seem to have largely brought about the changes Paul sought in this area.

However, linked to slower policies of redeployment, these changes may actually have exacerbated discrepancies in the Church of England. On the issue of clergy payment, Leslie Paul was aware that the Church of England had already made major changes; his proposals merely sought to accelerate them. On the issue of redeployment, he argued that the Church of England remained disproportionately rural in a predominantly urban society:

> The distribution of clergy is in inverse proportion to pastoral need. A pattern repeats itself time and time again: the greater the density of population the fewer relatively the number of clergy. But another pattern superimposes itself: the greater the density of population the poorer the pastoral results of the Church, the feebler its total impact. One might go further and say, the greater the density of population the more congregations approximate to ingatherings of the elect rather than to representative parochial congregations. And so the greater the density of population the more areas become mission areas against the problems of which the traditional parochial forms appear largely ineffective ... The *central* missionary problem of the Church of England is how to carry its faith and its life with urgency and meaning into the hearts of the busy, preoccupied, harassed urban multitudes whose very pattern of life seems to estrange them from the Church.[8]

---

[7] Paul, *Deployment*, p. 119.
[8] Paul, *Deployment*, p. 137 and his *A Church by Daylight*, Chapmans, London, 1973.

This vision lies at the very core of Leslie Paul's report. After all the data presented in the previous chapters, there must be some doubt about his assumption that it is urbanization as such which 'estranges' people from churches. Throughout the report he assumed that church decline was primarily an urban phenomenon. In reality, it has been seen repeatedly that, even at that stage, it was also a rural phenomenon. As already noted in Chapter 8, *Table 18* suggests that churchgoing decline has actually been faster than the mean rate over the last two decades in some of the most rural dioceses and slower in the most urban ones. Furthermore, data about churchgoing patterns in the United States was already at considerable odds with Leslie Paul's assumptions.

Nevertheless, the central challenge of Leslie Paul's report was in the area of clergy deployment. In 1958 almost half of the livings in the Church of England had populations of less than 1500, and of these almost half were one-church livings with populations of less than 1000. In the Diocese of Hereford parochial clergy on average each had 1054 people in their parishes, whereas those in the Diocese of Birmingham had 6607. In other words, there was a discrepancy of more than one-to-six. By 1999 this discrepancy has been reduced to under one-to-three, albeit with clergy in both dioceses having larger parishes.[9] Today full-time parochial clergy in Hereford on average each have 2981 people in their parishes, and those in Birmingham 7617.

Leslie Paul made a number of proposals to reduce this urban/rural discrepancy: bishops should be given power to reorganize areas; clergy freehold should be turned instead into a ten-year leasehold; clergy should be allowed to retire at 65; at 70, freehold/leasehold should automatically be lost; group and team ministries should be fostered; extra-parochial ministries in universities and in industry should be increased; ordinands should be directed to urban areas of pastoral need during their first five years of ministry; patronage should be transformed into a staffing or appointments advisory system, with private patrons represented only on regional boards; and a directory of vacancies should be established and made available to clergy intending to move.

Today almost all of these proposals have become a reality somewhere in the Church of England. However, as has happened so often in the past, few have been implemented systematically. The *ad hoc* changes that have been introduced may even have made overall structures more confused and complex. Team ministries have perhaps been most successful in implementing them, yet patronage and freehold remain intact in many more traditional parishes. Within teams, fixed-term appointments have now been widely accepted. Voluntary retirement at 65 and compulsory retirement at 70 have applied to all clerical appointments since the mid-1970s. Stipendiary, but extra-parochial, ministries have also grown. In 1977 they constituted 2.4 per cent of all stipendiary diocesan clergy; in 1985 they were 2.8 per cent; in 1990 they were 3.1 per cent and in 1999 they were 3.3 per cent.

---

[9] For the present-day statistics that follow, see *Church Statistics: Some Facts and Figures about the Church of England*, The Central Board of Finance of the Church of England 1991; a few additional figures were also kindly supplied by Mr Douglas Fryer, then of the Statistics Unit, Church House, Westminster.

In the countryside, multi-church benefices have become the norm and have reduced the traditional role of private patrons. Some patrons now advertise when a parish is vacant. There is also a full-time clergy appointments adviser, who is increasingly used by patrons and by those seeking new livings. Under the Pastoral Measure, bishops have long had powers to suspend livings and to reorganize areas; and under the Patronage Measure, parishes also have had a greater say in the appointment of incumbents. Designated local ecumenical projects also allowed almost all of the changes envisaged by Leslie Paul. For several years before 1994 when women were finally ordained in the Church of England, a number of these projects even allowed women ministers, from participating Free Churches, to celebrate the Eucharist in what would otherwise have been regarded as Anglican churches.

However, in one crucial respect the situation is now radically different from that envisaged by Leslie Paul. He assumed that ordinands would continue to be predominantly young, unmarried men who could be directed in increasing numbers for five years to urban training parishes. In fact, in 1990 less than a third of those ordained deacon into full-time ministry were aged under 30 (in Leslie Paul's time it was three-fifths). His own predictions about the number and typical profile of future ordinands can now be seen to have been highly misleading.

Specifically, Leslie Paul argued that, 'providing the Church of England maintains its efforts to attract and train candidates for the ministry, greater numbers of young men will become clergymen'.[10] He predicted that by 1970 there would be 809 deacons ordained; in fact, there were just 437. By 1980 the number had reduced to 309, with an additional 119 deacons ordained into non-stipendiary ministry. By 1990 there were 282 male and 79 female deacons ordained into full-time ministry, and 77 males and 42 females into non-stipendiary ministry. A majority of curates today are middle-aged, married, have a family, and are already experienced in the secular world. With children at school, and frequently with a spouse in an established career, it is perhaps not surprising that today they tend to serve just a single curacy before becoming incumbents.

Since 1975 the major instrument to effect changes in rural–urban clergy deployment in the Church of England has been the 'Sheffield Formula'. It was explicitly designed to:

> Enable the Church, over a period of years, to use the manpower that was available in the most effective way possible, and in a manner which would ensure fairer shares as between dioceses than the existing distribution, based on historical patterns rather than present needs, provided.[11]

The formula has sought to apportion the total number of full-time stipendiary clergy between dioceses on the basis of a number of factors weighted differently: diocesan populations, diocesan areas, numbers on electoral rolls, number of churches, and (since 1988) average Sunday attendances.

---

[10] Paul, *Deployment*, p. 297.

[11] *Church Statistics: Some Facts and Figures about the Church of England*, The Central Board of Finance of the Church of England, London, 1991, p. 16.

Leslie Paul envisaged a great expansion of stipendiary clergy. To improve clergy–population ratios he argued that the 15 488 full-time clergy in 1961 (with an average population each of 2838) should be increased to 17 581 (to reduce this population to 2500) and ideally to 29 301 (to reduce it to 1500). On this basis he calculated that by 1991 there would have needed to be 21 761 full-time clergy to achieve the 2500 ratio and 36 268 to achieve the 1500 ratio. In fact by 1991 there were 10 480 male and 596 female full-time, stipendiary clergy (with an average population each of 4340). Given this huge discrepancy, it is not surprising that rural/urban redeployment resulting from the Sheffield Formula has also been accompanied by worse clergy–population ratios in both areas. Paradoxically, it has also been accompanied by an increased economic subsidy to rural areas – a subsidy that has not stopped rural attendances declining faster than urban ones.

This can be seen by comparing the five most urban dioceses (London, Southwark, Birmingham, Manchester and Liverpool) with the five most rural ones (Hereford, Carlisle, Sodor and Man, Lincoln and Truro). In Leslie Paul's time, 31 per cent of the stipendiary clergy in these ten dioceses were deployed in the rural ones (serving 14 per cent of the total populations); by 1990 this reduced to 27 per cent (serving 17 per cent of the populations). In the early 1960s rural stipendiary clergy were each responsible on average for 1763 people; by 1990 this had increased to 3179. In contrast, the populations per urban clergy had only increased from 5136 to 5762.

Yet this pattern of redeployment has also been accompanied by an increased economic subsidy to the remaining rural clergy. In Leslie Paul's time, the latter each raised on average £998 in parish giving (when, as just noted, minimum stipends averaged £800–49); by 1990 parish giving per rural clergy had risen only to £5641 (when minimum stipends were double that amount and actual costs quadruple). Parish giving in relation to urban clergy, in contrast, had meanwhile risen from an average of £1661 to £9856. In neither case did parish giving keep pace with inflation. However, the effect of parish giving increasing at little more than half the rate of inflation has been to redistribute economic resources in favour of rural parishes. These figures clearly show that, despite some redeployment, rural parishes were still being subsidized disproportionately to urban ones.

Furthermore, this increased subsidy did not prevent attendances in the most rural dioceses from declining faster than those in the most urban dioceses. Between 1968 and 1989 average attendances in the five most urban dioceses declined from 276 370 to 185 300. In relation to their populations this represents a decline from 2.3 per cent to 1.8 per cent. The latter is a decline over the twenty-one years of 24.8 per cent. Over the same period average attendances in the five most rural dioceses declined from 98 970 to 73 100. In relation to their populations, this represents a decline from 5.3 per cent to 3.3 per cent. This, in contrast, is a decline over this period of 37.4 per cent.

All of this suggests the ironic conclusion that a radical policy of implementing equal payment among clergy, regardless of levels of parish giving and allied to more gradual policies of rural–urban redeployment, actually increased the problem of subsidy in the Church of England. Leslie Paul's own warning quoted a few pages ago – that 'to attempt a few piecemeal reforms which may save face but leave the central missionary problem to the conurbations unresolved'[12] – sadly proved to be prophetic. Even the structural changes initiated by Archbishop George Carey in the 1990s (such as the introduction of the Archbishops' Council and the Decade of Evangelism) have done little if anything to reduce churchgoing decline in Britain.

2

Of course churchgoing decline is not unique to Britain. However, the wealth of historical data used in this book is unique. Evidence of churchgoing decline elsewhere in the Western world can certainly be traced, but for the most part this evidence is comparatively recent. For example, in Australia those recording a no-religion option in the national population census have increased from 6.7 per cent in 1971 to 16.6 per cent in 1996, and those claiming in opinion polls to go to church at least once a month have declined from 47 per cent in 1950 to 24 per cent in 1993.[13] Similarly, in Canada opinion polls suggested a decline in those claiming to have gone to church or synagogue in the last seven days from 65 per cent in 1940s to 30 per cent in the 1990s, with this decline just as evident amongst Catholics (especially in Quebec) as amongst Protestants, and a decline in the same period of children going to Sunday school or church from 60 per cent to 26 per cent.[14]

Even in the United States, despite much evidence of comparative resilience of religious participation, there is also tentative evidence of recent decline. Gallup Polls over the past fifty years have suggested comparatively high levels of regular churchgoing at approximately two-fifths of the population, yet in the 1950s this rose to almost half of the population. And the blunt Gallup question 'What is your religious denomination?' shows an increase in no-religion responses in five decades from 2 per cent to 11 per cent. Until the mid-1960s the *Yearbook of American and Canadian Churches* charted overall membership of religious bodies in the United States, both Christian and non-Christian, measured against the total population. This suggested a remarkable rise from 16 per cent in 1850, to 36 per cent in 1900, to 47 per cent in 1930, to 57 per cent in 1950, rising finally to 64.3 per cent in 1965. Using the same basis of measurement, this level was still 64.5 per cent in 1970, but had declined to 59.5 per cent in 1980 and to 59.3 per cent in 1990.

Many European countries have also seen a recent decline in churchgoing and with it a measurable decline in specifically Christian beliefs. For example, the two sets of surveys conducted by the *European Value Systems Study Group* showed a

---

[12] Paul, *Deployment*, p. 171.

[13] See Philip J. Hughes, *Religion in Australia: Facts and Figures*, Christian Research Association, Kew, Victoria, Australia, 1997, and Philip J. Hughes, Craig Thompson, Rohan Pryor and Gary D. Bouma, *Believe it or Not: Australian Spirituality and the Churches in the 90s*, Christian Research Association, Kew, Victoria, Australia, 1995.

[14] See Reginald W. Bibby, *Fragmented Gods: The Poverty and Potential of Religion in Canada*, Irwin Publishing, Toronto, 1987, and Reginald W. Bibby, 'Going, Going, Gone: The Impact of Geographical Mobility on Religious Involvement', *Review of Religious Research*, vol. 38, no. 4, 1997, pp. 289–307.

decline in mean weekly churchgoing rates during the 1980s in ten European countries from 49 per cent to 29 per cent, with a particularly sharp decline in the 18–24 age-group from 43 per cent to just 18 per cent.[15] These surveys also detected a decline in the same countries in belief in God from 85 per cent to 79 per cent and in heaven from 53 per cent to 49 per cent. In addition, they provided evidence of clear generational differences consonant with the EVSSG figures for Britain cited in Chapter 8. And, in their survey of evidence in the 1990s from the *International Social Survey Programme* Nan Dirk De Graaf and Ariana Need conclude that 'most countries (Britain, western Germany, eastern Germany, United States, Hungary, Italy, Ireland, Norway, Austria, Poland, and Slovenia) show a large decline in church membership between 1991 and 1998, and a much smaller decline in church attendance and belief in God'.[16] Only Russia showed significant increases in all three areas.

Again, using a rather longer time-frame, *Der Spiegel* commissioned an attitude survey in West Germany in 1967 which it repeated in 1992.[17] During that twenty-five year period declared weekly churchgoing declined sharply from 25 per cent to 10 per cent and, amongst a series of beliefs, a belief in God declined from 68 per cent to 56 per cent and in Jesus as the Son of God from 42 per cent to 29 per cent.

Evidence, then, of growing secularity in the Western world appears to be overwhelming. The future seems clear. Participation in religious institutions (predominantly Christian) will continue to decline. Within two generations we can expect, on current trends in Britain, that only 31 per cent of the elderly there will report that they had been 'brought up religiously at home', 22 per cent of the middle aged, and just 12 per cent of the young (and possibly even less if the non-religious parent in a mixed union prevails). As a result, explicitly Christian beliefs of any variety will be held by only a small section of the population and most people, old as well as young, will see themselves as having no religion and will be increasing prepared to express scepticism about any form of religious (especially theistic) belief. Thus within two generations secularity and religious scepticism will have triumphed both in Britain and in most other countries within the modernized, Western world. The population of the United States, apart from the more secular California, may be comparatively resilient, but on this basis it too will eventually follow the ineluctable modernity and secularization evident elsewhere in the West.

---

[15] See Jan Kerkhofs, 'Between "Christendom" and "Christianity"', *Journal of Empirical Theology*, vol. 1, no. 2, 1988, pp. 88–101. For specifically British EVSSG data see Mark Abrams, David Gerard and Noel Timms (eds), *Values and Social Change in Britain: Studies in the Contemporary Values of Modern Society*, Macmillan, London, 1985, and Noel Timms, *Family and Citizenship: Values in Contemporary Britain*, Dartmouth, Aldershot, 1992.

[16] Nan Dirk De Graaf and Ariana Need, 'Losing Faith: is Britain alone?', in R. Jowell, J. Curtice, A. Parrk, K. Thomson, L. Jarvis, C. Bromely and N. Stratford (eds), *British Social Attitudes: the 17th Report*, Sage, London, 2000, p. 129.

[17] See Jack D. Shand, 'The Decline of Traditional Christian Beliefs in Germany', *Sociology of Religion*, vol. 59, no. 2, 1998, pp. 179–84.

3

Yet there are other, more awkward, pieces of evidence suggesting that growing Western secularization is not the whole of the story. There are already indications in the data just set out that churchgoing decline has not been an entirely linear, unambiguous process, either between or across denominations, neither in Britain nor elsewhere in the Western world, and especially not in the United States. In addition, to focus so exclusively upon declining Christian participation and beliefs may be to miss other religious forms brought with new immigrants or re-emerging within the indigenous population. As a result, predictions based only upon linear secularization may well be far too simplistic. Despite the fact that such predictions have often been made by sociologists going all the way back to Comte, they may owe more to ideology than to empirical observation.

Evidence pointing to a rise in churchgoing in York between 1837 and 1851 has already been noted. Throughout Britain in the first half of the nineteenth century there was very extensive building of new churches and chapels as well a general increase in the number of services that they offered of a Sunday. Anglican parishes that had been neglected for years received a resident incumbent, sometimes for the first time since medieval times, with a new parsonage and a renovated or newly built church. Rural churches that had often had an irregular provision of Sunday services now had a regular pattern of two or three services. Urban churches, which frequently had a single service in the afternoon in the eighteenth century, now had morning and afternoon services and Sunday schools as well as evening services for adults. Free Churches competed vigorously in both rural and urban areas, providing an abundance of new churches and chapels and frequently several alongside each other even in larger villages. The 1851 census reveals clearly just how successful all of this was. In some areas of Britain more than half of the total population was in church or chapel at a single point on the census day and there was sufficient space in all of these churches and chapels for most of the population. Ironically, the conductors of the census were worried that not everyone *was* attending church on that Sunday and that a reason for this might be that there were still insufficient church buildings to serve the population. In reality, 1851 may well have been a high point both in British churchgoing and in church provision compared with the immediate centuries before, rivalling the remarkable period of church building by immigrant Normans in the eleventh and twelfth centuries. The mid-nineteenth century appears to have been the most recent peak of religious participation in Britain, just as the mid-twentieth century was apparently that for the United States.

Again, although regular attendances within most denominations in Britain and in much of the rest of Europe have been declining since the 1960s, their pattern is much more varied before that date. It has already been seen that in urban areas Anglicans have experienced the longest-term decline, whereas Roman Catholics had a century of steady growth (albeit perhaps exaggerated by Irish immigration) or consolidation in many areas, as they did in the United States, before experiencing recent decline. It has also been the inclusive denominations, such as Episcopalians, in the United States which have experienced long-term decline, whereas more exclusive denominations, such as Southern Baptists, or 'sects', such as the Mormons, which have experienced considerable growth.[18] The relative resilience, until recently, of overall levels of churchgoing in the United States has often been contrasted with European decline. Yet in both contexts predictions about linear and unambiguous secularization appear far too simplistic. There seems to be more than one process operating between and across denominations even within Europe, let alone within the United States. Migration may be an important variable accounting, in at least some circumstances, for such variations. In Britain in the first half of the nineteenth century, rural migration to cities and large towns was associated not simply with estrangement from churches but also with new religious attachments.

A more recent example of a similar process is that of South Korea.[19] There the three decades up to 1990, but not beyond, were characterized both by extremely rapid urbanization and industrialization and by a phenomenal growth of Roman Catholic and Protestant church membership and also the building of a rich variety of Protestant churches (as well as Buddhist temples). In contrast, Japan, which (like Britain) urbanized in the nineteenth century, has experienced no comparable twentieth century growth in formal religious participation.

Immigration has also been strongly associated with religious growth and change in Britain. The steady growth from the mid-nineteenth century of Roman Catholics after emancipation, until the mid-twentieth century, closely matched patterns of Irish immigration. As seen in earlier chapters, it was accompanied by an Irish rather than a continental European pattern of church building. Characteristically a single building was used on a Sunday morning for multiple masses with churchgoers expected to travel in from some distance. In contrast, Anglicans and many continental European Catholics expected to have a local church even within small communities. This pattern persists to the present with Catholic churches typically placed in small towns rather than villages. In York, as Chapter 9 showed, there are now slightly more Roman Catholic than Anglican church attendances on a typical Sunday, yet there are still twenty-four Anglican churches there to the Roman Catholic seven. Roman Catholics now represent approximately a third of total churchgoers in England as a whole, and yet they own only a tenth of the churches (although, with the sharp decline in mass attendances since the 1960s, Roman Catholic bishops in urban areas such as Liverpool are now, like their Anglican counterparts, facing a considerable surfeit of church buildings).

The first half of the twentieth century saw a series of waves of Jewish immigration following persecution in Russia and continental Europe. In cities such as London and Liverpool this resulted in the building of many Orthodox, Liberal and Reformed synagogues. Towards the end of the twentieth century other waves of immigration saw a considerable growth in the Muslim population of Britain (accounting now for 3–4 per cent of the general population). With this has also come a rapid building of rival mosques – there are now more than fifty in Bradford alone and prestigious central mosques in cities such as London and Edinburgh. Although fewer in number, Sikh and Hindu temples have also been built in urban areas. Taken together they have radically changed the visible religious map in some,

[18] See Roger Finke and Rodney Stark, *The Churching of America: Winners and Losers in Our Religious Economy*, Rutgers University Press, New Brunswick, NJ, 1992.
[19] See further my *Changing Worlds*, Continuum, London, 2002.

but certainly not all, parts of Britain and offer a challenge to a theory of linear secularization.

This varied pattern is also reflected in the data from attitude surveys already mentioned (see *Table 20*). Alongside a pattern of declining Christian beliefs and growing scepticism is another pattern of persisting, and sometimes increasing, non-traditional or non-institutional religious beliefs. Belief in reincarnation and in horoscopes has been held consistently by a quarter of the population over the last three decades. About half of the population also apparently believes in those foretelling the future. Over the past fifty years the proportion of people believing in ghosts has also doubled: a third of the population now has this belief, even though only half claims actually to have seen a ghost. Although many people express scepticism about these beliefs, they hardly support a theory of linear secularization.

Attitude data also suggest that there are remarkable continuities (as well as some changes) in the beliefs and values of churchgoers across several decades and across different cultures. Perhaps it is not surprising that British churchgoers in the 1960s and 1990s have similarly high levels of belief in a personal God or in life after death – and, indeed, that similar levels can be detected amongst churchgoers in continental Europe, Australia and North America. It is, though, interesting that British and Northern Irish, or Canadian and American, churchgoers have very similar levels of belief even though these levels differ widely among non-churchgoers in their countries. So in Britain and Canada, where churchgoing levels are comparatively low, differences between the beliefs of churchgoers and non-churchgoers are more pronounced than those in Northern Ireland and the United States, where churchgoing levels are higher. Yet in all of these contexts the levels of basic Christian belief among churchgoers themselves are remarkably similar (whatever their other obvious differences).

Just to give a single example, using results from the *World Value Survey*[20] of the early 1980s for the United States and Canada, there are close similarities amongst weekly churchgoers in the two countries on their beliefs in God (99 per cent+), in life after death (USA 88 per cent and Canada 86 per cent), in the soul (98 per cent and 97 per cent), in heaven (98 per cent and 95 per cent), in sin (96 per cent and 90 per cent), in their taking time to pray (97 per cent and 92 per cent), and in their disbelief in reincarnation (78 per cent and 73 per cent). They differed sharply only on their belief in the devil (81 per cent and 64 per cent) and in hell (86 per cent and 67 per cent). Yet among those who 'rarely attend', there were sharp differences on most of these items of belief: life after death (70 per cent and 60 per cent), heaven (78 per cent and 62 per cent), sin (84 per cent and 66 per cent), taking time to pray (72 per cent and 62 per cent), and some difference on God (95 per cent and 88 per cent), the soul (85 per cent and 79 per cent) and disbelief in reincarnation (72 per cent and 62 per cent).

More significantly, there is now abundant evidence that participation in voluntary service in the community is characteristically high among churchgoers.

---

[20] See Samuel H. Reimer, 'A Look at Cultural Effects on Religiosity: A Comparison Between the United States and Canada', *Journal for the Scientific Study of Religion*, vol. 34, no. 4, 1996, p. 452. For a rather different interpretation in the 1990s, see Graaf and Need, 'Losing Faith: is Britain alone?', pp. 119–36.

In terms of a wide set of stated attitudes and behaviour, churchgoers throughout the Western world have a strong sense both of moral order and altruism.[21] For example, in the two sets of surveys of the *European Value Systems Study Group* in the early 1980s and 1990s churchgoers in Britain, and more widely in Europe, were two or three times more likely than other people to be involved in some form of voluntary service. Even when specifically church-related voluntary service was taken out of the analysis, it still appeared that churchgoing was a highly significant variable, indeed at least as significant as gender and social class. Again, *British Household Panel Survey* data in the 1990s suggest that members of religious groups are more than three times as likely as non-members to be involved in voluntary service. They were also disproportionately involved in all of the other caring groups – such as community groups, environmental groups, Scouts and Guides – as well as in self-help groups – such as tenants groups, parents associations, pensioners groups and political parties. The Australian *National Church Life Survey* of 1991 also found that 27 per cent of churchgoers in the survey were 'involved in wider community care/welfare/social action'. This was especially the case amongst churchgoers in the more liberal denominations: in the Uniting Church the level of involvement was 36 per cent of churchgoers and within the Anglican Church it was 32 per cent.

4

A more complex picture of the past and present is beginning to emerge. There are indications of growing secularity and scepticism, but alongside these there appear to be other counter-trends. What responsible speculations might be made about possible future patterns of religious participation and belief in Britain and elsewhere in the Western world?

Both among some rural migrants to urban areas and among some overseas immigrants there appears to be a concern for identity. It is well known that English expatriates, missing their culture, can become more regular churchgoers, involved in the English-speaking Anglican Cathedral in Hong Kong, say, than they might have back at home. Throughout Britain's former colonies it is, perhaps, not surprising that there are a disproportionate number of St George's churches built by the English and St Andrews' churches built by the Scots. Indeed, as a retired section of the British population gravitates to the coast of Southern Spain, so English-speaking congregations are still being established there to serve their need for cultural identity. If the future in the West is characterized at all by radical internal migration (perhaps this time from urban to rural areas) or by immigration from overseas, then renewed religious participation may well be a result. A part of the continuing vitality of American churches may be a result of this. Successive waves of new religious minorities, as well as distinctive immigrant groups within long-established denominations (such as the fast-growing Hispanic Catholics in Southern California), continue to bring their own religious enthusiasm to the United States. This is not, of course, to claim that migration and/or immigration are *always*

---

[21] For this see my *Churchgoing and Christian Ethics*, Cambridge University Press, Cambridge, 1999.

and everywhere associated with renewed religious enthusiasm, but simply to note that they can indeed be. Mobility is an important factor associated with religious change – whether in terms of increasing or even declining levels of religious participation.

However, in Britain immigrant groups have not usually been able to retain their distinctively religious identity intact indefinitely. Just as the effects of rural–urban migration eventually wear off, so do those of immigration from overseas. Many of the synagogues built in London and Liverpool by newly arrived Jewish immigrants have now been closed. Intermarriage between Jews and Gentiles has contributed to a sharp decline in the practice of religious rituals in the household and religious scepticism is expressed by many British and continental European Jews today. Significant cultures of observant Jews, such as the Sephardi Jews in Gibraltar, are becoming increasingly rare outside the United States (and have long been a minority even within Israel). British Catholics have also experienced a considerable increase in intermarriage with non-Catholics in the second half of the twentieth century and increasing difficulties in retaining the religious loyalties of their young. Set within a dominant culture in which a majority of neither young nor old are religious participants, it becomes increasingly difficult to retain a separate religious identity. Inevitably the young ask, 'Why do I have to go to mass?' or 'Why do I have to eat kosher food or go to synagogue?', when a majority of their other friends have no corresponding religious practices. As a result, apart from small enclaves of Orthodox Jews, most British Jews today live largely secular lives, and British Roman Catholics may now be following a similar path.

Will young Muslims in Britain (or, indeed, in continental Europe, Australia or the United States) be any different? At present they represent a distinctive set of religious enclaves, concentrated particularly in a number of urban areas. Muslim leaders and parents naturally press for the establishment of Muslim schools in Britain, mock Christians for not taking their own faith seriously and demand a more significant role for Muslim institutions in British life. If they are as successful in retaining this distinctive cultural identity as British Catholics have been, then this may remain an important part of the religious map both within parts of Britain and within continental Europe for several generations to come. Yet if the young rebel, as British Jews soon did and as Catholics eventually did, then this culture may not be as secure as it seems to be at present. Whatever its longevity, its eventual demise appears likely. More than that, even if it survives relatively intact for several generations, it is likely to remain a religious *enclave*. The broader populations may well visit the more spectacular central mosques out of interest or curiosity, but they are unlikely themselves to become practising Muslims in any significant numbers. Unlike the conquering Norman immigrants in the eleventh century, who themselves may have remained as enclaves within England for several decades, more recent Irish Catholic, Jewish or Muslim immigrant enclaves have been in no position eventually to 'persuade' the population at large to join them.

Even the attitude data, evident in *Table 20*, suggesting a strong minority persistence of non-traditional religious beliefs in the British population do not modify this judgement. As yet, there is little clear evidence that these beliefs are grounded in any particular institution or communal practice. So-called New Age beliefs are characteristically eclectic and may well lack wider social significance.

Nevertheless, problems of personal identity will remain for individuals, especially when confronted with the vicissitudes of life. New Age beliefs, however lacking in social function, may well be symptomatic of problems of personal identity – as well as a general dissatisfaction with Christianity and secularism alike. What institutional religious options are likely to remain to meet these problems in the future?

One obvious option is exclusive religious groups with a strong sense of separate identity, whether in the form of small-scale sects or new religious movements or in the denominational form of congregations that become more exclusive and sectarian. At present, the latter appear to be growing everywhere in the Western world at the expense of inclusive denominations, sometimes ensuring that overall religious participation remains comparatively high (as in the United States or Northern Ireland) but more often not (as in Britain, Europe, Canada and Australia). As a growing section within most Western societies becomes explicitly secular and sceptical, so those religious groups who are confident about their own separate identity and beliefs are apparently more likely to survive than those who are not. Sometimes the present situation in the West is depicted as the culture of postmodernity and, at other times, as simply fragmented post-industrial society. On either basis it is argued that the future will increasingly consist of incommensurable groups (some religious and some secular) in which individuals will seek reassurance and certainty in a situation of confusing pluralism. In terms of this scenario, there will no longer be *any* dominant meta-narratives in Western societies – neither those of the long-distant Christian past nor those of the more recent secular Enlightenment.

Now this is a distinct possibility for a map of the future in the West. Nonetheless, it still has some flaws. The most obvious is that it is remarkably difficult in a changing world for groups, whether religious or not, to retain a consistent reassurance and certainty which remains credible to all of their followers. Rigorous exclusive sects such as the Jehovah's Witnesses have long known that such consistency is only possible if members are excluded as soon as they deviate from official teaching. In a sceptical world they lose or exclude many members and, despite mighty efforts in evangelism, find overall growth in the West extremely slow. Other groups, such as Pentecostalists, tend to become fissiparous. They typically recruit strong-minded individuals looking for reassurance and certainty, who then fall away or form new groups when they disagree with their leaders or fellow members. The higher the demand for commitment, the more likely may be the possibility of disillusionment.

Attitude data again confirm that consistent levels of distinctiveness are not apparent even among regular churchgoers.[22] As already mentioned, churchgoers are more concerned about moral order and altruism than the population at large. Yet neither value is absent in the general population nor consistently present among churchgoers. Furthermore, on specific moral or belief issues there are usually variations of opinion amongst churchgoers themselves. So, whereas it is true that most Catholic churchgoers tend to oppose abortion or euthanasia, there are some

---

[22] For this again see my *Churchgoing and Christian Ethics*.

who do not. And, throughout the Western world, it has long been established that lay Catholic opinion on contraception differs markedly from that of the Pope. Even Mormon birth-rates in the United States are at variance with conservative Mormon teaching on birth-control.

What of those individuals who continue to take an active part in more inclusive religious denominations? In terms of present data this is the group which still appears to be declining in most of the Western world. In Britain and Europe more widely this group is closest in ethos to a general population which has learned from the bitter experience of past centuries to be deeply suspicious of religious zealots (reinforced strongly of course by September 11). This is a group that is particularly active in the community at large and, without which, much community service would be lost. Yet, for the moment at least, it faces an uncertain future. In the first half of the twentieth century most children in the West were socialized through Sunday schools and their equivalents. Thus familiarized with church culture, they retained many of its beliefs and values as adults and returned to its worship at key moments of the calendar or life-cycle. Faced with some crisis in identity (migrating, having children, retiring, or being bereaved) they could even return to regular attendance. Changes in the second half of the twentieth century – especially in Britain, most other European countries, Australia, and Canada – made all of this more difficult for the twenty-first century. Children became more reluctant to go to Sunday school or church while their parents stayed at home, or they came with their parents but never established a pattern of independent churchgoing once they left home and were among non-churchgoing friends. As a result, few adults in the future, even when faced with a crisis of identity, will be able to 'return' to church. They will never have acquired the language, symbols or ritual of church culture and are likely to find it strange rather than reassuring. Searching for meaning beyond the ambiguities of life, they will find difficulty in decoding the meanings offered within institutional worship.

In this situation boundaries between inclusive denominations are likely to become increasingly fluid for new churchgoers. A pattern already becoming established among British University students today, may become more widespread in all age-groups. Some denominations committed to older but disappearing loyalties will face further attrition if not extinction. In contrast, those inclusive denominations seeking to attract new members may find that much of their worship is family oriented non-sacramental worship. Whereas many inclusive denominations in the late twentieth century became accustomed to a diet of eucharistic worship, those in the twenty-first century may discover that this is actually a recipe only for socialized Christians. To attract the religiously unsocialized at a point when they are searching for meaning in their lives, they may need to provide less formal worship and, indeed, provide it less often than once a week. In many rural areas there is already developing a pattern of fortnightly or monthly worship.

If this is the future, then it will involve some social cost. Attitude data suggest strongly that those who attend only once a month have less distinctively Christian beliefs and values than those who attend weekly. And those who attend weekly, having become accustomed to a regular eucharist, are likely to be impatient with a non-sacramental diet. Perhaps they will have to resort instead to conferences or retreats to supplement this diet.

All of these options assume that thoroughgoing secularity is not the only option remaining in the future within Western societies. Secularity is indeed likely to be a strong and growing feature in many Western countries. If most of those aged 18–24 in, for instance, Britain and the Netherlands remain committed to 'no religion' as they grow older, then explicit secularity is likely to become dominant. In turn, this dominant secularity may result in a decline of the sort of voluntary service in the community currently associated with churchgoers. Nonetheless, other more varied patterns, resulting from migration, immigration and a human tendency to search for meaning, especially at moments evoking a crisis of personal identity, may also remain features of the Western religious map in the future. On this basis the future is likely to be ever more fragmented, with varied pockets of secularism and persistence existing alongside each other.

Whichever scenario finally unfolds, I fear that, at least in Britain, the empty church will still predominate.

Tables

Table 1 Cumbrian churches

	Rural areas[1]	Small towns[2]	Larger towns[3]
1821 population	3,797	12,370	24,776
Seats:			
CE (%) pop.	50.8	32.3	33.7
Free	6.6	6.0	21.4
RC			2.4
Attendances: CE	28.3	20.9	21.0
% full: CE	55.7	64.6	62.3
1851 population	3,941	16,794	28,664
Seats:			
CE	63.2	29.1	35.7
Free	17.6	23.4	26.5
RC			2.4
Attendances:			
CE	17.0	20.1	25.8
Free	10.6	13.6	14.6
RC			4.4
% full:			
CE	13.4	34.4	36.1
Free	30.1	29.2	27.6
RC			93.0
1902 population	3,129	35,863	45,467
Seats:			
CE	79.6	15.6	21.1
Free	25.4	23.2	26.2
RC		1.7	2.0
Attendances:			
CE	13.2	4.6	5.8
Free	2.0	7.3	10.8
RC		2.2	5.4
% full:			
CE	8.3	14.8	13.6
Free	3.9	15.8	20.7
RC		66.8	135.6

Table 1 (cont.)

	Rural areas[1]	Small towns[2]	Larger towns[3]
Church of England Comparisons			
1861 communicants	10.9	3.0	7.0
1900 communicants	10.7	3.2	3.0
1989 communicants	15.4	3.4	3.0
1861 Sunday school	8.8	6.0	7.5
1900 Sunday school	8.7	8.7	5.6
1989 Attendances: adult	5.7	2.5	2.3
1989 Attendances: child	6.9	2.2	2.5
Totals: all Churches			
Seats:			
1821	57.4	38.3	57.5
1851	80.8	52.2	64.5
1902	105.0	40.5	49.3
Attendances:			
1821 (est.)	32.4	24.6	36.7
1851	27.6	33.7	44.8
1902	15.2	14.1	22.0

Notes:
1 Rural areas = Bassenthwaite, Dean, Emmerdale, Haile, Loweswater, Lorton, Netherwasdale, and St John's Beckermet.
2 Small towns = Arlecdon, Brigham, Cleator, Clifton, Cockermouth, Distington, Egremont, Harrington, Hensingham, and Lamplugh.
3 Larger towns = Whitehaven and Workington.

Table 2 Church of England comparisons: 1821–51

	1821	*1851*
Rural districts[1]		
Population	46,474	52,201
Total attendances (% pop.)	23.7	20.6 and 35.4[4]
Seating	40.9	43.4
Large Towns[2]		
Population	220,275	437,089
Total attendances	10.7	10.0 and 20.4[4]
Seating	21.0	18.0
Conurbations[3]		
Population	226,988	679,337
Total attendances	10.1	9.4 and 17.0[4]
Seating	14.7	15.2

Notes:
1 Rural districts = Ulverstone, Leybrun, Garstang, and Askrigg.
2 Large towns = Bolton, Blackburn, Burnley, Chester, Lancaster, Macclesfield, Oldham, Rochdale, Salford, Stockport, Warrington, and Whitehaven.
3 Conurbations = Manchester and Liverpool (towns for 1821; Metropolitan boroughs for 1851).
4 1851 attendances: first figure = morning + Sunday school; second figure = Index.

Table 3 Free Church comparisons: 1829–51

	1829	*1851*
Rural districts[1]		
Population	39,237	44,096
Total attendances (% pop.)	1.1	2.9 and 5.9[4]
Seating	5.4	9.2
Large Towns[2]		
Population	246,607	407,006
Total attendances	11.5	8.7 and 18.0[4]
Independents	4.0	3.0 and 5.7[4]
Wesleyans	4.0	2.4 and 4.7[4]
Other Methodists	1.5	1.6 and 4.1[4]
Baptists	0.6	0.8 and 1.7[4]
Various	1.4	0.9 and 1.9[4]
Conurbations[3]		
Population	307,201	679,337
Total attendances	11.3	6.9 and 13.2[4]
Independents	2.7	1.5 and 2.5[4]
All Methodists	4.8	3.1 and 6.4[4]
Baptists	1.4	0.6 and 1.5[4]
Various	2.5	1.6 and 2.8[4]
Large towns[2]		
Total seats	17.6	17.4
Independents	5.4	5.0
Wesleyans	4.5	4.5
Other Methodists	2.8	3.9
Baptists	1.5	1.5
Various	3.5	2.5
Conurbations[3]		
Total seats	12.9	14.4
Independents	3.0	3.0
All Methodists	5.2	6.1
Baptists	2.7	1.6
Various	1.9	3.6

Notes:
1 Rural districts = Lancaster and Ulverstone.
2 Large towns = Blackburn, Bolton, Burnley, Bury, Lancaster, Oldham, Preston, Salford, Warrington, and Wigan.
3 Conurbations = Manchester and Liverpool (towns for 1829; metropolitan borough for 1851).
4 1851 attendances: first figures = morning + Sunday school; second figure = Index.

Table 4 Church of England and Free Churches compared: 1834–51

	Church of England % pop.	Free Churches % pop.
1834 (pop. 272,453)		
Hearers	9.6	18.7
Hearers and Sunday school	13.9	29.2
1851 (pop. 482,780)		
Morning and Sunday school	7.4	12.4
Morning and evening – Sunday school	11.6	20.9
Morning or evening – Sunday school	6.5	11.8
Index	15.1	26.6

Note:
Sample consists of Bradford, Burnley, Coventry, Hull, Lancaster, Nottingham, Sheffield, and York.

Table 5 Three towns compared

1830s

Town	Population	CE seats	CE attendances	Free seats	Free attendances
Penzance (1839)	10,621	2,847	1,780	5,170	5,021
Stockton (1837)	8,000	1,610	850	3,195	1,610
York (1837)	28,000	12,181	5,763	6,500	7,635
Aggregate % pop.		35.7	18.0	31.9	30.6

1851s

Town	Population	CE seats	CE attendances	Free seats	Free attendances
Penzance	11,745	2,780	3,100	5,107	4,521
Stockton	10,172	2,810	2,100	3,845	2,153
York	36,303	12,181	10,117	10,479	8,807
Aggregate % pop.		30.5	26.3	33.4	26.6

Table 6 Sunday school enrolments: England and Wales

Date	Enrolment nos.	% total population	% population – 15 years	CE as % population – 15 years	Others as % population – 15 years
1818	477,225	4.1	11.5	5.5	6.0
1833	1,548,890	10.8	30.3	13.6	16.7
1851	2,407,642	13.4	38.0	14.8	23.2
1891	5,238,445	18.1	51.4	21.2	30.2
1901	5,549,059	17.1	52.6	22.1	30.5
1911	5,684,295	15.8	51.4	22.0	29.4
1921	4,875,480	13.5	46.7	19.1	27.6
1931	4,319,904	10.8	45.8	19.1	26.7
1951	2,845,346	6.5	30.0	13.9	16.1
1961	2,105,908	4.6	20.4	10.1	10.3

Notes:
Calculations of population under 15 years for 1818 and 1833 based on 35.5 per cent estimated total populations and calculations of relative denominational enrolments based on numbers of Sunday schools; 1891–1961 enrolment numbers do not include RCs and sects: enrolment number for 1891 contains 1895 number for Presbyterians in Wales, 1898 number for Congregationalists, and 1900 number for Baptists.

(*Sources*: 1818–51 'Education Census (1851)'; 1891–1961 'Churches and Churchgoers' by R. Currie, A. Gilbert and L. Horsley.) In MARC/Europe 1989, English Sunday school attenders represented 1.3 per cent total population or 6.7 per cent child population (CE 2.5 per cent and Free Churches 4.2 per cent).

Table 7 Liverpool

	1851	*1881*	*1891*	*1902*	*1912*
Total population (morning/evening):	375,955	552,508	629,548	704,134	746,421
Attendances					
CE (% pop.)	15.3	9.8	10.5	9.6	7.7
Free	10.7	12.7	11.9	10.8	8.7
RC	13.9	(10.4)	(9.5)	(9.0)	(10.2)
Overall	39.9	32.9	31.9	29.4	26.6
Free Church attendances:					
Cong./Independ.	1.77	1.41	1.38	1.28	1.03
Baptist	1.01	2.10	1.52	1.57	0.98
Presbyterian	1.49	1.85	1.83	1.55	1.00
Wesleyan	2.62	2.79	2.45	2.56	2.19
Prim. Methodist	0.25	0.51	0.36	0.37	0.25
Other Methodist	2.31	1.91	2.18	1.71	1.33
(All Methodist)	(5.17)	(5.21)	(4.98)	(4.64)	(3.78)
Sub-total	9.5	10.6	9.7	9.1	6.8
Salvation Army	–	0.19	0.28	0.07	0.03
Unitarians	0.31	0.36	0.21	0.18	0.13
Free Gospel	0.16	0.12	0.08	0.08	0.06
Bethel	–	0.05	0.07	0.06	0.02
Church of Christ	–	0.13	0.11	0.10	0.07
City Mission	0.11	–	0.39	0.35	0.14
Nondenom./Small	0.64	1.29	1.05	0.89	1.45
Sub-total	1.2	2.2	2.2	1.7	1.9

Table 7 (cont.)

	1851	1881	1891	1902	1912
Seats:					
C of E	16.0	14.0	14.3	13.6	13.1
Free	12.5	15.5	16.0	15.3	14.4
Cong./Independ.	2.08	1.95	2.17	2.01	2.07
Baptist	1.51	2.49	2.36	2.17	1.94
Presbyterian	2.08	2.35	2.29	2.22	1.69
Wesleyan	2.29	2.88	3.15	3.34	3.07
Prim. Methodist	0.37	0.59	0.50	0.57	0.48
Other Methodist	2.51	2.35	2.40	2.33	2.15
(All Methodist)	(5.16)	(5.83)	(6.05)	(6.24)	(5.70)
Sub-total	10.8	12.6	12.9	12.7	11.4
Salvation Army	–	0.24	0.43	0.18	0.08
Unitarians	0.48	0.41	0.36	0.31	0.26
Free Gospel	0.15	0.29	0.24	0.16	0.17
Bethel	–	0.16	0.25	0.15	0.11
Church of Christ	–	0.19	0.12	0.11	0.14
City Mission	0.14	–	0.55	0.55	0.24
Nondenom./Small	0.92	1.58	1.23	1.15	1.98
Sub-total	1.7	2.9	3.2	2.6	3.0
% Seats full					
C of E	54.1	36.1	37.1	36.3	29.6
Free	45.2	43.6	37.6	37.1	31.9
Cong./Independ.	43.8	36.7	31.4	31.7	25.0
Baptist	36.7	43.2	33.8	36.4	25.3
Presbyterian	38.0	39.7	34.1	38.1	29.9
Wesleyan	57.7	49.2	36.4	38.6	36.1
Prim. Methodist	34.7	43.4	38.1	33.1	25.9
Other Methodist	47.4	40.6	46.3	36.8	31.0
(All Methodist)	(51.1)	(45.1)	(40.3)	(37.4)	(33.3)
Sub-total	45.3	42.4	36.5	36.0	30.0
Salvation Army	–	55.4	29.4	22.1	20.8
Unitarians	43.8	44.8	29.2	30.0	27.8
Free Gospel	54.9	24.7	20.3	25.9	17.9
Bethel	–	15.8	16.7	28.3	14.1
Church of Christ	–	48.2	47.3	46.1	24.5
City Mission	50.0	–	70.9	63.7	58.4
Nondenom./Small	41.9	64.2	59.0	52.8	48.9
Sub-total	44.4	50.6	43.3	44.5	41.6

Table 7 (cont.)

C. of E. oldest churches compared: attendances

	Seats	1821[1]	1851	1881	1891	1902
St Anne	800	650	414	59	171	120
St Andrew	1,100	1,000	1,050	1,931	584	Closed
Christ Church	2,300	1,400	3,200	501	616	460
St George	1,000	700	650	68	22	Closed
Holy Trinity	1,500	1,000	← 1,000[3]	640	840	999
St John	1,500	1,200	3,500	332	301	Closed
St Matthew	600	300	1,200	1,029	915	270
St Mark	2,500	1,700	2,392	570	160	140
St Nicholas	2,500	1,500	750	387	1,435	1,210
St Paul	3,000	1,200	800	275	147	Closed
St Philip	1,500	1,000	1,500[2]	117	432	300
St Peter	2,000	1,500	1,000	1,482	1,132	1,049
St Stephen	650	400	620	599	233	87
St Thomas	1,000	550	850	272	381	219
Totals	21,950	14,100	18,926	8,262	7,369	4,854
% seats full						
1821 churches			43.1	18.8	16.8	15.8
Later churches			50.5	41.5	43.1	39.1

Notes:
1 1821 congregations = attenders: 1851–1902 = morning/evening attendances.
2 Morning/afternoon attendances.
3 Missing entry supplied by nearest complete entry (see arrow).

Table 8 Twenty-eight large towns[1]

	1851	1881
Total population	946,553	1,981,816
Attendance (morning/evening):		
Mean as % pop.	37.2	35.4
Morning	18.3	15.3
Evening	18.9	20.1
Mean:		
CE	13.8	12.7
Free	20.6	20.4
RC	2.8	2.3
% churchgoers:		
CE	37.1	35.9
Free	55.4	57.6
RC	7.5	6.5
Churches:	664	1,626
Pop. per church	1,426	1,219
Attendance per church	530	431
CE churches:	204	456
Pop. per church	4,640	4,346
Attendances per church	641	551
Free churches:	432	1,110
Pop. per church	2,191	1,785
Attendances per church	451	364
RC churches:	28	60
Pop. per church	33,805	33,030
Attendances per church	932	766
Seating as % of population:	43.8	41.3
CE	18.8	14.2
Free	23.7	25.6
RC	1.3	1.5
% seats:		
CE	42.9	34.4
Free	54.1	62.0
RC	3.0	3.6

Table 8 (cont.)

	1851	1881
% seats full:		
CE (morning)	40.4	40.4
CE (evening)	33.3	48.9
Mean	36.8	44.7
Free (morning)	37.5	31.7
Free (evening)	49.2	47.8
Mean	43.4	39.8
RC (morning)	146.6	98.7
RC (evening)	74.7	58.6
Mean	110.6	78.6
Free Churches compared:		
Congregationalist churches:	74	154
Attendances per church	581	392
Attendances as % pop.	4.5	3.1
Seats as % pop.	5.0	4.2
% seats full	45.5	36.7
Wesleyan churches:	91	226
Attendances per church	586	429
Attendances as % pop.	5.6	4.9
Seats as % pop.	6.5	5.9
% seats full	43.6	41.6
Other Methodist churches:	101	289
Attendances per church	437	299
Attendances as % pop.	4.7	4.4
Seats as % pop.	4.7	6.3
% seats full	49.5	34.8
Baptist churches:	77	136
Attendances per church	471	445
Attendances as % pop.	3.8	3.1
Seats as % pop.	4.1	3.7
% seats full	46.5	41.3
Presbyterian churches:	8	26
Attendances per church	230	325
Attendances as % pop.	0.2	0.4
Seats as % pop.	0.4	0.6
% seats full	24.3	33.2
Isolated congregations:	81	246
Attendances per church	201	195
Attendances as % pop.	1.7	2.4
Seats as % pop.	3.1	3.2
% seats full	28.2	37.7

Table 8 (cont.)

	1851	*1881*
Salvation Army churches:		33
Attendances per church		1,314
Attendances as % pop.		2.2
Seats as % pop.		1.8
% seats full		61.5
Overall Free Church comparison:		
Mainstream denominations:		
Attendances as % pop.	18.9	15.8
Seats as % pop.	20.7	20.6
% seats full	45.6	38.2
Isolated and Salvation Army:		
Attendances as % pop.	1.7	4.6
Seats as % pop.	3.1	5.0
% seats full	28.2	46.2

Effects of Weather and Census Method on Attendances

	1851	*1881*
All towns:		
CE attendances (% pop.)	13.8	12.7
Free attendances	20.6	20.4
Overall	34.4	33.1
(1851 pop. 946,553)		
Fine-weather towns:		
CE attendances	14.0	13.6
Free attendances	19.4	21.6
Overall	33.5	35.2
(1851 pop. 240,621)		
Bad-weather towns:		
CE attendances	12.3	12.0
Free attendances	22.3	21.0
Overall	34.6	33.0
(1851 pop. 448,149)		
Clergy-return towns:		
CE attendances	11.0	12.6
Free attendances	20.4	19.5
Overall	31.4	32.1
(1851 pop. 435,097)		
Enumerated towns:		
CE attendances	13.0	10.9
Free attendances	20.3	21.6
Overall	33.3	32.5
(1851 pop. 381,601)		

Table 8 (cont.)

	1851	1881
Fine weather/clergy-return towns:		
CE attendances	10.0	12.2
Free attendances	16.1	19.3
Overall	26.1	31.5
(1851 pop. 153,793)		
Bad weather/enumerated towns:		
CE attendances	11.0	9.8
Free attendances	22.0	24.3
Overall	33.0	34.1
(1851 pop. 172,149)		

Note:
1 Large towns = Barrow, Bolton, Bradford, Burnley, Burslem, Coventry, Darlington, Derby, Gloucester, Gosport, Hanley, Hull, Ipswich, Leicester, Longton, Newcastle-upon-Lyme, Northampton, Nottingham, Peterborough, Portsmouth, Rotherham, Scarborough, Sheffield, Southampton, Stoke-on-Trent, Warrington, Whitehaven, and Widnes.

Table 9 Sheffield – Church of England

	1851	1865	1868	1877	1881	1884
Estimated population	135,310	201,603	223,511	266,622	284,410	296,359
St Peter	1,800	1,500	3,300	2,600	2,190	1,200
Holy Trinity, Wicker	1,550	750 →	750	400	803	1,100
St George	2,100	1,000	1,350	2,000	2,455	2,400
St James	225 →	225 →	225	450	852	850
St John	1,600	120	70	600	703	750
St Jude, Eldon	189	200	220	500	728	545
St Jude, Moorfields	50	800	1,200	328 →	328 ←	328
St Luke, Dyers	25		80	130	449	450
St Luke, Hollescroft	50	150	210	290	344	
St Mary	832	1,500	850	964 →	964	700
St Paul	701	1,000	1,100	1,100	948	450
St Philip	1,250	1,500	1,350	1,525	1,661	1,450
St Thomas, Crookes	210	500 ←	500	622 →	622	830
Christ Church, Pitsmoor	306	200 →	200	750	1,543	600
Christ Church, Attercliff	254	950 →	950 →	950	782	800
Christ Church, Heeley	370 ←	370	184 →	184 →	184	140
Christ Church, Fulwood	194	150 →	150	347 →	347	200
Ecclesall	455	775 →	775	588 →	588	600
St Thomas, Brightside	70	110 →	110	150	275	220
Holy Trinity, Darnall	60	135 →	135	399 →	399 ←	399
St Matthew		500	600	600	391	650
St Simon		300	700	300	360	275
St Stephen		1,300	700	700	763	500
St Michael			800	759 →	759 ←	759

Table 9 (cont.)

	1851	1865	1868	1877	1881	1884
St Silas			250	800	954	700
St Andrew				600	1,102	650
St Barnabas				900	761	450
St Bartholomew				283 →	283	575
St Mark				800	1,250	1,600
St Mary, Walkley				600	612	1,100
All Saints				800	1,192	700
St John the Baptist				300	867	850
St Matthias					963	1,200
Emmanuel					369	500
Carbrook					671	1,100
St John, Ranmoor					512 ←	512
St Peter, Heeley					1,182	800
Missions		180			1,744	335
Totals						
1851 churches	12,291	11,935	13,709	14,877	17,165	14,012
All churches	12,471	14,035	16,759	22,319	31,900	27,268
Total attendances: % pop.	9.2	7.0	7.5	8.4	11.2	9.2
Seats: % pop.	13.8	11.2	10.9	11.1	11.5	11.1
% seats full	33.5	31.0	34.3	37.8	48.7	41.6
Date	1851	1865	1868	1877	1881	1884

Note:
Other dates: 1924 seats 40,800 = 8.3 per cent; 1956 attendances *c.* 12,500 = 2.4 per cent; diocesan attendances 1961 = 2.1 per cent and 1985 = 1.7 per cent. Missing entries supplied by nearest complete entries (see arrows).

Table 10 Kingston-upon-Hull – Church of England

	1851	1865	1868	1877	1884	1912	1931	1947	1953	1969	1990
Estimated population	84,600	107,353	114,622	141,302	167,965	279,260	313,366	300,000	300,000	300,000	285,000
Holy Trinity	972	800	1,700	2,000	1,900	1,600	1,000	800	850	375	115
St Mary	839	550	750	1,400	1,630	596	100 →	100	155	75	26
St James	1,410	1,200 →	1,200 →	1,200	1,350	550	210	38			
St John	1,062	1,700	1,400	500	650	124					
St Luke	300	325 ↓	325 ↓	325	325	260	220	30			
St Stephen	1,027	1,000	900	900	1,300	350 →	350	30	30	17	17
Mariners	1,030	850	500	475	250						
St Peter	1,200	750 ↓	750	250 ↑	250	330	260	40			
St Mark	160 ↑	160 ↑	160 ↓	350	350	215	26				
Christ, Sculcoates	1,000 ↑	1,000	1,000	1,400 ↓	1,400	450	450	48	170	34	52
St Mary, Sculcoates	350	250 ↓	250	100	90	700	250	80	130	40	30
St Paul, Sculcoates	1,000 ↑	1,000	1,100	900	1,050	250	200	40	55	70	
St Barnabas				500	500	320	230	160	80	12	
St Jude				1,250 ↓	1,250	500	950	140	80		
St Matthew				350	300	925	300	140	140	88	48
St Andrew, Drypool				800	650	530	600	120	105	110	
All Saints, Sculcoates				850	900	1,050	600	300	180	70	
St Silas, Sculcoates				345	560	358	450	110	110		
St Thomas					830	300	200	ns	90	58	
St Clements, Sculcoates					280	62	140				
St Philip, Sculcoates					420	240	395				
St Augustine						640	550	180	325	105	160
St Cuthbert						245	250	60	100	100	99
St Michael All Angels						350 ↑	105 ↑	105	200	66	24
St John the Baptist						450	850	185	130	65	
Transfiguration						750	470	370	280	80	

Table 10 (cont.)

	1851	1865	1868	1877	1884	1912	1931	1947	1953	1969	1990
St Nicholas							410	150	105	124	121
St Saviour							210	24	100	50	45
St John, Drypool							333	70	94	36	
St Mary and Peter							250	50	60		
St John, Newland							800	450	550	325	437
St Columbo, Drypool							700	245	160	320	207
St Aidan, Drypool							200	165	105	84	34
Ascension								172	135	73	45
St Martin								280	315	110	155
St Alban								450	335	210	95
St George, Marfleet								36	80	80	⎫
St Giles, Marfleet									50	195	⎬ 184
St Philip, Marfleet								↓	80	80	⎭
St Faith										40	
Missions						1,705	186	15			
Totals											
1851 Churches	10,350	9,585	10,035	9,800	10,545	5,425	3,066	1,206	1,390	541	240
All Churches	10,350	9,585	10,035	13,895	16,235	13,850	12,245	5,183	5,379	3,092	1,894
% pop.	12.2	8.9	8.8	9.8	9.7	5.0	3.9	1.7	1.8	1.0	0.7
Seats	14.9	11.7	11.0	12.0	11.1	8.6	7.1	6.9	6.6	7.7	5.4
% full	41.1	38.1	40.0	40.9	43.6	28.7	27.5	12.5	13.5	7.7	6.1
Date	1851	1865	1868	1877	1884	1912	1931	1947	1953	1969	1990

Notes: Other dates: 1834 = 6,400 'hearers' (13.8 per cent pop.), 9,800 seats (21.1 per cent pop.); 1881 = 13,772 attendances (8.9 per cent pop.: 35.7 per cent full); 1904 = c. 16,095 attendances (6.4 per cent pop.: 38.3 per cent full). Missing entries by nearest complete entries (see arrows). ns = no service.

Table 11 Newcastle upon Tyne – Church of England

	1851	1866	1874	1878	1887
Estimated population	89,156	118,778	133,519	140,287	176,235
St Nicholas	2,900	2,450	1,950	2,050	3,500
All Saints	1,160	535	200	100	250
St Ann	800	610	150	400	270
St John	1,900	1,100	500	700	710
St Andrew	1,900	2,100	2,300	2,000	1,990
St Peter	680	1,150	550	← 550	450
St Thomas	1,900	→ 1,900	1,500	→ 1,500	1,600
St James, Benwell	522	620	360	← 360	400
St Paul	791	510	600	250	350
Byker, St Michael	150	320	480	625	430
Byker, St Anthony		170	← 170	150	200
Jesmond, Clayton		2,100	2,000	2,100	2,150
Christ Church		850	350	500	← 500
St Philip			450	350	600
St Stephen			550	600	950
St Matthew				360	440
St Cuthbert				340	330
St Mark					320
St Wilfred					143
St Luke					420
St Silas					1,200
St George					600
Jesmond Vale					400
St Augustine					400
St Jude					150
St Aidan					220
Totals					
1851 Churches	12,703	11,295	8,590	8,535	9,950
All Churches	12,703	14,415	12,110	12,935	18,973
% population	14.2	12.1	9.1	9.2	10.8

Note:
Missing entries supplied by nearest complete entries (see arrows).

Table 12 Inner Greater London

	1851	*1887*	*1903*	*1928*	*1979*	*1989*
Total population	2,362,236	4,100,000	4,470,304	sample	2,409,600	2,308,600
Attendances (morning/evening:						
Mean as % pop.	29.1	28.7	22.4	11.9	10.8	10.7
CE attendances	15.6	14.1	9.6	4.8	2.5	1.8
Free attendances	11.3	12.5	10.7	4.9	3.6	4.6
RC attendances	2.3	(2.1)	2.1	2.2	4.7	4.2
% attendances:						
CE	53.5	47.1	42.8	40.0	23.2	16.9
Free	38.7	45.6	47.8	41.6	33.3	43.4
RC	7.8	7.3	9.3	18.4	43.4	39.7
Churches:	1,086	2,284	2,626		1,424	1,556
Pop. per church	2,175	1,795	1,702		1,692	1,484
Attendances per church	634	516	382	224	182	156
CE churches:	458	872	1,014			451
Pop. per church	5,158	4,701	4,409			5,119
Attendances per church	804	663	424	304		91
Attendances per service	494	367	231	152		
Free churches:	592	1,344	1,512			926
Pop. per church	3,990	3,051	2,957			2,493
Attendances per church	450	382	317	158		104
Attendances per service	247	225	189	87		
RC churches:	36	68	100			179
Pop. per church	65,618	60,294	44,703			12,897
Attendances per church	1,482	1,266	936	350		539
Seating as % of	29.2	33.8	35.7		18.7	20.2
population:						
CE	17.1	16.5	17.3			5.9
Free	11.0	16.1	16.6			12.0
RC	0.8	1.2	1.7			2.3
% Seats full:						
CE (morning)	54.2	43.7	31.3			
CE (evening)	45.4	44.5	28.9			
Mean	50.3	44.1	30.3			
Free (morning)	50.7	37.7	31.8			
Free (evening)	56.6	47.5	37.0			
Mean	53.6	43.1	34.6			
RC (morning)	203.3		95.8			
RC (evening)	112.3		28.1			
Mean	164.2	90.3	63.4			

Note: Seats estimated for 1903–89.

Table 13 London – detailed comparisons

	Number of churches/chapels				Aggregated attendances as % pop.			Mean seats full as % pop.		
	1851	1887	1903	1914	1851	1887	1903	1851	1887	1903
Church of England	458	872	1,014	1,155	15.6	14.1	9.6	50.3	44.1	30.3
Roman Catholic	36	68	100	120	2.3	2.1	2.1	164.2	90.3	63.4
Free Churches	592	1,344	1,512	1,443	11.3	12.5	10.7	53.6	43.1	34.6
Total	1,086	2,284	2,626	2,718	29.1	28.7	22.4	55.2	47.0	33.9
Free Churches:										
Cong./Independen.	161	248	219	203	4.90	3.05	2.36	58.6	39.8	35.7
Baptist	130	259	283	241	2.49	2.98	2.43	56.0	46.5	37.5
Presbyterian	23	60	68	67	0.70	0.82	0.55	47.2	47.6	31.4
Wesleyan	98	146	159	141	1.64	2.01	1.75	44.6	42.7	37.5
Prim. Methodist	21	44	57	60	0.11	0.26	0.30	40.2	36.3	35.1
Other Methodist	46	60	56	48	0.67	0.33	0.35	61.2	33.7	41.6
(All Methodist)	(165)	(250)	(272)	(249)	(2.42)	(2.61)	(2.40)	(48.0)	(40.6)	(37.7)
Sub-total	479	817	842	760	10.51	9.45	7.74	54.3	42.5	36.5
Brethren	3	16	137	138	0.01	0.12	0.38	31.5	45.0	19.2
Salvation Army	–	44	94	78	–	0.80	0.50	–	50.2	16.3
Unitarian	9	16	23	25	0.07	0.08	0.08	34.3	26.0	18.2
Friends	9	15	17	19	0.05	0.06	0.07	30.9	18.8	21.3
Foreign Prot.	9	17	28	29	0.06	0.06	0.06	38.6	18.9	14.9
Cath. Apostolic	6	8	9	7	0.12	0.06	0.07	60.2	34.0	40.9
Nondenom./Small	77	411	362	387	0.46	1.90	1.85	47.4	49.0	53.0
Sub-total	113	527	670	683	0.76	3.08	3.00	44.9	45.0	30.5

Note:
Additional source for 1914: H.W. Harris and M. Bryant, 'The Churches and London'. *Daily News*, 1914.

Table 14 Chelsea

	1851	*1887*	*1903*
Population	53,725	73,079	70,190
Attendances:			
CE (morning) (% pop.)	9.9	5.7	6.2
CE (evening)	9.1	8.2	5.5
Total	19.0	13.9	11.7
Free Churches (morning) (% pop.)	3.6	4.1	3.0
Free Churches (evening)	4.5	7.3	4.7
Total	8.1	11.4	7.7
Overall: + chapels, but – RCs	29.9	28.0	21.5
Free Churches compared:			
Presbyterians	1.49	1.34	0.84
Congregationalists	0.76	3.51	1.95
Baptists	0.83	0.69	1.33
Wesleyan Methodist	4.02	1.04	0.50
Other Methodists	0.37	0.37	0.20
Catholic Apostolic	0.47	0.39	0.42
Mormons	0.15	–	–
Nondenominational	–	2.76	1.08
Salvation Army	–	0.98	0.28
Disciples of Christ	–	0.29	–
Moravians	–	–	0.05
Christian Science	–	–	0.79
Brethren	–	–	0.23

Table 14 (cont.)

Main churches and chapels compared:

	1851	1887	1903
GAINS			
Catholic Apostolic, College St	250	288	292
Baptists, Chelsea Chapel	–	506	935
St John's Missions	–	470	562
Independent Welsh Chapel, Randor St	–	162	184
GAINS AND LOSSES			
Holy Trinity, Sloane St	1,995	1,408	2,251
St Saviour, Walton St	1,055	541	655
Christ Church, Christchurch St	1,084	431	550
Old Chelsea Church, Cheyne Walk	850	1,039	675
Wesleyan, Justice Walk	50	156	52
LOSSES			
St Luke, Sidney St	2,897	2,451	1,156
Independent, Markham Sq.	–	1,399	808
Park Chapel, Park Walk	1,777	1,087	397
Presbyterian St Columba, Pont St	–	878	592
St John, Tadema Rd	–	804	684
Salvation Army, Riley St	–	713	105
Independent, Edith Grove	–	641	395
Wesleyan, Chelsea Church, Sloane Trinity	1,400	560	296
St Simon, Moore St	–	560	260
St Jude, Turk's Row	542	364	361
C of E, Oakley Mission, Manor St	–	259	184
United Methodist, Marlborough Sq.	–	178	86
United Methodist, College Pl.	–	94	57
Church Army Mission, Marlborough St	–	79	73

Table 14 (cont.)

Church of England Attendances:

	1851	1858	1862	1883	1887	1900	1903
St Luke	2,897	2,600	1,800	1,000	2,451	1,200	1,156
Old Christ	850	450	450	375	1,039	450	675
Christ	1,084	600 ←	600	446	431	1,100	550
Park	1,777	1,000	900	1,200	1,087	850	397
Holy Trinity	1,995	1,000	1,100 ←	1,100	1,408	2,050	2,251
St Jude	542	700	800	200	364	361 →	361
St Saviour	1,055	1,500	1,600	800	541	950	655
Sub-total	10,200	7,850	7,250	5,121	7,321	6,961	6,045
St Simon			450	500	560	350	260
St John				1,050	804	875	684
Missions					1,470		1,253
Total	10,200	7,850	7,700	6,671	10,155	8,196	8,242
% pop.	19.0	14.6	12.9	9.1	13.9	11.1	11.7

Comparison of Sunday school attendances:

	1851	% pop.	1903	% pop.
CE:				
Morning	922		524	
Afternoon	699		2,117	
Evening	109		–	
Total	1,730	3.2	2,641	3.8
Free churches:				
Morning	676		236	
Afternoon	370		–	
Evening	120		1,341	
Total	1,166	2.2	1,577	2.2
Overall attendance	2,896	5.4	4,218	6.0
Index		43.3		34.7

(CE attendance for 1903 = 77.0% of 1901 Sunday school membership.)

Note:
Missing entries supplied by nearest complete entries (see arrows).

Table 14 (cont.)

Comparison of men, women and children as % total attendances:

1903	Men	Women	Children
Inner Greater London			
(– Sunday school and afternoon):	26.6	41.2	32.3
CE	22.9	43.8	33.3
Free	30.1	37.9	32.0
RC	25.5	45.7	28.8
Chelsea			
(– Sunday school and afternoon):	22.4	47.5	30.1
CE	20.8	44.5	34.6
Free	26.4	48.2	25.4
RC	18.9	60.0	21.1
Chelsea			
(+ Sunday school and afternoon):	18.5	38.4	43.1
CE	16.7	35.2	48.1
Free	22.2	39.4	38.4
RC	17.8	55.6	26.6

Inner Greater London – by age groups:
Child attendance (morning and evening + Sunday school (est.) = 50.0% pop. under 15
Adult female attendance (morning and evening) = 26.1% female pop. 15 and over
Adult male attendance (morning and evening) = 18.5% male pop. 15 and over

Table 15 Birmingham

	1851	*1872*	*1892*
Population	232,841	343,787	346,798
Attendances: Index	35.0		45.0
Morning/evening as % pop.	27.6		24.2
Morning	13.7		9.3
Evening	13.9		14.8
Morning/evening:			
CE	12.4		10.9
Free	12.4		11.5
RC	2.8		1.7
% churchgoers			
CE	45.0		45.0
Free	45.0		47.7
RC	10.0		7.3
Churches:	87	155	197
Pop. per church	2,676	2,218	1,760
Attendances per church	740		425
CE churches:	23	46	71
Pop. per church	10,124	7,474	4,884
Attendances per church	1,259		532
Free churches:	61	102	120
Pop. per church	3,817	3,370	2,890
Attendances per church	475		333
RC churches:	4	7	6
Pop. per church	58,210	49,112	57,800
Attendances per church	1,617		1,013
Seating as % of population	27.6	30.8	30.7
CE	12.6	13.8	14.1
Free	14.2	16.1	15.8
RC	0.6	0.9	0.9
% seats:			
CE	46.0	44.9	45.8
Free	51.7	52.1	51.4
RC	2.3	3.0	2.8
Seats full:			
CE (morning)	48.8		33.9
CE (evening)	52.7		46.5
Mean	50.7		40.5
Free (morning)	40.5		29.7
Free (evening)	48.9		48.5
Mean	44.4		40.0
RC (morning)	315.6		132.4
RC (evening)	159.4		72.3
Mean	245.2		102.4

Note: 1892 population represents same wards as 1851.

Table 15 (cont.)

	1851	1872	1892
Free Churches compared:			
Congregationalist churches:	11	17	15
Attendances per church	526		454
Attendances as % pop.	2.5		2.0
Seats as % pop.	2.7	3.2	2.2
% seats full	47.0		47.4
Wesleyan churches:	14	16	15
Attendances per church	463		634
Attendances as % pop.	2.8		2.7
Seats as % pop.	3.3	4.0	2.9
% seats full	42.2		54.6
Other Methodist churches:	10	19	13
Attendances per church	309		278
Attendances as % pop.	1.3		1.0
Seats as % pop.	1.3	1.7	1.5
% seats full	50.2		35.9
Baptist churches:	10	19	23
Attendances per church	634		345
Attendances as % pop.	2.7		2.3
Seats as % pop.	2.9	3.1	3.7
% seats full	46.9		31.4
Presbyterian churches:	1	5	3
Attendances per church	591		257
Attendances as % pop.	0.3		0.2
Seats as % pop.	0.3	0.7	0.5
% seats full	42.2		21.4
Isolated congregations:	15	26	46
Attendances per church	444		193
Attendances as % pop.	2.9		2.6
Seats as % pop.	3.6	3.3	4.1
% seats full	41.7		37.1
Salvation Army churches:	–	–	5
Attendances per church			498
Attendances as % pop.			0.7
Seats as % pop.			0.8
% seats full			45.8
OVERALL FREE CHURCH COMPARISON:			
Mainstream denominations:			
Attendances as % pop.	9.6		8.3
Seats as % pop.	10.6	12.7	10.8
% seats full	46.5		40.5
Isolated and Salvation Army:			
Attendances as % pop.	2.9		3.3
Seats as % pop.	3.6	3.3	4.9
% seats full	41.7		38.8

Table 15 (cont.)

Church of England attendances:	1851		1887	1892	
	Morning	*Evening*	*Morning*	*Morning*	*Evening*
St Mark, Ladywood	335	350	510	261	290
St Margaret	260	185	120	202	360
St Thomas	1,435	1,650	391	769	735
St Luke	659	546	333	308	375
St Martin	1,700	2,000	334	291	2,300
Bishop Ryder's	700	700	455	238	391
St Bartholomew	800	850	29	60	92
St Peter	300	500	192	65	106
St Philip	784	537	563	684	722
Christ Church	720	700	584	298	756
St Paul	600	400	430	330	382
St Mary	1,100[1]	1,600[1]	720	518	768
St George	1,130	1,340	319	→ 319	465
St Stephen	300	400	276	125	220
All Saints	294	181[2]	310	214	584
St John Baptist, Deritend	256	224	225	240	450
Holy Trinity, Bordesley	1,000	1,200	857	1,123	1,303
St Andrew, Bordesley	247	150	117	18	38
St Matthew, Duddeston	233	226	339	→ 339	394
St James, Duddeston	600	700	201	505	414
Edgbaston Parish	275	200[2]	435	647	580
St George, Edgbaston	550	300	828	825	570
Totals	14,278	14,939	8,568	8,379	12,295

Notes:
1 Estimated figure.
2 Plus afternoon attendances.
Missing entries supplied by nearest complete entries (see arrows).

Table 16 Eight large towns[1]

	1851	1902–4
Population	210,929	573,863
Attendance:		
Mean as % pop.	43.8	26.6
Morning	21.3	12.3
Evening	22.5	14.3
Mean:		
CE	17.9	9.5
Free	23.0	14.2
RC	2.9	2.9
% attendances:		
CE	40.9	35.7
Free	52.5	53.4
RC	6.6	10.9
Free Church attendances compared (– York):		
Congregationalists	4.1	1.6
Wesley	7.3	4.9
Other Methodists	7.4	3.5
Baptist	1.0	0.7
Presbyterian	0.6	1.3
Isolated	2.1	1.4
Salvation Army		0.7

Note:
1 Large towns = Chester, Hull, Lincoln, Middlesborough, Wallasey, Whitehaven, Workington, and York.

Table 17 Newspapers and religion (August 1969 and July 1990 compared)

	Total religious content		*% deemed hostile*		*Peak religious content*		*% religious letters*	
	1969	*1990*	*1969*	*1990*	*1969*	*1990*	*1969*	*1990*
Times	0.8	0.7	17	6	1.2	1.9	5	5
Telegraph	0.5	0.7	11	11	0.7	3.6	6	4
Guardian	1.1	0.5	13	1	1.8	3.1	6	4
Independent		1.4		2		2.7		8
Daily Express	0.5	0.4	11	12	1.6	2.3	1–	3
Daily Mail	1.0	0.5	18	30	2.5	2.5	3	3
Mirror	0.6	0.4	12	12	1.3	1.4	7	1–
Sun	0.8	0.5	28	47	1.2	2.4	4	1–
Sketch/Star	1.0	0.4	35	25	1.8	3.0	4	1–
Mean	0.8	0.6	18	16	1.5	2.5	4.5	3.2

Table 18 Anglican diocesan usual Sunday attendances as % pop.

	1968	*1973*	*1978*	*1985*	*1989*	*1994*	*1999*
Bath	6.4	5.8	4.6	4.1	4.2	3.6	3.0
Birmingham	2.1	2.0	1.6	1.5	1.5	1.4	1.1
Blackburn	4.1	3.7	3.3	2.9	2.9	2.5	2.1
Bradford	3.1	2.8	2.5	2.0	2.0	1.9	1.7
Bristol	3.4	2.9	2.7	2.4	2.5	2.1	1.8
Canterbury	4.5	3.6	3.1	2.9	2.7	2.5	2.5
Carlisle	5.4	4.7	4.1	4.0	4.0	3.3	2.7
Chelmsford	2.6	2.3	1.8	1.9	1.7	1.6	1.4
Chester	3.6	2.9	2.8	2.8	2.6	2.5	2.1
Chichester	5.6	4.5	4.0	3.3	3.3	3.0	2.6
Coventry	3.4	2.9	2.6	2.4	2.3	2.2	2.2
Derby	2.8	2.7	2.2	2.1	2.2	1.9	1.9
Durham	2.7	2.3	2.0	1.9	1.8	1.5	1.3
Ely	5.0	4.5	3.8	3.5	3.1	2.8	2.3
Exeter	6.0	5.0	3.7	3.2	3.2	2.9	2.6
Gloucester	5.6	4.8	4.2	4.0	4.0	3.5	3.1
Guildford	4.4	3.6	3.4	3.4	3.0	2.9	2.5
Hereford	6.5	5.6	5.2	4.5	4.4	4.2	3.2
Leicester	3.4	2.9	2.4	1.9	2.0	1.8	1.6
Lichfield	3.2	2.7	2.4	2.0	2.0	1.9	1.7
Lincoln	4.2	3.5	3.3	2.7	2.6	2.2	1.9
Liverpool	2.8	2.5	2.4	2.2	2.2	2.0	1.8
London	2.1	2.0	1.7	1.7	1.6	1.6	1.6
Manchester	2.5	2.1	2.1	2.0	1.8	1.7	1.5
Newcastle	3.2	2.4	2.3	2.2	2.1	1.9	1.6
Norwich	5.4	4.5	4.0	3.7	3.2	2.9	2.4
Oxford	4.2	3.4	3.1	2.9	2.8	2.7	2.3
Peterborough	4.5	4.0	3.0	2.8	2.7	2.5	2.3
Portsmouth	3.7	3.2	2.7	2.3	2.3	2.2	1.9
Ripon	3.3	2.8	2.7	2.6	2.3	2.0	1.9
Rochester	3.7	3.3	2.8	2.6	2.6	2.5	2.1
St Albans	3.5	3.0	2.6	2.7	2.4	2.2	1.9
St Edmund	5.3	4.6	3.8	3.7	3.9	3.7	3.2
Salisbury	5.9	5.1	4.6	4.5	4.2	3.8	3.4
Sheffield	2.1	2.0	1.7	1.7	1.7	1.6	1.4
Sodor & Man	6.2	5.0	3.8	3.4	3.4	3.2	2.6
Southwark	2.6	2.2	2.0	1.8	1.8	1.8	1.6
Southwell	3.0	2.3	2.6	2.1	1.9	1.7	1.5
Truro	5.8	5.9	4.2	3.7	3.4	3.1	2.7
Wakefield	2.6	2.4	2.2	2.0	1.8	1.6	1.5
Winchester	4.5	3.8	3.2	3.2	3.1	2.9	2.3
Worcester	4.4	3.4	2.8	2.6	2.5	2.1	1.8
York	3.5	3.0	2.5	2.4	2.5	2.2	1.8
Overall	3.5	3.0	2.7	2.5	2.4	2.2	1.9

Table 19 York: Church of England attendances

	1837	1851	1865	1868	1877	1884	1912	1931	1947	1953	1969	1989	2001
All Saints Pavement	130	618	350	← 350	420	400	520	190 →	190	365	49	90	46
All Saints North St	100	186	240	505	400	320	205	85 →	85	14	27	35	41
Holy Trinity Goodram	180	193	← 193	With St Maurice								Close	
Holy Trinity Kings Ct	70	46	100	180	150	200	With St Sampson						
Holy Trinity Micklegate	158	600	375	← 375	275	300	445	450	375	195	190	60	13
St Crux	60	200	100	← 100	200	Demolished							
St Cuthbert	670	440	315	385	165	230	210	236	110	← 110	370	Close	
St Denys	140	130	150	225	175	100	188	220	60	55	50	19	22
St Helen	240	155	400	350	250	← 250	330	340	165	185	255	70	13
St John	300	650	650	600	65	65	235	70	With Holy Trinity Mickle				
St Lawrence	30	140	150	410	← 410	700	550	575	175	250	170	96	65
St Margaret	30	860	550	350	199 →	199	140	90	22	70	47	Close	
St Martin Coney	60	150	240	140	230	170	With St Helen						
St Martin Mickle	180	← 180	320	150	425	320	180	130	With Holy Trinity Mickle				
St Mary Bishophill Sr/St Clement	280	← 280	275	375	1170	680	780	650	245	210	120	50	76
St Mary Bishophill Jr	85	150	280	300	200	200	215	45 →	45	85	68	31	22
St Mary Castlegate	110	← 110	135	← 135	400	800	510	140	80	60	20	Close	
St Maurice	180	440	200	345	160	550	500	140	240	200	Demolished		
St Michael le Belfrey	280	895	650	350	375	900	570	100	55 →	55	Close	750	503
St Michael Spurriegate	110	60	138	78	With All Saints then St Mary Castle Close								
St Olave	120	793	793	← 793	500 →	500	1200	550	370	196	145	140	130
St Sampson	220	360	220	275	250	← 250	270	69	10	Close			
St Saviour	960	1080	450	550	150	100	115	210	Close				
Holgate/ St Paul		500	600	500	550	800	450 →	450	200	365	153	340	249

Table 19 (cont.)

	1837	1851	1865	1868	1877	1884	1912	1931	1947	1953	1969	1989	2001
School room/St Thomas		215	500	500	500	400	380	325	178	260	128	115	57
St Barnabas							250	170	80	95	77	49	42
St Luke							222	90	83	56	85	170	128
Suburban churches								2220	1678	2230	1555	1399	986
Total	4693	9431	8374	8321	7619	8434	8465	7545	4446	5056	3509	3414	2393
% pop	16.8	26.0	20.7	19.0	15.4	17.0	11.1	8.6	4.2	4.8	3.5	3.4	2.4

Notes: Other dates: 1901 = *c.*9145 (11.8 per cent pop.); 1935 = 6935 (7.8 per cent); 1948 = *c.*4152 (3.9 per cent). Missing entries supplied by nearest complete entries (see arrows).

Table 20 Traditional religious belief in Britain

	% of British population				
	1940/50s	*1960s*	*1970s*	*1980s*	*1990s*
Belief					
God		79	74	72	65
God as Personal	43	39	32	32	31
God as Spirit or Life Force	38	39	38	39	40
Jesus as Son of God	68	62		49	
Life after death	49	49	37	43	46
Heaven		52	55	53	
Hell			21	26	27
Devil	24	28	20	24	27
Disbelief					
God		10	15	18	27
Jesus as just a man/story	18	22		38	
Life after death	21	23	42	40	41
Heaven		33	35	37	
Hell			68	65	64
Devil	54	52	70	64	67
Non-traditional religious belief in Britain					
Belief					
Reincarnation			24	26	25
Horoscopes			23	26	26
Foretelling future			48	54	47
Lucky charms			17	19	18
Black magic			11	13	10
Exchange messages with dead	15		11	14	14
Ghosts	15		19	28	32
Disbelief					
Reincarnation			53	57	59
Horoscopes			72	69	67
Foretelling future			41	40	46
Lucky charms			79	78	78
Black magic			82	82	86
Exchange messages with dead	59		79	77	80
Ghosts	64		73	65	58

Notes: Table 20 updated both from that first published in Robin Gill, C. Kirk Hadaway and Penny Long Marler, 'Is Religious Belief Declining in Britain?', *Journal for the Scientific Study of Religion*, vol. 3, no. 3, 1998 and a later version in my *Churchgoing and Christian Ethics*, Cambridge University Press, Cambridge, 1999, (see this book for full source references).

Sources: *God:* [Mass Observation 1947]; ITA 1968; Gallup 1968, 1973, 1975, 1979, 1981, 1986, 1989, 1993, 1995, 1999; NOP 1980; EVSSG 1981, 1990; STV 1985; MORI 1985, 1989 (2 surveys) 1998; IBA 1987; BSA 1991, 1993, 1998. *God as Personal/Spirit*: Gallup 1947, 1957, 1963, 1979, 1981, 1986, 1989, 1993; ABC 1964; ITA 1968; Harris 1974; EVSSG 1981, 1990. *Jesus*: Mass Observation 1947; Gallup

1957, 1963, [1979], 1981, 1986, 1989, [1993]; ABC 1964. *Life after Death*: Gallup [1939], 1947, 1957, 1960, 1963, 1968, 1973 (3 surveys), 1975, 1978, 1981, 1986, 1988, 1986, 1993, 1995, 1999; Mass Observation 1947; Gorer 1950, 1963, ABC 1964, Harris 1970, 1974; NOP 1980; EVSSG 1981, 1990; STV 1985, 1989; BSA 1991, 1998; MORI 1985, 1989, 1998. *Heaven*: Gallup [1968], 1973, 1975, 1979, 1981, 1986, 1989, 1993, 1995, 1999; EVSG 1981, 1990; STV 1985; MORI 1985, 1989, 1998; BSA 1991, 1998. *Hell*: [Gorer 1950]; [Gallup 1968], 1973, 1975, 1979, 1981, 1986, 1989, 1993, 1995, 1999; EVSSG 1981, 1990; STV 1985; BSA 1991, 1998. *Devil*: Gorer 1950, 1963; Gallup 1957, 1963, 1968, 1973, 1975, 1979, 1981, 1986, 1989, 1993, 1995, 1999; ABC 1964; EVSSG 1981, 1990; STV 1985; MORI 1985, 1989; BSA 1991. *Re-incarnation*: Gallup [1968], 1973, 1975, 1979, 1981, 1986, 1989, 1993, 1995; EVSSG 1981, 1990; STV 1985; MORI 1998. *Horoscopes*: [Gorer 1950]; Gallup 1973, 1975, 1978, 1981, 1986, 1988, 1989, 1993, 1995; STV 1985; MORI 1989, 1997, 1998; BSA 1991. *Foretelling*: Gallup 1973, 1975, 1978, 1981, 1986, 1988, 1989, 1993, 1995. *Lucky Charms*: [Gorer 1950]; Gallup 1973, 1975, 1978, 1981, 1986, 1988, 1989, 1993, 1995, BSA 1991. *Black Magic*: Gallup 1973, 1975, 1978, 1981, 1986, 1988, 1989, 1993, 1995. *Exchange Message with Dead*: Gallup 1940, 1957, 1973, 1975, 1978, 1981, 1986, 1988, 1989, 1993, 1995. *Belief in Ghosts*: Gorer 1950; Gallup 1950, 1973, 1975, 1978, 1981, 1986, 1988, 1989, 1993, 1995; MORI 1997, 1998.

Index

DATE DUE
